D0205939

THE 'SPECIAL RELATIONSHIP'

THE 'SPECIAL RELATIONSHIP'

Anglo-American Relations Since 1945

EDITED BY

WM. ROGER LOUIS

AND

HEDLEY BULL

CLARENDON PRESS · OXFORD

1986

Oxford University Press, Walton Street, Oxford OX2 6DP

Oxford New York Toronto
Delhi Bombay Calcutta Madras Karachi
Petaling Jaya Singapore Hong Kong Tokyo
Nairobi Dar es Salaam Cape Town
Melbourne Auckland

and associated companies in
Beirut Berlin Ibadan Nicosia

Oxford is a trade mark of Oxford University Press

Published in the United States
by Oxford University Press New York

British Library Cataloguing in Publication Data
The 'Special relationship': Anglo-American
relations since 1945.
1. Great Britain—Foreign relations—
United States   2. United States—Foreign
relations—Great Britain   3. Great Britain
—Foreign relations—1945-   4. United
States—Foreign relations—1945-
I. Louis, William Roger   II. Bull, Hedley
327.41073   E183.8.G7
ISBN 0-19-822925-9

Library of Congress Cataloging-in-Publication Data
The Special relationship.
Includes index.
1. United States—Foreign relations—Great
Britain.   2. Great Britain—Foreign relations—United
States.   3. United States—Foreign relations—1945-
4. Great Britain—Foreign relations—1945-   .
I. Louis, William Roger, 1936-   .   II. Bull, Hedley.
E183.8.G7S74 1986   327.73041   86-8472
ISBN 0-19-822925-9

Printed in Great Britain
by the Alden Press, Oxford

Foreword

W E are pleased to present a volume resulting from the first collaboration between the Ditchley Foundation of Enstone, Oxfordshire, England, and the Woodrow Wilson International Center for Scholars in Washington, DC. The collaboration grew out of a desire to combine perspectives in a review of the evolution of the relationship between the United States and the United Kingdom over the forty years since the end of the Second World War. Would the 'Special Relationship', enormously strengthened during the years of war, atrophy as Britain became, after much hesitation, a part of Europe? Would a review of certain critical concerns shared by the United States, Britain, and Europe reveal differences in attitudes and policies that had grown wider over four decades?

Our two institutions brought to these questions different traditions of enquiry. The Wilson Center is an institution for advanced research with a strong commitment to the printed word. Ditchley Park has no scholarly infrastructure, sees its vocation in the organization of high-level transatlantic conferences, and attaches more importance to the spoken word at the conference table than to the written reported results. The Wilson Center suggested that substantial papers should be prepared for each conference and where possible circulated in advance. This was easily agreed, and papers were invited from contributors on both sides of the Atlantic. This volume is built upon those papers, with additions generated as a result of conference discussion and argument.

We decided to concentrate upon three sets of issues: strategic concerns, defence, and arms control; finance, trade, and development; decolonization, North–South relations, and perspectives on the Third World. These three foci, each the subject of a separate conference, were set within an historical frame (the first conference) and an analytical summing up (the fifth conference). The conferences were held between September 1984 and May 1985, alternately at the Wilson Center and Ditchley Park. Rapporteurs' summaries of each have been published by the Ditchley Foundation and short notes on the series have appeared in Ditchley Newsletters. This volume is their full and permanent record.

Evocations—or sceptical assessments of—the famous 'Special Relationship' recurred throughout our conferences. The essays gathered here attempt to define the real nature of that relationship from the viewpoint of the mid-1980s. The revised essays also reflect the discussions by participants in the conference series, who represented a mix of those responsible for policy—in several instances responsible for the actual policies under discussion—together with scholars and analysts who had written on the history and consequences of certain policies or alternatives to them.

From the outset two distinguished scholars of international affairs began to shape the conference essays into a coherent volume. Professor Hedley Bull of Oxford, the editor on the British side, was one of the original planners of the series, and continued to guide us by his insight and high intellectual standards until his untimely death from cancer. His death laid the burden of the final editorial tasks almost entirely on Professor Roger Louis of the University of Texas, whose careful scholarship and shaping vision we most appreciate.

The Ditchley Foundation is grateful to the German Marshall Fund of the United States which gave a grant toward the travel expenses of the British participants in the three conferences held in Washington. Ditchley was much helped in the collaboration with the Wilson Center by Charles Muller, the Administrative Director of the American Ditchley Foundation, and his staff. The Wilson Center acknowledges the generous support of the Ford Foundation through its grant to support international activities at the Wilson Center. Both institutions appreciate the hospitality of the British Embassy in Washington and the personal interest taken in our proceedings by Sir Oliver Wright, the British Ambassador.

PROSSER GIFFORD
The Wilson Center

REGINALD HIBBERT
The Ditchley Foundation

Preface

HEDLEY BULL died on 18 May 1985, the day after the last Ditchley Foundation–Woodrow Wilson Center conference finished discussing the past, present, and future of the 'Special Relationship' between Britain and the United States. From the beginning the project represented a partnership, and it is melancholy to pen this note without him. Yet it is gratifying to complete the book, and I believe he might have been pleased.

The 'Special Relationship' was not the theme of the conferences. The organizing idea, as is stated in the Foreword, was to analyse the relations between The United States and Britain during the forty years of a tempestuously changing world. In discussions designed to study contemporary problems at least as much as the historical background, the label 'Special Relationship' seemed to prejudice the debate. One of the more stringent critics of that term, Dean Acheson, would have felt at home with our approach. He once commented about the 'stupidity' of writing about a special relationship, at least officially, and urged his American colleagues to suppress their 'sentimental' impulses. Nostalgia is a scarce commodity in relations between nations. Throughout the book hard questions are asked about terms of trade, military links, and common policies toward the Soviet Union. This line of enquiry is far more revealing about the nature of the relationship than what David Watt has called the rhetorical nonsense, sometimes majestic and often moving, yet neverthless nonsense, that has frequently been written about the relations between the two countries. Yet the idea of an intimate connection, a 'Special Relationship', would not go away. Indeed it haunted the discussions. Eventually it was referred to as the ghost, ever present yet elusive, derided by some but acknowledged by all. What then was the 'Special Relationship'? Why was it 'special'? Was it a good thing? What has become of it? Has it run its course?

Since the book has an introductory chapter as well as a conclusion, it would be impertinent to answer those questions here, but it may be useful to summarize certain points. The chapter by David Reynolds discusses not only Churchill and the origins of the alliance but also Britain's decline and the rise of the United States as a global power. The other historical chapters pursue this theme, Bradford Perkins dealing with the critical period when it became apparent that Britain was losing ground as a world power, D. C. Watt with the subtle yet vital distinction between the perception, or myth, and the reality of power, and Alistair

Horne with the 'special relationship within the special relationship' between Prime Ministers and Presidents, among others, Macmillan and Kennedy. Richard Ullman's chapter stresses a point essential to the volume as a whole: the 'Special Relationship' endured because of the *Pax anti-Sovietica.*

Margaret Gowing explains the origin of the British nuclear deterrent and the significance, past and present, of the scientific and technological gap between Britain and the United States. Samuel Wells discusses the evolving European defence systems and concludes that another special relationship—this one between the United States and the Federal Republic of Germany—will be the determinant in the Western alliance. Sir James Eberle examines the links between the military services and co-operation in the field of intelligence—the 'C³I' or 'Command, Control, Communications, and Intelligence' systems. 'The British military establishment', he writes, 'still maintains a degree of experience and capability that cannot be ignored.' The chapter by Ernest May and Gregory Treverton argues that agreements on air bases and missiles, service arrangements, and intelligence co-operation will continue to be significant, even though British influence on American strategic policy has been and will be slight. In budgetary and political rivalry, each of the American services seeks support of its sister services in Britain (the reverse is also true, as Admiral Eberle points out). Yet, as May and Treverton conclude, the links will eventually erode. They remind the reader of Britain's economic as well as military decline: in 1950 the British GNP still rivalled that of France and West Germany combined; by 1970 Germany had excelled it and France had matched it; by 1985 Britain's GNP per capita was less than Italy's.

In the economic chapters the theme of the 'Special Relationship' is less prominent than in others, but nevertheless, as Richard Gardner writes, the founding of the post-war economic order by a handful of British and Americans was an act of creative statesmanship. No one now believes that 'a new Bretton Woods conference' could reorder the world's economic system, but is it possible to hope for the calibre of constructive internationalism that inspired international economic policy two generations ago? Stephen Marris is troubled not only by the present leadership but by the principles of the Thatcher–Reagan economic philosophy. In his view the world is headed for a new crisis and a world-wide recession. Like Gardner, he argues for a return to co-operative efforts to manage the world economy. Marris's chapter is notable for connecting British and American issues with those of the European Community and Japan, but it is not conspicuous for its optimism. He believes in 'making constructive use of the crisis'. Sir Arthur Knight's chapter also argues that sustained Anglo-American dialogue might help to avert the crisis itself. Here, as in the chapters on defence, American policy is viewed in relation to British membership in the European Community, and a link may be found between economic and defence policy in the British response to the Strategic Defense Initiative: 'Janus-like as ever, the British have also been more positive than others about direct involvement in SDI'. Whatever the fate of SDI, the point that emerges from the economic chapters is that the debt crisis subsumes Anglo-American relations and overshadows everything else. In Richard Portes's words, 'the debt problem could itself become the crisis we feared for the international monetary system and domestic financial systems'. These economic themes spill over into the discussion about the non-European world, where the United States and Britain have effectively collaborated in rescheduling debts. The crisis is world-wide, and it can be better understood by taking into account the reasons behind the call by the former colonies of Britain and Europe for a 'New International Economic Order'.

In the next part of the book Lord Beloff marshalls political and philosophical arguments to indict the United States for failure to fill the political void left by the dissolution of the British Empire. The *Pax Britannica*, he writes, has disappeared and a *Pax Americana* has not yet arisen. Decolonization in his view has proved to be a catastrophe. My own chapter challenges his assumption that the United States should replace the British system. It argues that decolonization was inevitable and that the Americans on the whole struck a balance between the demands of their British allies and the aspirations of the nationalists. The eclipse of British power and American-Soviet rivalry in the Middle East are the themes of Sir Harold Beeley's chapter. Lord Saint Brides develops the argument that the end of the British Raj in India constitutes a successful episode of decolonization, and that successive British and American governments have effectively collaborated while maintaining, on the whole, good relations with India and Pakistan. Roderick MacFarquhar demonstrates that the marked Anglo-American rivalries in China before 1949 have played themselves out, but the chapter, as a historical case study of civil war, Communism, and liquidation of Western economic investment and military influence, has much to say indirectly about other parts of the world, notably Africa and Latin America.

The African chapter by James Mayall connects with the themes of the economic section and, while explaining the continent's 'low priority', it assesses problems of trade and development in tropical Africa as well as the British and American response to the African campaign against South Africa as a 'pariah state'. William Rogers also deals with economic issues, notably the debt crisis, but he is mainly concerned with the different British and American views of the Falklands crisis, the Grenada invasion, and Central America. Wherever else the 'Special Relationship' might endure, he explains, in Nicaragua 'the United States elbowed its way to a responsibility which left little room for European involvement'. The paradoxes, if not the dangers, of the American variant of British informal imperialism are especially acute in Latin America. This is one of the historical lessons to be taken from Edward Mortimer's chapter, which draws together the themes in this part of the book. Americans may not see themselves as the successors to the British Empire, but through British eyes the problems of 'ruling indirectly' are remarkably similar.

No account of Britain's transformation from a world power into a medium-size Atlantic and European power would be complete without the context of the Commonwealth. This perspective is the purpose of the chapters by A. P. Thornton and J. D. B. Miller. Thornton's is mainly historical and develops the theme that the special relationships within the Commonwealth rest on 'a particular set of intangible values' comparable to those of the Anglo-American connection. Miller's traces the meaning of the 'Special Relationship' in the Pacific and concludes with a sober assessment similar to David Watt's in the Introduction: 'the special relationship, fruitful and attractive as it has been, flourishes only in Atlantic water and European soil'.

Perhaps the salient point of the book is that the 'Special Relationship' is no longer decisive in American policy, if indeed it ever was. To the extent British influence remains significant, it will be in military links and political counsel. Playing the part of a superpower is a lonely business. In the words of May and Treverton, the 'Special Relationship' amounts to 'a sense of company in a confusing, unfriendly world'. Here the historic American and British friendship will probably endure because of mutual trust, but the relationship cannot be taken for granted, as will be clear from Sir Michael Howard's chapter.

Was it a good thing, and will it continue? There are gloomy prognostications in this book, not merely that the 'Special Relationship' was less heroic a venture than has been commonly believed, but also that it may have run its course. To provide a final word of introduction, I wish to draw briefly on the robust optimism of George McGhee as well as the foreboding of Sir Michael Howard.

Ambassador McGhee, who held official responsibilities during some of the critical periods of post-war Anglo-American relations, chaired the third conference held at the Wilson Center that dealt with British and American perspectives on the Third World. His remarks should be understood as part of the discussion about the dissolution of the British Empire and whether or not the United States should be viewed as its successor. Mr McGhee's is a realist view. He warns against the nostalgia for the British Empire and the false optimism that a *Pax Americana* might somehow lead to stability reminiscent of an earlier age. He does not believe the British 'lost' their empire but rather that it was a casualty of post-war nationalism. He believes still less that the Americans aspired to replace the *Pax Britannica* with their own influence. Even decolonization, the most controversial of Anglo-American subjects, should be seen as part of 'the extraordinary degree of cooperation between the two countries in making global decisions, which was, I believe, without precedent'. Here is his assessment of the past and future of the 'Special Relationship':

There is still a 'Special Relationship' based on our common ancestry, which provides our two countries a common cultural, political and philosophic heritage. I believe such ties will continue to exist. We must, however, realize the increasing limitations in the practical value of this tie, which has been greatly reduced from the period when we fought Hitler together as allies, to the present situation in which Britain has become an integral part of the European community. The decrease in effectiveness of the tie also reflects the greater difference that now exists in the relative power and influence of our two countries in the world. I believe, however, that something 'special' still exists between us, and I for one welcome it and wish it a long life.

As a reaffirmation, Mr McGhee's remarks provide a positive theme that runs through many of the chapters.

Sir Michael Howard's chapter ends the book on a note of scepticism and warning. The 'Special Relationship' may not endure. The societies of the two countries may be evolving in different directions. To many Americans now in ascendancy, Britain consists of a far-away people of whom they know nothing. They regard the world beyond the United States as an arena for confrontation with the Soviet Union. In Britain itself the wave of the future may belong to those who are indifferent to Soviet expansionism and who look upon the United States 'with a dislike sometimes bordering on hatred'. This sober assessment does much more than to warn us against complacency. The 'Special Relationship' is a touchstone of our common heritage and our historic traditions. Like liberty itself, it requires constant vigilance.

I wish to thank Lord Beloff, William R. Braisted, Mary Bull, and Janice L. Tuten for their assistance in preparing the book for publication. Mary Bull also compiled the index. The Clarendon Press allowed me to read in typescript Robin Edmonds, *Setting the Mould: The United States and Britain 1945–1950*.

W.R.L.

December 1985

Contents

List of Contributors

SIR HAROLD BEELEY (MA, Oxford), KCMG, CBE, was Lecturer in Modern History at the universities of London and Oxford before World War II, when he entered the British Foreign Office. In 1946 he served as Secretary to the Anglo-American Committee of Inquiry on Palestine. His diplomatic posts included Baghdad, 1951–3, and Washington, 1953–5. He was Ambassador to Saudi Arabia in 1955 and to Egypt 1961–4 and 1967–9. He is President of the Egypt Exploration Society.

LORD BELOFF (D.LITT., Oxford), KT, FBA, F.R.HIST.S., FRSA, is Emeritus Professor of Government and Public Administration at Oxford University and an Emeritus Fellow of All Souls College. He holds honorary doctorates from Pittsburgh University and Bowdoin College (USA); Bishop's University (Canada), the University of Buckingham and the University of Aix-Marseille III (France). He is working on *Imperial Sunset*, vol. ii, *Dream of Commonwealth 1921–1942*. Vol. i, *Britain's Liberal Empire*, was published in 1969.

ADMIRAL SIR JAMES EBERLE, GCB, studied at Clifton College, RNC, Dartmouth and Greenwich, and has been the Director of The Royal Institute of International Affairs since 1984. He has written extensively on international affairs and defence strategy. He served as C-in-C, Fleet, and Allied C-in-C, Channel and Eastern Atlantic, 1979–81; and C-in-C, Naval Home Command, 1981–2. He retired from the Royal Navy in 1983.

RICHARD N. GARDNER (D.PHIL., Oxford) is Professor of Law and International Organization at Columbia University. At Oxford he studied as a Rhodes Scholar. He served as United States Ambassador to Italy, 1977–81, and as Deputy Assistant Secretary of State for International Organization Affairs, 1961–5. His books include *Sterling–Dollar Diplomacy: The Origins and the Prospects of our International Economic Order* and *In Pursuit of World Order: U.S. Foreign Policy and International Organization*.

MARGARET GOWING (B.SC. (Econ.), LSE), CBE, FBA, F.R.HIST.S., is Professor of the History of Science at Oxford University. She is joint author of *British War Economy* and *Civil Industry and Trade* (in the British History of the Second World War, Civil Series). As historian of the United Kingdom atomic energy project, she has published three volumes: *Britain and Atomic Energy 1939–1945*; *Independence and Deterrence 1945–1952*: vol. i *Policy Making* and vol. ii *Policy Execution*. She is working on another. She holds an honorary D.LITT. of Leeds and Leicester, and D.SC. of Manchester Universities.

ALISTAIR HORNE (MA, Cambridge) was partly educated in the United States and is a Fellow of St Antony's College, Oxford. At Cambridge he delivered the Lees Knowles Lecture in 1982 (published in 1984 as *The French Army and Politics: 1870–1970*) and in 1980–1 he was a Fellow at the Woodrow Wilson International Center for Scholars. His books include *The Price of Glory: Verdun 1916* (Hawthornden Prize), *To Lose a Battle: France 1940*, and *A Savage War of Peace: Algeria 1954–62* (Wolfson Literary Award). He is the official biographer of Harold Macmillan.

SIR MICHAEL HOWARD (D.LITT., Oxford), F.R.HIST.S., FBA, is Regius Professor of Modern History at Oxford University where he has also been Fellow of All Souls College, 1968–80, and Chichele Professor of History of War, 1977–80. His numerous publications include *War and the Liberal Conscience*, *The Continental Commitment*, and *The Causes of War*.

SIR ARTHUR KNIGHT graduated in 1938 from the London School of Economics where he is now an Honorary Fellow. He served in the British Army 1940–6 having joined Courtaulds, Ltd. in 1939. He was chairman of Courtaulds 1975–9 and of the National Enterprise Board 1979–80. He has served as vice-chairman of the Royal Institute of International Affairs and is the author of *Private Enterprise and Public Intervention: the Courtauld Experience*.

WILLIAM ROGER LOUIS (D.LITT., OXFORD), F.R.HIST.S., is Kerr Professor of English History and Culture at the University of Texas. He studied as a Marshall Scholar at Oxford where he has also been a Visiting Fellow of All Souls College. His books include *Imperialism at Bay*, and *The British Empire in the Middle East*. He is currently completing *The Last Three Viceroys* and editing, with Prosser Gifford, *African Independence*.

RODERICK MACFARQUHAR (PH.D., LSE) is a Professor of Government at Harvard University. He was a Member of Parliament (Labour) 1974–9, and the founding editor of *The China Quarterly*. He has been a Fellow at the Woodrow Wilson International Center for Scholars. His publications include *The Hundred Flowers Campaign and the Chinese Intellectuals*, *China under Mao*, *Sino-American Relations, 1949–1971*, *The Forbidden City*, and *The Origins of the Cultural Revolution*, vols. i and ii.

STEPHEN MARRIS (PH.D., Cambridge) is Senior Fellow, Institute for International Economics. He has served as Economic Adviser to the Secretary-General of the Organization for Economic Co-operation and Development, and was the first editor of the OECD *Economic Outlook*. He has been a Visiting Professor at the Brookings Institution and holds an honorary degree from the University of Stockholm. His most recent works are *Managing the World Economy: Will We Ever Learn?* and *Deficits and the Dollar: The World Economy at Risk*.

ERNEST R. MAY (PH.D., UCLA) is Charles Warren Professor of History at Harvard University where he teaches the history of international relations. His books include *The World War and American Isolation* and *Imperial Democracy*. His most recent works are, as editor, *Knowing One's Enemies: Intelligence Assessment Before the Two World Wars* and, as co-author (with Richard E. Neustadt), *Thinking in Time: The Uses of History for Decision Makers*.

JAMES MAYALL (BA, Cambridge) is Reader in International Relations, London School of Economics, where he specializes in African affairs. He has been a Visiting Professor of Government at Dartmouth College in 1982 and 1984. He is the author of *Africa: The Cold War and After*; and has edited *The Community of States: A Study of International Political Theory*, and, with Cornelia Navari, *The End of the Post-War Era*.

J. D. B. MILLER (M.EC., Sydney, MA, Cambridge), FASSA, has been Professor of International Relations at the Australian National University since 1962. He has also held posts at Sydney, Leicester, and the London School of Economics, and (as a visitor) at Columbia, Yale, Princeton, and Cambridge. His books include *The Commonwealth in the World*, *The Politics of the Third World*, *Britain and the Old Dominions*, *The EEC and Australia*, *Survey of Commonwealth Affairs 1953–69*, and *Norman Angell and the Futility of War*.

EDWARD MORTIMER (MA, Oxford) is a Fellow of All Souls College, Oxford. He was Foreign Specialist and Leader-Writer at *The Times* 1973–85, and Senior Associate, Carnegie Endowment (New York), 1980–1. He is the author of *France and the Africans 1944–1960*, *Faith and Power—The Politics of Islam*, *The Rise of the French Communist Party, 1920–1947*, and co-author and co-editor of *Eurocommunism—Myth or Reality?*

BRADFORD PERKINS (PH.D., Harvard) is Professor of History at the University of Michigan and has been President of the Society for Historians of American Foreign Relations, and Commonwealth Fund Lecturer at University College, London. His books include *The First Rapprochement*, *Prologue to War*, *Castlereagh and Adams: England and the United States, 1812–1823*, and *The Great Rapprochement: England and the United States, 1895–1914* (winner of the Bancroft Prize).

RICHARD PORTES (D.PHIL., Oxford) is Professor of Economics, Birkbeck College, University of London, and Director of the Centre for Economic Policy Research in London. He was an American Rhodes Scholar and then a Fellow of Balliol College, Oxford, and has taught at Princeton and at Harvard. He is a Fellow of the Econometric Society and has held a Guggenheim Fellowship. His books include *Planning and Market Relations*, *The Polish Crisis*, and *Deficits and Detente*.

DAVID REYNOLDS (PH.D., Cambridge) is a Fellow and the Director of Studies in History at Christ's College, Cambridge, where he teaches the history of international relations. He has lectured and researched extensively in the United States, including a year as Charles Warren

Fellow at Harvard. His book, *The Creation of the Anglo-American Alliance, 1937–41*, was awarded the Bernath Prize in 1982. One of his current projects is a study of Anglo-American relations in the twentieth century.

WILLIAM D. ROGERS (LLB, Yale) is senior partner in the Washington law firm of Arnold and Porter. He was Deputy Co-ordinator of the Alliance for Progress, 1961–5, and Henry Kissinger's Assistant Secretary of State for Latin America and Under-Secretary for International Economics until 1977, with a sabbatical at Cambridge, 1982–3. Author of *The Twilight Struggle* and numerous articles, he is currently preoccupied with the restructuring of the debt of Brazil and Venezuela.

LORD SAINT BRIDES (BA, Oxford), GCMG, CVO, MBE, PC, was educated at Bradfield and Balliol. He was British High Commissioner in Pakistan, 1961–6 and in India, 1968–71; Permanent Under-Secretary of State, Commonwealth Office, and Privy Counsellor, 1968; and British High Commissioner in Australia, 1971–6. Since becoming a Life Peer in 1977, he has been a Visiting Fellow at the Universities of Chicago, Pennsylvania and Texas at Austin, and also at Harvard and Stanford. He is working on his South Asian memoirs, to be entitled *Travelling Hopefully*.

A. P. THORNTON (D.PHIL., Oxford), F.R.HIST.S., has taught in Oxford, Aberdeen, the West Indies, and, since 1960, at Toronto University. He participated in the D-Day Landing, European Campaign 1944–5. He is a Fellow of the Royal Society of Canada, and was a Smuts as well as a Commonwealth Fellow at St John's College, Cambridge. He is the author of *The Imperial Idea and Its Enemies, Doctrines of Imperialism, The Habit of Authority, For the File on Empire*, and *Imperialism in the Twentieth Century*.

GREGORY F. TREVERTON (PH.D., Harvard) is a Lecturer at the Kennedy School of Government, Harvard University. He served on the staff of the Senate Select Committee on Intelligence and as staff member for Western Europe on the National Security Council during the Carter Administration. He was Assistant Director of the International Institute for Strategic Studies in London, 1979–81. He is the author of *The 'Dollar Drain' and American Forces in Germany, Nuclear Weapons in Europe*, and most recently, *Making the Alliance Work: The United States and Western Europe*.

RICHARD H. ULLMAN (D.PHIL., Oxford) is Professor of International Affairs at Princeton University. At Oxford he was a Rhodes Scholar. He has served as a member of the staff of the National Security Council and in the Office of the Secretary of Defense, as Director of Studies at the Council on Foreign Relations, as a member of the Editorial Board of the *New York Times*, and as Editor of *Foreign Policy*. He is the author of a three-volume study of *Anglo-Soviet Relations, 1917–21*, and many other works.

D. CAMERON WATT (MA, Oxford), F.R.HIST.S., is Stevenson Professor of International History, London School of Economics. He was an editorial assistant on *Documents on German Foreign Policy 1918–1945*, as well as editor of the *Survey of International Affairs*, 1961–3, and is currently working as the official historian of *The Organisation of British Defence Policy, 1945–1964*. His books include *Personalities and Policies, Too Serious a Business, European Armed Forces and the Approach to the Second World War*, and *Succeeding John Bull*.

DAVID WATT (MA, Oxford) was Director of the Royal Institute of International Affairs, 1978–83, and is a former Fellow of All Souls College, Oxford. He has been dramatic critic of the *Spectator*, Common Market correspondent of the *Daily Herald*, Washington correspondent of the *Financial Times*, and joint editor of the *Political Quarterly*. Since 1981 he has been a regular contributor to *The Times*.

SAMUEL F. WELLS, Jr. (PH.D., Harvard) is Associate Director of the Woodrow Wilson International Center for Scholars and directs its European Institute. He has taught diplomatic history and defence studies at the University of North Carolina at Chapel Hill and in 1977 founded the Wilson Center's International Security Studies Program. He is co-editor and contributor to *Economics and World Power* and *Limiting Nuclear Proliferation* and the author of numerous articles on diplomatic and security affairs.

I

Introduction: The Anglo-American Relationship

DAVID WATT

THE essays in this volume are primarily concerned with plotting the course—some would say the rise and fall—of the 'Special Relationship' between Britain and the United States as it has developed from 1940 to the present. But it is an important preliminary to understanding this unusual phenomenon to place it in a longer historical perspective. The first thing that must strike anyone who thinks objectively about the Anglo-American relationship is the contrast between its coolness for most of its duration and its warmth in modern times. Only for a mere forty-five years in total, corresponding to much less than a quarter of the life of the American Republic, has it amounted to what might be called an 'alliance'.

It is not altogether easy to rescue this fact from beneath the mountain of rhetoric that now enshrines it. Every British Prime Minister from Churchill onwards has made it his business to suggest that 'our joint aims', 'our common heritage', and other emblems of 'the unity of the English-speaking peoples' have the patina of great antiquity. Equally, from the moment the United States entered the last World War, leading American politicians began to pay their own lip-service to the notion that there is a natural and immemorial affinity between the two countries; and though one hears less of this from the American side of the Atlantic than twenty years ago, it still reappears today from that quarter as an occasional basis of flattery or reproach.

This has been a powerful and often beneficent myth, and it was no doubt emotionally valid for Churchill himself, and later Macmillan, with their American family connections. But it does not bear critical inspection. At the popular level, a shared language and a joint adherence to the common law did not make our nineteenth-century forebears feel any very close affinity. The average Englishman, right up to World War II, regarded the Americans as surpassingly strange and largely irrelevant (though the cinema and popular music had perhaps begun to soften this view among the young in the 1930s). The general

American image of the British for 150 years was of a nation of more or less menacing snobs, and almost every successive wave of immigration into the United States from the Irish famine onwards added to the sum of Americans who either had a positive animus against Britain or at least had no particular cultural bias in her favour.

At the level of state relations, it is true that for most of the nineteenth century, and certainly after the settlement of the *Alabama* claims in 1872, there was no great reason for hostility between Britain and the United States. But neither was there any pressing need for them to come to grips with each other at all. It suited the British (with only occasional qualms) to leave the Caribbean and most of the Pacific to a relatively harmless power, thus freeing themselves to concentrate on the higher priorities of their imperial lifelines and the balance of power in Europe. It was equally convenient to the United States to leave the British Navy in protective control of the Atlantic. There was a certain objective congruence of interest here which survived the German attempt in 1897 to disrupt it; but there was no explicit understanding.

America's late entry into the First World War created a genuine alliance for the first time, but it was an odd kind of partnership, intense while it lasted but also curiously remote. The Americans were determined to maintain their freedom of manœuvre at all costs. President Wilson, in order to avoid accusations of foreign entanglement, invariably insisted that the United States was not an ally of the Allies but an 'associate' and kept American representation in the Supreme War Council to a discreet minimum. The Allies themselves, at the political as well as the military level, were inclined to patronize the American contribution and, considering that until the summer of 1918 there were no more than the equivalent of nine American divisions on the Western front out of more than 170, they had some justification. The turning-point came when, in the desperate situation of June 1918, the Allied Prime Ministers were obliged to make their famous appeal to Wilson: 'There is great danger of the war being lost unless the numerical inferiority of the Allies can be remedied as rapidly as possible by the advent of American troops.'

Whatever may be argued about the subsequent contribution to victory of the additional 300,000 American soldiers shipped over in answer to this call, Wilson was afterwards in a position of moral equivalence and even superiority to the Europeans. This greatly increased his influence at the peace conference. It also made an indelible impression on British foreign policy, which has never entirely ceased from that moment to see the American connection as being, on balance, a potential aid to the furtherance of British interests rather than as being neutral or a positive hindrance.

Even so, the joint experience of World War I still did not succeed in bringing about a deepening of the Anglo-American relationship in the inter-war years. This failure was largely due to the American withdrawal into isolation which frustrated a number of tentative British attempts to draw the United States into multilateral political and economic enterprises. But it also owed something to the British reversion to pre-war imperial preoccupations, which were now tinged with a new element of rivalry and fear of American power on the economic and strategic (particularly naval) planes. Anglo-American relations at the outbreak of World War II were about as distant as it is possible to imagine between 'friendly' powers and, of course, infinitely less warm than British relations with the French.

It is worth labouring this contrast between the situation prior to the fall of France and the situation after it (the important change in American, as well as British, attitudes dates from that event rather than from Pearl Harbor), for it makes the essential point to which the essays in this book bear witness—namely that the underlying basis of the Anglo-American relationship has always been interest and not, in the first place, emotion. Sentiment has indeed flourished in the soil that interest has watered, and has itself borne fruit, but it cannot be relied on to remain a vigorous and fertile plant for more than a limited period when interest on one side or the other is withdrawn.

In its broad outlines, the historical framework of the last forty-five years illustrates this proposition. The United States was confronted in 1940, as in 1916, with the prospect that its interests, which had become global, would be seriously threatened if the balance in Europe were destroyed and the continent dominated by a single power. The destruction of France not only made this a very possible outcome, and would almost certainly have forced America into the war eventually, irrespective of the Japanese attack. It also made the alliance with Britain obligatory; no other serious resistance to Germany was available. Once this enterprise had been brought to a successful conclusion the United States showed every sign of reverting to its old unilateralism, if not actual isolationism, and to the pursuit of its latent rivalry with Britain and the British Empire. Roosevelt played with the idea of American non-alignment between Britain on the one hand, colonialist and slave to immoral practices such as the balance of power, and on the other a paranoid, obstreperous, but ultimately manageable Soviet Union. This course was ruled out by another crisis in Europe. The continent was again threatened by a single power whose global pretensions were evidently turning out to be even more menacing than Germany's had been. Once more, with France, Germany, and Italy prostrate, an intimate alliance with Britain was the only possible expedient. As

Professor Ullman remarks, 'without the spectre of Soviet expansionism seemingly ever present . . . the Anglo-American relationship might have taken quite a different course'. But the intimacy and cordiality of the relationship was conditional on Britain's remaining the single most effective adjutant in the task of containing the Soviet Union and its allies. This condition applied for ten years after the war but was gradually dissolved as British power diminished and other allies, above all Germany, were revived.

At the point we have now reached, Britain is still an important ally of the United States. She remains, moreover, a *more* important ally than her size and economic strength would justify, for her situation has some unique features. Possession of nuclear weapons, membership of the Security Council, access to political and military intelligence, political stability, and willingness (at any rate hitherto) to devote an unusually high proportion of GNP to military purposes—all these are valuable to the United States. British membership of the European Community is an asset of even greater importance, but it is an ambiguous one. On the one hand, so long as Britain maintains her Atlantic outlook, it helps to keep the Europeans from neutralist and protectionist excesses. On the other hand there is a dual risk: first, that Britain will be seduced into European heresies herself and, second, that a Britain that appears to be too close to the United States will be regarded by her Community partners as a 'bad European' and will therefore lose her utility. This situation ensures that British views are taken into account in certain specific areas of policy. But they are no longer strong enough to ensure either (*a*) a purely British veto over any single American policy (except where, as in the case of bases in Britain, British sovereignty is directly involved) or (*b*) a purely British ability to influence the general direction of American foreign policy.

The question of where, along this path, the 'Special Relationship' can be said to have ended is to some extent a semantic one. My own definition, which would require the degree of British influence that I have just defined, implies that the 'special relationship' in the broad sense ceased to exist in the early 1960s and perhaps even earlier. On the other hand it is clear from a number of the essays which follow that in some specific areas of policy (particularly, as Professors May and Treverton and Admiral Eberle show, in certain military and intelligence matters) a close functional connection has lasted up to the present.

The question of how far sentiment has affected the logical train of events is one of the central themes of this book. In the first place, as David Reynolds explains, once confidence had been established it smoothed the working of the war-time alliance. It is debatable to what extent Roosevelt and Churchill ever really liked or even fully understood each other; certainly, neither was always entirely frank with the other. But it is obvious that they established an unusual degree of ·personal communication and a reasonable degree of mutual trust. At lower levels, military and official, habits of easy intercourse also took root and many permanent friendships were formed. This kind of sentiment survived the war, and continued in the first ten years of peace. The sense of overall common purpose and mutual need which the Truman and Eisenhower Administrations shared with their British counterparts made it possible, until the end of the 1950s at any rate, for politicians and officials in Britain and the United States to converse with an openness and regularity that was exclusive and on a different level from the normal cordiality of allies. This resulted in an instinctive understanding of the political and emotional patterns and constraints of the other side and greatly increased speed and ease of operation in any joint enterprise. As for the mystique created by Churchill, it has and was deliberately intended to have the effect of providing a climate of public opinion in which it was easier for both governments, if they so wished, to override special interests and nationalist objections to mid-Atlantic compromise. This has become a more and more fragile instrument, particularly in the United States where special interests are institutionalized, but it has played some part even as recently as the Falklands crisis.

Common sense, as well as the testimony of innumerable participants, confirms the operational importance of these links. But how far did they ever cause the American government to decide to act in a way which the logic outlined earlier would not have dictated anyhow? There certainly were plenty of instances, even at the height of the 'special relationship', in which they failed to prevent American administrations following a very cold-blooded course. Professors Perkins, Gardner, Watt, Gowing, and Louis, as well as Sir Harold Beeley, elaborate some of the most notable examples of the first post-war phase: the abrupt ending of Lend-Lease, the insistence on sterling convertibility, the refusal to share nuclear technology, the exclusion of Britain from the ANZUS Pact, the failure to join the Baghdad Pact, and, most traumatically of all, the stop on the Suez operation. To what extent these unpleasantnesses were due to a simple, overriding consciousness of American national interest and how much to the strong residue of anti-colonial moralism analysed by Professors Beloff and Louis is arguable. What is certain is that in each case pro-British sentiment was relatively easily overcome even in the heyday of the 'Special Relationship'. Moreover cases of the opposite kind are, almost by definition, unsubstantiated. One can speculate, for instance (as Alistair Horne does), that Harold Macmillan's emotional appeal to President Kennedy at Nassau in 1962 powerfully affected the decision to provide Britain with Polaris as a replacement for Skybolt.

But the arguments from national interest (which included, on the negative side, the danger of being seen to let down a major ally) were finely balanced: and one cannot be absolutely sure that Kennedy would have replied any differently to a cooler approach from a Prime Minister who had not taken pains to cultivate a personal relationship with him. Similarly, in the case of the Falklands it is tempting to guess that the Latin American faction within the State Department might have defeated the Atlanticists if the European protagonist had been France instead of Britain; but this is not at all certain. There were plenty of good arguments for opposing General Galtieri and backing a major member of NATO and these arguments might well have prevailed even without the pro-British emotions of the Secretary of State and the Secretary of Defense.

It appears from these examples that these major incidents are not very helpful for isolating and assessing the importance of emotion. So many factors were at work that individual motives cannot be satisfactorily separated out. The same applies, for slightly different reasons, to the World War II period, when the parity of power between the two partners made the element of feeling, in a sense, less important. The obvious fact that in many areas the United States simply could not act successfully without British acquiescence and co-operation meant that the emotional and ideological links seldom, if ever, had to bear the whole weight of the relationship. For these reasons it seems better to take the years after 1946 as the test, and to take them as a whole. On this basis it appears that what I have rather loosely called sentiment did have one substantial though not easily definable effect.

The simplest way to describe this is, perhaps, by noting the tolerance shown by successive American administrations towards British disagreement with them. Considering the state of economic and, later, strategic dependence to which Britain was rapidly reduced after the war, there has been remarkably little cracking of the American whip. The Suez 'veto' was one exception; the heavy economic pressure on the Callaghan government at the end of 1977 was possibly another. But there has been a long list of British 'aberrations', beginning with Palestine and the recognition of Communist China, continuing with Eden's Indo-China initiatives and Macmillan's insistence on summitry, and ending with Denis Healey's establishment of the Eurogroup and Wilson's refusal to send even a token British contingent to Vietnam. All these discommoded the United States at the time—to put it no higher—but though the Americans naturally argued their case or circumvented British opposition in some other way, they did not often demand that Britain desist on pain of American sanctions, explicit or otherwise. It is true that there existed, in each of these instances, other practical restraints against

American retaliation. Nevertheless it is possible to detect in the correspondence of all American Presidents and British Prime Ministers from Truman and Attlee to Nixon and Wilson a certain consideration, even deference, on the American side which was not so often displayed—at any rate until the 1970s—towards other allies. Macmillan's famous classical analogy (Greece = Britain: Rome = United States) was far-fetched as well as self-serving. But it did catch something of the sense on both sides that America was undertaking a global role that Britain was passing on. Never mind that this renunciation was not entirely voluntary; never mind that a number of British politicians and commentators regretted—and, as Lord Beloff's essay makes clear, still regret—the transition and believed that the Americans were making a poor fist of it. The fact remained that Britain had been there before. At the beginning—for instance, when the British inability to hold Greece and Turkey led to the Truman Doctrine—there was some grumbling about 'pulling British chestnuts out of the fire' (to quote a Congressman at that time). The fear of being sucked into Britain's nefarious imperial machinations was persistent. Later (in Henry Kissinger's opinion too late), this was replaced by a desire to profit from British experience and even to help sustain lingering British influence in the Third World for as long as possible. Later still, it has turned into profound exasperation with all Europeans, including the British, for not sharing with the United States the assumptions and burdens of a global struggle with the Soviet Union (a divergence whose growth can be traced in most of the essays in the non-European section of this book as well as in Professor Ullman's discussion of East–West relations). Nevertheless, for some years the notion of a torch being handed on cast a something of a sunset glow over the relationship, as seen from Washington, and enhanced the arguments against undermining the British by too many hard choices or bullying tactics.

That, of course, like most of the points I have discussed so far, represents matters from the American side. The perspective offered by the British contributors to this volume alters the picture considerably, though not perhaps as drastically as might be supposed. One is initially inclined to accept, as a working hypothesis, the common idea that the British have been much more sentimental about the relationship than the Americans; or, in other words, that they believed their own Churchillian propaganda and were frequently misled by it. It is a proposition which has received a lot of backing from the Europeanists in British public life, to whom it has become virtually axiomatic that our failure to 'catch the European bus' in the mid-1950s was almost entirely due to a national obsession with the special relationship. Closer investigation, to say nothing of a reading of these essays, shows that things were much more complicated.

For one thing the thesis does not take account of the strong currents of anti-Americanism that have flowed continuously on the left and right wings of British politics ever since 1945, often subterranean but apt to spring to the surface at moments of crisis. Since these are not discussed specifically elsewhere they are worth a brief mention here. The basic elements of the British left's hostility have not varied much over the years: a dislike of capitalism, a desire to think well of 'socialist' states if at all possible, and, above all, a belief (with a long lineage going back beyond George Lansbury and Ramsay MacDonald to the nineteenth-century origins of the Labour movement) that, since conflict in international relations is due to injustice and misunderstanding rather than clashes of legitimate interest, it is the mission of socialists to take a moral stand and to avoid power politics and blocs. These views informed the 'Keep Left' group, led by Michael Foot and Richard Crossman, which attacked Bevin's 'excessive subservience' to the United States in the late 1940s; they provide the instinctual basis for the Labour Party's defence policy published in August 1984. Experience had forced the non-Communist left to modify their opinion of the Soviet Union somewhat from the unclouded admiration of the war years; but the psychological difficulty of this shift has been eased by the gradual substitution of the United States for Britain in the villain's role of chief 'imperial' power. This last transformation, which corresponds, of course, to developments in the real world that have already been discussed, assumes special significance in Britain because it enables a whole segment of liberal opinion, spreading much wider than the left proper, to transfer feelings of guilt about the British imperial past to American shoulders—which are then cudgelled with redoubled vigour. More generally, however, it has produced a comfortable state of mind in which the two superpowers are lumped together in the same moral category and a new infusion of vitality is imparted to the old attack on power blocs and alliances.

The new American right, which has joyfully discovered these quite antique phenomena in the last couple of years, appears to regard them as symptomatic of a new and general degradation of British will. They are wrong on both counts. Anti-Americanism of the type I have just described may have broadened its appeal since the Vietnam War, and again since the election of Ronald Reagan, but it is as old as the Cold War and has been very consistently held in check among the wider public, as countless opinion polls have demonstrated, by the common-sense perception that the United States is infinitely less of a potential menace to Britain than the Soviet Union and that the British need the Americans to help protect them from the Russians. The fact that the main opposition party in Britain became committed after 1979 to a position which, in effect if not quite in principle, contradicted this popular view was chiefly a result of the hermetic convolutions of its internal politics at that time; a party which had stuck to the bipartisan policies of the 1945–79 era might have had a better chance of winning power in 1983. On the other hand it would be wrong to suggest that this left-wing critique of the American connection has been wholly without influence on policy—especially when Labour has been in office, but even, indirectly, when it has not. Attlee and Bevin were able to face it down by weight of prestige and personality, but it caused immense difficulties and divisions at the time of the Korean War. It suffused the nuclear disarmament movement in the late 1950s which in turn affected the Macmillan government's attitudes to East–West relations. It was the origin of the Wilson government's decision to stand aloof from Vietnam. And it has reappeared with renewed force in the 1980s.

Right-wing anti-Americanism has been less obviously influential. The right has been generally resentful of the Americans' usurpation of British power, either out of pure national pride or on the more elevated ground, laid out by Lord Beloff, that the United States helped to destroy a beneficent British world system without putting anything effective in its place. But these sentiments have been overtrumped by an even greater dislike of others. Resistance to Communism, clearly at the top of the right's priorities, has been difficult to sustain without at least some co-operation with the strongest anti-Communist power in sight. Opposition to British membership of the European Communities, another obsession, has also softened opposition to the United States whose alliance (along with the Commonwealth) has had to be presented as the only credible alternative. Nevertheless there have been periods when anti-American feelings within the Conservative Party have boiled over. Anyone who wants a strong taste of these sentiments, even in the immediate aftermath of allied victory in World War II, should read the debate in the House of Commons on 13 December 1945 when the terms of the American loan were grudgingly approved, with 100 MPs opposed and 169, including Churchill himself, abstaining. Again, after the Suez débâcle, the 'Suez Group' of Tory MPs was a thorn in Macmillan's flesh throughout his Ministry, opposing not only every step in the dissolution of the Empire in Africa, but also every sign of 'weakness' in the face of American pressure as well. Had he not succeeded in pulling off the Nassau agreement with Kennedy he might have been in very grave difficulties with his own party. Subsequent manifestations have had less practical effect, but have still made a great deal of noise from time to time—the most recent being the Falklands War (so long as it looked as if the United States proposed to remain an impartial mediator in the dispute) and the Grenada affair.

It is obvious, then, that some quite important groups on the wings of British opinion have always been less than enchanted with the special relationship. But it is also true that the pro-American centre has not been quite so intoxicated by mid-Atlantic rhetoric as is sometimes alleged. Innumerable quotations (of which Sir Roger Makins's comments on American policy in the Middle East, cited by Professor Louis in Chapter 16, provide one excellent example) can be produced to show that British policy-makers have usually had a pretty hard-headed appreciation of what they were doing in relation to the United States. Stated crudely, their purpose has been to use the American connection to maintain British interests and security at a reasonable financial cost. They have from time to time miscalculated the degree to which the Americans would permit themselves to be manipulated or underestimated the price they would exact, but the fundamental British illusion has had much more to do with the old vision of Britain as a major independent actor on the world stage than with any very profound belief in the combined destiny of the English-speaking peoples. Ernest Bevin, for instance, who is rightly given the credit for dragging the United States back into the European arena in 1945 and 1946, never had any doubt that what he wished to do ultimately was to restore Britain's *ante bellum* position. The Americans were essential to Britain's economic recovery and also, while that recovery was taking place, to her security. He was determined that the United States should not lapse into isolation again and was therefore prepared to compromise a number of important issues, including Palestine, rather than sour Anglo-American relations. But his underlying attitude was summed up in a minute, written in January 1946, opposing a suggestion of Attlee's that we should withdraw from the Mediterranean: 'Let us wait till our strength is restored and let us meanwhile, *with US help as necessary* [my emphasis], hold onto essential positions and concentrate on building up U.N.O.' Those positions where the necessity of American help was accepted by Bevin were mainly limited to the realms of East–West strategy and economic recovery in Europe. Throughout the Attlee Cabinet's discussions of policy towards Africa, South-east Asia and the Indian subcontinent the American angle was rarely considered relevant at all; in the Middle East, it was regarded as an intrusive and usually very unhelpful factor. Bevin and Attlee would have relied on American help in the nuclear field if they could have got it, but neither had the slightest hesitation in going ahead with the British nuclear weapons programme when American co-operation fell through; it seemed the natural thing to do.

The slow death of this easy assumption about an independent status and freedom of manœuvre has in my view been the crucial and traumatic British experience in the last thirty years. The growing disparity between British and American power was, of course, one important element of this but it is a mistake to think that it was, or always seemed, the most important one. British governments were aware that their strength and influence were shrinking in each of Churchill's three famous overlapping circles—the Commonwealth, the Atlantic, and Europe—but the fact that the process advanced at different rates at different times and in different places muddled them and occasionally led them to believe that in one area or another it had stopped or even been reversed. The confusion was increased in the case of the Commonwealth by the sense of movement; the very act of negotiating, and then granting, independence in a succession of dependencies gave an illusion of power—that is, until the dependencies began to run out.

Psychologically speaking, the declension was marked by three phases. In the first, just described, the loss of power was mainly felt in the Atlantic and European 'circles'. The American loan and the abandonment of Palestine (essentially forced by the United States) signalled the one and the British withdrawal from Greece and Turkey the other. The decision to leave India, which looks objectively the most significant symptom of decline in this period, did not really seem so at the time, being generally regarded (in spite of the chaos of partition and the opposition of zealots like Churchill) as a statesmanlike gesture which had in any case been foreshadowed for the last twenty-five years.

In the second phase, roughly the 1950s, British attention turned primarily to weaknesses in the Empire circle. At the beginning of this period General Templer's remarkable victory in Malaya shored up the British position in the Far East for another decade, but the situation elsewhere showed that Bevin's dream of eventually re-establishing the world role on something like the old scale would have to be abandoned. The old Middle Eastern sphere of influence (Egypt and Iraq) began to crumble and following a deliberate decision of Macmillan's, the African empire was disposed of at breakneck speed. Meanwhile the British delusion of strength, or at least business as usual, was maintained in Europe and the Atlantic. Eden upstaged Dulles with the Geneva negotiations on Indo-China; Macmillan irritated Eisenhower by his independent summit manœuvres with the Russians; almost all British politicians cold-shouldered the infant movement for European integration.

From the same psychological point of view, the third phase (the 1960s) was perhaps the most interesting, for it brought matters to a crucial decision point. The decision in question was not, as was then claimed by General de Gaulle and is still often claimed today, one between Europe and the United States. For the vast majority of British policy-makers, this was a false dichotomy. The United States was in Europe; Europe needed the United States. To maintain close security links with America and to try to retain some influence in Washington, whatever else one was doing, was only a matter of realism. De Gaulle's anti-American posturings seemed petty and dishonest since France ultimately relied on the United States as much as anyone else; they were also stupid, since to indulge in America-baiting without the strength to stand on one's own was to lose influence for no purpose. The debate in Britain was much more to do with a choice between unilateralism or multilateralism. The left and the right wanted various forms of independent national self-assertion—the right tending to imperial nostalgia, the left to little Englandism or, in the case of sublimated imperialists like Hugh Gaitskell, to visions of the new Commonwealth as a way of prolonging '1000 years of history'. As Macmillan and company perceived it, on the other hand, none of these options any longer offered a satisfactory degree of influence. Britain was running out of entry cards in Washington, and was 'losing out', as the phrase went, in Europe as well. A far more co-operative form of alliance diplomacy was therefore required in which a residual world position, easy relations with the United States and security and economic interests in Europe would, as it were, be pooled. This line of argument suited the United States as well, not so much because of a desire to have a 'Trojan Horse' in Europe (which is what the French alleged) as because the utility of the British as a major partner, under the old assumptions, was becoming hopelessly compromised by sheer weakness and the idea of using what was left of British power to build a more solid (and perhaps less expensive) European 'pillar' to the alliance was, in spite of possible drawbacks, extremely attractive on balance.

In one sense, de Gaulle actually proved Macmillan's case for him. By excluding Britain from Europe, and preventing the 'pool' being made for another decade, he forced a demonstration of the inadequacy of the 'independent' option. The Wilson years were a painful series of economic and political retreats made more humiliating by Wilson's own tendency to grandiose pretensions of power and statesmanship. Economic weakness brought on the withdrawal from east of Suez; and this in turn reduced British importance to the United States. Britain's influence in Europe was effectively nullified by the French. The Commonwealth, in spite of the ideals and pretensions described by Professor A. P. Thornton, was a broken reed, so far as offering Britain a serious global standing was concerned. Wilson's final desperate attempts to reopen the question of European entry, against all his own past views and the instincts of his party, were the most convincing proof of who had won the main argument.

Having said that, one has to admit that a subsidiary argument of a Europe-versus-the-United States kind has subsequently been forced on the British. Edward Heath recognized, as perhaps Macmillan did not, the emotional importance to the Europeans of a British 'commitment' to the Community. This appeared to mean, as in childish initiation ceremonies, proving the point by doing the thing you least like to do—in this case being nasty to the Americans. Heath duly obliged. As Henry Kissinger says in his memoirs: 'Heath dealt with us with an unsentimentality quite at variance with the special relationship. The intimate consultation by which American and British policies had been coordinated in the post-war period was reduced to formal diplomatic exchanges.' More substantially he snubbed Kissinger's Year of Europe in 1973 and later the same year joined other European countries in refusing to allow American planes to use British bases to reinforce the Israelis in the Arab-Israeli war. The last of these gestures was arguably an early example of a real conflict of interest between Europe on the one hand and the United States on the other, but the rest do not seem, in retrospect, to have been either necessary or effective. They merely alienated the Americans without greatly improving Britain's relations with the Community. The same could probably be said in reverse of the opposite tactic, tried by James Callaghan, of trying to establish a particularly close and avuncular relationship, à la Macmillan, with President Carter; it aroused European suspicions without paying any great dividends in Washington.

Margaret Thatcher's stance has been more equivocal—partly because it has actually been less consistent. Having started with a strongly anti-European instinct and an admiration for President Reagan's brand of conservatism (in many ways similar to her own), she was naturally disposed to assume that the 'Special Relationship' was alive and would remain efficacious if she built on her empathy with the President. On the other hand, not only has her government necessarily become more and more enmeshed in European Community affairs, but she has also had to swallow some humiliating demonstrations of the modern limits of British influence in Washington, notably the Grenada affair and the loss of an enormous telecommunications contract to French competitors in spite of her personal intercession with the President.

The truth of the matter is that since the 1970s Anglo-American relations, considered entirely by themselves, have ceased to be very important or very interesting. To be either, they have to be viewed in the context of American–European relations, a fact which strips them of some of their remaining sentimental trimmings. Leaving aside anachronistic red herrings like the Falklands and Grenada, the great question for the future has nothing to do with special relationships. It is how far European and American interests are going to diverge, and if so how to manage this divergence. Where there are serious disputes, the Anglo-American relationship forged in World War II will not prevent Britain lining up with increasing regularity on the European side, for all sorts of hard-headed reasons to do with geography and economics. Where history and sentiment come in is in enabling Britain to avoid two psychological traps. One, into which the French are particularly prone to fall, is to lose sight of the fundamental interdependence of the United States and Europe and make empty anti-American gestures in order to satisfy national pride. The other, which is the peculiar tendency of the Germans, is to see the European-American relationship in the excessively blinkered focus of immediate domestic political and economic concerns and therefore to veer, sometimes quite wildly, between fear of being abandoned and fear of being a pawn in American hands. Britain's true value to the United States at present is not as a 'Trojan horse' in Europe, still less as an independent adjutant in world affairs; to the extent that she is successfully tempted by American blandishments or nationalistic nostalgia to be either, she loses her ability to play the modern role for which she is best suited by temperament and historical experience. That role is to act emphatically as the European power she has actually become, but to bring to European counsels the important elements of pragmatism, balance, and global perspective that are her distinguishing characteristics. In future this may often, as Edward Mortimer implies in his reply to Lord Beloff, entail a multipolar view of the world which the United States finds disconcerting and even hostile. But the essays in this volume demonstrate that the British have developed since 1940 the important ability to understand the American mind better than any of their European partners. They are able to say, on the basis of long experience and in all sincerity, that trans-Atlantic conflicts of interest are manageable even among unequal partners provided there is a minimum of shared objective and provided both sides are prepared to devote real energy to cultivating the habits of close and civilized intercourse.

HISTORICAL

2

Roosevelt, Churchill, and the Wartime Anglo-American Alliance, 1939–1945: Towards a New Synthesis

DAVID REYNOLDS

INTRODUCTION: THEMES AND INTERPRETATIONS

THE wartime alliance was Winston Churchill's creation. That is a statement about historiography as much as history. Churchill popularized the term 'Special Relationship' in his Fulton speech of 5 March 1946—an eloquent appeal for the USA to perpetuate the wartime Anglo-American alliance into the post-war era.[1] He also used his war memoirs, the six-volume history of *The Second World War* published between 1948 and 1954, in part to develop the same theme by laying 'the lessons of the past before the future'.[2]

In his memoirs Churchill depicted the wartime alliance as the outgrowth of an underlying cultural unity—the 'English-speaking peoples'. Between the world wars improvident leaders and indifferent publics in both countries had thrown away the hard-won victory. But, he argued, following his own accession to power in 1940 at a time when a 'warm-hearted friend' of Britain occupied the White House, a special relationship blossomed. This 'gradually became so close that the chief business between our two countries was virtually conducted by these personal interchanges between him and me. In this way our perfect understanding was gained.'[3] Throughout *The Second World War* Anglo-American relations generally appear in a roseate hue, with little evidence of suspicion or controversy. Indeed Churchill admitted to Eisenhower that the final volume, which appeared in 1954 when the two men headed their respective governments, had been carefully vetted by him to ensure 'that nothing should be published which might seem to others to threaten our current relations in our public duties or impair the sympathy and understanding which exists between our countries'.[4]

---

[1] Winston S. Churchill, *Complete Speeches*, ed. Robert Rhodes James (New York, 1974), vol. vi, p. 7289.

[2] Winston S. Churchill, *The Second World War* (6 vols., London, 1948–54), vol. i, p. vii.

[3] Ibid., ii, p. 22.

[4] Churchill to Eisenhower, 9 Apr. 1953, Presidential Papers, Whitman File, Box 16 (Dwight D. Eisenhower Library, Abilene, Kansas).

For a generation Sir Winston's interpretation of the Anglo-American relationship was definitive for statesmen, scholars, and publics on both sides of the Atlantic. Historians copied his broad picture even if they differed on details, colour, or tone. Over the last decade, however, a very different image of the wartime alliance has emerged from the work of specialist scholars who have burrowed into the newly opened archives in both countries. It is in fact a double image, as suggested by the titles of some of their books: 'ambiguous partnership', 'competitive co-operation', 'allies of a kind'.[5] Set against the celebrated story of common cause against the Axis—Lend-Lease, the Battle of the Atlantic, and Operation OVERLORD—is the more chequered Anglo-American relationship in the Pacific and Middle East. Attention has also been paid to less familiar aspects of the war, such as the negotiations over decolonization or economic policy, which sometimes reveal acrimonious rivalry for long-term position and advantage.

From this perspective the wartime alliance is seen as part of a longer and larger story, namely the decline of Britain and the rise of the United States as major world powers. While Britain sacrificed a quarter of her national wealth and suffered a fatal blow to her Asian empire, the war pulled America out of prolonged depression, set off a boom in consumer as well as war production, and enabled her to extend her influence in the Pacific, East Asia, and the Middle East—areas where before she had frequently taken second place to Britain. World War II, then, marked a decisive moment in the shift of world power, and each government often formulated policy with one eye on the Axis and the other on its rival ally.

The theme of ambivalence has also been extended into studies of the Roosevelt–Churchill relationship. While not denying its intimacy or importance, recent historians have noted the mutual suspicion that characterized its early stages when neither was sure of the other's fidelity. Later, as the alliance blossomed, it remained an unequal partnership—warmer on Churchill's side than Roosevelt's and reflecting, particularly as the war progressed, the imbalanced bargaining power of the two nations. 'What do you want me to do—stand up and beg like Fala?' asked the premier at one particularly humiliating moment in 1944, likening himself to the president's dog.[6]

[5] Robert M. Hathaway, *Ambiguous Partnership: Britain and America, 1944–1947* (New York, 1981); David Reynolds, *The Creation of the Anglo-American Alliance, 1937–41: A Study in Competitive Co-operation* (London, 1981); Christopher Thorne, *Allies of a Kind: The United States, Great Britain and the War against Japan, 1941–1945* (London, 1978). For a similar approach see James R. Leutze, *Bargaining for Supremacy: Anglo-American Naval Relations, 1937–1941* (Chapel Hill, 1977); Wm. Roger Louis, *Imperialism at Bay, 1941–1945: The United States and the Decolonization of the British Empire* (Oxford, 1977); Mark A. Stoler, *The Politics of the Second Front: American Military Planning and Diplomacy in Coalition Warfare, 1941–1943* (Westport, 1977).

[6] John M. Blum, *From the Morgenthau Diaries* (3 vols., Boston, 1959–67), vol. iii, p. 373, during the OCTAGON conference at Quebec in Sept. 1944. On their early relationship see James Leutze, 'The

Appreciation of the larger context in which both men operated has also led historians away from the Churchillian preoccupation with the two national leaders. As Lord Halifax once remarked, the Prime Minister was usually 'pretty bored with anything except the actual war',[7] and Roosevelt often got bored even with that. Neither kept close track of economic or imperial issues, and historians enquiring into these humdrum but vital aspects of the alliance have been forced to examine the government departments in Whitehall and Washington and to assess the ideas of middle-level civil servants such as Keynes, Harry White, and Harley Notter who often determined the agenda for transatlantic negotiation. This in turn has necessitated closer study of the policy-making élites in both countries.[8]

Such a divergence from the 'great man' theory of history, often informed by recent political science analyses of how bureaucracies function, highlights the difficulty of talking about governments pursuing unitary, coherent policies. This is particularly true of the United States, where the co-ordinating forces usually apparent in British decision-making were generally absent. The presence of a much higher proportion of 'outsiders' in senior American government posts, the lack of a cohesive Cabinet to formulate common policy or of a presidential secretariat to implement it—all these impeded clear decision-making even within the Executive. Add the greater formal powers of Congress over foreign affairs, the relative lack of party discipline, the operations of a multitude of organized lobbyists, and the unrestrained media attention (which led one frustrated British official to complain that in Washington 'you either do no business at all or you do it through the newspapers'[9])—and one has a political system in which it was far more difficult for Roosevelt than for Churchill to translate personal preference into national policy. Frequently American leaders were forced to have a 'public' and a 'private' policy on key issues—one for domestic consumption, the other for diplomatic negotiation—though the two could not always be kept from conflicting, as indicated by the Anglo-American row over Greece in December 1944.[10]

Secret of the Churchill-Roosevelt Correspondence: September 1939–May 1940', *Journal of Contemporary History*, 10 (1975), 465–91; David Reynolds, 'Roosevelt, the British Left and the Appointment of John G. Winant as US Ambassador to Britain in 1941', *International History Review*, 4 (1982), esp. 408–9. See also Warren F. Kimball, ed., *Churchill and Roosevelt: The Complete Correspondence* (3 vols., Princeton, 1984).

[7] Halifax to Eden, 5 Jan. 1942, Hickleton Papers, A4.410.4.15 (Churchill College, Cambridge).

[8] Pioneered by D. C. Watt. See his *Personalities and Policies* (London, 1963) and *Succeeding John Bull: America in Britain's Place, 1900–1975* (Cambridge, 1984).

[9] Sir Frederick Phillips, quoted in David Reynolds, *Lord Lothian and Anglo-American Relations, 1939–1940* (Philadelphia, 1983), p. 52.

[10] On 5 Dec. 1944 the State Dept. issued a press release apparently critical of British intervention in Greece, much to London's fury. In fact, US policy-makers basically agreed with British policy in

Not that US officials were above citing domestic pressures as a convenient justification for policies they themselves ardently supported—as Neville Chamberlain once observed, Congress was the 'Mr Jorkins' of American negotiators.[11] Nor was British policy-making immune from bureaucratic wrangling, or from domestic political pressures (over the Second Front or Imperial Preference). But even if Whitehall did not always run, as Lord Halifax once suggested, like a smooth passenger train in comparison with Washington's jolting freight train,[12] his contrast was broadly accurate. A good deal of Anglo-American friction, from the 'Destroyers-for-Bases' negotiations of 1940 to the abrupt termination of Lend-Lease in 1945, was attributable to the problem of managing the domestic politics of US foreign policy.

This is a reminder not to push the 'revisionist' interpretation of the alliance too far. Much of the acrimony stemmed from the intense, complex, highly public debate within which transatlantic negotiations were conducted. Diplomacy, after all, is the art of reconciling the inevitably divergent viewpoints of independent, sovereign states. The fact of eventual agreement on common, if compromise, policies is surely as important as the colourful disputes through which those agreements were often reached. That is one point to be emphasized in what follows. The other qualification to 'revisionism' is that we should not permit the story of America's rise and Britain's decline to become overstated. Like many long-range trends it does not always help us understand short- and medium-term events. Neither the closeness of the wartime alliance nor the growing American dominance within it are straightforward guides to the outcome of particular wartime negotiations, let alone to the nature of the relationship in the post-war period. A fuller understanding of the alliance requires analysis of its origins in 1939–41 and then a look at four of its most important facets—often with a glance ahead into the Cold War era.

CREATING THE ALLIANCE, 1939–1941

However natural it may seem in retrospect, the wartime alliance was the

Greece, as long as it was discreet enough not to offend the US public. Their statement, hastily drafted, was an attempt to appease domestic opinion and remind the British of the need for prior consultation, but it struck a chord in the USA and precipitated sustained American media criticism of Britain, to which the British press replied in kind. See Hathaway, *Ambiguous Partnership*, ch. 6, and Lawrence S. Wittner, *American Intervention in Greece, 1943–1949* (New York, 1982), pp. 22–6.

[11] Chamberlain, memo, Sept. 1934, para. 11, Neville Chamberlain Papers, NC 8/19/1 (Birmingham University Library). (Mr Jorkins figures briefly in Dickens's *David Copperfield* as the mild but unseen junior partner in the law firm of Spenlow and Jorkins, always cited by Mr Spenlow as a ruthless and obdurate taskmaster who prevented him from showing generosity to clients and staff.)

[12] Halifax to Eden, tel. 865, 21 Feb. 1944, Foreign Office Correspondence, FO 954/30B (Public Record Office, Kew, London—henceforth PRO).

result of an unforeseen and unique crisis: the fall of France in May–June 1940.[13] Prior to that Anglo-American relations had been cool and distant. Chamberlain and his colleagues, disillusioned by the history of American isolationism since 1919, had little faith in the likelihood of speedy and substantial American help. Their appeasement diplomacy and Phoney War strategy were predicated on that assumption. The Prime Minister and some of his Conservative colleagues also feared that dependence on the United States would make Britain vulnerable to American economic pressure and to renewed 'Wilsonian' peacemaking. In the United States the strength of domestic isolationist opinion and Franklin Roosevelt's own weakened political position ruled out an overtly interventionist policy. In any case F.D.R., though anxious to see Hitler contained, had no wish to become embroiled in another European war, and his policy was therefore to help Britain and France acquire the munitions they needed to deal with Hitler themselves. Thus, during the winter of 1939–40 neither country sought or expected a close association. In fact, British policy-makers were thinking of a long-term 'special relationship' with France rather than the United States.

All was transformed in 1940. That long, hot spring Hitler overran much of north and north-west Europe in a matter of weeks. Most devastating of all and completely unexpected, despite the outpouring of retrospective wisdom, was the abrupt collapse of France. Allied strategy of holding Germany by land, while strangling her by sea and bombarding her from the air, lay in ruins. Britain was left alone, bereft of significant allies, and her tiny army had abandoned much of its modern equipment on the continent. US assistance was therefore essential—for survival let alone victory—and Britain's new leader, Winston Churchill, deluged Roosevelt with impassioned pleas for munitions, ships, aircraft, raw materials, and even immediate American entry into the war. Yet Washington was not initially receptive. The immediate response to France's collapse was a panic-stricken concern for America's own defences. Even Roosevelt shared the widespread scepticism about whether Britain could survive alone—personal doubts and political considerations again pointing in the same direction. It was only after Congress had been bypassed, the Republicans squared, and the British cajoled into a hard bargain that Roosevelt agreed to the Destroyers-for-Bases deal in September 1940. The importance of this was more symbolic than real—neither side was to benefit tangibly for many months—and, despite the striking American gesture of support for Britain, it was not until the November presidential election was over and F.D.R. had won an unprecedented third term that the embryonic alliance took shape.

[13] This section summarizes the argument of Reynolds, *The Creation of the Anglo-American Alliance*.

Between January and March 1941 Roosevelt steered the Lend-Lease bill through a divided Congress. It was a testimony to his imagination and political skill—avoiding a new war debts tangle by offering munitions on terms to be decided later, and eliciting for the first time from Congress a clear commitment to his policy of 'material aid to the opponents of force'. Previously Churchill had entertained doubts about Roosevelt's sincerity and favoured a hard-bargaining approach to the United States involving periodic threats about the possibility of a compromise peace if US aid were not forthcoming. But the announcement of Lend-Lease and the visit of Roosevelt's confidant, Harry Hopkins, in January 1941 convinced him that F.D.R. was indeed Britain's 'best friend'. From then on his tactic for the rest of 1941 was to minimize all peripheral differences with the United States and to provide Roosevelt with the diplomatic 'molasses' he needed to sweeten American opinion. Get America into the war—that was his pre-eminent objective. All else was secondary.

Churchill hoped that the Americans would be drawn in through incidents with German U-boats. From April 1941 F.D.R. cautiously and incrementally extended the US Navy's patrolling operations in the Atlantic until, by September, the Americans were escorting Allied convoys across much of the ocean with instructions to shoot at any Axis vessels seen in the vicinity. Privately Roosevelt warned the British of the persistence of anti-war sentiment in Congress and encouraged Churchill to believe that he was trying to provoke an 'incident' that would take the issue of peace or war out of his hands. Historians disagree about Roosevelt's candour on this point: perhaps he was now anxious to get into the conflict, or perhaps he was just telling the British what they wanted to hear. He may have felt less pressured after the German invasion of Russia in June had relieved the threat to Britain and therefore to the United States. At any rate the situation remained uncertain in early December 1941. Periodic clashes between American and German vessels had led to loss of American lives but no *Lusitania*-style public outcry; American merchant ships were now free, after the close-fought repeal of parts of the Neutrality Act, to go to Britain and Russia, but F.D.R. was not planning to move rapidly. The British were becoming progressively more disenchanted and impatient. But in the end the issue was decided in the Pacific and not the Atlantic.

The crisis of mid-1940 had left a vacuum in the Far East. The European colonial powers were unable to stand up to renewed Japanese pressure and the defence of their Asian interests necessarily devolved on the United States. The Americans had two major weapons at their disposal. One was the main American fleet, which since April 1940 F.D.R. had kept at Pearl Harbor, some 2,000 miles from its West Coast bases. The other was Japan's reliance on raw materials ultimately controlled by the United States, particularly oil, and her supplies were restricted in late summer 1940. American policy was to deter Japan from further expansion while not provoking her into war, it being generally agreed in Washington that Germany was the major threat to American interests. That policy worked until mid-1941, but the German attack on Russia, which reduced the pressure in Europe, intensified the crisis in Asia because the Soviet Union was no longer able to threaten Japan. Again F.D.R. hardened American policy, reinforcing the Philippines with heavy bombers and approving a further cut-back in oil supplies. But it seems that Washington 'hawks' transformed this into a full-scale embargo, thereby accelerating Japan's deadline for turning from diplomacy to war in search of its sphere of influence in East and South-east Asia.

During all this Britain had little say in American policy, yet she would suffer more from an Asian war. For the Americans, preoccupied by the Atlantic and suspicious of British imperialism, would not send their own main fleet west of Hawaii to protect Britain's Asian possessions. It was not until late October 1941 that the firmer American policy in the Atlantic permitted the Royal Navy to dispatch even a token force of capital ships to Singapore. In the end, however, the fundamental cause of the Far Eastern débâcle was not the divergence of Anglo-American interests, but a mutual underestimation of Japan. Though expecting war in South-east Asia by December 1941, virtually no one in London or Washington predicted the vehemence and scope of Japan's onslaught. The attack on Pearl Harbor brought the United States into the war, but it was only the beginning of a sustained and brilliant series of Japanese combined operations across the western Pacific which in six months decimated Western forces and toppled the European empires. It also presented the newly consummated alliance with an unanticipated global crisis that was to bedevil Allied strategy for the rest of the war.

ANGLO-AMERICAN STRATEGY FOR GLOBAL, COALITION WARFARE

The broad outline of that strategic debate is familiar and easily summarized.[14] The basic principle in 1942 remained 'Germany First': contain Japan and concentrate on overcoming Hitler, after which

---

[14] Basic official histories for the USA are Maurice Matloff and Edwin M. Snell, *Strategic Planning for Coalition Warfare, 1941–1942* (Washington, 1953), and Maurice Matloff, *Strategic Planning for Coalition Warfare, 1943–1944* (Washington, 1959); and, for the British, the series of *Grand Strategy* volumes under the general editorship of Sir James Butler (6 vols.; London, 1956–76). See also Michael Howard, *The Mediterranean Strategy in the Second World War* (London, 1968), and Stoler, *Politics of the Second Front*.

Japan's defeat would follow. In April 1942 the two governments agreed on a buildup in Britain (BOLERO) with a view to invading the continent in strength in 1943 (ROUNDUP) or even on a small scale later in 1942 (SLEDGEHAMMER). After the British vetoed the latter operation, Roosevelt and Churchill revived the idea of invading Morocco and Algeria (TORCH) and linking up with British forces from Egypt to drive the Axis out of Africa. TORCH began in November 1942 and led on to the invasion of Sicily the following July and of the mainland of Italy in September 1943. But meanwhile the American-dominated Allied forces in the Pacific had regained the initiative from the Japanese whose expansion had been finally checked on the edge of India, the mid-Pacific, and Australasia in mid-1942. MacArthur's forces worked north from Australia, taking two grim years to recapture the Solomons and New Guinea, while Admiral Nimitz gradually won the Pacific islands west of Hawaii. With major theatres of operation in the Mediterranean and the Pacific, each devouring the output of the Allied arsenals, it was not until the summer of 1943, after intense argument, that the two governments firmly committed themselves to invading north-west Europe (OVERLORD) in the spring of 1944. Even then divergences over operations in Burma, the Balkans, and the south of France distracted from that effort, and once on the continent in June 1944 there were sharp disagreements about the extent, speed, and direction of the thrust into Germany. The Reich surrendered in May 1945, and the Americans, now on the periphery of the Japanese home islands and sceptical about the depth of Britain's commitment to the Pacific, rapidly transferred their forces to Asia. But the final bloody offensive was forestalled by Japan's surrender in August 1945, after belated Russian entry into the Pacific war and the dropping of the two atomic bombs.

Why did the two governments find it difficult to concert their strategy? In part because each had a fundamentally different approach to winning the war, particularly in the European theatre. Extrapolating from the 'Germany First' principle, the American military planners wished to bring the Nazi forces to an early engagement on the continent. They, and especially General Marshall, the Army Chief of Staff, favoured a concentration in Britain as prelude to ROUNDUP-OVERLORD and the avoidance of peripheral operations, notably in the Mediterranean, which would dissipate Allied resources. Behind such thinking lay the military traditions of the Civil War and America's abundance of manpower and resources. In contradistinction to the United States' classical strategy of applying overwhelming power to annihilate the enemy's forces, Britain favoured a more indirect approach. Relatively weak in manpower, but richly endowed with naval strength and global economic resources, British strategists had traditionally emphasized a war of seapower and blockade. This inclination was reinforced by memories of the Great War carnage and by the disasters of 1940 which made the prospect of a land victory on the continent seem remote and Utopian. Better to wear the Axis down, concentrating on Hitler's weaker partner, Italy, and engaging in areas where Britain still had a foothold, notably North Africa, as a way of gradually 'closing the ring'. Underlying this strategy, and now often forgotten, was the assumption that the end would come through not the conquest but the collapse of Hitler's Reich. Bombing and blockade would help break the German war economy; peripheral operations on several fronts and aid to the European resistance movements would facilitate a political collapse. Late into the war the British still entertained hopes that the re-entry of Allied armies on to the Continent would be the *coup de grâce* rather than *guerre à outrance*.

Divergent national interests as well as differing strategies also help explain the conflict of policies. Undoubtedly US suspicions of Britain's imperial preoccupations were exaggerated: the British never had a coherent 'Mediterranean strategy' and Churchill's 1944 flirtations with operations in the Balkans and Aegean were frowned on by his own Chiefs of Staff. Nevertheless, the Middle East *was* an area of particular importance to Britain, commanding the sea route to India and access to vital oil fields, and undoubtedly this influenced strategic thinking in London. Moreover, at heady moments of success in Italy, such as mid-1943 and mid-1944, British leaders did talk as if that was the crucial theatre. Similarly, Britain's emphasis on South-east Asia reflected her interest in recovering lost territory in Burma, Malaya, and above all Singapore, which Churchill described in 1944 as 'the supreme British objective in the whole of the Indian and Far Eastern theatres'.[15] His 1944 advocacy of major operations in Italy and in South-east Asia also owed something to a desire to assert Britain's independence and military prowess in an alliance increasingly dominated by American power and propaganda. But the Americans, too, did not formulate strategy in a political vacuum. Nurtured on the idea of a special Sino-American relationship and burning to avenge the humiliation of Pearl Harbor, American planners made it clear that the Pacific and the subsequent Allied occupation of Japan were to be American shows. Despite American mythology *neither* government fought the war without considering its longer-term objectives.

These conflicts of national attitude and interest should not be overstated, however. Some of the rows were intra-national in character:

---

[15] Churchill to Chiefs of Staff, 12 Sept. 1944, Prime Minister's Operational Correspondence, PREM 3, 160/6 (PRO).

the US Navy, for whom Japan had been the real enemy since 1919 and
the war in Europe offered little scope for major naval operations,
naturally fought the Army for greater resources in the Pacific; the
deadlock over British strategy in South-east Asia in 1944 involved the
Prime Minister and his Chiefs of Staff in 'perhaps their most serious
disagreement of the war';[16] and British and American bomber commanders often joined forces against both their governments to secure
priority for the strategic air offensive against Germany. Nor should one
overstate Anglo-American differences in the conduct of warfare. As
democracies, placing a high value on individual human life, neither
government could contemplate the more liberal use of manpower
characteristic of the Russians. In that sense both advocated the 'indirect'
approach. Such concern for domestic opinion also played a decisive part
in the details of strategy. With many Americans obsessed by Japan, and
twenty to thirty per cent inclined towards a negotiated peace with
Germany,[17] it is little wonder that F.D.R. was adamant that he needed
some kind of military operation in Europe in 1942 to keep 'Germany
First' alive. He therefore backed TORCH against his military advisers
once SLEDGEHAMMER was abandoned. Nor should one underrate similar
pressures on Churchill at this time for a Second Front to aid Russia and a
victory for the persistently humiliated British army.

Though understandable, however, TORCH was to cast its shadow over
the rest of the war. As Marshall feared, it made a sustained diversion of
resources into the Mediterranean inevitable, and the postponement of
action in north-west Europe also strengthened the US Navy's argument
to concentrate on the Pacific. Had resources been unlimited, conflicts of
interest might not have arisen. But even the vast American arsenal could
not prevent crucial logistical bottle-necks from emerging, notably in
merchant shipping in 1942–3 and landing craft in 1943–4. With
insufficient equipment to supply three major theatres and a dozen
secondary ones, everyone could not be satisfied. By 1943 the 'Germany
First' principle had been significantly eroded, and Marshall's 'strategy
of concentration' was replaced by planning for 'a multi-front' war.[18]

Yet TORCH and its associated decisions were not entirely to 'blame'.
After the fall of France, Germany could not be defeated in the manner of
the Great War. After the disasters of the winter of 1941–2 Japan could
not be put on the backburner to the extent envisaged before Pearl
Harbor. Those who argue that VE Day could have occurred much

[16] John Ehrman, *Grand Strategy*, vol. v. *August 1943–September 1944* (London, 1956), p. 425.

[17] Richard W. Steele, 'American Popular Opinion and the War against Germany: The Issue of
a Negotiated Peace, 1942', *Journal of American History*, 65 (1978), 704–23.

[18] Robert W. Coakley and Richard M. Leighton, *Global Logistics and Strategy, 1943–1945*
(Washington, 1968), p. 798.

earlier[19] must ponder not just the intricacy of alliance politics but also the ramifications of global war.

IMPERIALISM—FORMAL AND INFORMAL: THE AMERICAN CHALLENGE, THE BRITISH RESPONSE

As we have seen, strategic debates were bedevilled by Americans' historic suspicions of the British empire. SEAC (the South-East Asian Command), for instance, was quickly glossed by Americans as 'Save England's Asian Colonies'. Such suspicions were part of an American's birthright, and they were not unwarranted, but, as British policy-makers liked to observe, they went with an ignorance of some colonial realities and also a tendency to assume that the American model was universal in its applicability. A case in point was Secretary of State Cordell Hull's claim that the United States' relationship with the Philippines was 'a perfect example of how a nation should treat a colony or dependency'.[20] Even more profound, however, was the blindness on both sides, perpetuated in some historical writing on the subject, about the complex methods by which great powers influence underdeveloped clients. American sanctimoniousness about imperialism reflected the fact that, apart from the aberration of the Spanish-American war, it had generally eschewed formal rule in overseas dependent territories. By contrast its twentieth-century expansion generally followed 'informal' methods of commercial and financial penetration, most notably in Latin America. Historically this had also been the preferred method of British expansion, particularly in the Victorian era: 'informally if possible, formally if necessary',[21] Egypt being an excellent example. Nevertheless, formal empire-building had been a feature of British policy in the late nineteenth century in Africa and again in the Middle East after World War I, and in general Britain's network of global influence relied much more than America's on direct rule.

As 'informal imperialists' the Roosevelt Administration mounted a sustained and high-sounding challenge in World War II to Europe's formal empires. The Atlantic Charter of August 1941 had been mainly directed towards the European war, but its rhetoric about self-determination was quickly appropriated by American policy-makers for use against colonialism in general. F.D.R. talked about putting all colonies under international trusteeship, while the State Department,

[19] e.g. Walter S. Dunn, Jr., *Second Front Now—1943* (University, Ala., 1980); John Grigg, *1943: The Victory that Never Was* (London, 1980).

[20] Cordell Hull to William Phillips, 18 Nov. 1942, Hull Papers, Box 50 (Library of Congress, Washington).

[21] John Gallagher, *The Decline, Revival and Fall of the British Empire*, ed. Anil Seal (Cambridge, 1982), p. 99.

though gradualist, tried repeatedly to tie the British to firm timetables for independence. The most intense intervention came in India in the spring of 1942. Churchill, a bitter opponent of the 1935 Act extending self-government, wanted to postpone any further transfer of power. But American pressure, combined with the military threat from Japan and demands from within his own Cabinet, necessitated the Cripps mission to negotiate a programme of immediate Indianization and Dominion status promptly after the war. Roosevelt took a personal interest, pressing his own proposals and trying to prevent a breakdown, and in the end only a veiled threat of resignation from Churchill made him desist.[22]

In 1942–3 the American challenge to empire was acute, as the Cripps mission and the July 1943 Declaration on the Colonies attest. But the British were able to ride out the storm. In part they did so through creating several regional consultative commissions on the model of the one proposed by the 1943 Declaration, through which the Americans could be involved in colonial reform and development (and in its financing) without having a significant say. In part, too, they funded development and welfare projects of their own, notably through the 1945 Act under which the Foreign and Colonial Offices prised £120 million from the habitually tight-fisted Treasury. But, in addition to appeasing the Americans by limited concessions, the British also benefited from the fact that the Administration's policy shifted in the last year of war. The Joint Chiefs of Staff (JCS), and especially the Navy, had never liked the trusteeship idea. They were adamant that the United States needed to acquire selected territory of its own—notably the mid-Pacific islands formerly under Japanese control, which would provide a valuable network of sea and air bases for civil and military purposes after the war. Talk of general trusteeship would also complicate relations with Russia, now wooed as an ally in the Pacific war, and would make America's continued possession of Puerto Rico and the Virgin Islands a little difficult to justify. With Roosevelt's backing, therefore, the JCS whittled down the State Department's proposals so that UN trusteeship was simply applied to existing League of Nations mandates and captured enemy territory. Although at Yalta Churchill pontificated, Hong Kong, the Gambia, and other British dependencies were no longer in danger. And after the Prime Minster's warning in

---

[22] Churchill told Hopkins that 'I could not be responsible for a policy which would throw the whole sub-continent of India into utter confusion while the Japanese invader is at its gate' and that while 'I should personally make no objection at all to retiring into private life' Cabinet and Parliament would take the same view of the matter. Draft tel. to Roosevelt, 12 Apr. 1942, communicated verbally to Hopkins, PREM 4, 48/9 (PRO). On Churchill and India see Thorne, *Allies*; Gary R. Hess, *America Encounters India, 1941–1947* (Baltimore, 1971); and Raymond Callahan, *Churchill: Retreat from Empire* (Wilmington, Del., 1984).

1942 and the ebbing of the Japanese tide, India was never again a crisis issue in Anglo-American relations.[23]

This was, nevertheless, a pyrrhic victory. Two years after Yalta the British were surrendering their troubled mandate in Palestine and preparing to evacuate the Indian subcontinent, the historic heart of empire. Decolonization resulted not only from indigenous nationalist pressures, often accentuated by Japan's humiliation of white power in the Pacific war, but also from the impact of the whole conflict in undermining the economic foundations of Britain's global power. Since the beginning of the century 'invisible earnings' from shipping, financial services, and foreign assets had balanced Britain's chronic trade deficit. But World War II necessitated a massive programme of external disinvestment, particularly in Latin America, India, and South-east Asia. The flow of invisible earnings abated and former clients were transformed into creditor nations able to buy out British properties. Their willingness to hold their credits as sterling balances in London helped preserve the reserve currency status of sterling, but the costs of global commitments became increasingly difficult to sustain. Often the Americans were the main beneficiaries. The United States supplanted Britain as the dominant Western influence in Saudi Arabia and China, and the Pacific crisis of 1941–2 enabled them to draw Australia and New Zealand into the American defence orbit. Whatever he might assert to the contrary, Churchill *had* presided over a turning-point in the liquidation of the British Empire.

But the picture of an ailing imperial giant overwhelmed by the inexorable tide of decolonization and progress is too simple.[24] For one thing, that was not how British leaders saw the situation. In May 1947 Foreign Secretary Ernest Bevin stated categorically that 'His Majesty's Government do not accept the view . . . that we have ceased to be a great Power.'[25] They remained determined to hold on to their gobal position, particularly by less burdensome, informal means. They still hoped, for instance, to utilize the manpower and resources of India—the real disaster in their view was not independence but partition—and the recession of British power in South Asia was counterbalanced by determined programmes of resource development in Britain's African territories.[26] Likewise, despite the loss of Palestine, the search for viable

---

[23] See Louis, *Imperialism at Bay*.

[24] As is emphasized by Gallagher, *Decline, Revival and Fall of the British Empire*, pp. 73–153; also R. F. Holland, 'The Imperial Factor in British Strategies from Attlee to Macmillan, 1945–63', *Journal of Imperial and Commonwealth History*, 12 (1984), 165–86.

[25] *Parliamentary Debates* (Commons), 16 May 1947, col. 1965.

[26] On Africa see the important debate in Wm. Roger Louis and Ronald Robinson, 'The United States and the Liquidation of the British Empire in Tropical Africa, 1941–1951', in Prosser Gifford and Wm. Roger Louis, *The Transfer of Power in Africa: Decolonization, 1940–1960* (New Haven, 1982),

alternative centres of British military power in the Middle East continued in Iraq, Libya, and Egypt.

Of course there was self-delusion aplenty here, but it should not obscure the fact that until the 1960s Britain *did* remain a truly global power. Moreover, that fact was not regarded with unequivocal distaste by the Americans, who still felt ambivalent about Britain's formal empire. Though they often regarded it as the epitome of dated Old World imperialism, it also included bases and natural resources of inestimable value in containing common enemies. Roosevelt had acknowledged this in the battle against the Axis; Truman took the same line as he sought to contain communism. We shall not appreciate the intricacies of the post-war Anglo-American relationship unless we remember that Britain's role as a world power did not end in 1945, and that this role was regarded by the United States as a blessing as well as a curse.

TOWARDS A NEW ECONOMIC ORDER

Economic wealth was the basis of global power and the foundation of grand strategy. Allied victory in the war owed much to the successful mobilization and deployment by the British Empire and the United States of their combined resources. In 1939 the two of them accounted for about sixty per cent of the world's industrial production and controlled roughly three-quarters of its mineral wealth. But the Axis victories of 1940–2 revolutionized the situation, giving them dominion over a third of the population and mineral resources of the globe.[27] In 1942 the British and Americans developed a network of combined committees to handle the economic prosecution of the war. Based in Washington—a sign of where ultimate power lay—and by no means immune from internecine conflicts, these were nevertheless a signal advance on the grudging co-operation of World War I and an unusual instance of inter-allied partnership.

Using their superiority in resources and shipping, Britain and America were able to reconstruct the blockade, shattered in 1940. In particular the USA gradually brought much of Latin America within the Allied orbit, satisfying her own deficiencies in tin and ferro-alloys and denying the Axis crucial supplies such as Chilean copper. On occasions, of course, the operation of the blockade provoked serious Anglo-American disagreement. The case of Argentina proved particu-

pp. 31–55; John Flint, 'Planned Decolonization and its Failure in British Africa', *African Affairs*, 82 (1983), 389–411; and Robert Pearce, 'The Colonial Office and Planned Decolonization in Africa', ibid., 83 (1984), 77–93.

[27] Alfred E. Eckes, Jr., *The United States and the Global Struggle for Minerals* (Austin, 1979), pp. 75, 84.

larly vexatious in 1944. The State Department considered the Peronist Farrell government to be pro-Nazi and hoped to topple it through a comprehensive trade embargo. The British—having considerable economic interests in the country, needing Argentine beef and wheat, and viewing the regime as nationalist not fascist—wished to sign a long-term meat contract. The issue reached the Roosevelt–Churchill level, and only the retirement of Hull and the imminent end of war facilitated a compromise solution.[28]

Behind the disputes about blockade policy, which mirrored similar arguments about how to treat Franco's Spain, lay a sensitivity to postwar national economic interests, for Argentina was one of the remaining countries of dominant British influence in a Western hemisphere increasingly under US economic control. The European war had once again enabled the New World 'to fatten on the follies of the Old',[29] and the argument over Argentina was paralleled by similar disputes over commodity agreements, merchant shipping, and commercial aviation.

A good instance of the underlying economic rivalry and of how it was handled diplomatically is the case of Middle Eastern oil.[30] The British had established a dominant position in Iran and Iraq after World War I, but the United States had secured concessions in Saudi Arabia in the 1930s and, as concern mounted in 1943 about declining US oil reserves, so did the rivalry and suspicion between British and American oil companies in which both governments became involved. But their fears proved exaggerated and the two sides found it desirable and possible to reach an agreement, concluded in August 1944. This would expedite the orderly development of Middle Eastern reserves, now vital for the postwar international economy, with mutual respect for each country's concessions and recognition of the potential importance of oil sales for easing Britain's peacetime payments problems. In the event, well-orchestrated opposition from smaller American companies ensured that this agreement was never ratified by Congress—another reminder of the unmanageable domestic politics of US foreign policy. But the fact of the agreement is nevertheless significant. Vociferous rivalry, exaggerated

[28] See Randall B. Woods, *The Roosevelt Foreign Policy Establishment and the 'Good Neighbour'* (Lawrence, Kan. 1979); C. A. MacDonald, 'The Politics of Intervention: The United States and Argentina, 1941–1946', *Journal of Latin American History*, 12 (1980), 365–96; R. A. Humphreys, *Latin America and the Second World War* (2 vols. London, 1981–2), ii, chs. 6–7.

[29] Merrill D. Peterson, *Thomas Jefferson and the New Nation* (Oxford, 1970), p. 416, quoting a memo by Jefferson dated 12 July 1790.

[30] Phillip J. Baram, *The Department of State in the Middle East, 1919–1945* (Philadelphia, 1978); Michael B. Stoff, *Oil, War, and American Security: The Search for a National Policy on Foreign Oil, 1941–1947* (New Haven, 1980); Irvine H. Anderson, *Aramco, the United States and Saudi Arabia: A Study of the Dynamics of Foreign Oil Policy, 1933–1950* (Princeton, 1981); John A. DeNovo, 'The Culbertson Economic Mission and Anglo-American Tensions in the Middle East, 1944–1945', *Journal of American History*, 63 (1977), 913–36.

suspicions, eventual compromise that was mutually beneficial but usually closer to American than British goals—this was the general pattern for wartime economic disputes. In most cases, too, it was essentially an Anglo-American framework which was imposed on the other powers.

The most striking example of this pattern derives from the protracted transatlantic discussions about the post-war economic order. In the Depression the multilateral economy had disintegrated into several loose economic blocs, each pegged to a major currency and trading largely within itself. Britain's grouping coalesced around the sterling area and the system of Imperial Preference, established in 1932, which discriminated against imports from outside the British Empire. To parts of the Conservative party and some in the Treasury and Bank of England, this seemed to be a viable long-term policy for promoting British commerce and safeguarding the position of the City in international finance. And even non-ideologues in Whitehall generally believed in 1941–2 that retention of trade and currency controls would be essential, at least temporarily, for Britain's post-war recovery.

During the 1930s, however, the Roosevelt Administration had repented of its initial economic nationalism, dedicating itself to the re-creation of a multilateral world economy. Henry Morgenthau and the Treasury wanted an early return to convertible currencies and stable exchange rates, while Hull's State Department concentrated on the commercial impediments to multilateralism, with Britain's network of preferential tariffs and quotas at the top of their list. Little was achieved in the 1930s, despite the 1938 Trade Agreement, but real opportunities came with Britain's wartime dependence on the United States.

After prolonged negotiations in 1941–2 the State Department secured a general (and not unambiguous) commitment that part of the repayment for Lend-Lease would be an end to British economic discrimination. Similarly, in 1943–4 London's approval of the largely American drafts for the International Monetary Fund and the World Bank reflected her need to secure the continuation of Lend-Lease after Germany's defeat. And at the end of 1945 Britain's ratification of the Bretton Woods agreements and her commitment to sterling convertibility by 1947 was extracted from a resentful Parliament only because the abrupt termination of Lend-Lease that August (again in response to US domestic pressures) left the UK reliant upon an American loan tied to this ratification.

As one US Treasury official predicted in 1940, in the last analysis the British could only 'stand and deliver' when pressed by the United States.[31] It is also undoubtedly true, as British officials grumbled, that

[31] Butterworth to Morgenthau, 13 Dec. 1940, Henry Morgenthau, Jr., Diary, 339: 401 (Franklin D. Roosevelt Library, Hyde Park, NY).

the American conversion to Cobdenite values conveniently fitted the interests of a country able to dominate an open, global market economy. But it would be wrong to depict the Americans as international highwaymen, or the British merely as spiritual descendants of Lord North. For, like Cobden, the Roosevelt Administration believed that thriving world commerce was a vital precondition of peace (and one fatally neglected in 1919). Equally, the majority of British policy-makers favoured a return to multilateralism, *if the terms were right*. This meant the United States should belatedly accept its own responsibilities as the world's leading creditor and a major importing nation. Specifically America should promote international liquidity through gold and dollar loans and reduce its own tariff barriers. In the United States Treasury these obligations were acknowledged in principle. Here, then, was the basis of agreement.

Admittedly the balance of power in the alliance ensured that America's was the decisive voice. Harry White's draft for a fixed-size stabilization fund was adopted as the working basis for negotiation, rather than Keynes's broader idea of an international clearing bank with larger assets and controls over creditor as well as debtor nations. The British were also uneasy at US dominance over the new institutions and their location in Washington. But all this was secondary in the minds of most British policy-makers, haunted by 1919 and 1931, to the fact that the United States had finally committed itself to a policy of economic internationalism through which the world might return to multilateralism *without* exchange fluctuations, payments deficits, and domestic deflation. It was agreement on American terms, but offering real benefits to Britain. And, despite Administration efforts to avoid any hint of a 'Special Relationship', it was essentially a blueprint devised by Washington and London and then imposed by them on everyone else.[32]

But we cannot end this story of conflict and compromise in 1945 with the triumph of multilateralism and the creation of the International Monetary Fund and the World Bank. For the multilateral, one-world economy was still-born. The Soviets abstained, Europe was partitioned. After the abortive British experiment in 1947 even limited currency convertibility was not achieved until 1958, and the Americans encouraged western Europe to form its own economic bloc in the interests of security and containment. Under the circumstances it was the American Government and not the IMF or World Bank which assumed the main

---

[32] See Richard N. Gardner, *Sterling–Dollar Diplomacy in Current Perspective* (3rd edn., New York, 1980); Alfred E. Eckes, Jr., *A Search for Solvency: Bretton Woods and the International Monetary System, 1941–1971* (Austin, 1975); Armand Van Dormael, *Bretton Woods: Birth of a Monetary System* (London, 1978); Sir Richard Clarke, *Anglo-American Economic Collaboration in War and Peace, 1942–1949*, ed. Sir Alec Cairncross (Oxford, 1982).

responsibility for promoting liquidity and reconstruction within 'the free world' through relief loans, Marshall Aid, and overseas military spending. These issues lie beyond the purview of this chapter. But they remind us again that the significance of the wartime alliance can only be fully evaluated if we look beyond 1945.

AMERICA, BRITAIN, AND POST-WAR SECURITY

In contrast to their equivocations about economic co-operation with the United States, British leaders emerged from the crisis of 1940–1 convinced that sustained American support was essential to secure long-term political stability. This time the United States must involve itself in peace-keeping as well as peace-making, working in close concert with Britain in diplomacy and military policy. Churchill spoke for most when he stated in 1944: 'It is my deepest conviction that unless Britain and the United States are joined in a special relationship, including Combined Staff organization and a wide measure of reciprocity in the use of bases—all within the ambit of a world organization—another destructive war will come to pass.'[33]

But could such a relationship be achieved? One fear was that the 'betrayal' of 1919–20 would be repeated. Republican and isolationist gains in the 1942 mid-term elections appalled British leaders, spurring them to seek agreement on the fundamentals of the post-war order while they still had a basically well-disposed administration in power. And in the Foreign Office some, including Eden, counselled against placing all Britain's eggs in the American basket, calling for closer economic and defence co-operation with western Europe. Nevertheless, even the sceptics agreed that they must try their best to construct a durable Anglo-American partnership.

The other and opposite fear was whether Britain would be swamped in such a relationship. This was a nagging anxiety, but British leaders remained basically optimistic. Victorians and Edwardians, they thought not of Britain the island but Britain the centre of a vast empire, and they still expected to draw on manpower and resources not far short of America's or Russia's. They also comforted themselves with the idea that, although increasingly dwarfed by American power, they still possessed superior skill and experience which would allow them to manage the immature young giant. Eden likened the UK–US relationship to that of Austria with Britain after 1815.[34] Harold Macmillan, in what proved a more popular analogy, invoked classical precedent to explain his conception of the British role in Eisenhower's Allied Force

[33] Churchill to Richard Law, 16 Feb. 1944, PREM 4, 27/10 (PRO).
[34] James V. Forrestal Diary, 21 Apr. 1945 (Naval Historical Center, Washington Navy Yard).

Headquarters (AFHQ) in North Africa. Expansively he told one subordinate:

> We, my dear Crossman, are Greeks in this American empire. You will find the Americans much as the Greeks found the Romans—great big, vulgar, bustling people, more vigorous than we are and also more idle, with more unspoiled virtues but also more corrupt. We must run A.F.H.Q. as the Greek slaves ran the operations of the Emperor Claudius.[35]

This concept of an Anglo-American 'Special Relationship' was, however, a largely British invention. It never had the same currency in Washington, let alone among the American public for whom wartime co-operation was counterbalanced by the Revolutionary tradition, ethnic pluralism, and a strident, hypersensitive nationalism. The State Department dedicated itself to creating the United Nations Organization and to ensuring, through a vast public relations campaign, that this time Americans accepted the gospel of idealistic internationalism. Power politics, spheres of influence, and formal alliances were all *passé*— at least for public consumption. Privately F.D.R. himself had little faith in international bodies: their efficacy would depend, he believed, upon co-operation among the great powers in keeping the peace. That was closer to the British position, but by 1943 Roosevelt's world 'policemen' included China and Russia as well as Britain and the USA. China was seen by F.D.R. as a future power and, more immediately, as an American client—a 'faggot vote' in Churchill's contemptuous phrase. And Roosevelt's wooing of Stalin from mid-1943—when it was clear that Russia would survive and would have much to say about the peace settlement—was particularly alarming to Churchill. The 'Special Relationship' seemed in danger of becoming an eternal triangle. At Tehran and Yalta Roosevelt sedulously avoided the appearance of an Anglo-American front and went out of his way to consult Stalin *à deux*.

Nevertheless, the Anglo-American partnership *was* in a class of its own among wartime alliances, as a glance at two of its facets makes clear. In intelligence matters London and Washington began sharing evaluations in 1940–1, and after American entry into the war an extensive and generally unfettered network of collaboration developed, despite some friction between the Office of Strategic Services and the Secret Intelligence Service. Nothing comparable was achieved or envisaged with the Soviet Union: the Russians distrusted even gratuitous information and by late 1942 the best Western intelligence on the state of Soviet forces came through German intercepts and not information from Moscow.[36]

[35] Richard Crossman, 'The Making of Macmillan', *Sunday Telegraph*, 9 Feb. 1964, p. 4.
[36] F. H. Hinsley *et al.*, *British Intelligence in the Second World War* (3 vols., London, 1979–84), esp. vol. i, pp. 311–14; vol. ii, pp. 41–66; vol. iii, pt. 1, pp. 459–75.

A similar, though more chequered, partnership blossomed in atomic weapons research. Britain had pioneered this work in the late 1930s, but in 1940–1 the two programmes were pooled and development went ahead in the United States. In 1942–3, as American dominance became apparent, some of F.D.R.'s atomic administrators tried to exclude the British, but Churchill resisted and the agreement with Roosevelt at Hyde Park, NY, in September 1944 committed the two countries to continued collaboration in both the military and commercial fields after the war. In all this Britain was increasingly the junior, but she remained a partner. By contrast Roosevelt deliberately held back from offering atomic secrets to Russia, perhaps viewing these as a possible bargaining counter in future diplomatic negotiations.[37]

Indeed, with regard to Russia, both British and American leaders shared fundamentally similar attitudes, and we should not allow Republican 'Yalta mythology' or Churchill's reminiscences, both the product of the Cold War, to obscure this fact. For much of the war Roosevelt and Churchill were primarily concerned to ensure that the Soviet Union, bearing the brunt of the fighting until mid-1944, did not succumb or sign a compromise peace. That was far from certain until the summer of 1943. Even then, Russian support was still essential: Roosevelt was anxious to bring them into the war against Japan and both leaders, fearful of a resurgent Germany, desired continued Big Three co-operation after the war.

In the summer of 1944, as the Russian armies swept west and south into Poland and the Balkans, Churchill became more alarmed about Soviet intentions. The result was not confrontation, however, but a spheres-of-influence arrangement for South-east Europe, negotiated in Moscow in October. Roosevelt did not protest at this, although it smacked of the 'power politics' deprecated publicly by the State Department, and it was in essentially the same spirit that Roosevelt and Churchill negotiated at Yalta in February 1945. Having little alternative, they conceded Stalin's predominance in Eastern Europe, but the agreements on free elections and the Declaration on Liberated Europe were intended to prevent a Russian sphere of influence becoming a closed Soviet bloc. In his last months the President was determined to hold Stalin to the Yalta accords, without causing unnecessary friction, and Churchill's urgent telegrams to Truman during the spring were not the prelude to Cold War but a demand that the two Western allies try to

---

[37] Margaret Gowing, *Britain and Atomic Energy, 1939–1945* (London, 1964); Martin J. Sherwin, *A World Destroyed: The Atomic Bomb and the Grand Alliance* (New York, 1973); Barton J. Bernstein, 'The Uneasy Alliance: Roosevelt, Churchill, and the Atomic Bomb, 1940–1945', *Western Political Quarterly*, 29 (1976), 202–30.

negotiate their differences with Russia before troop withdrawals sapped their bargaining power.[38]

This gradual convergence of British and American policy into a firm (if still irenic) approach towards the Soviet Union may seem to take us neatly into the beginnings of the Cold War era. But once again it is misleading to extrapolate from the Anglo-American relationship in 1945. For one thing this disintegrated rapidly immediately the war ended. Though the dominant world power, committed unlike in 1919 to upholding the new international order, the United States nevertheless withdrew from Europe to some degree once hostilities ceased. (Roosevelt had predicted as much in 1943–4.[39]) The Truman Administration was intent on establishing its exclusive protectorate over Japan while Congress struggled to restrict overseas spending and to bring the boys home. Not until the economic crisis of 1947 did the United States intervene substantively in Europe, and in the interim Britain was the main adversary of the Soviet Union.

In 1947–8 the Truman Doctrine, the Marshall Plan, and the Berlin airlift all symbolized a new American commitment to Europe and it seemed as if the wartime alliance was being recreated. But appearances were deceptive. For most of the war continental Europe had been under enemy control: the United States and Britain were the only surviving Western democracies and their relationship constituted a main axis of international politics. By the late 1940s, however, France was a significant actor again, and increasingly America's designated partner in the transatlantic alliance was not Britain alone but Western Europe which the US hoped would be under British leadership. Thus, after the mid-40s hiatus a new *Atlantic* alliance had been created of which the

---

[38] For recent discussions from various angles see Robert Dallek, *Franklin D. Roosevelt and American Foreign Policy, 1932–1945* (New York, 1979); Elisabeth Barker, *Churchill and Eden at War* (London, 1978); Eduard Mark, 'American Policy toward Eastern Europe and the Origins of the Cold War, 1941–1946: An Alternative Interpretation', *Journal of American History*, 66 (1981), 313–36; Warren F. Kimball, 'Naked Reverse Right: Roosevelt, Churchill, and Eastern Europe from TOLSTOY to Yalta—and a little beyond', *Diplomatic History*, 9 (1985), 1–24.

[39] At Tehran in Nov. 1943 F.D.R. spoke of a one- or two-year occupation of Germany—see *Foreign Relations of the United States [FRUS]: The Conference at Cairo and Tehran, 1943* (Washington, 1961), p. 256. The following February he told the State Dept.: 'I do not want the United States to have the post-war burden of reconstituting France, Italy and the Balkans. This is not our natural task at a distance of 3,500 miles or more. It is definitely a British task in which the British are far more vitally interested than we are.' Roosevelt to Acting Secretary, 21 Feb. 1944, State Dept. Records, 740.00119 Control (Germany) /2–2144 (National Archives, Washington, RG 59). In Dec. 1944 the President, in conversation with one British diplomat, 'spoke of a United States withdrawal from Europe with a genial kind of fatalism which was somewhat depressing'. (Richard Law, memo, 22 Dec. 1944, Foreign Office General Political Correspondence, FO 371/44595, AN 154/32/45, PRO.) And at Yalta on 5 Feb. 1945 he reiterated 'that he did not believe that American troops would stay in Europe much more than two years'. See *FRUS: The Conferences at Malta and Yalta, 1945* (Washington, 1955), p. 617.

Anglo-American axis was only a part. Again the wartime alliance does not point us simply into the Cold War era.

CONCLUSION: THE 'SPECIAL RELATIONSHIP'

The wartime alliance was neither natural nor inevitable, but the consequence of the unexpected global emergency of 1940–1. It was a marriage of necessity, uniting two major states whose recent history had been one of peaceful rivalry. That rivalry subsisted even during the crisis of global war, and arguments about grand strategy, decolonization, economic blocs, and post-war security all reflected the larger divergence of national interests and ideals. Apart from the profits of direct wartime competition, for example in the Middle East or Latin America, the USA also benefited from the destruction of much of Britain's trading base: exports cut by 40 per cent, shipping by 30 per cent, £4.2 billion external disinvestment.[40] And the war brought the United States near the zenith of her world power, with territory in the Pacific and a dominant influence in East Asia, as well as a monopoly of atomic weapons.

The growing disparity between the two powers was not, however, always reflected in the outcome of specific wartime arguments. In 1940–1 America's war effort had scarcely got going, yet Britain was her suitor because of the desperate international crisis. By 1942 the United States was a co-belligerent and her war industries were in full swing, yet the relationship was at its most equal, and in grand strategy, for instance, the British largely called the tune. In the last year of the war America was the dominant partner, militarily and economically, and she used her leverage to obtain a post-war economic order on her own terms. Yet at the same time the American challenge to Britain's empire, presaged in bitter debates about colonialism, failed to materialize, and the two nations drew closer in their thinking on post-war security and on handling of the Soviet Union. Nevertheless, the broad trend was evident: the United States the dominant power, Britain weakened and increasingly dependent upon her. That was a leading theme of World War II.

Yet, although we can no longer see the wartime alliance in Churchillian terms, there is no denying its remarkable character. Instead of measuring it against the standards of international harmony proclaimed by Utopians or propagandists, we should take our criteria from the real world of alliance politics. No two sovereign states have identical interests; every joint endeavour involves prior debate and compromise; neither side is totally committed to the common cause but keeps a weather eye open for its own advantage. Accepting, then, that

[40] W. K. Hancock and M. M. Gowing, *British War Economy* (London, rev. edn., 1975), p. 548.

no alliance is perfect, we can acknowledge that this one was much less imperfect than most.

Anglo-American co-operation grew out of a sense of shared threat and mutual need. For Britain after the fall of France American aid was essential for survival, victory, and a stable peace. For disarmed America the British Isles and its fleet were initially the last bastion against Hitler and later the essential base for liberating the continent of Europe. Britain's empire, despite American disquiet, was generally supported as a vital supplier of Britain's needs (and also of some of America's own) as well as a bulwark against further Axis expansion. Similar ideals reinforced similar interests. Despite the legacies of the Revolution and mass immigration, the two countries shared a tradition of liberal, capitalist democracy, and this was all the more apparent in a world of totalitarian states glorifying violent change. Furthermore, the sense of common cause was accentuated by the shared language. Admittedly this had deleterious consequences, because it facilitated highly publicized arguments about the alliance among bureaucrats, soldiers, legislators, pressmen, and opinion leaders. But this was a sign that the relationship was unusually intense and extensive—involving more people and thus offering more scope for disagreement and misunderstanding. Anyone who doubts its remarkable, three-dimensional character should look at wartime alliances that tried to span a language barrier—Britain's with France, America's with China.

What were the legacies of this wartime co-operation? Firstly, it assisted in the reordering of international relations. The Nazi drive for hegemony was mastered. Germany was divided. And all three major Axis powers were democratized and integrated in a new international order directed by the United States along Anglo-American guidelines. The war, and the way it was fought, also facilitated the extension of Soviet power in Europe. Subsequent anxiety about Russian intentions prompted renewed Anglo-American co-operation in the late 1940s when the two countries played a decisive role in creating an Atlantic alliance that has lasted to the present day.

At an intellectual level the wartime alliance profoundly shaped foreign policy attitudes. In a way unimaginable to Neville Chamberlain it predisposed British leaders for a generation to think in terms of a 'Special Relationship' with the United States—not as the sole basis of British policy but as a principal element—and sometimes to romanticize the link. On the American side this was never the case, but the wartime experience did help ensure that, as America emerged to superpower status, her attention was directed primarily not towards the Pacific but Western Europe, with Britain as her main intermediary. For Americans, then, the intellectual legacy of the war was 'Atlanticism'—articulated by pro-Allied publicists in 1941, visualized in the cartographic revolution of the war, institutionalized in NATO in 1949. Atlanticism proved the dominant paradigm for a third of a century. Not until the 1980s has it been seriously questioned, with talk of a 'successor generation', the shift in America's centre of gravity to the south and west, and closer US ties with Hispanic America and the Pacific basin.[41]

Finally, the alliance forged enduring and important personal relationships at all levels of the two countries' officialdoms. The contacts at the top, between men such as Macmillan, Eisenhower, Marshall, and Ismay are the most obvious, but connections lower down, among middle-ranking officials later to rise to policy-making positions in the 1950s and early 1960s, were perhaps more significant as well as wider-ranging. These personal links did not guarantee agreement—witness 1956—but they did provide a firm framework for diplomatic interchange, and in the case of intelligence at least there was continuous institutional co-operation through the post-war era.

Nevertheless, we should not treat the wartime alliance as an exact paradigm for what followed. For that alliance was abnormally close—the temporary response to a temporary world crisis. Most of the joint enterprises of the war did not survive its end: the Combined Chiefs of Staff, the other Anglo-American war-making boards, the atomic alliance (strangled by Truman and Congress in 1945–6). Most of the panaceas for the post-war order, concocted jointly though closer to American than British ideals, also fizzled out—One World, the UN, the new multilateral world economy. In part failure was attributable to unforeseen Cold War circumstances, but the formulae were also intrinsically flawed because they grew out of the unusually simple pattern of international relationships in 1940–2, when Britain and the USA were the only major Western democracies left and Russia's future remained uncertain. Through war the two nations were forced together, but in peacetime the scope and complexity of diplomacy increased again for both powers. To American policy-makers, relations with Russia and the reviving countries of western Europe assumed new importance; for the British, despite the seductions of the 'Special Relationship', traditional links with the Empire and the Continent once more had to be taken into account. And Britain was not yet finished as a world power.

The wartime Anglo-American relationship was probably the most remarkable alliance of modern history. No two countries have ever been so completely 'mixed up together . . . for mutual and general advantage', to borrow Churchill's felicitous words from 1940.[42] Their co-operation

---

[41] On cartography see Alan K. Henrikson, 'The Map as an "Idea": The Role of Cartographic Imagery during the Second World War', *The American Cartographer*, 2 (1975), 19–53. Stephen F. Szabo, ed., *The Successor Generation: International Perspectives of Postwar Europeans* (London, 1982) is a good study.

[42] *Parliamentary Debates* (Commons), 20 Aug. 1940, col. 1171.

helped reshape the international order at a particularly malleable time and, despite the post-war upheavals, it set durable patterns for future attitudes and institutions. Yet the wartime relationship was also unusual because never again would the two countries be so closely matched in power and capability. After 1945 Britain's decline became apparent, even though she remained a genuine world power into the 1960s. And never again would the two nations be thrown so completely upon each other. In the post-war world greater American power and the multiplicity of America's and Britain's peacetime interests meant that each mattered less to the other. In more senses than one, the wartime alliance was truly a 'special' relationship.

3

Unequal Partners:
The Truman Administration and
Great Britain

BRADFORD PERKINS

SECRETARY of State Dean Acheson once discovered British and American diplomats working on a paper defining their countries' 'Special Relationship'. Horrified, he ordered all copies of 'the wretched paper' to be destroyed.[1] The Secretary believed that a special relationship did indeed exist. But he knew that efforts to define it would raise severe difficulties, since the British, who had coined the term and almost monopolized its use, woud seek to define it in expansive terms. Acheson feared that formalization of a privileged British position *vis-à-vis* the United States would disturb other allies and horrify American opinion.

In fact, during the Truman Administration the British did occupy a special position among America's partners, but it was not a relationship between equals. During World War II the Americans developed a sense of power, of righteous power. On the whole, despite criticism from isolationists of one stripe or another, they considered it their right, their duty, and their opportunity to lead the world. No ally, even the closest, could expect to change the directions of American policy. With the exception of the North Atlantic Treaty, the major moves in the Cold War on the Western side were American initiatives. On most of the initiatives, notably the Marshall Plan, the British were not consulted in advance.

Moreover, when Britain sought special privileges, she was, with the notable exception of the loan of 1945, almost always rebuffed. A good example is the atomic relationship. Because British science had contributed to development of the atomic bomb and because Roosevelt had made extensive promises to Churchill regarding post-war cooperation, the British thought they had a right to be considered partners. The Americans disagreed. As a result the British had no part in

---

[1] Dean Acheson, *Present at the Creation* (New York, 1969), p. 387.

formulation of the Lilienthal or Baruch plans, about which they had reservations, and played a very secondary role in the United Nations Atomic Energy Commission's unsuccessful efforts to establish international control. Similarly, they failed to get a reaffirmation of Roosevelt's pledge that Britain would be consulted before atomic bombs were used, although in 1950 President Truman nearly gave that assurance. Finally, repeated efforts to obtain scientific information from the Americans failed to achieve much.

In January 1947 a small Cabinet group secretly approved construction of a British bomb. (It is not clear when the Americans were first informed, or learned, of this decision.) In part, the decision was justified on the grounds of need for a weapon of deterrence. But, in the view of those who made the decision, the bomb was also required to 'hold up our position *vis-à-vis* the Americans'.[2] Without assistance from the United States—indeed, in the face of American arguments against a separate bomb programme—the British pressed ahead. In the autumn of 1952 they exploded their first atomic bomb.

'Looked at in isolation [from other aspects of the Anglo-American relationship],' Margaret Gowing has declared, 'these atomic energy negotiations would present a depressing picture of a super-power playing with a satellite.'[3] Britain, whose wartime services supported her claims, received more consideration from the Americans than any other power, but this was far from an admission of equality.

In somewhat the same way, wartime patterns of co-operation in the military and diplomatic areas were dismantled, to a large degree despite the wishes of those men on both sides of the Atlantic who had worked together during the war. Shortly after victory, the Combined Chiefs of Staff, a major instrument of co-ordination, was allowed to lapse, and when military officers, particularly in the two armies, attempted to carry on their liaison informally, the civilian authorities in Washington made their displeasure known. American diplomats continued to have closer contact with their British opposite numbers than any others, and in most cases their world-views were remarkably similar. However, at least until George Marshall became Secretary of State in 1947, and even then not in all areas, there was no real co-ordination.

Many British officials never really understood that the American service departments and the State Department were even less independent actors than British ministries and their chiefs, and that in those areas in which he chose to exercise his authority the President was not only independent but supreme. As a result, they sometimes felt misled or

---

[2] Francis Williams, *A Prime Minister Remembers* (London, 1961), p. 119.
[3] Margaret Gowing, *Independence and Deterrence* (London, 1974), vol. i, p. 320. For her own reconsideration of these issues in this volume, see Chapter 7.

mistreated, most notably during the Palestine imbroglio of 1945–8, when American diplomats showed sympathy for the British position, had many of the same attitudes toward Jewish statehood, and wanted to work for compromise between Arabs and Jews, only to have President Truman reject, or even ignore, their counsel.

In 1945, when Truman's succession worried the British, one anonymous official wrote, 'One can only hope that the dignity of his new office will reveal in him hitherto unsuspected qualities which will render him equal to his enormous responsibilities.'[4] Truman brought to the White House some traditional prejudices against perfidious Albion, and at first he sought to keep his country above and separate from the Anglo-Soviet quarrel he foresaw. As he turned in an anti-Soviet direction his reputation in Britain began to climb. Both Labour and the Tories welcomed his re-election in 1948.

The British did not, particularly during the first months of his tenure, get along well with James F. Byrnes, whom they considered both arrogant and inconstant. During the London meeting of foreign ministers in September 1945, Byrnes's free-wheeling angered Bevin, the Foreign Secretary, and the Cabinet agreed that 'it was impossible for us to work with [the Americans] if they constantly took action . . . without prior consultation with us'.[5] When Byrnes arranged for a conference at Moscow in December without informing Bevin, the Foreign Secretary considered refusing to attend. Not surprisingly, there was practically no Anglo-American co-operation during the meeting.

Subsequently, tactics were better co-ordinated between the Americans and the British (and to a lesser degree the French), but there was little doubt that Byrnes, George Marshall, and then Dean Acheson were the leading figures. During the Berlin blockade of 1948–9, for example, the three Western powers orchestrated their negotiations with Moscow. When secret Soviet-American exchanges began, however, the British were informed no more than the French until a settlement had been outlined.

Neither before nor after Truman's election in his own right in 1948 could he ignore the restraints of Congressional and national opinion. Concern that moving too far, too fast would alienate both may, as Seyom Brown argues, help to explain 'the Truman administration's early gropings toward a coherent foreign policy'.[6] However, once the administration struck out on a decisive line it never suffered important checks at the hands of Congress. To mobilize support it sometimes acted in ways the British found questionable. At times it excused refusals to

---

[4] Quoted in Robert M. Hathaway, *Ambiguous Partnership* (New York, 1981), p. 133.
[5] Hugh Dalton, quoted in Daniel Yergin, *Shattered Peace* (Boston, 1977), p. 131.
[6] Seyom Brown, *The Faces of Power* (rev. edn., New York, 1983), p. 32.

meet British requests, as in atomic matters, with the argument that agreements must be made 'palatable to Congress'.[7] Usually this was a ploy to excuse decisions it wished to take. British worries, frequently expressed, about the baleful effects of the American political system were largely unjustified.

In Britain, the electoral landslide of 1945 committed the country to socialism. Of course, as Clement Attlee stressed in an address to Congress in November 1945—'You have heard that we are Socialists, but I wonder just what that means to you'[8]—it was socialism in the British style, moderate and democratic. Still, much American criticism might have been anticipated. As it was, Britain's socialism—'a very long step toward communism', in one Congressman's view[9]—was used as an argument against the loan of 1945, but never became an important theme. American officials might deplore the British swing to the left, but they had the good sense not to say so in public, then or later.

One reason, no doubt, was their broad satisfaction with the foreign policy of the Labour government. In the face of the emerging conflict with the Soviet Union, the Attlee cabinet disregarded such things as international working-class solidarity and the idea that 'Left speaks to Left'. When Attlee and Bevin replaced Churchill and Eden in the middle of the Potsdam Conference, the Americans were surprised to find that this meant no change in policy. In his first address to the House of Commons, a speech which 'spread dismay through the Left Wing',[10] the new Foreign Secretary declared that 'The basis of our policy is in keeping with that worked out by the [wartime] Coalition Government'[11] in which he and the Prime Minister had served.

Bevin and Attlee were under no illusion that, in the central arena of Soviet–Western relations, Britain could follow a truly independent policy. They, their colleagues, and Foreign Office officials might chafe at America's management of the conflict with Russia, but they dared not defy her. As the Permanent Under-Secretary of the Foreign Office expressed it early in 1947, with Britain weak and Russia threatening, 'too great independence of the United States would be a dangerous luxury'.[12]

Why Attlee selected Bevin rather than Hugh Dalton as Foreign Secretary in 1945 is unclear, but, once made, the Prime Minister's commitment was firm. Attlee was readier to accept the limits on British power, more prone to compromise with the Soviet Union, and more

[7] D. Cameron Watt, *Succeeding John Bull* (Cambridge, 1984), p. 96.

[8] Quoted in Kenneth Harris, *Attlee* (London, 1982), pp. 280–1.

[9] Jesse Wolcott, quoted in Justus D. Doenecke, *Not to the Swift* (Lewisburg, Pa., 1979), p. 61.

[10] Edward J. Meehan, *The British Left Wing and Foreign Policy* (New Brunswick, 1960), p. 71.

[11] Quoted in Hugh B. Berrington, *Backbench Opinion in the House of Commons* (Oxford, 1973), p. 51.

[12] Sir Orme Sargent, quoted in Victor Rothwell, *Britain and the Cold War* (London, 1982), p. 270.

critical of American behaviour. However, while he sometimes gently questioned Bevin's policies, in the end he usually mobilized Cabinet support for them and dealt firmly with critics from Labour's left wing. Averell Harriman was one of the few Americans who appreciated Attlee's 'ability to bring the quarrelsome elements in his party together'.[13]

Although Bevin knew that his country's freedom of action was limited, he sought to preserve as much as possible and to develop influence that might be a substitute for power. He fostered ties with Commonwealth countries, only to find some of them looking first to the Americans for protection. He assumed a leading role in European politics, without however committing Britain to regional organizations which might limit her sovereignty. (Since progress toward European integration was an American preoccupation, British reluctance to go beyond circumscribed limits caused tension with the United States.) Finally, Bevin sought partnership in Western leadership: close but not sycophantic ties with Washington. The Foreign Secretary did attain a measure of influence, but the Americans simply would not allow others, even those who shared their outlook, to determine major lines of policy. They tended, a Foreign Office memorandum of 1947 rightly observed, 'consciously or unconsciously . . . to claim leadership of any forces in the world which are willing to stand up to excessive Soviet pretensions'.[14]

Under the circumstances, especially given Bevin's warm temper, penchant for alcohol, and the poor health that finally drove him from office in 1951, it is not surprising that he often complained about or resisted the Americans. He hated James F. Byrnes; he did not get on well with George Marshall, who thought him both slow and, more damning to Marshall, disorganized; and (primarily because of Truman's policy on Palestine) he positively detested the President, who reciprocated his feelings. Of the Secretaries of State, only Dean Acheson appreciated him: 'Ernest Bevin was as honorable and loyal a colleague as one could wish'.[15]

Far more important, however, was Bevin's agreement with the Americans that the Soviet challenge was the most important fact in international affairs. Indeed, he reached that conclusion before they did. At Potsdam, Bevin's anti-Soviet venom troubled Byrnes, and during other conferences in 1945 he was much firmer than the Secretary of State. From time to time, Bevin spoke of being alert to the possibility of compromise with the Soviet Union, and during the Korean War he

---

[13] W. Averell Harriman and Elie Abel, *Special Envoy to Churchill and Stalin* (New York, 1975), p. 550.

[14] Rothwell, *Britain and the Cold War*, p. 434.

[15] Dean Acheson, *Sketches from Life* (New York, 1961), p. 1.

explored avenues to settlement in ways that disappointed Washington. On the whole, however, he pursued policies as firm as those of the United States, despite occasional prodding from Attlee, who for example suggested in January 1947 that, before embarking on all out resistance to the Soviet Union, 'we seek to come to an agreement with the USSR'.[16]

During an almost unique moment of *bonhomie*, an interlude in the tense talks over Korea in December 1950, Truman and Attlee commiserated with one another over their respective domestic oppositions. Soon, in April 1951, Aneurin Bevan was to resign, essentially over the British commitment to rearmament. Yet despite the attention it attracted, down to the end the Labour Left was no more able than Truman's opposition to defeat government policy. This was so not only because the government could usually count upon Conservative support for its Cold War policies but also because of inherent weaknesses of the Left. While the Left could easily stir up a commotion at annual party conferences and in the House of Commons, denouncing Bevin's anti-Soviet, pro-American position, it neither could nor wanted to bring down the government. Left-wing MPs neither pressed their motions on foreign policy to a division nor voted against those of the government, preferring the symbolic act of abstention. Moreover, their numbers were usually small. About a hundred MPs abstained from voting on NATO in May 1949, but there were only about two dozen 'persistent offenders' in the Commons.[17] Finally, the Marshall Plan, at first attacked as an instrument of American economic domination, undermined criticism from the left when it proved instead to be a major contribution to European recovery. The rebels irritated their superiors, but they did not deflect policy any more than did Truman's opponents on Capitol Hill.

The two traditional themes of discord, imperialism and trade practices, failed to keep the nations apart after 1945. American anti-imperialism had always been more noisy than determined, and the Attlee government's retreat from empire in any case reduced the target. Freedom for India, the chief subject of anti-imperial agitation during World War II, virtually disappeared as an object of American concern after 1945. In the Middle East, where, particularly because of the oil factor, rivalry might have been expected, the reverse was the case. Although some in Washington thought otherwise at first, London welcomed American petroleum investments because they implied political involvement that would buttress British efforts. For its part, the State Department, at least in some areas, discouraged American companies who considered challenging British interests. On the whole,

---

[16] Alan Bullock, *Ernest Bevin: Foreign Secretary* (New York, 1983), p. 349.
[17] W. L. Guttsmann, *The British Political Elite* (London, 1963), p. 270.

particularly as the Cold War deepened, 'The United States supported the British Empire as the predominant regional power'.[18]

Two episodes involving Iran show that this generalization must not be overstressed, that reservations about British imperialism lingered. In the early stages of the controversy over the continued presence of Soviet troops sent to Iran to protect wartime supply routes, the Americans avoided a leading role, primarily because they had not yet settled on an anti-Soviet tack but also because they had doubts about British activities. Only in early 1946 did they take the lead in efforts which led to Soviet withdrawal. When the British later stumbled into a collision with Iranian nationalism, Secretary Acheson repeatedly urged compromise. ('The old Kipling approach did not work', he told Ambassador Franks.[19]) Before and after Iran's nationalization of the Anglo-Iranian Oil Company in 1951, the Secretary worked steadily to get negotiations going, angering himself and the British alike. Of course, broader calculations entered into American policy, but anti-imperialism played a part.

Britain's anger at American officiousness regarding Iran was as nothing compared to her fury over Truman's interference in the Palestine question. Indeed, this caused more friction between the two governments than any other episode, spilling into the public arena in a way that, for example, disagreement over the atomic relationship never did. The intractable nature of the problem was itself inevitably a cause of frustration, but both sides indulged it.

At the end of the war, demands resumed for increased Jewish immigration into Palestine and, by Zionists, for creation of a Jewish state. Britain, the mandatory power, faced a dilemma. The Cabinet itself was divided and often critical of Bevin, who, however, kept control of policy. In principle the Foreign Secretary did not oppose immigration and even some Jewish self-rule, although he did oppose the creation of a Jewish state. He sought a settlement that would at least be tolerated by Arabs and Jews and would certainly not have to be enforced by British arms, and he wanted to preserve, as a legacy of empire, Britain's political standing and influence in the Arab states.

To accomplish these ends, Bevin sought a compromise between Arabs and Jews—at a time when the gap between the two sides was too great for even the most talented, impartial conciliator to bridge. Moreover, in effect he defined compromise as the minimum the Arabs said they would accept—and this was very little indeed. He also sought to involve the United States, both to share the burden and as an additional weight for compromise—at a time when all Americans, emphatically including the

[18] Wm. Roger Louis, *The British Empire in the Middle East* (Oxford, 1984), p. 102.
[19] Quoted in Gaddis Smith, *Dean Acheson* (New York, 1972), p. 339.

President, had no stomach for involvement. Success was unattainable; as George Marshall confessed to English visitors in the fall of 1947, the British 'had been the victims of an impossible situation and considerable unjust criticism'.[20]

In the United States, Truman monopolized policy-making. While the President only belatedly came down firmly behind Jewish statehood and frequently fulminated against Zionist leaders, from the summer of 1945 onward he pressed for large-scale immigration into Palestine. But he expected the British—whose willingness he doubted—to make this possible on their own, declined to support efforts for a compromise by negotiation, and above all refused to consider helping to impose one. 'I have no desire to send 500,000 American soldiers . . . to make peace in Palestine', he said in 1945,[21] and he never wavered from this determination. In short, he wanted to propose, leaving it to the British to dispose. One can only sympathize with Attlee's complaint that 'the Americans . . . forever lay heavy burdens on us without lifting a little finger to help'.[22]

Two episodes highlight the gap between Truman and the British. Late in 1945 the British arranged an Anglo-American Committee of Inquiry on Palestine, with the primary purpose of making the United States share in responsibility. The committee's report was a compromise package that called for the immigration *ab initio* of 100,000 Jews and the creation, in time, of a binational state, not separate Jewish and Arab ones. The President endorsed the first recommendation but ignored the rest. Attlee, speaking in the House of Commons for emphasis, thereupon stated that this would not do, and that the United States must take its share of responsibility in Palestine.

In the autumn of 1946 the British believed, almost certainly wrongly, that they were on the verge of convening a conference that might produce a compromise founded on the principle of a binational state. Learning that Truman intended to issue a statement on Yom Kippur, they begged that it be delayed a mere week to give them time to complete plans for a conference. The Americans refused, explaining that the President had to speak before the Republican leader, Thomas A. Dewey, did so. Truman's statement, actually somewhat equivocal but taken as an endorsement of partition, undermined Jewish compromisers and further alienated the Arabs. 'I shall await with interest', Attlee wrote frostily, 'to learn what were the imperative reasons which compelled this precipitancy.'[23]

---

[20] Quoted in Louis, *The British Empire in the Middle East*, p. 480.
[21] Quoted in Zvi Ganin, *Truman, American Jewry, and Israel* (New York, 1979), p. 32.
[22] Quoted in Louis, *The British Empire in the Middle East*, p. 419.
[23] Quoted in Harris, *Attlee*, p. 396.

Such behaviour irritated even pro-Zionist British but positively infuriated Bevin. As early as 1945 a Jewish agent reported, 'Bevin's anger and fury against the United States are unimaginable'.[24] Privately and—alas!—publicly, he charged Truman with pandering to the Jewish vote. When, in February 1947, Britain threw in her hand and tossed the issue to the United Nations, Bevin complained in the House of Commons, '... I cannot settle things if my problem is made the subject of local elections'.[25] In fact, although Jewish pressure was only one factor influencing Truman, Bevin had good reason to complain that the President had been unhelpful throughout.

Although the problem of Palestine had imperialist overtones, both on the British side and among American critics, imperialism was never central to the nations' disagreement. A closely related issue, what Americans liked to describe as economic imperialism and the British preferred simply to call the sterling system, produced one sharp controversy but otherwise less tension than might have been anticipated.

'Popular memory', two economists have written, 'dwells upon the Cold War. But for a time, the financial struggle with Britain loomed as large in our policies.'[26] So also argue revisionist historians. Clearly so-called 'multilateralist' thought influenced United States policy. Leaders stressed the virtues of open trade, frequently without admitting that the United States would be a special beneficiary. Britain, at the centre of the sterling system, stood at the head of a different kind of world.

However, the Americans seldom drove home their case. Imperial Preference was a striking example of the kind of barrier to trade (and American opportunities) they disliked, but the Americans did not make its abolition a condition of help to Britain. The General Agreement on Tariffs and Trade, concluded in 1947, included a compromise so favourable to the British that it provided 'little practical benefit' for American trade.[27] British state trading—bulk purchases of agricultural goods by intergovernmental agreements, for example—never came under heavy attack, although the practice ran directly counter to American principles. And the Americans allowed negotiations to establish an International Trade Organization, designed to codify American hopes, to dwindle away into nothing.

The great exception to this generalization is the loan of 1945. In December, John Maynard Keynes and Assistant Secretary of State Will Clayton arranged for a loan to Britain of $3.75 billion. In return,

[24] Moshe Shertok, quoted in Bullock, *Bevin*, p. 178.
[25] Quoted in Michael J. Cohen, *Palestine and the Great Powers* (Princeton, 1982), p. 234.
[26] David P. Calleo and Benjamin F. Rowland, *America and the World Economy* (Bloomington, 1973), p. 38.
[27] Richard N. Gardner, *Sterling–Dollar Diplomacy* (2nd edn., New York, 1969), p. 360.

Clayton extorted a promise soon to make sterling freely convertible and a pledge to ratify the Bretton Woods agreements that were expected to lead to a multilateral world system. 'We loaded the British loan negotiations with all the conditions the traffic would bear', he bragged.[28]

The agreement came under sharp British attack, and the cabinet defended it only tepidly. Nearly a hundred MPs opposed it in the House of Commons, and the Conservatives, partly to prevent a party split, abstained *en masse*. 'It is aggravating', complained *The Economist*, 'to find that our reward for losing a quarter of our national wealth in the common cause is to pay tribute for half a century to those who have been enriched by the war'.[29]

Until convertibility took effect in July 1947, the British economy appeared to be recovering remarkably. 'If we keep going . . . as we have since V-J Day the shortages and frustrations which still afflict us will disappear like the snows of winter', the Chancellor of the Exchequer exulted.[30] Following convertibility, however, there was a run on the pound, and the loan evaporated. As permitted in an emergency by the loan agreement, Britain suspended convertibility. An orgy of recrimination broke out in Britain. The American insistence on convertibility so soon had proved a serious mistake, economically and politically.

Granting this, the financial terms had otherwise been generous— funds to an amount Keynes considered satisfactory, a liberal settlement of the Lend-Lease account, a very low rate of interest, and a long repayment schedule. Moreover, convertibility and a few minor matters aside, the British did no more than in the past: they agreed only to enter negotiations to remove other trade barriers, and little came of this promise later on.

Above all, the loan was the first American commitment to European recovery. The Truman Administration moved as it did for a multitude of reasons—to work toward a multilateral world helpful to the United States and others alike, to strengthen an economy vital to world stability, and, though administration officials muted this point, to support a partner in the struggle against Communism. Revisionists' objection that 'idealism played no role whatsoever in the matter'[31] is as naive as Keynes's hope that Washington would simply give money in gratitude for wartime contributions.

Various factors explain the American failure to press harder for a multilateral world. Domestic support was never unanimous; many

---

[28] Quoted in Robert J. Donovan, *Conflict and Crisis* (New York, 1977), p. 186.
[29] Quoted in Bullock, *Bevin*, p. 203.
[30] Quoted in Gardner, *Sterling–Dollar Diplomacy*, p. 307.
[31] Joyce Kolko and Gabriel Kolko, *The Limits of Power* (New York, 1972), p. 63.

doubting businessmen and Congressmen were certainly unwilling to accept the tariff reductions and other sacrifices necessary to achieve such a system. Moreover, as the Cold War deepened, even such zealots as Will Clayton recognized that allied economies were too precarious to expose to radical change: 'when it came to choice, American opinion subordinated the immediate enforcement of multilateralism to the political and economic interests of the Western World'.[32] Certainly by 1947 the Americans had more or less put the campaign for a new trading world into moth-balls. An issue which might well have produced serious tension between the English-speaking powers ceased to do so.

The Americans would not have been so concerned about Britain's trading practices in 1945 had they really understood her weakness. This failure to comprehend also helps to explain why the Truman Administration at first looked upon itself as an arbiter between Britain and the Soviet Union, a concept that made no sense unless Britain had the strength to act independently. Although many in the bureaucracy, taking an anti-Soviet line, dissented, even as late as December 1945 an interdepartmental group believed that the United States 'must act as mediator and conciliator between Britain and Russia'.[33] This position meant that, until well into 1946, London and not Washington was the major target of Soviet propaganda.

By the spring of 1946 the Americans had moved toward the British position. Thereafter, regarding Europe, which both considered the most important battleground in the struggle with the Soviet Union, there were no significant disagreements. Both believed that Moscow sought to extend its domination and that this effort must be met with a policy the Americans christened 'containment'. (George Kennan's famous 'long telegram' of February 1946, which formulated or at least defined the emerging view, had its counterpart in similar messages from Frank Roberts, minister in the British embassy at Moscow, with whom Kennan often exchanged ideas.)

Both also believed that the threat was not so much military as political and psychological. What they feared was that, largely as a result of economic distress, Europe would unravel. Bevin worried in particular that France would go communist; in July 1947 he told the American ambassador that 'If... no action is taken by the United States until late fall or winter, he thought that France, and with her most of Europe, would be lost'.[34] The answer was to rebuild national economies and,

---

[32] Gardner, *Sterling–Dollar Diplomacy*, p. 346.

[33] State-War-Navy Coordinating Committee, quoted in Terry H. Anderson, *The United States, Great Britain, and the Cold War* (Columbia, Mo., 1981), p. 87.

[34] Bullock, *Bevin*, p. 424.

consequently, political will. This fundamental agreement in analysis overwhelmed all differences at other levels.

Both felt that European recovery required German participation. There were differences between the two occupying powers—over the level of industry to be permitted in Germany; over reparations, which the British continued to remove in small quantities until as late as 1949; over British zonal authorities' support for socialist politicians and their dabbling in socialization schemes; and over occupation costs, which the British tried to shift to the Americans. But in the teeth of Russian and French opposition they worked in tandem to rebuild West Germany, first as an economic factor (the primary motive for the agreement of December 1946 to unite the British and American occupation zones) and then as an independent state.

Events in Greece showed both the coincidence of views and the asymmetry of power. There, beginning in 1946, the royalist government faced a rising supported by the Soviet Union and its satellites. The British committed troops and money, but the burden soon became too much to bear. The Chancellor, Dalton, argued for pulling out, and Attlee wrote to Bevin in December, 'I am beginning to doubt whether the Greek game is worth the candle'.[35] At first Bevin resisted, then he hoped to arrange to share the burden with the United States, but in February 1947 he gave in: 'I think Mr. Dalton is justified. We get no help from the Greeks'.[36] He told Washington that Britain would leave Greece in six weeks' time. In March the President addressed Congress, promulgating the Truman Doctrine and calling for aid to Greece.[37]

The ground for what appeared to be a dramatic change in American policy had in fact already been prepared. Trickles of American assistance had been going to Greece for some time, although the Americans were reluctant to get deeply involved, partly because they feared that they would be accused of pulling British chestnuts from the fire. However, as early as October 1946 they told the Greeks that substantial aid could be expected if they reformed their government. Bevin himself had given Byrnes a good indication of the way in which the wind was blowing the previous December, and Acheson, then Assistant Secretary, has been told to begin planning before the British note arrived. 'The Americans', as Daniel Yergin has written, 'were primed for crisis.'[38]

In Alan Bullock's words, in going along with his colleagues Bevin agreed to a step he 'had hitherto refused to take and took only with

---

[35] Quoted ibid., p. 340.
[36] Quoted in Anderson, *The United States, Great Britain, and the Cold War*, p. 168.
[37] Truman also asked for aid to Turkey, where the British similarly laid down their burdens.
[38] Yergin, *Shattered Peace*, p. 281.

considerable misgivings, partly because it meant admitting publicly Britain's inability to go on playing an equal role with the Americans, but, even more perhaps, because he was unsure how the Americans would take it'.[39] The first reason is generally accepted; the second is more debatable. Of course Bevin could not know—and the Truman Administration did not know—how Congress would respond to a radically new line of policy, but, though he and others had grumbled at American indecisiveness down to that time, he surely must have divined how the administration would react to a British withdrawal from Greece. And he may well have realized that it would be much easier, politically, for the Truman Administration to take unilateral action rather than arrange the Anglo-American collaboration he had desired.[40]

Bruce R. Kuniholm argues that, tacitly at least, by the end of 1946 there was agreement that 'The British were to continue their aid to [Greece and other countries in the region] as long as possible, and to serve as a kind of front for the United States in order that American policies not appear provocative, but there was little question that they were gradually giving way to the Americans.'[41] Ernest Bevin regretted that factors of power made this so, but he welcomed the American commitment.

On the heels of the Truman Doctrine came George Marshall's speech at the Harvard commencement of 1947, offering to support a European effort at reconstruction. Bevin, the first European leader to pick up Marshall's invitation, quickly arranged to see the French foreign minister and, with him, convened the conferences which led to the multinational response Marshall required. Like the Americans he felt that the Russians should be invited to take part but hoped they would not; he expected the Kremlin to decline but feared that it might decide to participate, seizing an opportunity to work for conditions the United States was bound to reject or merely delaying the completion of a programme which Bevin believed must not be delayed. After the Russians withdrew from a Big Three conference at Paris, British representatives played leading roles in efforts to produce a plan acceptable to the Americans.

Nevertheless, British and American views differed. Above all, the British sought to cast themselves in a leading, at least semi-independent role. One of Bevin's aides envisaged a situation in which 'Europe under

[39] Bullock, *Bevin*, p. 369.

[40] In fact, at American urging the British continued aid at a modest level, and British troops remained in Greece until after the end of the civil war in 1949. A plan to withdraw them in the summer of 1947 angered Marshall, who complained of the British that 'They are far too casual or free-handed in passing the buck of the international dilemma to [the] U.S.' Bevin managed to block withdrawal at the time. Quoted in Bullock, *Bevin*, p. 470.

[41] Bruce R. Kuniholm, *The Origins of the Cold War in the Near East* (Princeton, 1980), p. 383.

American water[ing]-cans handled by British gardeners blossoms into a happy . . . garden of Eden'.[42] When Will Clayton and Ambassador Lewis Douglas met with the Inner Cabinet a fortnight after Marshall's speech, they faced a barrage of arguments 'that Britain ought to be regarded as the partner of the USA in helping Europe rather than "lumped in" with the other European countries'.[43] Clayton felt confident enough to reject this idea without even consulting Washington. There must be, he said, an all-European plan developed by equals.

Even before Marshall's speech, *The Economist*, often critical of American domination, had argued that in this emergency 'the United States [should] use its great power to knock [European] heads together and impose agreement'.[44] This too was not what British leaders had in mind. They were happy to have the United States embark upon a programme of aid, but they at first scoffed at the idea of a 'plan', a conception which Foreign Office officials described as 'eyewash designed to extract dollars from a reluctant Congress'.[45]

Once convinced that a 'plan' was the key, the British went only part way in the direction the Americans desired. They accepted the American view that the European plan should be more than a loosely co-ordinated set of 'shopping lists' from individual countries, but they were reluctant to create the mechanisms for co-ordination the Americans had in mind. The British were not the only Europeans who caused difficulty—the French resisted the idea that German economic recovery should be stressed—but they were the ones who most angered the Americans.

When Clayton came to Paris at the end of August he declared that a draft report prepared by the Europeans was 'disappointing and would constitute a prejudice to the success of the Marshall program'.[46] That opinion was underscored by American diplomatic notes to the participating countries a few days later objecting that the 'whole program gives little more than lip service to principles of European self help and mutual help'.[47] In the end, Washington agreed to accept the European report as 'provisional', with the intention, later carried out, of forcing modifications during negotiations in the United States. The plan got under way.

---

[42] Quoted in Rothwell, *Britain and the Cold War*, p. 284.

[43] Bullock, *Bevin*, p. 413.

[44] Quoted in Ernst H. van der Beugel, *From Marshall Aid to Atlantic Partnership* (Amsterdam, 1966), p. 57.

[45] Quoted in Rothwell, *Britain and the Cold War*, p. 279.

[46] Van der Beugel, *From Marshall Aid to Atlantic Partnership*, p. 79.

[47] Robert Lovett, quoted in John Gimbel, *The Origins of the Marshall Plan* (Stanford, 1976), p. 215.

Subsequently, the British dragged their heels on the construction of all-European institutions. Along with others, they blocked plans to give the Organization for European Economic Co-operation real, continuing powers. They resisted creation of a European Payments Union, only agreeing in 1950 after the proposal had been watered down. And Britain declined—'her great mistake of the postwar period', in Acheson's opinion[48]—to join in the Schumann Plan, which initiated the movement toward European economic union. Unpleasant Anglo-American exchanges marked negotiation on these issues, but, particularly because the Department of State had mixed feelings, the Americans never used their full power to force their views.

Congress appropriated $13.3 billion in Marshall aid, and Britain, which received $3.2 billion, was the largest beneficiary. European production rose by one-third from 1948 to 1951, and, although the European Recovery Programme's contribution to this growth cannot be measured, it was the most important factor. The threat of European political deterioration, the menace which inspired Ernest Bevin to orchestrate a favourable response to Marshall's overture, had been dissipated.

As the Marshall Plan got under way, European and American leaders began to consider a further step, a military alliance. Here Bevin played a perhaps even more prominent role. His initiatives were welcomed by Washington, and both proceeded on the basis of very similar analyses of the military situation. In the framing and implementation of the North Atlantic Treaty, however, there were differences of approach which once again showed that the 'Special Relationship' by no means meant total identity of views.

In January 1948 Bevin proposed an alliance between his own country, France, and the Benelux nations. Although on its face primarily directed at a possible German *revanche*, the Brussels pact, signed in March, also committed the signers to resist a Soviet attack. No more than anyone else did Bevin expect the Brussels treaty to lead to effective defence. Indeed, no buildup of forces followed. He sought to create a vehicle for military co-operation with the United States and, by showing Americans that Europe was prepared to do its share, to lessen resistance to what would be a shattering departure from the American tradition against alliances, especially peacetime ones. The Brussels treaty was, 'in Bevin's eyes, really little more than a carefully arranged trigger for an American commitment'.[49]

Neither Bevin nor the Americans believed that the Soviets planned to invade Western Europe, but they agreed that if war came by accident or

---

[48] Acheson, *Present at the Creation*, p. 385.
[49] Richard J. Barnet, *The Alliance* (New York, 1983), p. 129.

miscalculation the Red Army could easily sweep to the English Channel. They did believe, as negotiators of the North Atlantic Treaty later reported to their governments, that the looming presence of overwhelming Soviet forces created 'a justifiable sense of insecurity among the peoples of Western Europe'. The visible deterrence of a defence treaty including the United States would go far to 'restore confidence among the peoples of Western Europe'.[50]

For the British and Americans, the matter was a little more complicated. Sharing a belief that several European governments only feebly held control, they feared that a combination of subversion within and the Soviet menace from abroad would produce a collapse. 'The problem at present', a State Department summary stated in March 1948, 'is less one of defense against overt foreign aggression than against internal fifth-column aggression supported by the threat of external force, on the Czech model. An essential element in combating it is to convince non-Communist elements that friendly external force comparable to the threatening external force is available.'[51] While this could not be said publicly, for the British and Americans, 'NATO was designed as a political response to a political threat',[52] although a political threat supported by military power.

The structure of defence was discussed even before the Brussels negotiations ended. At first, Bevin sought an arrangement that would give Britain a privileged position as partner in an Anglo-American-Canadian alliance that would bestow support on the Brussels powers. The Americans would have none of this. Indeed, for a time they were unsure whether they should make any formal commitment to European defence, at least not until they saw what the Europeans would do on their own ('You are in effect asking us to pour concrete before we see the blueprints'[53]) and until Congress had acted on the European Recovery Programme. However, in March 1948, just as the Brussels treaty was signed, Bevin gave up his search for preference. He suggested a single pact binding the United States to Europe. Secretary of State Marshall immediately replied, 'we are prepared to proceed at once in . . . discussions on the establishment of an Atlantic security system. I suggest the prompt arrival of the British representatives early next week.'[54]

Marshall invited only the British and Canadians to opening discussions, but in June the talks were broadened to include France and the Benelux powers. Negotiations proceeded slowly, partly because the

[50] Quoted in Thomas H. Etzold and John Lewis Gaddis, eds., *Containment* (New York, 1978), pp. 146–7.
[51] John D. Hickerson, quoted in Escott Reid, *Time of Fear and Hope* (Toronto, 1977), p. 19.
[52] Barnet, *The Alliance*, p. 129.
[53] Lovett, quoted in Bullock, *Bevin*, p. 522.
[54] Quoted ibid., p. 530.

Americans had no desire to conclude them before their presidential election. There was much haggling over the rigour of the pledge. In deference to the need to win Senate approval, the treaty stated that, while an attack on one should be considered an attack on all, each state would follow its own constitutional procedures in deciding how to meet it. Finally, in April 1949, the North Atlantic Treaty was signed. At the ceremony, according to Dean Acheson, by then Secretary of State, a marine band played 'I've Got Plenty of Nothing' and 'It Ain't Necessarily So'.[55]

In keeping with the Anglo-American conception of the nature of the Soviet threat, the first military plans provided only for 'forces sufficient to convince any would-be aggressor that he would not by quick marches gain easy victories'.[56] Soon, events beginning with the Soviet's first atomic explosion in the autumn of 1949 hastened the process which transformed NATO into a true military alliance supported by massive force. During this process the British sometimes disappointed Washington, but quarrels were usually muted. Washington tolerated their lack of enthusiasm for German rearmament and refusal to join the European Defence Community, the intricate device developed to make German rearmament palatable to France. In the American view, despite these matters Britain's contributions to NATO were second only to those of the United States in strength and reliability.

By contrast with European ones, Asian issues never entered deeply into the Anglo-American government relationship until the Korean War. The British resented their lack of influence on MacArthur's regime in Japan. They resented even more the way the Americans, principally through the agency of John Foster Dulles, rammed through a peace treaty with Japan with 'a determination mounting at times to ruthlessness in dealing with opposition'.[57] They felt positively cheated that Dulles told them the Japanese would be free to recognize either the Nationalists on Taiwan or, as they hoped, the People's Republic at a time when Prime Minister Yoshida had already secretly committed Japan to Taiwan.[58]

Still, differences over China were more important. The British ministers' refusal to endorse the Kuomintang exposed them to vicious attack in the United States, either as Communist sympathizers or as greedy materialists ready to accept China's loss of freedoms. For their

[55] Acheson, *Present at the Creation*, p. 284.

[56] David S. McLellan, *Dean Acheson* (New York, 1976), p. 166.

[57] Acheson, *Present at the Creation*, p. 539.

[58] On the other hand, the British would have been 'little short of naive' to think that the Truman administration would really leave the Japanese a free choice. (Roger Buckley, *Occupation Diplomacy* [Cambridge, 1982], p. 177.) Dulles's trickery allowed the British to maintain consistency without jeopardizing the treaty; the fault was in allowing Yoshida's promise to become known.

part, the British simply could not understand the American policy of support for Chiang Kai-shek. Both diplomats and politicians 'displayed [contempt] in private for American naivety, ignorance, and sheer professional incompetence'.[59] To this, the Left added attacks on the United States for its support of counter-revolution. Yet the two governments shrank from confrontation, not least because they considered China a side-show compared to the European theatre and each understood the domestic political problems of the other.

When London considered recognizing Peking in the autumn of 1949, the Cabinet explained to the Americans that continued support for the Nationalists would only drive the Chinese Communists, who were at least as nationalist as they were communist, in the direction of Moscow. A more moderate approach would teach them the economic advantages of ties with the West even as it would expose Soviet imperialistic ambition. By this time Acheson was drifting toward ultimate recognition. As he made clear to London, however, he hoped that the leading Western powers would move together so that the Chinese could be compelled to observe what he considered their international obligations, economic and diplomatic.

Nevertheless, in October 1949 the Foreign Office announced that it intended to arrange recognition, and this was formally extended in January 1950. Bevin, perhaps apologetically, explained to Acheson: 'There are some factors which affect us specially, not only our interests in China but the position in Hong Kong, and also in Malaya and Singapore where there are vast Chinese communities.'[60] The Secretary replied philosophically through Franks that '. . . the views of states differ and each has to act upon his own immediate and long-term self interest.'[61]

The British move evoked howls of public protest in the United States.[62] However, Downing Street appears to have believed that Washington, although immobilized by American opinion, was really not displeased as the Americans recognized the value of Western contacts with Peking and the chance to test the reaction of the People's Republic of China. Above all, British officials expected the Truman Administration to follow their lead as soon as it dared.

[59] Alan Bullock, in Yonosuka Nagai and Akira Iriye, eds., *The Origins of the Cold War in Asia* (New York, 1977), p. 100.

[60] Quoted in Robert J. Donovan, *Tumultuous Years* (New York, 1982), p. 87.

[61] Quoted in McLellan, *Acheson*, p. 202 n.

[62] A British public opinion poll showed that the government's decision was disapproved in that country, too. However, even the Conservative leaders saw that recognition was inevitable; Eden's only complaint was that the government had acted prematurely, before co-ordinating policy with the United States. Moreover, the English-speaking members of the Commonwealth declined to follow Britain's lead.

The outbreak of the Korean War in June 1950 ended any chance of that. Almost everyone in Britain, even Bevanites, agreed that North Korean aggression had to be met. However, the war also strained ties, partly because the British, unlike the Americans, believed that they saw an opportunity to develop a Sino-Soviet split. They also feared that the Far Eastern war would divert American energies from Europe, a real danger, perhaps, but one of which Washington was well aware. Finally, they worried that American truculence, or 'MacArthurism', would trigger World War III.

Throughout the war Britain showed herself more interested in negotiation than victory and more worried about confronting the Chinese than the Americans. Shortly after the war began, the British ambassador in Moscow explored the possibility of a return to the status quo ante. He reported, and Bevin passed word on to the Americans, that while the Soviets seemed favourable they would probably link a cease-fire with the withdrawal of American protection from Taiwan and the bestowal of UN membership on Peking. Truman and Acheson reacted with anger, firmly refusing to negotiate on these items 'under the duress and blackmail then being employed'.[63] Reluctantly, the British dropped the project.

On the other hand, the British fully shared the euphoria which followed MacArthur's counter-offensive after the Inchon landing in September. They favoured exploitation of this success by action north of the thirty-eighth parallel. At America's behest they sponsored a UN resolution, passed in October, calling for all-Korea elections. The resolution did not call for unification by force, but it did recommend that 'all appropriate steps be taken to ensure conditions of stability' prior to the elections,[64] a euphemism understood by everyone. 'The principal American ally', Trumbull Higgins observes, 'had not re-strained Washington at the decisive moment.'[65]

At about the same time the British became uneasy about possible Chinese intervention in the war. Bevin urged Acheson to issue a statement reassuring China and to permit participation by the People's Republic in UN debates on Korea. However, when Acheson responded that 'we should not be unduly frightened at what was probably a Chinese Communist bluff',[66] Bevin did not press the point.

As MacArthur pushed forward, British generals suggested stopping at the narrow waist of North Korea, and Churchill and other Conservatives publicly endorsed the idea. But the Labour government refused to

[63] Acheson, *Present at the Creation*, p. 418.
[64] Quoted in David Rees, *Korea: the Limited War* (New York, 1964), p. 101.
[65] Trumbull Higgins, *Korea and the Fall of MacArthur* (New York, 1960), p. 55.
[66] Quoted in Joseph C. Goulden, *Korea* (New York, 1982), p. 283.

criticize MacArthur's advance, and only a few days before Chinese
intervention became known Attlee exultantly declared in the House of
Commons that the war was near an end.

The truth is that, although the British never admitted the fact, 'like
Truman and Acheson, Attlee and Bevin did not think that the objective
of a united Korea would really provoke a massive Chinese counter-
action'.[67] There was, in short, concern without urgency. Had it been
otherwise, Britain would have had misgivings about the unification
resolution it so strongly pushed and would much more forcefully have
counselled caution.

On the last day of November, as UN forces crumpled before the
Chinese, Truman held a press conference. In a series of clumsy answers
he seemed to suggest that the United States was considering use of
atomic bombs, even that the decision would be left to General
MacArthur.[68] This created an uproar on both sides of the Atlantic, and
Attlee interrupted a session of the House of Commons with an
announcement that he would fly to Washington for consultations.

There, he carried the ball almost alone, since illness kept Bevin home.
He quickly gathered, so Acheson recalled, that 'alarm over the safety of
our troops would not drive us to some ill-considered use of atomic
weapons' but he argued that, nevertheless, 'the position of our forces was
so weak and precarious that we must pay for a cease-fire to extricate
them'. These payments might include withdrawal from Korea (here
Acheson exaggerated), abandonment of Taiwan, and acquiescence in
Peking's entry into the United Nations. The Secretary replied by
touching on a raw nerve: the American people, he said, could hardly be
expected to 'follow a leadership that proposed a vigorous policy of action
on one ocean front while accepting defeat on the other'.[69] Attlee
dropped his argument. For their part, the Americans tacitly but clearly
dropped their insistence on pursuing unification (a goal, it should be
repeated, that had also been Britain's) but made clear they did not
intend to evacuate the peninsula unless driven into the sea. They would
settle for restoration of the thirty-eighth parallel. Attlee thereupon
pledged his country to fight by America's side to prevent defeat, a pledge
he repeated publicly. Then he flew home.

The whole affair was grotesque. Attlee allowed it to be understood
that he had scotched a project (which Truman in fact had never
planned). He had flaccidly abandoned proposals for concessions to
China. Then he had pledged to fight to the end with the Americans.

[67] Rees, *Korea*, p. 147.

[68] The matter had in fact been discussed within the government, although not at the
Presidential level, but the Army rejected the idea on military as well as political grounds. On the
other hand, Truman ordered bomb parts sent to the Far East.

[69] Acheson, *Present at the Creation*, pp. 481–2.

Small wonder that Truman wrote in his diary, 'The position of the British is, to say the least, fantastic. We cannot agree to their suggestions. Yet they say they will support us whatever we do!'[70] What the President failed to confess was that his own indiscretion had caused most of the problem in the first place. What he failed to recognize was that the British position remained essentially what it had been in June 1950: belief in Korean defence combined with a hankering for compromise with China that gave way in the face of American obduracy.

The same pattern persisted during the rest of the Korean War. 'Britain', a historian has recently written, 'retreated quickly from the United States' side when American officials talked of strong sanctions against Red China or a UN censure of the Communist Chinese intervention.'[71] Instead, she concocted a plan calling for a unified Korea to be arranged at a conference of the United States, the Soviet Union, the People's Republic, and herself, with the issues of Taiwan and Chinese representation in the UN not excluded from discussion. The Americans, though outraged, allowed the resolution to pass, correctly anticipating that the Chinese would refuse to accept it. When the Americans then insisted that this made condemnation of China even more logical, the British nearly decided to oppose it, agreeing only when the UN resolution of February 1951 had been watered down on the issue of sanctions.

Subsequently, although giving general support to the Americans in peace negotiations, they occasionally irritated the Americans by suggesting a more moderate course than Washington wished, particularly on issues respecting the return of prisoners of war. On the other hand, Herbert Morrison, Bevin's successor at the Foreign Office, agreed in May 1951 that if the Chinese launched air attacks on United Nations forces an extension of the war into China would be called for, and in September he also agreed that the war would have to be stepped up if peace talks broke down.

The British and American governments had never been able to co-ordinate Asian policies as they had European ones, but the differences between them were not as extreme as critics of 'MacArthurism' or 'British appeasement' suggested. Both looked at Asia in terms of the Cold War, although the British believed that the People's Republic could be weaned from Moscow whereas the Truman administration, except briefly before the Korean War, did not. Both considered Asia a side-show compared to Europe, but both agreed that Korea could not be abandoned, not least because of the psychological effect on Europe.

Historians are drawn, almost necessarily because of the nature of their

[70] Quoted in Robert H. Ferrell, ed., *Off the Record* (New York, 1980), p. 203.
[71] D. Clayton James, *The Years of MacArthur* (Boston, 1985), vol. iii, p. 539.

sources, to emphasize discord. Position papers, correspondence, memoirs—all are far more likely to record disagreement than agreement. Tacit understandings, by their nature, are rarely documented. It is true that 'while the United States viewed [the Special Relationship] as an instrument for American system-building, Britain, belying the postwar realities, saw it as the pillar of her own diametrically opposed design for reinstating herself as a major power'.[72] But there is real danger that, pursuing this theme, differences between the two governments may be allowed to overshadow the far more fundamental common ground.

This would be both a pity and an error. In the era of Truman and Attlee, the relationship between the two nations—though less intimate and slightly more troubled than their wartime alliance—was truly remarkable, in part precisely because Britain was undergoing the traumatic shock of passage from the ranks of superpowers. The British often employed the metaphor of Greece and Rome to describe the Anglo-American relationship: the British wisdom of ages and the American strength of arms would combine to defy their enemies. The metaphor was more a hope—and a vain one—than a reality. The Americans, like the Romans, never permitted challenge to their authority. But the two modern nations, stimulated by nearly identical views on the nature of the challenge they faced, did forge ties of unusual closeness and, indeed, tolerance.

[72] R. B. Manderson-Jones, *The Special Relationship* (London, 1972), p. 20.

4

Demythologizing the Eisenhower Era

D. CAMERON WATT

DWIGHT D. EISENHOWER was elected President of the United States in November 1952 and inaugurated in January 1953. During his Presidency he faced three British prime ministers, all of whom thought of him as a long-standing friend, both personal and of Britain, as a result of the contacts they had with him while he was in command of the Allied armies in North Africa (1942–3) and in Western Europe (1943–5). Winston Churchill had succeeded Clement Attlee as Premier after the general election held in November 1951 had produced a Conservative majority. He was an old man whom gossip, much of it traceable to the supporters of his heir apparent as leader of the Conservative party, Anthony Eden, depicted as approaching senility, garrulous, indecisive, and forgetful. He was however to stay in office, in the hope of achieving a summit conference and an alleviation of East–West tensions, until February 1955, when he finally resigned.

His successor, Anthony Eden, who had resigned as Foreign Secretary in February 1938 as a result of disagreements with Premier Neville Chamberlain over the alleviation of Anglo-Italian tensions, had rejoined the wartime coalition, first as Secretary of State for the Dominions, then as Secretary of State for War, and, finally, from January 1941 as Foreign Secretary, a post to which he had returned in November 1951 with the Conservative victory. He was to lead his party to victory in the 1955 general election. He was a proud, arrogant, and nervous man, deeply resentful of criticism who took opposition very personally and who was *persona non grata* to the right wing of his own party. He had come to believe, wrongly, in his own myth as the man who had fought appeasement. His career was to end with his resignation on health grounds in January 1957 after the disaster of the British intervention at Suez in November 1956, an intervention condemned by the United Nations under Eisenhower's leadership, after Eisenhower's overwhelming success in the Presidential elections in that month. The British withdrawal was eased in form by the intervention of Canada's Foreign Minister, Lester Pearson, but it was an outright humiliation none the less, for no one more than Eden's Foreign Secretary, Selwyn Lloyd, widely represented as merely Eden's messenger boy or poodle.

Eden's successor, after a mysterious period of consultation, was not, as many had expected, R. A. Butler, then one of the most powerful figures in the Cabinet and architect, during the period of Conservative opposition after their defeat in the 1945 general election, of the so-called 'new Conservatism'. Instead it was Harold Macmillan who, like Churchill himself, had an American mother. Macmillan had represented Britain with the rank of Cabinet Minister at Eisenhower's headquarters in North Africa in 1943. In Churchill's cabinet between 1951 and 1955 he had headed the Ministry of Housing, making it the outstanding success story in domestic politics of that administration. He had served Eden in quick succession as Minister of Defence, Foreign Secretary, and Chancellor of the Exchequer—the post he occupied during the Suez incident. His relations with Eden were difficult and unhappy. Unlike Rab Butler, who had served Neville Chamberlain as Under-Secretary of State for Foreign Affairs and spokesman in the House of Commons for Chamberlain's foreign policy, and who the inner circles of the Conservative party knew to have flirted with the idea of a negotiated peace with Hitler in the summer of 1940, Macmillan had been a consistent opponent of appeasement from 1936 onwards.

When Eisenhower became President, he inherited a world very different from that of 1945. The United States headed an alliance with Britain, Canada, and the states of Western Europe, Italy, Greece, and Turkey which was formed to balance the conventional military strength which the Soviet Union maintained in Eastern Europe. Indeed Eisenhower had served as Commander in Chief of NATO's forces from the winter of 1950 until his resignation to accept the Republican nomination in 1952. During this period NATO had been reformed and extended: reformed to acquire a permanent civilian secretariat led by a British Secretary-General, Lord Ismay, who had been at the centre of British defence policy-making since 1936; extended to take in Greece and Turkey. On paper it faced a further extension. In response to American urging, Hitler's former victims in Western Europe had agreed at the time of the outbreak of the Korean War to the rearmament of the West German state. On French initiative, however, and with the encouragement of that very powerful lobby of American policy-makers who saw the creation of a United Europe as the only way in which American withdrawal from Europe could be achieved, as well as a desirable end in itself, it had been proposed that West German rearmament should only be permitted within the framework of a European army. These proposals, seen by European federalists, themselves an influential, if largely bureaucratic, élite within the governments of Western Europe (though not in Britain or Norway) as a logical second step to the formation of the European Coal and Steel Community, seemed to have been achieved by the Treaty of Paris signed in the summer of 1952. No French government, however, faced with the deep and abiding hatred of Germany which was the legacy of three German invasions of France over the previous eighty years, and conscious of Communist hostility on the left and the hard core of support for de Gaulle on the right, could dare submit the Treaty for ratification by the French National Assembly.

The world seemed to be changing even faster in the technology of warfare. The war in the Pacific had ended with the use of America's two atom bombs, the product of a programme in which American engineering genius had built on the scientific achievements of a team of British, French, and refugee European physicists, and on the uranium which was obtained only from Canada and the Belgian Congo. Ignorant of the wartime Churchill–Roosevelt agreements on sharing the outcome of their joint effort, the United States Congress had in 1946 passed the McMahon Act which denied Britain's access to the products of what was seen as a purely American achievement. Britain had embarked on her own atomic weapons programme. So had the Soviets. By 1952 both the Soviets and Britain were firmly established in the nuclear arms race, which had made an enormous jump in 1952 with the explosion of the first US fusion weapon. The Soviets were to follow suit in 1953 and Britain in 1957. France had by then also entered the race, which was to move to yet a third level with the substitution of the long-range missile for the bomber as its delivery vehicle. In 1958 the Soviets stole a march on America by putting the first man-made satellite into orbit around the earth. The missile race was even more expensive than the bomb race in terms of money for research and development. By 1958 the British missile programme was running into serious financial trouble. One of the last acts of the Eisenhower regime in the summer of 1960 seemed to have solved this by agreeing to allot part of the Skybolt missile programme to Britain, and, failing Skybolt (so it was understood in Britain), the submarine-based Polaris missile. This followed the repeal of the McMahon Act in 1958, and the conclusion of agreements providing for an interchange of knowledge between the British and American nuclear programme, an interchange from which Britain benefited much more than the United States, and to which France was allowed no access whatever.

The French experience during Eisenhower's presidency seemed to confirm the view of France as a has-been power entertained in Roosevelt's entourage during World War II. The Fourth Republic was racked by continuous political crisis. Its decolonization process was long, bloody, and studded with defeat, first in Indo-China (where the Americans, for all their contempt for the French, were to do no better if not a lot worse in the next decade) and then in Algeria. Threatened with an army *coup d'état*, France turned towards the local Cincinnatus, General de Gaulle, who, behind a smoke-screen of rhetoric about France's cultural supremacy and invocations of *La Gloire*, hid the nastiest of wars between military and assassinatory-minded conspirators and a spectrum of equally unsavoury secret police organizations, and manœuvred France towards the evacuation of both French forces and the settler element in the population of Ageria. De Gaulle's great weapon was provided him by the Europeanist élites of the Fourth Republic, Italy, West Germany, and the Benelux countries who, baulked in their hopes of a European Defence Community (EDC) in 1954, had turned the following year to the *rélance* of Europeanism which was to produce in January 1957 the two Rome treaties, establishing Euratom and the European Common Market.

The British were not far behind, though too far as it was to prove. Under Macmillan's stimulus they had proposed in that same month a wider free trade area which Austria, Switzerland, Sweden, Norway, Denmark, and Portugal supported. The real issue turned on which way West Germany would go. West German industrial and financial interests were known to favour the free trade area over a common market. Even in Benelux sentiment was divided. But for the Chancellor of West Germany a close tie with France was the only protection he had against the possibility of an Anglo-American-Soviet deal over the corpse of German reunification. Sure of this, de Gaulle was able in November 1958 to veto further talks on the reconciliation of the Common Market and the Free Trade Area, as he was in January 1963 to veto British accession to the Common Market. For de Gaulle America belonged less in Europe than did Soviet Russia, dreaming as he did of the expulsion of the one and the break-up of the other, a united Europe from the Atlantic to the Urals. Between his image of Franco-American relations and those entertained by the President and the foreign policy élites in Washington there could be no reconciliation. Britain, not West Germany, was the sufferer.

The reasons were only in part economic, though the economic ones were serious enough. The 1950s were the decade of rapid industrial growth on the European continent, with first the German and then the French economic miracles. British growth was rapid too, but slower than that of her European competitors and Britain's financial system, still carrying the burden of financing much of the world's trade in primary products, was racked by repeated losses of confidence in the stability of sterling as vast floods of hot money poured out of London to its funk-holes in Zurich, Rotterdam, or New York, only to ebb back as soon as it became clear that no other financial centre could offer, or wanted to offer, the skills and faculties—and risks—that were available in London. When raw material prices ran high London carried the risk. In 1957, it was said, Ghana, Malaya, and Kuwait, cocoa, copper and oil, were responsible for three-quarters of the sterling balances. Three years later cocoa was a drag on the market, copper not much better. Oil kept London going, as three-quarters of Europe's oil supplies came from countries and via companies who banked in sterling.

This is the background against which this paper is written. There is one further element, that of the decolonization process as it applied to Britain. This greatly misunderstood and misrepresented process was not a simple one. Moreover, the events which are usually subsumed under it are of two quite different sorts. The first was the transfer of power in Britain's former colonies and possessions in Africa and South-east Asia and the West Indies. These were not without stress, conflict, or minor colonial wars (the Mau Mau rising in Kenya or the long guerilla conflict in Malaya, for example). And in one case, Rhodesia, things were to go badly wrong in the 1960s and 1970s. But on the whole the progression was orderly, reasonable and, where it came to grief, as it undoubtedly did, it was where colonialist rule had been insufficiently secure to breach the underlying structures of power and authority, and where it was only a matter of time before local politicos reverted to the violent and tyrannical disorder which had so often persuaded the Victorians of the virtues of empire.

The other process was the dismantlement of the 'informal' British empire in the Middle East. This 'empire by treaty' with states to whose birth Britain had in many cases been the midwife, Iraq, Libya, Transjordan, and the Sudan, for example, depended on the agreements concluded with the ruling élites of Arab *effendis* and *bimbashis* which the break-up of the Ottoman Empire had thrown up in 1918. The process of adjusting to the social pressures and the rise of new élites, often based on minority sects, threatened by the breakdown of the Ottoman system which had preserved their religion- and family-based laws and communal self-government within the overall decentralization of Ottoman authority, would have been a difficult one even without the problems posed by the creation of the state of Israel. In 1945 Britain had treaties of alliance with Egypt, Transjordan (as it then was), and Iraq. British forces occupied southern Iran, Syria, and the Lebanon, mandated Palestine, the colony of Cyprus, Cyrenaica, and Libya. A network of treaties preserved the British position in the Gulf. As such Britain became, even before Israel, the one unifying factor against which all the emerging élites, especially the students, the journalists, the would-be professional men, and the young officers, could unite. All of them challenged the existing holders of wealth, land ownership, power, and status in the separate Arab countries.

By 1954 they had found themselves a hero figure in the leader of the 1952 revolution in Egypt, Colonel Gamel Abdel Nasser. Cairo radio rallied them, Egyptian money financed them (it was clumsily and ineffectively opposed from time to time by Saudi money), and the educated élites among the Palestinian refugees combined with Egyptian-trained schoolteachers throughout the Middle East to propagate their ideas among the young. Nasser intervened in the old rivalries between Hashemite and Saudi, and between Damascus and Baghdad, for the leadership of the movement for the restoration of Arab self-esteem and dominance over the lands between Turkey and Iran in the north and the Sahara and the African mountains in the south, which was so misunderstandingly discussed in the West as Arab nationalism. He bankrupted Egypt in the process and his country fought and lost four wars, three against Israel and one in the Yemen. He accepted the Union offered him by the intellectual Arab socialists of Damascus and mishandled it so badly that Syria broke away after only two years. He was forced to abandon the long Egyptian dream of the unity of the Nile valley. He saw the overthrow of the Hashemite dynasty in Baghdad, but came no nearer commanding the loyalty of the Iraqis. He saw the regimes in the Lebanon and Jordan preserved by American and British aid and intervention. In the cause of Egyptian independence he mortgaged Egypt to the Soviets for arms and aid in building the High Dam in Aswan. He was, save in the manner in which he personified Arab resentment of the European conquest of the civilization of Islam in the eighteenth and nineteenth centuries, an unmitigated disaster as much for his own country and the Middle East as for Britain. At his death the political map of the Middle East remained as it had been established by Britain and France in 1919 and modified by Israel and Transjordan in 1949 and 1967. His role was created by Dulles, Eden, and Eisenhower; and he ensured that the contraction of British power which was imperial but not colonial (save in Aden and Cyprus) would be unredeemed by any signs of grace or statesmanship, on the part of any of the participants in the process.

Central to this process was the extraordinary inability of the US government to pursue a consistent course of conduct towards Egypt in the period from 1955 to 1956. The decision to 'cut Nasser down to size' involved in the decision (taken without consultation with the British partners) to withdraw the offer of a loan for the construction of the High Dam at Aswan ended with the 'cutting down to size' of the British and French, America's allies. The ill-timed and ill-judged reversion to Dulles's anti-colonialist and anti-imperialist past at the famous press conference held when Britain and France were looking for American aid in forcing a new international regime for the Suez Canal on Egypt convinced Eden and the French that America had changed sides in midstream. The consequent Anglo-French intervention in collusion with Israel and the element of deception involved in this led to American invocation of the General Assembly against Britain and France after their vetoes had blocked action by the Security Council. America rather than Egypt used the oil weapon against Britain by refusing to allow American oil companies to consult with the British, Dutch, and French on rerouting oil at sea once the Canal had been blocked. America refused to help sterling against the tide of hot money which passed out of London at the signs of British weakness and defeat.

This took place against a background of change in the Soviet position. Stalin's death in 1953 was followed by a distinct weakening in Soviet control over her satellites, a weakness which showed itself first in the quick suppression of the East German rising in the summer of 1953 and in the rigidity of the Soviet position over arms control and over Germany demonstrated at the summit of 1955. But Khrushchev's invocation of de-Stalinization in his bid for the succession to Stalin's leadership unleashed forces that the Soviet Union could no longer control. The restoration of nationalist Communism in Poland in 1956 nearly led to Soviet intervention. What saved Poland was the fear of German revanchism which kept her loyal to her alliance with the Soviets. Hungary felt no such threat or constraints and the Red Army extinguished the Hungarian revolution in blood. But Khrushchev steadily lost influence over China and over the leaders of other Communist parties, bitterly discredited as they were in the West by the campaign against Stalin and the scenes of suppression in Budapest.

Khrushchev sought to reassert his leadership by the 'ultimatum' he issued over the status of the West in Berlin in November 1958 and the threat to sign a separate peace treaty with East Germany which would hand over control of access to Berlin to a state the West did not recognize. Macmillan tried to reason with him, and Khrushchev himself toured America, but the 1960 Paris summit, already clearly headed for failure, was destroyed by Khrushchev over the U-2 incident. Eisenhower's last months in office were spent listening to Khrushchev thump the rostrum of the United Nations podium in the centre of New York with his shoe. More ominously, Khrushchev had maintained himself in power against the challenge of his rivals with the aid of the Red Army. The Soviet Union was now an oligarchy, even a pluralist oligarchy, rather than the tyranny Stalin had made; and the internal cohesion it was to develop could only be maintained by complete *immobilisme* on the domestic front, an *immobilisme* to which Khrushchev himself was to fall victim four years later. These are the realities against which discussion of the relations between Britain and America in the 1950s has to be conducted. How they were perceived at the time and how those perceptions changed between 1960 and 1980 is another story.

Any historian of Anglo-American relations who contemplates the history of the 1950s can only be struck by the contrast between the rhetoric and the realities of alliance. To the generation which left British universities at the end of the 1940s and entered political activity in the 1950s, this decade was pre-eminently the era of Atlanticism—crowned as its end by the election of President Kennedy and the last golden age of Anglo-American co-operation between Kennedy and Macmillan. To the first wave of writers who reviewed this period, that curious *mélange* of backward-looking commentators, political fixers, memoirists, writers of biographies, myth-makers, and second-guessers whose initial occupation of the field makes the task of the professional historian coming after so much more difficult, the fifties were the era of inevitable British decline, a decline the more marked both by the failure of contemporary British statesmen to realize it and by the speed with which Britain's European rivals, unencumbered by the debris, actual and intellectual, of empire, raced ahead of her in terms of investment and economic growth. It was a decade in which, to use Dean Acheson's memorably cruel but inaccurate phrase, Britain 'lost an empire' but failed to 'find a rôle'.

The real archival evidence for the study of the 1950s is only now beginning to become available. But it is already evident to the first scouts of the armies of professional historians who wait like the Anglo-American armies in Britain in the initial weeks of June 1944 for the battlefield to enlarge itself sufficiently to accommodate them, that they will have an unusually difficult knot of subjective misperceptions to disentangle before they can begin to make sense of the historical realities these obscure. Not only will they have to decode the whole misleading babel of interpretations, perceptions, political mythologies, and personal eye-witness accounts, which the writing of the 1960s and 1970s has already created, to sort out the misunderstood from the wilfully misleading, the invented, and the contradictory. They will also have to cope with the contemporary misperceptions and illusions which influenced policy-makers so much. They will have to decide, for example, whether Churchill's actions in the years 1952–5 were as senile as British and American pressmen, and through them Eisenhower and his cabinet, were persuaded they were by Anthony Eden's acolytes. They will have to decide whether Eisenhower's frequent absences on the golf course, already a matter of comment to British political diarists during his first term, really showed him to be the amateur bungler that American Democratic party propagandists depicted him as being. They will have to decide how far John Foster Dulles has to carry the blame for the course of American policy in the Middle East and in the Far East in the years he was Secretary of State. They will, on the British side, have to rethink the picture his enemies painted of Selwyn Lloyd as the Urban District Council Chairman out of his depth. They will have to come to terms with the image of himself so elaborately and cleverly documented at such length by Harold Macmillan. They will have to decide whether Macleod's period at the Colonial Office was that of the far-sighted statesman or more akin to that of the driver of a dump truck anxious only to rid himself of a load of potentially lethal pollutants irrespective of the ecological damage he will do to wherever he sheds his load.

They will, however, face much more difficult tasks than these that are concerned mainly with the reassessment of individuals, and with comprehending the psychological and social climate which produced and conditioned contemporary perceptions of them. Most difficult, and yet most essential of all is the need to assess the contemporary policy-makers' perceptions of the political and power relationships between their own countries and governments and those of their allies and their opponents. If, as seems at least arguable, those perceptions were mistaken, and if what was significant in the history of the 1950s was not the actual decline of British power but the general belief in its occurrence, then the contemporary historian will face a dual task: first, of examining the working out of the effects of those misperceptions, and secondly, of explaining how they came to arise.

In no sphere does this task seem so essential as in the assessment of Anglo-American relations in the 1950s. Not only was this the period in which what, at least on the American side, had been intended to be a temporary military and economic commitment and, at least on the British side, had been hoped was a temporary dependence, became seemingly permanent; it was also the period in which the decline of British prestige and authority became perceived as irreversible. To that process of decline American policy and American misperceptions were perhaps, outside political and economic mismanagement of economic development and investment in Britain, the major contributor. Nemesis was to make itself felt in the 1960s, when President Johnson looked in vain for British aid in South-east Asia, and when the British withdrawal east of Suez left a void into which all the United States could do was to thrust, to his ultimate downfall, the Shah. The illusion of American omnipotence, to use Denis Brogan's telling phrase, was rudely revealed with the capture of the American embassy in Tehran and the disastrous farce of President Carter's attempt to rescue its staff, who had been seized as hostages.

What the historian, assessing the history of Anglo-American relations in the 1950s, has to do is to explain why American policy-makers so misunderstood the power relationship between Britain and the United States in the 1950s; why they failed to understand the degree to which the sources of British power and influence were at risk in the 1950s, and the degree to which their own actions and policies were contributing to translating these risks into reality; and why they failed to understand the degree to which the consequences of their actions and policies were weakening America's own position by extending the areas in which American interests were vulnerable, where Britain's presence had once protected them.

So far as the consequences of American actions are concerned, they can be seen in four areas: in the destruction of the British position in the Middle East begun in the 1940s in Palestine and Saudi Arabia; in the polarization of conflict in Indo-China and South-east Asia inherent in American policy toward South Vietnam and Indonesia; in the failure to take more advantage of the succession crisis in the Soviet Union on Stalin's death; and in the persistent US pressure for the loosening or dismantlement of the sterling area, and of sterling as the most important alternative to the dollar as one of the world's great trading currencies. Central to this process is the disastrous year of 1956, the year which began with the Prime Minister being fêted in Washington. Though Harold Macmillan noted perceptively in his diary that Eden had found the President 'very well and—as usual—very friendly also', his later commentary continues 'like so many of these conversations there was little tangible effect'.[1] That same year was to end with the American ambassador, Winthrop Aldrich, in clandestine communication with Macmillan and Butler, on the need to replace the Prime Minister.[2] It is a curious comment on the one-sidedness of Anglo-American relations today to reflect how little stir Aldrich's revelation of this eleven years later caused in either country. One needs only to imagine American reactions had it been alleged that Eden and Macmillan had been in contact with Vice-President Nixon the previous year during the period of the President's heart attack with a view to establishing friendly relations with the President's successor.

Macmillan, once the succession to Eden had been successfully negotiated, was to launch what in some respects was a highly successful effort to re-establish relations of trust and confidence between himself and President Eisenhower. Dulles's death and his succession by

[1] Harold Macmillan, *Riding the Storm, 1956–1959* (London, 1971), pp. 91–2.
[2] Winthrop Aldrich, 'The Suez Crisis: A Footnote to History', *Foreign Affairs*, 45 (1967).

Christian Herter, a man who genuinely believed in the Atlantic Community and was devoid of Dulles's somewhat John Knoxian attitude to international relations, made his task easier.[3] But even with this success, which involved the repeal of the McMahon Act, the American decision to intervene in the Lebanon in July 1958 was taken without any consultation with Britain, despite earlier agreement that such an operation, if undertaken, would be preceded by mutual consultation. British caution in reaction to Khrushchev's threat in November 1958 to make a separate peace with East Germany and isolate the Western allies in West Berlin was denounced in the Pentagon as weak and defeatist, if not positively treacherous. Macmillan's visit to Moscow in the spring of 1959 was widely denounced in Washington as a lapse into appeasement. And Macmillan's appeals to Eisenhower in November 1959 and March 1960 for support against French efforts to divide Europe economically were rudely and unsympathetically rebuffed by Eisenhower and Douglas Dillon.[4] Eisenhower's own moves towards the second summit conference and the sympathetic hearings he gave to Macmillan's views on the issue of the nuclear arms control negotiations were to bring upon the President accusations from the Pentagon of being too much under British influence. It is hardly surprising that Eisenhower was to revenge himself by denouncing the American 'military-industrial complex' in his farewell address.

Compared with Macmillan's partial success in refurbishing Anglo-American relations to which contemporary British diplomatic observers were inclined to feel that the sudden American discovery of the Soviet technological lead in space had greatly contributed,[5] the record of Anglo-American relations under Churchill and Eden is a sorry and deplorable story, which it would take much too long to examine in detail on this occasion.[6]

On the British side much of the misfortune which was to strike Anglo-American relations in 1956 can be laid at the door of Lord Avon's (i.e. Anthony Eden's) tenure of the Foreign Office and of 10 Downing Street. Lord Avon's ability to understand the Americans was as limited as his ability to convince himself of American respect for his advice and

---

[3] After the Democratic victory in the 1960 elections Herter was involved in the unofficial moves to set up an Atlantic Assembly and in the issue in 1961 of the now-forgotten Atlantic Declaration. Macmillan, however, believed Herter to lack the authority Dulles exercised over the State Department or the President. Harold Macmillan, *Pointing the Way, 1959–1961* (London, 1972), p. 71.

[4] Macmillan, *Pointing the Way*, pp. 59, 214–16. Private evidence of Lord Harlech.

[5] Statement by Sir Roger Jackling at the London University Institute of United States Studies Conference on Anglo-American relations since 1945, June 1984.

[6] The evidence is set out in my forthcoming essay 'Eisenhower and Churchill: The race to the Summit, 1952–1954': and in ch. 6 of my book *Succeeding John Bull: America in Britain's Place, 1900–1975* (Cambridge, 1984).

criticism was unbounded. In part this can be blamed on his acceptance of Churchill's and Sumner Welles's not entirely disinterested, and now largely discredited, version of the origins, fate, and consequences of the rejection of Roosevelt's famous message to Chamberlain of January 1938,[7] by no means the only example of Lord Avon's ability to convince himself of the truth of the legends others had woven around him. In part it lay in the very considerable and largely unsung success Sir Roger Makins, the British Ambassador in Washington for most of Eisenhower's first term, enjoyed in establishing relations of confidence with the State Department and with Dulles.[8] In part it lay in the very genuine ease of communication which Dulles and Eden enjoyed in 1952–3, when both were opposed to Churchill's summit ambitions and both contemptuous of France's flounderings in the effort to avoid the ratification of the Paris treaty of 1952 establishing a European Defence Community.[9] This co-operation was to break down very badly over the Indo-China issue in 1954. Eden's success in rescuing West German rearmament out of the collapse of EDC in the autumn of 1954 rekindled Dulles's admiration. But the course of American policy over the Baghdad Pact, over Saudi Arabian claims on the Buraimi oasis, over Cyprus, and over Anglo-Egyptian relations were to destroy this confidence entirely. Writing in November 1953 in preparation for the Bermuda summit, Dr Raynor, the head of the State Department's British Commonwealth and North European Affairs department, was to sum it up admirably. On the Near East, he wrote,

The British, rightly or wrongly, appear to feel that we have not given them the public support in the area which they feel is required in order for them to carry out their agreed primary responsibility for the defence of the area and to protect their interests . . .

It should be noted [he concluded] that the British, from the Governmental point of view feel that as problems arise, area by area, which involve their interests, we are prone to give too great weight to the local area considerations and not enough weight to the British interests at stake.[10]

This feeling was to manifest itself very strongly in the last five months of 1956, months in which the issue of an Anglo-French union first mooted in the dark days of 1940 was again, if only briefly, considered in Whitehall—not so much as an anti-German measure, but as one which

---

[7] See Winston S. Churchill, *The Gathering Storm* (London, 1948), pp. 196–9.

[8] Dulles regarded Makins's replacement by Sir Harold, later Lord Caccia, in 1956, as an inherent part of the deception he believed Lord Avon to have practised upon him. Cf. his bitter complaint to Macmillan in Dec. 1956, *Riding the Storm*, p. 179, diary entry of 13 Dec. 1956.

[9] See David Carlton, *Anthony Eden, A Biography* (London, 1981), pp. 300–2.

[10] *Foreign Relations of the United States, 1952–1954*, vol. v, pt. 2 (Washington, DC, 1983), pp. 1715–18, Raynor to MacArthur, 16 Nov. 1953.

would strengthen Britain against a hostile America.[11] As Harold
Macmillan wrote, mulling in the late 1960s over the events of 1956,

We could not believe that Eisenhower . . . who had commanded our great
armies and shown such generous appreciation of British qualities of tenacity
and courage would allow our rights and our interests to disappear in a fog of
argument or sentiment.[12]

Lord Avon anticipated him a decade earlier: 'We could hardly foresee
that the US government would harden against us on almost every point
and become harsher after the ceasefire than before.'[13]

In the light of the most recent American work on the Eisenhower
presidency, it is interesting to note the degree to which John Foster
Dulles, both at the time and later, was made the scapegoat for America's
role during and after the Suez crisis.[14] This is the more surprising when
it is realized that for much of the worst period of American action against
Britain, the month of November 1956, Dulles was in hospital being
treated for the cancer which was ultimately to kill him. It was not he but
Cabot Lodge, America's representative at the United Nations, Herbert
Hoover, Jr., the Assistant Under-Secretary in the State Department,
and George Humphrey, the Secretary to the Treasury, at whose hands
British interests were most mishandled and British representatives in
America were most humiliated. None of this could have taken place
without Eisenhower's support, encouragement, and approval. It was
Eisenhower who withdrew the invitation given on 7 November to Eden
and Guy Mollet to come to Washington. The move from the Security
Council to the General Assembly was authorized by Eisenhower.
Eisenhower refused to see either Selwyn Lloyd or Robert Menzies, the
Australian premier. Lester Pearson, the Canadian intermediary who
played the most active part in mobilizing the United Nations so as to
provide a way by which the withdrawal of Anglo-French forces would
not be followed by an Egyptian counter-offensive, had more trouble
with Cabot Lodge than with either the Egyptian or Soviet representatives. The refusal of American approval for the co-operation between
the major oil companies necessary to the rerouting of Europe's oil
supplies once the Canal had been blocked, Humphrey's resistance to
Britain exercising her legal right to withdraw funds from the IMF to
back sterling, were all actions undertaken with the President's active
approval.

Where Dulles cannot escape blame is for the equivocations over the
Suez Canal Users Association, his inability to resist beating the anti-

[11] Private information.
[12] Macmillan, *Riding the Storm*, p. 104.
[13] Sir Anthony Eden, *The Memoirs of Anthony Eden: Full Circle* (London, 1960), p. 561.
[14] Robert Divine, *Eisenhower and the Cold War* (Oxford, 1981), pp. 19–23.

colonial drum at the crucial press conference of 1 October 1956, and his steady retreat from the consequences to Britain and France of his decision to 'cut Nasser down to size' by the manner of his withdrawal of the Aswan Dam loan offer. Here too it now seems that he was governed entirely by Eisenhower's determination that nothing should threaten his election campaign image of the man of peace. It is impossible to read the detailed accounts, buttressed by citations from his diaries, given in Macmillan's memoirs, of his meetings with Dulles on 24 August 1956, with Eisenhower on 25 September, or with Humphrey the following day, without feeling that there was, whether wrongly or not, an element of deceit practised upon Britain, an element, interestingly enough, against which Winthrop Aldrich warned Macmillan in early September.[15]

These observations are purely historiographical in implication. Their burden is to call attention to the degree to which President Eisenhower's central role has so far largely been omitted from the historiography of this blackest of periods in Anglo-American relations. It is time now to turn to his responsibility for the misperceptions of British power and British interests, the failure to understand the effects of American policy towards Britain and British interests on America's own position in the world, and the failure to recognize the limitations of American power which underlay them.

This chapter will now limit itself to attempting to establish four contentions, three at least of which are valid not only in the context of Anglo-American relations in the 1950s but to the context of American foreign policy today. The first is that President Eisenhower and his advisers, having lived through the experience of America's partial mobilization during World War II, never understood or distinguished between mobilizable power *in posse* and mobilized power *in esse*. When Eisenhower became President, despite his most recent experience in command of NATO's forces, and his intellectual awareness that America's direct contribution to the land defence of Europe was marginally greater than that of the Netherlands, but nowhere near the level of forces that, once EDC became fact, France could or West Germany was expected to produce in the front line of European defence, he behaved and planned as though the relationship between the United States Army in Europe and her European allies was as it had been in January 1945, when he had five American armies, one Anglo-Canadian, and one French under his command. His 'New Look' in defence would, if anything, have diminished America's contribution in men under arms to Europe's defence. It was not, moreover, for another three years after his election that he was to abandon the view that the

American commitment in Europe's defence was a purely temporary one. In another man, more aware of the deterrent power of the Strategic Air Command (SAC) and of nuclear weapons, such an attitude would have been comprehensible. But the evidence of Eisenhower's views on nuclear disarmament expressed at Bermuda in December 1953, his dismissal of the atomic bomb as a purely military weapon, and his failure to appreciate the revolutionary effect of the hydrogen bomb urged on him by Churchill on the evidence of the Eniwetok tests, makes it clear that his attitude towards a future war in Europe was at that time still dominated by the experience of 1944–5.[16] The enemy's capacity to wage war could be weakened by air bombardment; but wars could only be won by the destruction of the enemy's army on the battlefield. What he could not understand was why the British would not show 'some common sense' and 'agree to let us give the French a few [atomic] arms and spray them around in Indo-China'.[17]

The available statistics suggest that when Eisenhower took office, despite the heavy US engagement in Korea, British and American armies in being were at about the same strength (some twelve American to eleven and a half British divisions). America's store of atomic weapons and the ability of America's long-range bombers to deliver them were greatly in excess of the capacity of the RAF. But the RAF's bases in Cyprus and in Iraq gave Britain a reach into Soviet Central Asia and the Caucasus that SAC was only to enjoy once her forces had been deployed in Turkey, Saudi Arabia, and Pakistan. Indeed, as late as 1958 the ponderousness of American intervention in the Lebanon (the whole operation came to a dead halt with the congestion of the Adana air base and the United States army arrived in the Lebanon equipped with atomic howitzers), compared with the mobility demonstrated by the supporting British moves into Jordan, Libya, and around the Gulf, said little for American ability to make her power felt where it mattered. America's military and financial potential was enormously greater than that of Britain. America's actual strength was greater than that of Britain, but not that much greater. It was also a lot further away and a lot less prepared for use where it might be needed. It is ironic that Eisenhower and his cabinet, so anchored in the mental preconceptions of 1944–5, should have regarded Churchill's views as the prehistoric survival, and their own as the last word in modernity.

The second contention is that Eisenhower and his advisers, not having

---

[16] Sir John Colville, *Footprints in Time* (London, 1978), pp. 240–1. Sir John attended the Bermuda conference as Churchill's private secretary. He kept a very full diary.

[17] Hagerty Diary, entry of 24 June 1954, directly quoting Eisenhower on the subject of British efforts to secure an American commitment to consult Britain 'before using atomic weapons anywhere anyhow'.

taken a direct part in the negotiation of the North Atlantic Alliance in 1948–9 or in the military, strategic, diplomatic, or political input into that alliance, shared the common American view of it as a progressive act of American grace, a military-political version of a Wilsonian commitment to world peace, a purging of the American sin of withdrawal from the League of Nations for which European opinion ought to be, and regrettably rarely was, duly and properly grateful. Fortress America, a retreat into a nuclear armed isolation, was always in their view a perfectly acceptable (if in a global and Wilsonian sense, immoral) military alternative. They were too young to have shared in Roosevelt's realization in November 1938 that America's first line of defence lay on the Rhine, a realization which in any case, after the furore consequent on his voicing this view in private to members of the Senate Foreign Relations Committee in January 1939, he kept entirely to himself. Nor had they played any substantial part in the deliberations of the US Chiefs of Staff and their planners in 1948, or their view that the passage of Middle Eastern oil or West European industry into Soviet control would be a disaster which would tilt the balance of power against the United States. When the question had arisen as to how American acceptance of the alliance urged on her by Britain, France, and Scandinavia could be justified to Congressional and public opinion, Truman's advisers had urged that, like Marshall Aid before it, it should be defended as a short-term American commitment to rehabilitation of Europe, to get Europe 'on to her feet and off our back'. Short-term political expediency has established the myth that America's commitment to the defence of Europe was an act of grace for which European opinion ought to be, but unfortunately often is not, properly grateful. Such a belief carries the often-stated corollary that European failure to follow America's lead could be punished by the withdrawal of American protection. Grace given can also be withheld. It is not that common, indeed, it has never been that common, for American voices to be heard urging the absurdity of such a viewpoint, or its irreconcilability with American insistence on the limitation of strategic imports from Europe into the Soviet Union. Even the Finlandization of West Europe would be an irretrievable disaster for the United States. It is high time that American historians of Anglo-American or American-European relations in the NATO period begin demythologizing American historiography on this point. It is too late perhaps to disillusion the present generation of American policy-makers. But there are always their successors to consider.

Underlying this historiographical problem there is another question which needs the most serious examination. Did the American obsession with the federalizing of Western Europe ever make sense? The

Community of today in no way resembles the vision pursued with such vigour by Harriman and Hoffman, among others, under the Truman Administration. The political obsession with European unity in the form of the European Defence Community delayed the rearmament of West Germany for four crisis-fraught years. The belief that Euratom and the Treaty of Rome were the pathfinders for a federal Europe played directly into the hands of President de Gaulle and threatened to confront America with a closed trade group entirely alien to American economic doctrine. In 1963 the concept of the Multilateral Force was to nullify the effects of America's Cuban missile crisis victory. Its ultimate absurdity was to be seen in 1965–6, when the Pentagon was seriously discussing 'taking out' French nuclear capacity and de Gaulle expelled NATO's headquarters from Paris. The American pursuit of European unity, or rather the attempt to force it on reluctant allies, has resulted in the separation of European defence co-operation in NATO from European economic, financial, and political relationships in the European Community. For more than thirty years American political discussion of relations with her European allies, and the historiography of those years of discussion, has been obsessed with the pursuit of an illusion. 'To dream the impossible dream' may have been an admirable characteristic in Don Quixote. It does, however, seem an odd basis for the conduct of the foreign policy of a superpower, and an even odder concept for its historians to take on board. 'The pursuit of the inconceivable by the incomprehending'; or 'The tyranny of geographical concepts over political reality': I offer these two titles to my American colleagues. As Alan Milward has shown in his masterly study of European recovery between 1947 and 1952, the pursuit of a federal United States of Europe was to deliver American power and freedom of decision into the hands of European national governments, particularly into those of France and West Germany.[18]

The last contention is that in yielding to the illusions of anti-colonialism America did a great deal to render more difficult the inevitable transition from European nineteenth-century colonial rule to independence. The history of the British, French, and Dutch overseas empires had shown long before John Foster Dulles became Secretary of State the transition of imperial thought from direct colonial rule to the development of colonial governments in which the indigenous inhabitants were to play an increasingly prominent and important part. The problem was, of course, enormously complicated where, as in the Dutch East Indies, Algeria, Rhodesia or South Africa, a settler population of European origins but native birth had sprung up. In the original dominions the early development of independence and the mass inrush

[18] Alan S. Milward, *The Reconstruction of Western Europe, 1945–1951* (London, 1984).

of European settlers internalized such problems so that Amerinds in Canada, Aborigines in Australia, Maoris in New Zealand present problems of interracial relations with which the greatest of all the now independent, once European-settled colonies, the United States itself, is only too familiar.

But in the main body of European colonial territories as they existed in 1939, for example, one could distinguish two forms of colonial rule, the progressive developmental models of French, British, and, after the trauma of Indonesia, Dutch colonial rule, and the stagnant, exploitative model of Belgian, Spanish, and Portuguese rule. Without the heavy external stimulus provided by American anti-colonialism in the early 1950s it is possible to conceive of a more gradual, less pell-mell rush toward independence, one which would have done less to augment the drain on the economies of the colonial powers arising from their attempt to control or halt the pace of decolonization, and more to reduce catastrophes such as the panic Belgian withdrawal from the Congo in 1960 or the gratuitous delivery in 1962–3 of the inhabitants of Western New Guinea to the colonial rule of Indonesia.

In this process the belief that America's eighteenth-century war of independence would confer on her the leadership of the new independent states, or that the minute *déclassé* and *déraciné* Europeanized élites who claimed to represent the colonial peoples were converts to American democratic ideals or could be so converted by brief and heavily subsidized periods with American universities, and that this would produce a permanent Americophile majority of new states at the United Nations is now beginning to be recognized as the illusion it was always maintained to be by the former colonial powers. As Macmillan put it in his memoirs, citing Robert Menzies, the Australian premier, by February 1957 Dulles was 'clearly becoming anxious about the djinn which he and Cabot Lodge had incautiously unloosened from the Afro-Asian bottle' as a result of their use of the General Assembly as a means of pressure on Britain, France, and Israel during the Suez crisis.[19] British disillusionment with the United Nations and with the workings of the Committee on anti-Colonialism was rapidly to lead to some serious but rather unreal talk of a separate organization for the 'free world'.

American disillusionment with the United Nations was to take longer. At a time when it has reached the point of serious proposals for American withdrawal from UNESCO and other UN special agencies, when a junior figure in the Reagan Administration has publicly invited the United Nations to withdraw itself from New York, when the deep sea mining companies are being urged to commit the United States

[19] Macmillan, *Riding the Storm*, p. 243.

government to direct conflict with the new UN Convention on the Law of the Sea, it is worth reflecting on whether the illusions of John Foster Dulles and of Eisenhower himself are not being turned inside out. Belief in the United Nations or rejection of belief in the United Nations are both inadequate substitutes for policy.[20] Nor can they be realistic guides to political discussions, unless prejudice is to become a substitute for rational calculation. The gratuitous cultivation of hostility, the instinct to add to one's known opponents is not rational conduct even for a nation of three thousand square miles and two hundred and twenty million inhabitants.

Behind the assault on British, French, and Dutch 'colonïalism', there lay a failure to comprehend the degree of strength the economies of modern Europe drew, not so much from their colonies (which were on the whole a drain on the domestic economies, though, save in time of major colonial campaigns, seldom a very severe drain) as from the international networks of trade, investment, and payments overseas which had come into existence concurrently with the growth of the Victorian colonial empires. Britain's earnings from the industries generated by her central role in the management, insurance, and financing of world shipping and of the cargoes carried in the world's shipping, let alone the oil earnings and the banking facilities available to the members of the sterling area, were of the first importance to Britain's economic well-being. In much the same way the aggressive arms salesmanship of the American military-industrial concept did much to destroy or retard the development of the British and French aerospace industries. Entrenched behind de Gaulle's defiance of economic costs, the French military aircraft industry survived and prospered. British industry by contrast took a terrible beating, its missile programmes progressively abandoned, its military aircraft programme surviving only by the development of the Harrier aircraft, a technological innovation neglected and in its earlier stages derided by its American competitors, intent on defeating the challenge of the TSR-2 and winning markets everywhere for the Starfighter and the F-107. In this atmosphere of high-powered salesmanship, it was difficult to discern much of the inter-Allied co-operation so often preached in Washington. The looseness of American social organization, the pluralization of American domestic power-centres, the long established relations of patronage and reward existing between American arms manufacturers and the American armed services were simply not amenable to presidential direction. If this had been admitted in the 1950s, little harm

---

[20] Speaking in the House of Commons on 1 Apr. 1975, Macmillan said that he had at Bermuda made it plain to Eisenhower 'our view that just trusting to the United Nations is not a substitute for a foreign policy'. (Cited by Macmillan, *Riding the Storm*, p. 259.)

need have been done. But it was to take until the 1970s before NATO procurement could be organized on a European basis, and much longer before that organization began to show results.

British politicians, commenting in retrospect on their experience of the Anglo-American relationship, are inclined to confine their comments to relations between presidents and prime ministers, secretaries of state and presidential advisers on national security problems and foreign secretaries, ambassadors, and senior political appointees to the Pentagon and the State Department. What has repeatedly defeated the achievement of true relations of confidence between allies, or more frequently the maintenance of relations of confidence and co-operation once established, has been the constant entry into the lower levels of presidential, treasury, State, and defence department advisers of new, inexperienced appointees, unlearned in the practices of alliance, culturally single-eyed in their conviction of the innate superiority of the American approach and the American view-point, conscious of American power and honed into competitiveness by the ethos of success, and concerned solely with the response of American constituencies to their actions and advocacies. For such individuals, the doctrine of interdependence, evolved by Macmillan in the last years of the Eisenhower presidency, was essentially rhetorical. The understanding that just as failure to react to the anxieties and interests of the various American constituencies where support was essential to the realization of administrative policy would result in the loss of support in Congress or in the electorate, so failure to heed the anxieties and interests of the differing constituencies of opinion among their allies on the eastern shores of the Atlantic would lead to their alienation and the weakening of inter-Allied co-operation, was a new, alien, and unwelcome doctrine. It was, and is, easier to believe in European ingratitude, European degeneracy, European propensity towards appeasement. Such constituencies after all play no part in the American electoral process—and it is through the electoral process that such new entrants are mainly able to emerge. Since 1976, the increasing dominance of American politics by men whose sole experience of politics has been competition to achieve election either for themselves or for those to whose public coat-tails they have attached themselves, has almost driven from American political discussion the issue as to how power once achieved should be exercised, let alone the existence of constituencies in no way part of the American electoral process, yet on whose support the effective exercise of power depends. Successive presidents have brought with them kitchen cabinets of driving, ambitious, yet inexperienced lawyers, business executives and quondam academics, for whom doctrine must of necessity fill the gaps that knowledge and experience simply cannot.

Since this development, itself a product of the disappearance of the old East Coast foreign policy establishment and of that younger generation which had experienced the realities of Anglo-American co-operation in Europe in 1943–5, is now itself a matter of history, it is essential that the myths of American power and invincibility inculcated by the insularity of so much historical writing on American foreign policy in this century be eradicated. In 1960–1 I had the extraordinary experience of sitting in on the weekly round-table discussions of current American foreign policy issues held under the chairmanship of Professor Arnold Wolfers at the Washington Center of Foreign Policy Research. Nothing in Britain, least of all the two years I had spent devilling for a Chatham House Study Group on British interests in the Mediterranean and the Middle East, had prepared me for discussion at once so broad-ranging, so intense, so sophisticated, or so stimulating. Yet such discussions needed the cool and authoritative direction provided by Wolfers, a Swiss historian and political scientist of distinction long before his arrival at Yale in the late 1930s launched him on his distinguished career in America. They needed too the presence of former State Department officials such as Paul Nitze or Charles Burton Marshall to provide a constant injection of political realities in the international sense. But their debates were held in private and had little reflection in academic teaching on American foreign policy.

What is needed today is a two-way movement, of political realism and political insight, not only into the current discussion of British and American foreign policy problems and relations but into the realistic assessment of the record of the past and its reinterpretation to the future entrants into the American policy-making process soon to emerge from the American educational system. The present version of American and British policies in the 1950s and 1960s is encrusted with myth, obscured by contemporary propaganda, misinterpreted by Anglophobes, anti-Americans, and spiritual descendants of Clarence Streit and pan-Anglo-Saxonists alike. It is essential that its course be rightly exposed and rightly understood, both in Britain and in America. For the effect of the myth of American omnipotence has been the strengthening of America's Soviet opponents as much as the weakening of her natural allies, which has been neither in America's interest nor, for that matter, in the interests of those nations who chose to ally their own prosperity, good fortune, and survival with that of the United States. By choosing to expose the mythology of the period, the alliance cannot but gain from a proper appreciation of its true basis in that pattern of interlocking cultures, interlocking experience, and interlocking society.

5

The Macmillan Years and Afterwards

ALISTAIR HORNE

THE 'Special Relationship', notes Henry Kissinger in a particularly eloquent passage in *White House Years*, is

particularly impervious to abstract theories . . . [I]t reflected the common language and culture of two sister peoples. It owed no little to the superb self-discipline by which Britain succeeded in maintaining political influence after its physical power had waned . . .

It was an extraordinary relationship because it rested on no legal claim; it was formalized by no document; it was carried forward by succeeding British governments as if no alternative were conceivable. Britain's influence was great precisely because it never insisted on it; the 'special relationship' demonstrated the value of intangibles.[1]

But, more than reflecting the 'common language and culture', or even trading interests, it was fundamentally based on mutual concern for defence against the enemy that threatened both partners. With the revival of the Anglo-American 'Special Relationship' after 1945, its dominant element continued to remain defence. 'It is easy to forget how dominant it was then and still is today', wrote Dr David Owen, former British Foreign Secretary.[2] It certainly was dominant when, in 1957, Macmillan and Eisenhower endeavoured to mend the holes in the fence rent by Suez.

In the 'Macmillan era' that was to begin, however, one needs draw attention straight away to a new triangular factor that was to affect the Anglo-American 'Special Relationship', much as Roosevelt's growing preoccupation with the Soviet factor did during the Second World War from mid-1943 onward. One might call it the 'French Connection', coupled with the name of Charles de Gaulle, who came to power in France the year after Macmillan took over from Eden in England. 'It could never be our interest', John Adams had declared a century and a half earlier, 'to unite with France in the destruction of England . . . on

---

[1] Henry Kissinger, *White House Years* (Boston, 1979), p. 90.
[2] David Owen, William E. Leuchtenburg, Anthony Quinton, George W. Ball, *Britain and the United States, Four Views to Mark the Silver Jubilee* (Heinemann in association with the United States International Communication Agency, 1979), p. 65.

the other hand, it could never be our duty to unite with Britain in too great humiliation of France.'[3] Duly translated into modern dress, this dictum of Adams became a key consideration of US policy toward Britain, notably from the accession of John F. Kennedy onward.

The Kissinger quotation evokes the essentially sentimental and mystical ingredients of the 'Special Relationship'. However, in private conversation Kissinger identifies various distinct occasions when he, or his predecessors, had benefited pragmatically from the Foreign Office's judgement, expertise, and that rare, intangible, quality of *Fingerspitzengefühl* (the British, he notes, usually seemed to come to conferences better prepared than their American opposite numbers). The more purely practical significance of the 'Special Relationship' was stressed, however, by McGeorge Bundy, referring to the Macmillan–Kennedy era: 'when you have dozens of situations in which you can in fact communicate with London to Washington and Washington to London in a way neither could with any other capitals'.[4] The importance of these old, custom-established channels of communication seemed to assume, more recently, a particular relevance at the time of the Falklands, in 1982, through the speed in which the whole British operation could be set afoot, by means of American collaboration over Ascension Island. Without continuance of what has been termed the 'residual defence relationship', the whole audacious expedition could almost certainly never have taken place.[5]

These residual defence relations, waning after the emergency of World War II and resuming again with the Cold War, were based on highly informal arrangements. For instance, there appears never to have been any formal agreement over the first establishment of US nuclear bases under the Attlee government; the United States Air Force commander in Britain, back in 1949, remarked how '. . . never before in history has one first-class power gone into another first-class power's country without any agreement. We were just told to come over and "we should be pleased to have you".'[6] Critical of Churchill's attempts to revive the old wartime relationship in the 1950s, Harold Macmillan (later Prime Minister) took the view that, in principle, informal and unorthodox methods of approach should be reserved only for very exceptional occasions. A decade later, however, this kind of unorthodoxy was exactly the medium through which his own relationship with

[3] Arthur Schlesinger, *America: the Perplexities of Power* (The Cyril Foster Lecture, University of Oxford, 26 May 1983), p. 3 (quoting John Adams).
[4] McGeorge Bundy, John F. Kennedy Memorial Library, Boston. (Hereafter referred to as JFKL.)
[5] John Baylis, *Anglo-American Defence Relations 1939–1980; The Special Relationship* (New York, 1981), Preface, p. xviii.
[6] Ibid., p. 35.

President Kennedy was able to blossom—notably at the potentially explosive Nassau Conference of December 1962.

Throughout his career, Macmillan in his relations with the United States was always deeply influenced by Winston Churchill, his hero. Like Churchill, he had been brought up by an American mother—a sternly ambitious lady from Indiana who could remember the Civil War—and, also like Churchill, his experience was based on practical wartime dealings, in North Africa and Italy as Churchill's 'Resident Minister', opposite number to Roosevelt's Bob Murphy. This brought him into close friendship with Eisenhower, a factor which had been denied Eden, his predecessor at No. 10, with calamitous results. As Eden's Foreign Secretary briefly in 1955, Macmillan had probably got on better with John Foster Dulles than any other Briton—or, at least, less badly. During Suez (which was definitely *not* Macmillan's 'finest hour'), although nominally he had been only on the fringe as Chancellor of the Exchequer, and sulking somewhat as a result of having been removed from the Foreign Office against his wishes, Macmillan managed to get the messages from his old friend Ike badly wrong. This was a result perhaps of excessive optimism derived from the happy wartime association that, somehow, mystically, things 'would all be right on the night' (a fundamental optimism Macmillan held about the nature of the 'Special Relationship', and he was not always mistaken).

The period of 1954–6 almost certainly represented the nadir of Anglo-American relations, and on coming to power in 1957 a much chastened Macmillan dedicated himself to restoring the old harmony with President Eisenhower. Suez had taught him some hard lessons about how easily communications between London and Washington could break down. These lessons helped him both in 1957 and later, in late 1962, when, once again, the 'Special Relationship' seemed threatened by the Skybolt crisis. In 1957 Eisenhower was also shaken and highly receptive to his wartime friend's overtures, and between them a remarkable recovery was effected. Eisenhower later designated their first meeting at Bermuda 'as the most successful international conference that I had attended since the close of World War II'.[7] Something of the intimacy of Casablanca and Cairo was resurrected. As a tangible result, Britain was given sixty Thor missiles, under the 'two-key' system.

The July 1958 *Agreement for Cooperation on Uses of Atomic Energy for Mutual Defence Purposes* (repealing the McMahon Act) was probably one of the most mutually beneficial accords ever achieved in peacetime. Under it Britain was able to receive technical information on production of nuclear warheads, as well as fissile material, and was the only nation

[7] Dwight D. Eisenhower, *The White House Years, Waging Peace 1956–61* (Garden City, 1965), p. 124.

to be so privileged—to the great distress subsequently of President de Gaulle. As a result Britain was enabled to manufacture her own smaller and more sophisticated warheads, which were required first for the ill-fated Blue Streak Missile and later for Polaris; the door was also opened to the purchase of marine nuclear propulsion plants for Britain's first nuclear submarine. In return the United States was granted British bases for her Polaris submarines, and full access to British thermo-nuclear know-how—which was by no means negligible. In the words of Andrew Pierre: '. . . the very act of nuclear-sharing . . . created an environment in which American trust in the British government deepened so that American officials discussed a wider range of military and political topics *more frankly with their British counterparts than with officials of other friendly nations*'.[8] Indirectly, one of the spin-offs of the new Macmillan–Eisenhower 'Special Relationship' was to be the disastrous Skybolt. Offered in place of Britain's scrapped Blue Steel, Skybolt was projected as a stand-off, long-range missile, with a highly complex guidance system designed to be fired from aircraft rather than land or sea. Its original attraction to the British Defence Chiefs was that it would keep the RAF's V-bombers going for another 'generation'.

The whole saga of Skybolt provides a prime case history in a breakdown and recovery of the 'Special Relationship', combined with the injection of a third dimension in the shape of 'the French Connection'.

In 1960 Eisenhower was replaced by Kennedy. There was immediate concern (shared not least by Macmillan himself) at how the 'Special Relationship' would work on a personal basis, between the avuncular Edwardian and the young Roman Catholic upstart a generation apart. But Macmillan was far from being the 'nice bumbling old man', as he was described at the time. Kennedy's astute ambassador in London, David Bruce, was closer to the mark when in a telegram to the State Department (but composed very much for the President's eyes), he gave the following assessment of Macmillan:

At times he gives the impression of being shot through with Victorian languor. It would be a mistake to infer from this that he is lacking in force or decisiveness, as it would be to deduce from what is called his 'Balliol Shuffle' that he is not capable of swift action. . . .

But this is no mean man. . . . He has charm, politeness, dry humor, self-assurance, a vivid sense of history, dignity, and character. To what extent he would bend conviction to comport with expediency one cannot say . . . my guess is that he will go far to suit otherwise discordant notes to the US President's harmony. . . .[9]

---

[8] Andrew Pierre, *Nuclear Politics: The British Experience with an Independent Strategic Force, 1939–70* (London 1972), p. 144.

[9] Telegram from Ambassador Bruce in London to Secretary of State, 12 Dec. 1961, Box 170, NSF, JFKL.

It was a brilliant prognostication.

The opening bars in the Macmillan–Kennedy concerto, however, were cautious and tentative. Mutual trials, like Khrushchev's brutal mauling of an inexperienced Kennedy in Vienna and the Berlin crisis of 1961, gradually brought them together. Following the disastrous Vienna encounter, Kennedy was suffering additionally with acute back pain. Macmillan, aided by his highly developed political antennae, immediately got it right by taking the President, informally, up to his study for a drink. Kennedy came to rely on the wisdom of his counsels; Macmillan gave advice on the Laos crisis that might have rescued subsequent American leaders over Vietnam: 'DON'T'.

Much has been written about this 'Special Relationship within the Special Relationship', the personal friendship, nay, affection for each other that grew between President and Prime Minister, and it and its impact on events should never be underestimated. Apart from the common bond of the war against the Axis, the principal interest shared by Roosevelt and Churchill had been in naval matters; it was fostered with utmost assiduity by the 'Former Naval Person' from their earliest correspondence. But the shared interests of Kennedy and Macmillan were both wider and deeper. The two men shared a profound sense of history and a similar, rare kind of Celtic humour, often bordering on black. For instance, at the time of the Bay of Pigs, a singularly unfunny period for Kennedy, Macmillan eased the strain by remarking: 'I could really perform my ultimate service to mankind if those Cubans had only shot down my plane; then you could have had your little invasion!' Or when, during the Laos crisis, Macmillan on a Potomac outing observed a small flotilla from a local high school and remarked: 'Looks like the Laotian Navy!'[10]

His humour invariably struck the right chord with the much younger President, while Macmillan was quite genuine in his obituary tribute to Kennedy in the House on Commons in November 1963: 'He was one of the best informed statesmen whom it has ever been my lot to meet, and he was altogether without pedantry or any trace of intellectual arrogance.'[11] On his side, Macmillan, with his American background, had the advantage of being rated by the American press as 'One of the very few living British politicians who can manage to sound convincingly patriotic without sounding anti-American'.[12]

By the time of their third meeting in Bermuda in December 1961, it was, to quote Arthur Schlesinger, '. . . as if they had known each other all

[10] Henry Brandon, JFKL Orals.
[11] Address by Harold Macmillan to the House of Commons on 25 Nov. 1963. *The Parliamentary Debates* (Hansard).
[12] Joe Harsch, *Christian Science Monitor*, 2 Apr. 1961.

their lives'; and, after that, adds Ormsby-Gore, 'it was almost like a family discussion when we all met'. His opposite number in London, David Bruce, was also not exaggerating when he declared that '. . . The frequence and frankness of their interchanges have few parallels in modern diplomatic intercourse.'[13]

This inner relationship was additionally reflected, indeed intensified, by the brilliant supporting cast of the 'two Davids'. Bruce's dispatches reveal him to have been one of the most outstanding American ambassadors ever sent to London, while Ormsby-Gore, a nephew of Macmillan as well as a long-standing personal friend of J.F.K., possessed (as a Welshman) a full measure of that eccentric Celtic humour that appealed to the President. He was undoubtedly one of Macmillan's most inspired appointments. 'We become very rigid, after we've reached a conclusion', Dean Rusk once explained of the Americans, but 'Lord Harlech [as Ormsby-Gore later became] had a knack of getting in the British view at the early stages, so we took them into account *before* we came to a final conclusion.'[14] Ormsby-Gore's privileged position with the White House became the envy of his fellow envoys; it also 'totally distorted the diplomatic corps set-up here', claimed Reston, while it even caused Dean Rusk to feel some resentment at being bypassed in the channels of communication between the two leaders.[15] During the Cuban missile crisis, Ormsby-Gore enjoyed the unique position of being invited to sit in on top-level sessions of the National Security Council. At the peak of that crisis, arrangements were also apparently made for him and his family to be brought to the safety of the presidential nuclear shelter in the Appalachian Mountains.

It was during Cuban missile week that the 'Special Relationship' reached a new peak, with Kennedy telephoning Macmillan to inform him of blow-by-blow developments at regular intervals. Allowing for the tense drama at the time, the transcripts of the conversations (curiously, taped only on the British side) make almost comic reading, with the President largely holding a monologue and the Prime Minister contributing sympathetic interjections that, subsequently, often sound rather vapid. (It is important, in the context, to note that Kennedy's telephone calls were purely informative and in no way seeking advice, or even endorsement; that may be relevant when considering subsequent, more contemporary tests of the 'Special Relationship', such as the Falklands and Grenada.) Other allies, like de Gaulle, Adenauer, and Diefenbaker, were also kept informed, though none with the same

[13] Arthur M. Schlesinger, Jr., *A Thousand Days: John F. Kennedy in the White House* (Boston, 1965), pp. 490–1; David Bruce Orals, JFKL.

[14] *Oral History Project*, JFKL; Schlesinger, *America: the Perplexities of Power*.

[15] James Reston Orals, JFKL.

degree of heart-to-heart unburdening to which the British Prime Minister was treated. The chief British contribution to that crisis, when the world stood on the brink of disaster (apart from the crucial, and pooled, information on the state of Soviet rocketry produced by the agent, Penkovsky) was to persuade Kennedy to accept what was for Khrushchev the face-saving compromise of reducing the quarantine line from 800 to 500 miles. The proposal was Ormsby-Gore's, acting entirely off his own bat, but with total support from Macmillan.

It seems quite wrong to suggest, as did some British commentators, that the missile crisis 'saw the death of Britain's "special relationship" with America . . .'[16] If anything, it brought the intimacy and trust between Macmillan and Kennedy to a new high-point, which was to have most important consequences for the next crisis: Skybolt.

The story of the dropping of Skybolt and its replacement is central to any account of Macmillan and the 'Special Relationship', but is highly complex; I will endeavour to deal with it as succinctly as possible.[17] Briefly, hints of problems with its guidance mechanism, and of pressure for its abandonment, had begun to seep out of the US government as early as 1960. In June 1962, the Defense Secretary Robert McNamara condemned limited nuclear forces operating independently as 'dangerous, expensive, prone to obsolescence and lacking in credibility as a deterrent'.[18] He reiterated this criticism in December, which aroused unsavoury suspicions in Britain, according to Macmillan: '. . . the failure of Skybolt might be welcomed in some American quarters [meaning George Ball and the 'Europeanists' within the State Department] as a means of forcing Britain out of the nuclear club.'[19]

Yet neither side broached the problem frontally for another six months, by which time a great head of mistrust had built up on the British side, and a first-rate rift loomed. The whole Skybolt saga was, to quote David Nunnerly,

. . . a crisis compounded of drama and deceit, of uncertainty and distrust, of muddled perceptions and disappointed expectations, of high political stakes both won and lost, of miscalculations and misjudgement, at times carefully concealed from the public eye, at times skilfully exposed for the public's benefit. . . [20]

The threat to the 'Special Relationship' so disturbed Kennedy that, once the skies had cleared, he commissioned Professor Richard Neustadt

[16] Baylis, *Anglo-American Defence Relations*, p. 75.

[17] For anyone wishing to examine it in greater detail, please see Colloquium to the Woodrow Wilson International Center for Scholars of 3 Mar. 1983, *The Skybolt Crisis, 1982*, by Alistair Horne.

[18] Speech at Ann Arbor, Michigan, 16 June 1962.

[19] Harold Macmillan, *At the End of the Day; 1961–1963* (New York, 1973), p. 343.

[20] David Nunnerley, *President Kennedy and Britain* (London 1972), pp. 127–8.

to conduct a full investigation (which resulted in a penetrating report, still partially classified) with the presidential brief: '. . . I want to emphasize the aspects of trans-Atlantic non-dialogue'.[21]

For how this all arose, one needs first to consider current distractions. Obviously transcending all others, there had been the missile crisis, just ended in November 1962. Said Sorenson: 'After Cuba, it seemed a small problem. All problems did.'[22] On Macmillan's side, there had been the 'Night of Long Knives' when he decimated his Cabinet that June, followed by a sharp fall in his personal popularity; the economy was in a bad way, unemployment was at a post-war record of 800,000 (compare this with three and a quarter million in 1985); there were troubles in Yemen, Aden, Brunei, Congo, and Rhodesia; China was attacking the Commonwealth nation of India; there was Berlin, and, above all, there was the issue of de Gaulle and British entry into the European Economic Community (EEC), which had entailed a long struggle within the country and the Commonwealth. 'I do not recall a time' Macmillan wrote in his diary on 9 December 1962, 'when there are so many difficult problems to resolve and awkward decisions', and he remarked plaintively on the current hostility and unfairness of the British press.

One now needs to mention the 'French Connection', the third party in the eternal triangle. Macmillan met de Gaulle at Champs in June 1962, in an effort to clear the way for British entry into the EEC. De Gaulle did not say 'yes' and did not say 'no', but to this day responsible Frenchmen insist that Macmillan deceived de Gaulle with promises of nuclear collaboration. This is open to challenge; the British view at the time was that Macmillan had simply said that if there were to be an attack on Europe at some future date, the United States might hesitate to use her nuclear armoury (a European view-point as valid in 1985 as in 1962), and that therefore 'some European deterrent was perhaps necessary'. At Champs de Gaulle made two points against British entry: it would alter the character of the Community, politically and economically, and Britain was too tied to the United States. Champs was followed by Rambouillet on 15–16 December, which ended in disaster, with a thoroughly crestfallen Macmillan admitting 'I thought the discussions about as bad as they could be from the European point of view'.[23] He did not relay his pessimism about British entry to J.F.K., not, I believe, out of any intent to deceive, but (*a*) because it was not in his nature to accept reverses or seek solace, and (*b*) because he was nervous about indiscretions in Washington, which, at that time, had a reputation in some British quarters as being 'government by leak!'

---

[21] *The Neustadt Report*, 'sanitized' text, JFKL.
[22] Sorensen interview, 23 Jan. 1981: Alistair Horne.
[23] Macmillan, *At the End of the Day*, p. 354.

One must also note the 'Europeanist Variation'. The State Department 'Europeanists', or 'Conceptualists', who were opposed to Britain's retention of the 'Independent Deterrent' that had long composed the main cornerstone of Macmillan's defence policy, consisted chiefly of George Ball, William Tyler, Walt Rostow, Bob Bowie, Henry Owen, and to some extent McGeorge Bundy at the National Security Council (NSC). They tended to share Dean Acheson's recently expressed views (that created an uproar in England and enraged Macmillan) about Britain's world role being 'played out', and they wanted to degrade the 'Special Relationship' in order to place American policy on more equal footing with Germany and France. Ball felt that the 'Special Relationship' had trapped the United States into undesirable policies; he identified three cardinal mistakes (all of them, in fact, Macmillan coups):

1. the 1958 amendment of the McMahon Act;
2. Eisenhower's 1960 promise to provide Britain with Skybolt;
3. the substitution of Polaris for Skybolt in 1962–3.

The 'Europeanists' were very much party to Kennedy's own fears (some of them conflicting):

—that the British deterrent would lead to nuclear proliferation;
—that the Germans would get a finger on the nuclear trigger;
—or, that the Germans would be in an inferior position if Britain got Polaris;
—or, that France and Germany would become the most powerful nations in Europe;
—that de Gaulle would be given an excuse to claim that the United States sought to dominate Europe if it aided perpetuation of the British deterrent;
—that he would be given an excuse for keeping Britain out of Europe.

As a result the 'Europeanists' thought up the Multilateral Force (MLF), a kind of nuclear first cousin to the ill-fated European Defence Community of the 1950s. MLF made many enemies. In the United States a hard-headed pragmatist like McNamara thought it had 'no military value'. In Britain the Minister of Defence, Peter Thorneycroft, condemned it as 'the biggest piece of nonsense that anybody had ever dreamed up, and a rather dangerous one'. At Nassau, expressing himself with moderation in front of the President, but damning it nonetheless effectively, Macmillan remarked that he foresaw difficulties in 'our fellows sharing grog with the Turks' aboard an MLF nuclear ship.[24]

When Macmillan returned home, thoroughly depressed, from Rambouillet on 16 December 1962, he found Skybolt had blown up in his

[24] *Oral History Project*, JFKL.

face. After he arrived for key defence talks on 11 December, McNamara let the cat out of the bag about dropping Skybolt; Thorneycroft flew into a rage (to which he seemed somewhat prone) at what looked like political ineptitude, or duplicity, on the part of the Americans; aided by leaks, the British press maximized the Government's discomfort and the apparent rift in the alliance.

There emerged several of what Neustadt has seen as 'mysteries', which may well be worthy of further discussion. Why did Washington delay so long before informing London of the abandonment of Skybolt? Why was London so slow to pick up the hints? (Neustadt's general conclusion, as synthesized by Henry Brandon of the *Sunday Times*, was that '. . . the writings were on the wall, but the British Government didn't believe them and didn't want to'.[25]) Why was J.F.K. so slow to realize the full gravity of political embarrassment the decision held for his friend, Macmillan?

One possible explanation lies in British inter-service rivalry, with the RAF determined to hang on to Skybolt for its survival; another, the 'distractions' afflicting both governments, outlined earlier. Another is the fact that Thorneycroft and McNamara spoke 'different languages'. As with Dulles and Eden, there was a mutual personal antipathy, and both were at odds throughout. Thorneycroft saw the Skybolt issue in terms of domestic politics; McNamara, in terms of technology and cost-effectiveness. Neustadt also suggests that McNamara was the 'loose nail' in a communication breakdown between the two leaders. In November, Macmillan requested three guarantees from Kennedy in the event of Skybolt being scrapped:

1. no publicity before a final decision;
2. no decision before consultation;
3. consultations as soon as possible.

But, says Neustadt, a distracted Kennedy forgot to pass these guarantees on to McNamara; hence McNamara's unguarded leak before seeing Thorneycroft in London.

Of such is the fabric of misunderstandings within the 'Special Relationship'. Both Thorneycroft and Macmillan flew into a rage, with Macmillan talking roughly (in private) about American perfidy, and (to Ormsby-Gore) about Dullesian threats of 'an "agonising reappraisal" of all our foreign and defence policy'.[26] The London talks broke up inconclusively, with abortive discussions on a substitute for Skybolt, and adjourned to Nassau, where the summit was already due to begin on 19 December.

[25] Henry Brandon, JFKL Orals.
[26] Ormsby-Gore, JFKL Orals.

The British delegation that arrived at Nassau was, in the words of Henry Brandon, 'the angriest' at any Anglo-American summit since the war. Other British journalists present also wondered whether it was purely hazard that the Bahamian band struck up 'Oh Don't Deceive Me' as Kennedy arrived on Air Force One. Thorneycroft was in a bullying frame of mind, prepared, if necessary, to walk out in a huff and blame it all on the Americans. McNamara and the 'Europeanists' were probably disposed to be equally combative; while Macmillan himself was in a hard-nosed mood, determined to ask for Polaris, or bust. Underlying all the preliminaries to Nassau was what Arthur Schlesinger afterwards aptly termed '. . . a Pinero drama of misunderstanding: Thorneycroft expecting McNamara to propose Polaris, McNamara expecting Thorneycroft to request it . . .'[27]

There was also the basic philosophic difference in attitudes to Skybolt/Polaris, as seen by Neustadt: 'The British didn't take the US problems with the precision guidance seriously; there were different attitudes, with the British wanting the weapon to hit a city, as a deterrent, *not* as precision targetting, which was the American interest'.[28] (One may note how today outlooks over Cruise seem to have switched, while parallels remain over Trident.) The British also showed—as indeed, they often have—some fundamental misunderstanding of how things actually work in Washington. Given the system of bureaucracy, once the Pentagon procurement machinery was already rolling it would have been extremely difficult for the President to have reverted to Skybolt by late November, let alone December. As Professor Michael Howard said (in the *Sunday Times* of 23 December 1962): 'Whitehall has been inexcusably naive if it really expected the US to develop at vast expense a weapon they no longer need, so that we could pursue a policy of which they disapprove; loyalty to allies has its limits.' On the other hand, the American team did not fully comprehend the acuteness of Macmillan's political predicament at home.

It now took what, in retrospect, seems like the almost miraculous intervention of the personal factor—the 'relationship within the relationship'—to cut through entrenched positions and save the day. It started with Ormsby-Gore travelling with the President aboard Air Force One, and putting across to him the extent of Macmillan's predicament. Kennedy replied with an offer of a fifty-fifty deal to develop Skybolt for Britain alone, which Ormsby-Gore regarded as a remarkable token of American good faith. At Nassau this was promptly, but gently, shot down by Macmillan, resorting to the kind of earthy humour he knew would appeal to Kennedy: '. . . although the proposed

---

[27] Schlesinger, *A Thousand Days*, p. 861.
[28] Richard Neustadt interview, 1 Jan. 1981: Alistair Horne.

marriage with Skybolt was not exactly a shot-gun wedding, the virginity of the lady must be now regarded as doubtful . . . the lady had already been violated in public. . .'[29]

At Nassau, on the eve of the summit, the two leaders walked together for a long time, without advisers, talking and joking about a whole range of subjects other than Skybolt, and displaying manifest affection for each other—to the apprehension of the Kennedy entourage, who feared (perhaps not without reason) that the Brits were going to get away with Uncle Sam's shirt. At the conference Macmillan followed this with a deeply moving bravura performance on what Britain had suffered in two World Wars, the cause of her present preoccupation with independent security.[30] He repeated the telling point, which he made to de Gaulle at Champs (and which appears to be equally relevant to the 1980s): Americans were currently willing to defend Europe, and had the means, but would they always have the will? He would trust this president, but what about his successors? He expressed determination to get Polaris, and persuaded Kennedy that de Gaulle would not be put out by this. (Whether he was right or wrong is another story.)

The results of Nassau were that the British got Polaris 'at a knock-down price not much more than half the original estimate', wrote the Defence Correspondent of *The Times* twenty years later: '. . . a bargain that for most of its life has cost the Government less than 2% of its defence budget'.[31] The British deterrent, rightly or wrongly, was preserved for another generation.[32] From Macmillan and Polaris to Thatcher and Trident was as from father to daughter. There were limitations imposed on the independent deployment of the weapon, but these were largely meaningless, as Macmillan pointed out: 'You don't fire it off as if it were July 4th or Guy Fawkes!'[33] MLF was torpedoed (though it took L.B.J. actually to sink it).

To this extent Nassau represented a great personal triumph for Macmillan, although the British press did not see it as such at the time. On the other hand, despite Kennedy making a subsequent offer to de Gaulle of a similar deal, Nassau was followed by de Gaulle's brusque veto of Britain's application to join the EEC, a shattering defeat for Macmillan's European policies. Even George Ball reckoned that in the course of time Nassau would have made no difference to de Gaulle's final decision, and that it was just a handy excuse. Dr David Owen, writing in

[29] Macmillan, *At the End of the Day; 1961–1963*, p. 358.

[30] Schlesinger, *A Thousand Days*, p. 790.

[31] *The Times*, 27 Jan. 1983.

[32] Writing in *Foreign Affairs*, Jan. 1963, Dean Acheson, for one, thought it 'a tragic misuse of resources', in that, for producing a nuclear capability equal to perhaps 2% of that of the United States, Britain would be forced to cut her conventional arms to a minimum.

[33] Ormsby-Gore, JFKL Orals.

1977, considered that 'psychologically, the whole offer had been handled apallingly', and that de Gaulle was justifiably huffed, which influenced his withdrawal from NATO in 1966. (On the other hand, might not de Gaulle, via Polaris, have obtained his costly *Force de Frappe* for virtually nothing?)

Other American critics charged Nassau with representing '. . . everything a conference of this sort should not . . . an impromptu occasion for sorting out the vastly complex problems in nuclear sharing and related questions of NATO politics, without the benefits of the intensive joint staff work that would normally (and necessarily) precede such a meeting',[34] and that it gave continental Europe a 'sense that our conceptions and our executions were alike erratic . . .'. Neustadt also regarded it as '. . . a case in point where J.F.K. did overrule his subordinates in order to help Macmillan. It was a case of "king to king", and it infuriated the court.'[35]

In terms of the 'Special Relationship', one of the most significant, and indeed truly remarkable aspects of Nassau was the speed with which, as after a violent thunderstorm, the air cleared, and business (i.e. defence talks) went on as usual between the two allies. Henry Brandon was not exaggerating when he described Nassau in its immediate aftermath as '. . . perhaps the most dramatic Anglo-American confrontation since Gladwyn Jebb put his feet on the table and began reading a newspaper when the US sought British support for a resolution endorsing the crossing of the 38th Parallel in Korea . . .'.[36] Nor was the London *Times* exaggerating when, looking back on Nassau from the vantage point of twenty years later, its current Washington correspondent, Nicholas Ashford, judged the Polaris agreement to represent '. . . the highest point that relations between the two countries ever reached since the war'.[37]

Ormsby-Gore (or Lord Harlech as he was now known) compared the rift caused at Suez with Nassau and remarked that hiccups between allies are inevitable and when they do occur, '. . . statesmen should try to minimize the damage they do to each others' interests and should heal the breach as fast as possible. In the two crises we have been examining, neither side gets many marks on the first count, both get high marks on the second.'[38] Yet if Nassau illustrates the capacity of the British and Americans to resolve a crisis within the 'Special Relationship', equally it throws up a vivid example of a failure to resolve an Anglo-French (and, to an extent, American–French) crisis, based—in contrast to the

[34] John Newhouse, *De Gaulle and the Anglo-Saxons* (New York, 1970; London, 1970), p. 213.
[35] *The Neustadt Report.*
[36] Henry Brandon, the *Sunday Times*, 23 Dec. 1962.
[37] Nicholas Ashford, *The Times*, 25 Jan. 1983.
[38] Lord Harlech, in 'Suez SNAFU, Skybolt SABU', in *Foreign Policy*, 2 (1971), 50.

'Special Relationship'—on years, indeed centuries, of mutual mistrust, but also simply on the age-old problems of linguistic *mésentendres*.

The recently published complete correspondence of Roosevelt and Churchill[39] includes letters that were never sent, notably by Churchill, a revealing aspect of their relationship. Churchill, in a rage, would count to twenty before he (or his staff) either redrafted or scrapped an abrasive communication. The 'Special Relationship' was kept afloat by Macmillan and Kennedy exercising similar restraints. Immediately after Nassau news was released that, after all, a successful test of the condemned Skybolt had just taken place—which threw Kennedy into a searing rage with McNamara. Macmillan's reactions were equally fierce. He had cause to wonder whether the Americans had in fact been telling the whole truth about Skybolt all along.

In contrast, however, Macmillan wrote to Kennedy the following day with utmost moderation: '. . . I enjoyed our talks in the Bahamas . . . but it was rather provoking that Skybolt should go off so well the next day. It would have been better if it had been a failure. However those are the chances of life.'[40] There are also several recorded instances of parallel restraint on Kennedy's side.

Before Macmillan resigned through illness in October, and before Kennedy was assassinated that November, their last act of collaboration was to sign the Nuclear Test Ban Treaty with the Russians. Macmillan always felt that if the Americans had been more forthcoming an even wider success might have resulted; nevertheless, he rates the Treaty his single greatest achievement while in office. Self-deprecatingly, he admits that 'perhaps we played the cards above their value' in the 'Special Relationship' with Kennedy. On the other hand, no alternative and equivalent alliance was open to Kennedy in the 1960s, and one is entitled to speculate what the two might have gone on jointly to achieve, had not both been removed prematurely. As it was, the Macmillan–Kennedy relationship undoubtedly marked the high-point of Anglo-American collaboration in the post-war world. As Averell Harriman, with his long experience of the 'Special Relationship' dating back to the 1940s, remarked to the author, the personal rapport in the Macmillan–Kennedy relationship even exceeded that of the original wartime compact of Churchill and Roosevelt:

On the other hand, from the standpoint of making decisions, there were far more far-reaching decisions which affected the two nations that were made between Roosevelt and Churchill . . . they had greater power and they worked together as a team during the war in a way two nations have never worked . . .'[41]

39 Warren F. Kimball, ed., *The Complete Correspondence: Churchill and Roosevelt* (Princeton, 1984).
40 Harold Macmillan, letter to John F. Kennedy, 24 Dec. 1962.
41 Interview with Averell Harriman, 28 Oct. 1980.

After 1963, relations—at least initially—continued to be good, especially on defence, but were never as warm and intimate. Then, gradually, a divergence of interests and the growing discrepancy in power between the United Kingdom and the United States began to have its effect. Relations between Harold Wilson and Lyndon Johnson cooled over the Labour Government's policy of withdrawal from east of Suez, and particularly over the lack of support over Vietnam—Johnson felt aggrieved that Britain could not even send 'a platoon of bagpipers', which he would have considered sufficient. On the technical level, however, close co-operation continued, leading to such secret defence deals as the granting to the United States of a telecommunications base at Diego Garcia in the Indian Ocean, in exchange for waiving research and development costs on Polaris. Personal relations between L.B.J. and Wilson were never good; though, strangely enough, Wilson managed to establish closer ties with Nixon.

By the mid-1970s, little remained of the global military partnership founded in World War II. Under Heath, the personal element in the 'Special Relationship' probably reached its nadir. This can be ascribed partly to the nature of Heath himself, and partly to his desire to impress the French with the new 'Europeanness' of Britain by replacing human transatlantic links with more formal state-to-state dealings. Relations were badly strained during the 'Yom Kippur' War of 1973, when Britain, because of oil interests, was reluctant to give Nixon the support required to help embattled Israel. In terms of rift, there was almost a repetition of Suez, in reverse.

In the opinion of David Owen (though obviously *parti pris*), relations improved with the advent of the new Wilson administration in 1974. Callaghan struck up a close working association with Henry Kissinger, one of the fruits of which was the Anglo-American initiative to try to break the log-jam over Rhodesia (although it actually took Thatcher and Carrington to finalize a deal on this issue). On the American side, perhaps no one has rated the intangible benefits of the 'Special Relationship', especially on the personal level, more highly than Henry Kissinger. In 1976, the Chairman of the United States Joint Chiefs of Staff stigmatized the British Armed Forces as 'pathetic': nevertheless, the United States bought a number of the Harrier jump-jets, the first direct operational aircraft purchase since World War I.

In the 1980s, a shared ideology brought Thatcher and Reagan closely together, but with none of the intimacy and warmth that characterized the Macmillan–Kennedy *entente*. As noted earlier, it was largely through long-established working rituals that the Falklands operation of 1982 was logistically feasible; while at the same time, the passing squall over the 1983 operation in Grenada revealed the level to which the British power base had sunk in US military thinking. On the nuclear side, Trident was acquired by Thatcher on preferential terms inherited from Polaris and Macmillan: so were criticisms of its desirability, and so was the habit of sharing nuclear secrets with the British, but not the French. Over the Cruise uproar, it became apparent once again how crucial it is for the United States to hold full consultations with an ally whenever new nuclear weapons are involved. (As Defence Minister Heseltine remarked to the author in 1984, it is the technical, rather than the political, aspects of any new nuclear weapon that, perversely, tend to provoke more alarm in British public opinion.) Once again, as with Skybolt, one finds the wrong questions being asked about Cruise, on both sides of the Atlantic.

To end, one may quote former Foreign Secretary David Owen on the perennial British dilemma—Europe or America?

All three relationships are important, but inasmuch as the Atlantic relationship is forged with one of the two super-powers in the world and sustains our very existence we must not be afraid to recognise it as having a very special quality . . . . The quality that makes this relationship so crucial is defence . . .[42]

[42] David Owen, William E. Leuchtenburg, Anthony Quinton, George W. Ball, *Britain and the United States, Four Views to Mark the Silver Jubilee*, p. 76.

6

America, Britain, and the Soviet Threat in Historical and Present Perspective

RICHARD H. ULLMAN

M O S T of all, the Anglo-American 'Special Relationship' has been about security—specifically, about the threat to security posed by the Soviet Union. The intimacy that the two governments (and, indeed, societies) have experienced over the course of more than four decades was born in the struggle against Hitler's Germany. But it would probably have died in the aftermath of the 1939–45 war had not Stalin's Russia sustained it. Now, four decades later, there is a possibility that the relationship will be substantially altered because of differences over the Soviet threat.

Without the spectre of Soviet expansionism seemingly ever present, as it was in the late 1940s and early 1950s, the Anglo-American relationship might have taken quite a different course. Even during the periods of most intense wartime collaboration there were serious divergences of view between Franklin Roosevelt and Winston Churchill, and even more serious ones between departments of the governments over which they presided. Like Churchill, Roosevelt made much of the partnership between the two English-speaking democracies, but he also saw the United States as playing a role in the post-war era that would separate it from both Great Britain and the Soviet Union, sometimes as a mediator between them, other times as a liberalizing force to offset what he took to be their narrower, more traditionally *realpolitik* concerns. American antipathy to the maintenance of Britain's colonial empire, competition for the oil resources of the Persian Gulf, differing notions regarding the future of the world trading system—these and other issues were bones of contention between London and Washington. They might well have been much more vexing. Had they been so, the insularity (indeed, latent xenophobia) that characterizes the populations of both democracies would very likely have made for an even more contentious relationship at the mass level. Despite the wartime collaboration, in 1945 there existed between the two countries few of the bonds of sentiment that tied the United Kingdom to the white Dominions of Canada, Australia, New Zealand, and South Africa.[1]

Yet Anglo-American frictions never grew to crippling proportions. The prospective challenge from Moscow had a powerfully concentrating effect on policy-makers' minds. And it largely diffused antipathies at the popular level. The Yanks had come to fight the Nazis. They would return to deter the Bolsheviks. For that they would need British bases—the 'unsinkable aircraft carrier', in the words of one critical account.[2] And they would come to depend upon British assistance in activities ranging from garrisoning Germany and patrolling the Atlantic to policing the Persian Gulf and fighting the war in Korea. Almost from the outset, this collaboration extended to the sharing of even the most secret intelligence information; it soon came to include substantial co-operation on matters relating to nuclear weapons as well.

If the Soviet threat has defined the contours of the Anglo-American 'Special Relationship', the United States (with the exception of the period immediately following the end of the war in Europe[3]) has taken the lead in defining that threat. Alarm bells generally rang louder in Washington than they did in London, or in the other capitals of Western Europe. It was the United States that decided to interpret North Korea's attack on South Korea as not only Soviet-sponsored but as perhaps a feint preceding an aggressive Soviet move in Europe. It was the United States that called NATO into being as a means of rearming West Germany. It was an American administration that, at the 1952 NATO ministerial meeting in Lisbon, set for the alliance force-level goals that proved politically impossible for any members to achieve.[4]

The United States led, but for the first two post-war decades it had willing followers. Washington's assessments of the threat posed by the Soviet Union and its allies did not differ markedly from those of its principal Western partners. (There was, however, considerably less consensus regarding the Peoples' Republic of China.[5]) In the United Kingdom, Ernest Bevin, Winston Churchill, Anthony Eden, and Harold Macmillan—the central figures in British foreign policy during

---

[1] See David Reynolds' contribution to this volume. For another recent commentary on the Anglo-American wartime relationship, see Warren F. Kimball's introduction to his definitive edition, *Churchill and Roosevelt, the Complete Correspondence*, vol. i. *Alliance Emerging, October 1933–November 1942* (Princeton, 1984), esp. pp. 12–20.

[2] Duncan Campbell, *The Unsinkable Aircraft Carrier: American Military Power in Britain* (London, 1984).

[3] See Bradford Perkins's chapter on the Truman Administration in this volume.

[4] For the force goals set by the NATO Ministerial Meeting at Lisbon in Feb. 1952, see Richard P. Stebbins, *The United States in World Affairs 1952* (New York, 1953), pp. 127–8, and Peter Calvocoressi, *Survey of International Affairs 1952* (London, 1955), pp. 32–6. For an excellent account of the ways in which the post-Korea rearmament strained Britain's economy and politics, see Joan Mitchell, *Crisis in Britain 1951* (London, 1953).

[5] See Roderick MacFarquhar's chapter on East Asia in this volume.

this period—shared to a considerable extent the outlook of Dean Acheson, Dwight Eisenhower, and even (once the rhetoric was stripped away) of John Foster Dulles. Moreover, they viewed the world from the perspective of the leaders of a state with global interests. This perspective set them apart from the political leaders of Fourth Republic France (despite its continuing colonial involvements) and of the newly formed Federal Republic of Germany. In both continental countries, concerns were much more narrowly focused upon Europe. 'Britain is going to continue to be what she has been, a Great Power', Oliver Franks declared in the first of his famous 1954 BBC Reith Lectures; a Great Power, he said, was a state whose 'action . . . can decisively affect the fate of other Great Powers in the world'. When Franks spoke those words (before Suez, it should be noted) the United Kingdom lacked the military capability of the United States, but it nevertheless had forces stationed around the world. With those forces came a concomitant sense of global responsibility as the head of the Commonwealth and as a genuinely Atlantic nation (*of* Europe but not wholly *in* it), capable of wielding influence on both its shores.[6]

For America's allies, as for the United States itself, the war in Vietnam was a watershed. But whereas many Americans came only eventually to believe that the entire involvement in Vietnam rested upon faulty assumptions regarding the degree to which the coming to power there of a Communist regime would jeopardize important Western interests, Europeans by and large came to this conclusion much earlier. Yet some, like Harold Wilson in London or a succession of Christian Democratic chancellors in Bonn, muted their criticism of their most important ally.

For Wilson's Labour government, the war in Vietnam was particularly problematic because the period of drastic American escalation, 1965–8, coincided with its decision to remove British forces from Aden and then (following the sterling crisis of 1967) sharply to reduce all other overseas garrisons with the exception of those in Germany. This meant, essentially, abandoning the last remnants of a once substantial British presence 'east of Suez', and—combined with London's inability to take more than rhetorical steps in opposition to Ian Smith's 'unilateral declaration of independence' in Rhodesia—it made clearer than ever the disparity between the extent of American and British involvement in the Third World. As Wilson's Cabinet colleague, Richard Crossman, noted in his diary in 1968, the Prime Minster decided early in the

---

[6] Oliver S. Franks, *Britain and the Tide of World Affairs* (London, 1955), pp. 7–8. 'Our enduring associations are within the Commonwealth, with the United States and with the nations of western Europe,' Franks said (p. 12) in a passage frequently cited. 'They are the three circles of our life and power.'

Vietnam War that Britain's role should be one of mediator between Washington and Hanoi, but that to be able to do so, 'standing close to the Americans is the price'. Crossman continued: 'I am convinced this is the central issue. The P.M. passionately thinks we have been effective and can still be important. [Minister of Defence] Denis Healey and I feel that we really can't play any part in the peace-making precisely because we have not been able to denounce the Americans.'[7]

The war in Vietnam and withdrawal from east of Suez were decisive events in a redefinition of British interests that focused, instead, on Europe. Significantly, on 2 May 1967 the British government formally applied for admission to the European Economic Community. Wilson and his successors—Labour and Conservative—found that interests are very much determined by power. When a polity no longer has the power to protect what it once defined as an interest, it begins to define its interests differently. Some that were thought to need active military protection turn out no longer to need it. Others turn out upon re-examination not to be interests at all. Within two years of the Anglo-French attempt forcibly to overturn Gamel Abdel Nasser's nationalization of the Suez Canal Company in 1956, policy-makers in London and Paris were regarding Egyptian operation of the waterway as utterly normal. By the time the Carter Administration took office in Washington in January 1977, less than two years after the fall of Saigon, the notion of a vital American interest in the survival of a non-Communist government in South Vietnam, once so staunchly asserted, seemed ancient history. Other examples of such redefinitions abound. In public life as in private, *faits accomplis* shape the ways people view the world around them. The mind adjusts. Phenomena one cannot affect seem less harmful than those one can.

Yet—in international if not in interpersonal relations—bipolarity has a powerful counteracting effect. The two leading members of a bipolar system experience imperatives that do not impinge upon lesser states. Each has a great incentive to extend its sphere of control until the other challenges it by pushing back. It is arguable that Soviet activities in Africa and Central America since the mid-1970s, when Moscow first acquired the ability to project power far beyond the Soviet Union's borders, stem more from a desire to narrow the range of choices open to the United States than from any estimate that the issues in contention

[7] Richard Crossman, *The Diaries of a Cabinet Minister*, vol. iii. *Secretary of State for Social Services 1968–1970* (New York, 1977), p. 236, entry for 24 Oct. 1968. Crossman frequently made similar comments; see pp. 289, 718, and 910. Wilson's own memoirs, however, while full of detail concerning his relations with both Presidents Johnson and Nixon over Vietnam, are singularly devoid of reflection on British (or his own) purposes. Nowhere does he present a rationale, either strategic or tactical, for his choices. (Harold Wilson, *The Labour Government 1964–1970: A Personal Record* (London, 1971).)

are of unique intrinsic value to the Kremlin. In this process the Soviets are merely following American footsteps. For years, ever since the famous NSC 68 planning paper of 1950, American policy-makers have tended toward the view that what has mattered most about any given piece of territory is whether or not it lies in their sphere or Moscow's.[8]

It is in this respect—defining the West's interests, and threats to those interests—that American thinking about foreign policy over the last quarter century has differed most from British. This is not to say that there has not been considerable overlap. In both societies, ever since 1945, there have been those who have regarded what they consider to be the relentlessly expansionist drive of the Soviet Union to be overwhelmingly the most important factor in world politics, reflected in turmoil and instability in many regions. For such observers, the Soviet threat is total; Moscow's ambitions are global, maximalist, and undifferentiated; and its efforts to dominate the world are ideologically motivated and limited only by the extent of Soviet capabilities or by barriers interposed by the West. Other analysts in both societies see Soviet behaviour as being driven not by expansionist ambitions but by defensive compulsions, as by and large reactionary rather than initiatory. For them the causes of instability in the Third World are to be found mostly in the dynamics of politics within individual countries and regions. The Soviets undoubtedly take advantage of that instability for their own purposes, but their role—either in engendering turmoil or nurturing it—is rarely decisive.

That views such as these are commonplace in debates over international politics in both Britain and the United States is scarcely surprising, given the extent to which the two English-speaking societies draw upon the same intellectual resources. Yet the two polities differ considerably in what might be called the location of the centre of gravity of thought. The first of these conceptions has for the most part been dominant in the United States, the second in Great Britain. That has not always been the case. During the two decades following World War II, as we have already noted, there was substantial conceptual congruence. At the governmental level, that was true, also, during the first two years of the Carter Administration; the general outlook of Cyrus Vance, Carter's Secretary of State—that Soviet motivations are essentially defensive—was very close to that of David Owen, the Foreign Secretary in James Callaghan's Labour government. Their collaboration began with their common effort to seek a solution to the problem of Rhodesia, but it soon extended to the other major issues on their agendas. Their

[8] See, among many works, John Lewis Gaddis, *Strategies of Containment: A Critical Appraisal of Postwar American National Security Policy* (New York, 1983), *passim*, but esp. pp. 89–126.

outlook was shared by Andrew Young, Carter's representative at the United Nations, and by most of the assistant secretaries who worked with Vance at the Department of State. Congruity did not, however, extend to what might be called the societal level. Vance's approach, with its orientation toward seeking regional accommodations and contextual explanations for instability rather than blaming the Soviets, was far too 'soft' for most Republican and many Democratic Senators and members of Congress—and also for Zbigniew Brzezinski, Carter's White House assistant for national security.[9]

In the American political context, Vance and his close colleagues were clearly untypical. Owen's orientation, on the other hand, was not drastically different either from that of his recent predecessors or from that of his successors, regardless of party. Where British governments of the past quarter century have differed markedly from one another over foreign policy has been in their approaches to particular problems of North–South relations, not in their approaches toward the Soviet Union, where all have pursued *détente* and all have defined the issues in contention between Moscow and the West in fairly specific and circumscribed rather than global terms. Even the Conservative government of Margaret Thatcher—much the most right-wing government in twentieth-century British history—has eschewed the globalist anti-Soviet rhetoric that has been a hallmark of the Reagan Administration's foreign policy.

The last two decades have demonstrated that the Anglo-American relationship—indeed, the relationship between the United States and all its NATO allies—can tolerate substantial differences over security policies. The Vietnam War and Middle East policy are but two of many issues where there have been substantial disagreements between Washington and most of its partners. Congressmen and Senators habitually complain that the allies do not sufficiently share the burden of Western defence, particularly the burden of responding to alleged threats outside Europe, and that their search for short-term commercial advantage has made their economies unnecessarily vulnerable to Soviet pressure. The European refrain is that American policies have heightened East–West tensions and have shattered *détente*.[10] Yet the heads of government have thus far managed successfully to contain these disagreements. And at the working level, particularly at the level of the alliance military command, effective co-ordination continues.

[9] For Vance's view of Owen, see Cyrus R. Vance, *Hard Choices: Critical Years in America's Foreign Policy* (New York, 1983), p. 262. Brzezinski's memoirs are full of comments on Vance, but see in particular, Zbigniew Brzezinski, *Power and Principle: Memoirs of the National Security Adviser 1977–1981* (New York, 1983), pp. 36–44.

[10] See Miles Kahler, 'The United States and Western Europe: The Diplomatic Consequences of Mr. Reagan', in Kenneth Oye *et al.*, *Eagle Defiant* (Boston, 1983), pp. 273–309.

These relationships might be considerably strained, however, if left-leaning parties come to power in the United Kingdom and the Federal Republic of Germany. Both the British Labour Party and the German Social Democrats are substantially more radical and left-leaning today than they were in 1979 and 1982, respectively, when they last governed their countries. Both have had a drastic shake-up of leadership[11] and reflect the currently much more radical and anti-American orientation of their activist rank-and-file members. They disagree with the Reagan Administration's policies in much of the Third World, and they are especially troubled by its nuclear weapons policies. They fear that the administration is not seriously interested in negotiated reductions of either strategic or intermediate-range nuclear weapons, and in their view, far from fulfilling Reagan's proclaimed goal of making nuclear weapons 'impotent and obsolete', his Strategic Defense Initiative (SDI) is more likely to be the engine of an unbridled arms race.[12]

A profound watershed will have been crossed if the parties of the democratic left in Europe begin to see the United States as part of the problem rather than as part of the solution. That will occur if it becomes generally perceived that the way in which Washington has defined the Soviet threat has in fact caused that threat to grow—for instance, in the form of yet further augmentations to Soviet and other Warsaw Pact forces facing NATO in Europe—and now makes accommodation impossible. Similarly, American policies in the Third World, such as the Reagan Administration's undeclared war against the Sandinista regime in Nicaragua, make it easy for Europeans to argue that in their external behaviour there is no meaningful difference between the United States and the Soviet Union and that the mere condition of being a superpower will inevitably cause them to act in a similar manner: both seek hegemony. Neither will tolerate political diversity within its sphere of influence. Therefore both are undeserving of aid or comfort or political support.

If such attitudes become widespread among Europeans—and there is a not insignificant danger that they will—they are likely to result in the

---

[11] James Callaghan and Helmut Schmidt are now elder statesmen in virtual retirement, while David Owen, it should be noted, was among the party notables who abandoned Labour in order to found and now (in Owen's case) lead the centrist Social Democratic Party.

[12] The British government is also distinctly cool to the SDI. Its summary of its *Statement on the Defence Estimates 1985* stated that it is 'anxious to prevent the spread of the arms race to space'. (Central Office of Information, London, Reference Services, 'Britain's Defence Policy: The 1985 White Paper', No. 243/85, June 1985, p. 2.) Foreign Secretary Geoffrey Howe was more blunt when, in a major address to the Royal United Services Institute, he compared the SDI to the Maginot Line and questioned whether it could be put into operation without 'generating dangerous uncertainty'. (*The New York Times*, 16 Mar. 1985, p. 1.) For an extensive commentary on British and European doubts, see John Newhouse, 'The Diplomatic Round', *The New Yorker*, 22 July 1985, pp. 37–55.

growth of unilateralism and therefore in a redefinition of the alliance. That will apply in particular to nuclear weapons. In the Federal Republic, a new SPD government might ask the United States to reduce or even remove the Pershing II intermediate-range ballistic missiles that are being deployed there in accordance with NATO's 1979 decision, and perhaps the ground-launched cruise missiles as well. In the United Kingdom, nuclear unilateralism might take either of two forms. If Labour returns to power soon, it may indeed act on its current policy of doing away with Britain's own nuclear force and removing all American nuclear weapons and nuclear bases from British territory and British waters.[13] Alternatively, if the Social Democratic–Liberal Alliance ever succeeds in forming a government—admittedly, not a likely development in the near future—it might move to eliminate at least some American nuclear forces while retaining some sort of independent British deterrent force. And it is even possible that a post-Thatcher Conservative government would be much less hospitable to American nuclear weapons if popular sentiment against them grows substantially.

The object of all these policies would be to uncouple Europe from the United States, at least to the degree that an American–Soviet war arising outside Europe would not bring Soviet nuclear weapons down on European cities. In its present mood the British Labour Party would go further and, by total denuclearization, attempt to remove Britain altogether from Soviet nuclear target lists. Washington would then be confronted, at a minimum, with a demand for a cafeteria-style alliance in which members would want some of the benefits of association with the United States without having to pay at least some of the costs.

It should be noted that the search for special alliance arrangements is not new. When Denmark and Norway joined NATO in 1949, they made clear that their membership would not entail basing foreign troops on their soil in peacetime. In 1957, when the alliance was in the process of deploying large numbers of tactical nuclear weapons, both Nordic countries declared that they would not accept them. In 1966 President Charles de Gaulle removed France altogether from the NATO military organization, retaining only a formal alliance with the other members. The separation still stands. As de Gaulle and his successors well knew, the facts of geography assure France of allied protection in any European war.[14]

---

[13] This policy was adopted at the Labour Party's annual conference in Oct. 1983 following the party's resounding defeat at the previous June general election. It was reconfirmed at the 1984 annual conference; the party stopped short, however, of approving a motion for the closure of all American military facilities in Great Britain. See *The Times*, 4 Oct. 1984, p. 4 and 6 Oct. 1983, p. 4.

[14] For the Nordic countries, see Robert K. German, 'Norway and the Bear: Soviet Coercive Diplomacy and Norwegian Security Policy', *International Security*, 7.2 (1982), 55–82. For France, see

De Gaulle's defection caused considerable annoyance in the other capitals of the alliance. Among other inconveniences, it required the removal of NATO's headquarters from Paris to Brussels. But it had long been coming, and it was seen as an inevitable development of Gaullist foreign policy. Therefore it inspired no retaliation from the United States or other alliance members. Eighteen years later, in February 1984, another defection occurred: on the other side of the globe and in the context of another alliance, the Labour government of New Zealand attempted to place its order at the American cafeteria by refusing to allow visits by nuclear-armed or nuclear-powered United States naval vessels. Yet, as Prime Minister David Lange made clear, he still regarded the tripartite ANZUS alliance (with the United States and Australia) as a pillar of his country's foreign policy.

Lange's *démarche* touched a particularly sensitive nerve in Washington, however. The Reagan Administration reacted with bitter hostility, seeing in it a portent of a general unravelling of alliances. 'Our differences with New Zealand', Secretary of State George P. Shultz said, 'raise the most basic questions about alliances and about alliance responsibilities in the modern world.' And he continued: 'If one partner is unwilling to make . . . sacrifices, others will wonder why they should carry their share of the burden. The result may be the gradual erosion of popular commitment to the common cause.'[15]

It was not the likely actual effect in the south-west Pacific of New Zealand's policy that inspired Washington's strong condemnation. For the US Navy, calling at New Zealand's ports is a pleasant but scarcely essential convenience. Yet the policy has been read—correctly—as a statement by a government, not merely an opposition, that the United States is now 'part of the problem', and that safety is more likely to come through distance than through proximity to American policies and American nuclear weapons. That, of course, is the British Labour Party's current refrain as well. For the Anglo-American nuclear relationship, therefore, events may come full circle again. Over the last forty-five years it has gone from intimate wartime collaboration in the development of the atomic bomb to a post-war period of chill as the United States Congress tried to monopolize the bomb and safeguard nuclear secrets, and then in 1958 back to the far-reaching collaboration between the two nuclear weapons establishments that has endured until now.[16] There is at least a reasonable chance that this collaboration may be circumscribed by a future British government.

François de Rose, 'The Relationship of France with NATO', *AEI Foreign Policy and Defense Review*, 4.1 (Washington: American Enterprise Institute, 1982), 23–6.

[15] *The New York Times*, 18 July 1985, p. 8.

[16] For a comment on that collaboration, see Alistair Horne's chapter on the Macmillan years in this volume.

If the United Kingdom does opt for denuclearization, the 'Special Relationship' between the two societies will atrophy. That is ironic, because American defence planners have historically been distinctly cool toward the British (and also, of course, the French) nuclear force, vastly preferring that the same resources be used instead to bolster the West's conventional capabilities. More conventional spending is not, however, a realistic alternative now. A British government that chooses the path of denuclearization would not do so to help the United States create a more efficient division of labour within NATO, but because of a conviction that more arms—nuclear arms especially, but arms of any sort—will not buy more security.

Although any government that asks American nuclear forces to leave will scarcely find Washington more obliging regarding collaboration on the conventional level, there is no reason to think that NATO as an alliance could not survive such an upheaval. Alliances have always had about them at least some aspects of a cafeteria. Commitments between sovereign governments are not total. Obligations, rules of engagement, and the like are always the subject of detailed negotiations. The question is not whether the cafeteria exists, but how much choice its managers allow.

Moreover, much depends upon what else is occurring within the alliance. British denuclearization would inevitably throw more of NATO's weight onto the American-German connection. That connection has been strained by the divisions introduced into German politics by the deployment, beginning in 1983, of the Pershing II and cruise missiles. There certainly is a potential for further strain if the Reagan Administration's Strategic Defense Initiative seems to be impeding American–Soviet arms reductions. But as long as the Germans do not seem to be trying to renegotiate the basis for their relationship with Washington, a future British government might have some leeway to do so.

Yet, if a British government were to pursue such a path—even if it encountered little counterpressure from Washington—it would be likely to find in the wake of doing so that there would not be much left of the Anglo-American 'Special Relationship'. For renegotiation would be confirmation that the world looks fundamentally different from Westminster (if not from Whitehall) than it does from Capitol Hill. That would apply most of all to assessments of the threat posed by Soviet nuclear weapons. And it might well be seen as applying as well to other dangers the West faces—foremost among them the upheavals in the Third World which some allege (and some deny) are the consequences of Soviet efforts at destabilization. That would not mean that British assessments of events, say, in the Persian Gulf or Southern Africa, would not be given a hearing in Washington. But they probably would not be given a privileged hearing. Rather, they are more likely to be on the same plane as views expressed by other European powers. And Americans for whom they were unpalatable would find it easier to label them as special pleading, and as such more easily disregarded.

This, it may be argued, is not drastically different from the situation that prevails today. British views are always welcome in Washington, but so are German or Israeli or Japanese views. They are given weight when they concern issues in which the government involved has either an obvious stake or recognized special knowledge. They are also given weight when they come from a leader who has a close personal relationship with the American president, the kind that Margaret Thatcher reportedly has with Ronald Reagan, but which a future prime minister—especially one from Labour—may well not have.[17] The difference is one of degree. But degree, after all, is what makes a relationship special.

Our discussion has dwelt perhaps excessively upon a scenario which, if not the worst case, would surely be regarded in Washington as fairly dire—the return to power in London of the Labour Party and its renegotiation of the basic terms of the Anglo-American security relationship. That is not an implausible scenario, but it is not the most likely one. It is much more likely that either the Conservatives will retain control of the government or else that there will be a centrist coalition—either left or right—in which the Social Democratic Party plays a crucial role. In either of these instances Britain's own nuclear force would be retained (although its 'modernization' through replacement of its current Polaris missiles with much more potent American Trident D-5s might be called off) and the United States would retain access to British bases for storing and deploying nuclear weapons.

Yet even in these eventualities, the future Anglo-American security relationship is likely to be at least somewhat troubled. Certainly that will be the case if the Reagan Administration is followed by one with a similarly all-encompassing view of the Soviet threat and a similar commitment to regaining strategic superiority over the Soviet Union. On the other hand, an American administration of a quite different *timbre*—one committed to strategic parity in the context of arms reductions and to the restoration of something like *détente* with Moscow—might come into conflict with a British government dedicated, like the present one, to retaining its own relatively powerful nuclear force. The Soviets argue, with some justification, that the British

[17] See, e.g., Newhouse's report on the degree to which Mrs Thatcher's objections caused Mr Reagan to modify important elements of his administration's approach to the SDI, 'The Diplomatic Round', pp. 44–5.

and French forces must be counted if there is to be any nuclear arms control in Europe. London and Paris argue just as strongly that their independent forces should be excluded from the totals to be negotiated between Washington and Moscow.[18]

That the bond between Washington and London has grown less 'special' over the course of four decades is scarcely surprising—a product in some respects of the alliance's success. Forged in global war and sustained by the urgent post-war need to deter aggression by a major common adversary, the Anglo-American relationship has gradually been transformed from a general to a limited partnership in good measure because war with the Soviet Union has, mercifully, never come. Both powers have been involved in wars—the United States far more deeply than the United Kingdom—but the wars have been 'out of area', and as such often as much a source of contention as of harmony. Together with the other European members of the alliance, the British now worry that the combination of American nuclear weapons policies and interventionism in the Third World will sour the possibilities for an accord with Moscow and exacerbate tensions that might otherwise be reduced.

When NATO was young, it was commonly said that the nations of the West must all hang together lest they hang separately. Today, however, hanging separately often seems the lesser danger. Moreover, for the United Kingdom the facts of geography make isolation, let alone hanging separately, unlikely. As France has done for two decades, Great Britain cannot help but draw decisive security benefits from a continuing firm American alliance with and military presence in West Germany. At least until that presence is dissipated, the United Kingdom can thus afford policies that enable it to have the cake of forward defence and yet still eat what appear to be the sweet fruits of denuclearization.

---

[18] On this point, see Richard H. Ullman, 'Out of the Euromissile Mire', *Foreign Policy*, 50 (1983), 39–52.

DEFENCE

7

Nuclear Weapons and the 'Special Relationship'

MARGARET GOWING

BRITAIN has been in the nuclear weapon business for forty-five years and, from the time an atomic bomb proved possible, has been determined to have an independent nuclear deterrent. Today, what Britain calls her independent nuclear deterrent is dependent on the provision of missiles, though not of nuclear warheads, from the United States, and Britain is the only individual country to which the United States supplies them. How did this very special atomic relationship come to pass? Here I shall return to its early historical development, lost as it is in the mists of history. For otherwise it is impossible to understand why Britain, now a medium-sized world power and a relatively low economic performer, has been determined to remain a nuclear power and to maintain her atomic relationship with the United States.

For the last twenty-seven years this relationship has been consonant with a smooth political relationship between the two countries but dissonant perhaps with the changes in Britain's political and economic realignments and, increasingly, with the relative economic, military, and political power of the two nations. Until 1958, however, as we shall see, the atomic 'Special Relationship' was far from smooth except briefly for three wartime years. For the most part the nuclear relationship was bitter, and the pride of achievement was all the greater when in 1958 the Americans signed an agreement ensuring the military nuclear collaboration that had lapsed in 1945. The bitterness and the pride were for many subsequent years prominent in the minds of British policy-makers.

Britain's special nuclear relationships with the United States derived from the fact that her scientists, including refugees from Germany, 'invented' the atomic bomb. This is often forgotten because the immense effort of the United States Manhattan project, which made the first bombs, overshadowed Britain's crucial role. In one of the strangest coincidences of history, discovery of the results of splitting a uranium atom came at the beginning of 1939 and the theoretical explanation was openly published three days before the outbreak of war. Although many scientists had speculated that uranium fission might provide an extraordinarily powerful explosive, the theoretical explanation encouraged scepticism.

Then in the spring of 1940 two refugee physicists at Birmingham University—Rudolf Peierls and Otto Frisch—explained how, with a five-kilogram lump of pure uranium 235 (the rare fissile atoms in a lump of ordinary uranium), a bomb could be made that would liberate the energy of several thousand tons of dynamite. Their memorandum led to the extraordinarily successful British Maud Committee, whose report in 1941 explained why an atomic bomb was almost certainly possible with uranium 235 and possibly with the new man-made element plutonium. This, together with nuclear power, might be made in nuclear reactors using ordinary, plentiful, unseparated uranium, interspersed with special materials called moderators. The British owed their interest in this bomb route to the arrival, as France fell, of two French scientists from a Paris team who had been the world leaders in this type of reaction. They had brought with them to Cambridge the total world stock of heavy water, the most efficient known moderator. After the war the British forgot their debt to France but General de Gaulle did not. British atomic relations with France were to conflict seriously with her relations with the United States.[1]

The Maud Committee had worked at a frantic pace, feeling the breath of their German competitors hot on their necks. The Germans did indeed launch a project which, most mercifully, floundered. Immediately after the Maud Report was completed it was shown to scientists in the still neutral United States where work on atomic bomb possibilities had been, like the German work, desultory and dispersed. It

---

[1] For the period up to the end of 1952 the histories sponsored by the United States and United Kingdom atomic energy organizations are the main source. For the United States these are: Richard Hewlett and Oscar Anderson, *A History of the United States Atomic Energy Commission*, vol. i. *The New World, 1939–46* (1962), Richard Hewlett and Frank Duncan, vol ii. *Atomic Shield, 1947–52* (1969)—both published by Pennsylvania University Press. For the United Kingdom they are: Margaret Gowing, *Britain and Atomic Energy 1939–45* (London, 1964); Margaret Gowing with Lorna Arnold *Independence and Deterrence* (2 vols.), vol. i. *Policy Making*; vol. ii. *Policy Execution* (both London, 1974). Booklets containing all the references to official papers used in the Gowing books can be obtained from the Historians' Office, United Kingdom Atomic Energy Authority, 11 Charles II Street, London SW1. Further volumes of the American and British histories are in preparation. Several other books cover the period from 1939 to more recent years. Especially valuable is Bertrand Goldschmidt, *The Atomic Complex* (American Nuclear Society, 1982) (trans. from French). The author, a Frenchman, participated personally and importantly in the scientific and political aspects of atomic energy both in France and the international atomic community from 1933 to the present. Other books relevant for nuclear weapons and the 'Special Relationship' are John Baylis, *Anglo-American Defence Relations 1939–1980* (London, 1981); A. J. R. Groom, *British Thinking about Nuclear Weapons* (London, 1974); Peter Malone, *The British Nuclear Deterrent* (London, 1984); Andrew Pierre, *Nuclear Politics: The British Experience with an Independent Strategic Force, 1939–70* (London, 1972); John Simpson, *The Independent Nuclear State; The United States, Britain and the Military Atom* (London, 1984).

was only when they read the brilliant Maud Report that Americans were galvanized into action. Without it World War II would almost certainly have ended before an atomic bomb was dropped. Britain's conception of herself as a nuclear power was born out of the Peierls–Frisch memorandum and the Maud Committee's Report.

At the end of 1941 the Americans, conscious that the British were so far ahead, proposed a joint project with them. But the British declined in a most superior tone, preferring instead collaboration through mutual exchange of information. And so they missed the bus. If the two projects had then become closely intertwined they could not easily have been pulled apart again. As it was, the Americans launched an all-out atomic effort even before Pearl Harbor and within six months they had far outstripped the British. In mid-1942 the British realized they must try to enter the American project on terms of equal partnership, but now the Americans did not want them and even the exchange of information ceased. The British could not proceed on their own and were cut off completely from the American project.

After a long struggle Churchill persuaded Roosevelt to sign, in August 1943, the Quebec Agreement, which allowed Britain to participate in parts of the American project and led to joint control of uranium supplies. The Agreement had two other important provisions: one was that neither side would use the bomb without the other's consent and the other was that neither country would communicate any atomic information to third parties except by mutual consent. Almost all the British scientists working on U235 and bomb calculations now joined the American project. The Americans would not have the Anglo-French reactor-plutonium team largely because they mistrusted the Free French and so it went to Canada where the project, after a bad start, flourished. Canada's role in the atomic story is important in the evolution of *her* power status. Britain's native project now closed down for the duration of the war as her scientists emigrated to North America. The biggest contingent in the United States was at Los Alamos where the bombs were fabricated, but no British scientists were admitted to the plutonium plants.

So in the end the British were the junior partners in the atomic project they had launched. Their status was apparent in the decision to drop the bombs on Japan: this was essentially an American decision although British consent was duly asked for and duly given. The British contribution to the $2 billion American project was small but it was of key importance in certain crucial areas and hastened decisively the dropping of the bombs on Japan.

After the Quebec Agreement Anglo-American atomic relations were fairly smooth, and in September 1944 Churchill and Roosevelt signed the Hyde Park (US) Agreement promising continued full atomic collaboration after the defeat of Japan. Churchill had no fear that the United States would maltreat or cheat the British. However, none of the American atomic people knew of the existence of the Agreement until after Roosevelt died, when they asked the British to supply a copy. The Minister at the British Embassy believed that the Americans wanted above all a post-war American atomic monopoly and that they profoundly mistrusted the British in anything to do with atomic affairs. 'The salad', he said, 'is heaped in a bowl permanently smeared with the garlic of suspicion.'[2]

Because of the crucial importance of British scientists' work in the wartime project there was almost no doubt in the minds of any politicians or scientists when the war ended that Britain must go at once into the nuclear business. A programme to produce plutonium was agreed upon a year or more before a clear decision was made early in 1947 to make atomic bombs. Henceforth an independent nuclear deterrent became a major objective of British policy. Why? First, there were strategic reasons. Secondly, there were reasons of status. Thirdly, and intimately connected with the other two, was the nature of Britain's relationship with the United States.

The 1947 decision to fabricate a bomb was not a response to an immediate military threat but arose from a fundamentalist and instinctive feeling that Britain must possess so climacteric a weapon. Alan Bullock's book on Bevin as Foreign Secretary has restored the significance of these first post-war months, which have so often been elided with the post-1948 period. At this time there was no United States commitment to aid Britain or the rest of Europe in another war and Britain could not rely on America to threaten the use of atomic bombs to serve British interests. In 1949, when NATO was created, America was committed to Europe but doubts persisted about her readiness to threaten retaliation in other people's interests.

The second reason for Britain's determination to possess nuclear weapons was her faith in her great-power status. The bomb which symbolized America's superpower status in 1945 also seemed to symbolize Britain's very high power status. The first Russian atomic test in 1949, three years before the British test of 1952, was a shattering moment of truth, but even then Britain fell only one step below the superpowers. Lord Cherwell—Mr Churchill's adviser—said that if Britain did not make atomic bombs she would rank with other European nations who had to make do with conventional weapons. 'If we are unable to make the bombs ourselves and have to rely entirely on the United States for this vital weapon we shall sink to the rank of a

[2] PRO ref. Cab/259, Campbell–Anderson, 29 Jan. 1945.

second-class nation'.[3] It was Henry Tizard, the Government's chief scientific adviser, who warned that if Britain continued to behave like a Great Power she would soon cease to be a great nation. 'Let us', he said, 'take warning from the fate of the Great Powers of the past and not burst ourselves with pride. (See Aesop's 'Fable of the Frog'.)'[4]

Britain's anxiety about her power status was closely intertwined with the third reason for her resolve to be a nuclear power: her relationship with the United States. The Hyde Park Agreement of 1944, being unknown to the American Administration, proved worthless. But at the end of 1945 the two new leaders, Truman and Attlee, also agreed that there should be full and effective atomic co-operation between their two countries and Canada. This assurance proved equally worthless. The McMahon Act, which Congress passed in July 1946, *inter alia* made illegal the passing of any classified atomic information to any foreign country, including Britain, with penalties including death or life imprisonment. Britain had no lobby for her atomic interest in Washington and was squeezed between the multilaterally-minded internationalists and the isolation-minded nationalists. All this reflected a more general American impatience with Britain, the importunate poor relation. So Britain counted for nothing in atomic energy affairs except that she was expected to help in acquiring uranium supplies.

In fact American collaboration was not crucial for building her atomic plants and a primitive bomb, but it was of the greatest political and strategic concern to Britain and, as time went on, essential for more advanced atomic weapon systems. So Britain refused to accept the closed door presented by the McMahon Act. Anglo-American atomic relations in the post-war decade were traumatic for the British. They ceaselessly sought the atomic collaboration they felt to be their due but this was denied them, in spite of occasional tantalizing hopes. Early in 1948 an atomic arrangement—called a *modus vivendi*—was signed which promised general, non-weapon, technological collaboration. In practice little was received although the promise had been dearly bought. For in the *modus vivendi* the British surrendered the clause in the wartime Quebec Agreement which said that neither country would use the atomic bomb without the other's consent—a clause which had outraged US Senators to whom the Agreement had been confidentially revealed.[5]

The British right was surrendered shortly before the British Government agreed in 1948 that United States bombers, potentially armed with atomic bombs, might be stationed in the United Kingdom. Britain

---

[3] No PRO ref. Department of Energy Cherwell folder *International Relations U.S.A.*, Cherwell–Prime Minister, 29 Dec. 1952.
[4] No PRO ref. Ministry of Defence file Def/42, undated memorandum.
[5] *Atomic Shield, 1947–52*, pp. 274–5.

now seemed to risk annihilating retaliation without even being first informed or consulted and this danger seemed acute when the Korean War broke out in 1950 and the Americans considered the use of the atomic bomb in the Far East. Attlee rushed to Washington, to restore the right of consent, or at least consultation, and he believed that he received from Truman a promise that the President would not authorize the use of the bomb without prior consultation with Britain and Canada. Truman indeed gave it to him. But because Congress vehemently opposed any limitation on the President's right to authorize the use of atomic weapons Dean Acheson, Secretary of State, ensured that no record of Truman's promise appeared in any American documents. In later life Acheson spoke admiringly of Attlee's success in achieving this promise and added 'we had to unachieve it'. Only later, in 1951, did Oliver Franks, as Ambassador in Washington, regain for Britain the right to consent before atomic bombs were used from bases in the United Kingdom: unlike the Quebec Agreement this did not apply to the use of bombs from overseas bases which might provoke retaliation on Britain.

Until 1949 Britain was determined to possess an independent deterrent which must be home-made; she simply wanted full exchange of information with the Americans, plus some scarce materials. Tizard noted that suggestions for concentrating atomic weapon production in North America had been greeted, as he put it, 'with the kind of horror one would expect if one made a disrespectful remark about the King'.[6] In late 1949 this belief was modified, partly because America's technological lead was clearly increasing as they built up industrial factory production of more efficient weapons while Britain was still struggling to produce one laboratory, Nagasaki-type bomb. The British and Americans therefore discussed a much deeper collaboration. Britain would produce some plutonium but send it and her weapon scientists to the United States, which alone would produce weapons. The United States would provide Britain with a stockpile of atomic weapons for her own use. The British Government had great misgivings, and Bevin was especially unhappy about placing British atomic capacity unreservedly in American hands. In a war it might be a matter of life or death for the British to use atomic weapons, but the Americans might refuse to supply them. He said Britain should make *no* sacrifice which would impair her ability to deal with the United States on equal terms.

These 1949 talks broke down. The Americans did not want to hand over a stockpile of bombs and the arrest of Fuchs, the British atomic spy, early in 1950 brought the talks to an end. When Churchill returned to office at the end of 1951 he believed he would get much further than

[6] No PRO ref. Ministry of Defence file Def/1J, Tizard–Elliott, 23 Sept. 1949.

Attlee with the Americans. He did achieve some consultation on the American strategic air offensive, about which no information whatever had been given to the British, but otherwise he was no more successful than Attlee. The two countries continued to work in watertight compartments, wasting effort, scientific manpower, and resources. Real collaboration continued only in uranium procurement where the British could help the Americans.

This then is the strange story of consonances and dissonances of nuclear weapon policy within the special relationship, in the crucial period up to the mid-1950s. Firstly, collaboration in the period of United States wartime neutrality. Secondly, complete breakdown in 1942 within an extraordinarily close military and political alliance. Thirdly, very close, though not complete, collaboration for the last two years of the war. Fourthly, complete breakdown in 1946 and 1947 as the general wartime 'Special Relationship' withered. Fifthly, a temporary thaw in atomic relations in late 1947 and 1948 within a more general *rapprochement*. Thereafter, until 1954, atomic energy relationships were totally different from those governing the rest of foreign and defence policy where the Anglo-American partnership was once more the mainspring of Atlantic defence. If the Anglo-American alliance should be dissolved, said a journalist, every military plan in the Pentagon would have to be torn up.[7]

Why this discrepancy? There was in the United States what Sir Roger Makins of the British Foreign Office called an ill-defined and almost unconscious feeling that atomic energy was and should remain an American monopoly both for military and industrial purposes. So the British deterrent had to be independent of the United States. It also had to be independent of Europe even though the Marshall Plan and NATO were bringing Britain closer to Western Europe. For under the remaining atomic agreements with the Americans, disclosure of atomic information to other countries was impossible without American consent which was never forthcoming. Britain had therefore to refuse the atomic collaboration France desired and turn down her simplest requests for help, despite the British wartime debt to the French scientists. Belgium got better treatment because the Belgian Congo was then the main source of uranium.

The first British atomic bomb test at Montebello in October 1952—mounted with no American help—seemed to be a demonstration of scientific and technical competence, a proof of Britain's status as a great, if not a super power. However, when American Congressmen were polled soon afterwards about atomic interchange with Britain one

---

[7] J. Alsop, *Washington Post*, 22 July 1949.

remarked, 'We would be trading a horse for a rabbit.'[8] Nevertheless, the demonstration of Britain's capacity to build successfully the full range of atomic plants, the bomb itself and in 1956 Calder Hall—the world's first industrial scale, land-based nuclear power plant to feed electricity into a grid—was to lead to a new, very special relationship.

In December 1953 came Eisenhower's Atoms for Peace speech. Next year the McMahon Act was amended, making possible individual bilateral agreements for exchange of information on civilian uses of atomic energy and on the external characteristics of nuclear weapons. In 1955 two bilateral agreements with Britain gave her favoured treatment.[9] Information on the design and fabrication of nuclear components of weapons was, however, still withheld. Ironically it was in 1957, soon after Suez and the nadir of Anglo-American relations, that Eisenhower and Macmillan forged a new nuclear partnership as the chief ingredient of a general policy of interdependence. This happened as nuclear deterrence became, in the 1957 Defence White Paper,[10] the very basis of Britain's defence policy.

Even before the first Russian Sputnik of October 1957 encouraged a pooling of nuclear efforts, the British had agreed to provide bases for Thor missiles and co-operation had already begun on nuclear submarines. In 1958 amendments to the McMahon Act permitted exchange of information about the design and production of nuclear warheads with, and also the transfer of fissile materials to, countries that had already 'made substantial progress in the development of atomic weapons'.[11] In July 1958, the day after these amendments were passed, an Agreement with Britain was signed.[12] In May 1959 a further Agreement enabled Britain to buy from the United States component parts of nuclear weapon systems and to make possible the exchange of British plutonium for American enriched uranium.[13] Soon the interdependence extended to delivery systems. In 1960, when Macmillan offered Eisenhower a forward base in Scotland for the new Polaris missile submarines, the President reciprocated with an offer to sell the land-based Skybolt missile. In 1962 at Nassau, after Skybolt was cancelled, President Kennedy agreed to sell Polaris to Britain.

These nuclear weapon agreements in the period from 1958 to 1962

---

[8] Representative Harris of Wyoming quoted in *Washington Star* 2 Jan. 1953.

[9] *Agreement for Cooperation Regarding Atomic Information for Mutual Defence Purposes*, Cmd. 9555 and *Agreement for Cooperation on the Peaceful Uses of Atomic Energy*, Cmd. 9560.

[10] *Defence: Outline of Future Policy, 1957*, Cmnd. 124.

[11] Public Law No. 85–479, 85th Congress, 2nd session.

[12] *Agreement for Cooperation on the Uses of Atomic Energy for Mutual Defence Purposes*, Cmnd. 537.

[13] *Amendment to Agreement between the Government of the United Kingdom of Great Britain and Northern Ireland and the Government of the United States of America for Cooperation in the Uses of Atomic Energy for Mutual Defence purposes of July 3, 1958*, Cmnd. 859.

gave Britain privileges extended by the United States to no other nation[14] and they were a very exclusive ingredient indeed in the wider 'Special Relationship'. They also ensured for Britain a more prominent role in general discussions of military and political policy. What was the cost to other relationships? The 1958 bilateral nuclear defence agreement was signed on 3 July 1958. On 1 June General de Gaulle had returned to office as President of France.

For Britain the symbol of Empire has gone but the symbol of the national nuclear deterrent remains. This chapter has been about the creation of this symbol. Without understanding its origin, which gave it such a key role in the special Anglo-American relationship, the tenacious attachment to it is not intelligible. The deterrent is here because it's here—because of past events and decisions which may be largely forgotten and may seem irrelevant but which have had a powerful incremental force. This force has been the greater because certainly until 1964 (the last date for which I have access to British government records) the complex factors involved in the deterrent, especially in the Anglo-American relationship, were a main preoccupation of Prime Ministers and a very select group of senior ministers and officials. Churchill referred to the subject as out of all relation to anything else in the world and his immediate successors clearly felt the same. Has the deterrent in recent years become just another problem within broader defence and foreign policy or does it retain its mystic significance?

The origin of the mystic significance may be answered historically. Some social scientists are contemptuous of historians' emphasis on chronology or the influence of individuals. But in the creation of Britain's deterrent and the 'Special Relationship' arising from it, both are crucially important. This is apparent if we indulge in that esoteric branch of history called counterfactual history—what might have happened but didn't. The basic scientific theory about fission was internationally available in September 1939, but without the Peierls–Frisch memorandum written in Britain in spring 1940 and the subsequent 1941 Maud Report—from which Britain developed her atomic status—World War II would almost certainly have ended before a bomb was used. Suppose the British had made no such contribution and had ended the war with no atomic project? Or suppose the great German physicist Heisenberg and his colleagues had written the equivalents and the Allies had not?

In 1941 Britain was the instigator and leader of the atomic project but then she became a suppliant: first for admission to the American project

[14] The United States was prepared to offer Polaris to France but discussions were abortive.

and then, after the war, for American assistance to her own project. In this decade, apart from the years 1943–5, the United States demonstrated to her closest ally not so much the discipline, but the arrogance, of power. This was more apparent because collaboration continued in certain atomic areas where the British could give help that the United States needed—in obtaining supplies of uranium (which was for a long time the potential limiting factor in the American project), in intelligence, and in securing bomber bases—after the wartime British right of consent before atomic weapons were used had been eliminated. The Americans believed that non-proliferation should begin with Britain and they did not want her to have a native atomic project. Yet this nuclear attitude prevailed side by side with great American generosity in the Marshall Plan and growing conventional military assistance. It proved counterproductive and Britain's refusal to be browbeaten, her relentless pressure for renewal of collaboration, after it was prohibited by the 1946 McMahon Act, her determination to pursue her own military and civil atomic project, and her scientific and industrial competence (not only in atomic weaponry but in aircraft) led to the unique Anglo-American military atomic collaboration—a new definition of transatlantic roles—which was signified by the various atomic Agreements after 1957.

1957 was a crucial year. Britain's atomic competence was shown by her first thermonuclear tests in 1957, but the era of missiles had arrived and here Britain had not the same competence she demonstrated in the V-bombers and indeed in submarines and nuclear warheads. Thor and Sputnik were portents of a race in which Britain could not independently compete. However, the two sets of Macmillan–Eisenhower talks in 1957 promised interdependence and the McMahon Act was amended in 1958 to permit American assistance to the British weapon programme. Thor missiles were to be stationed in Britain. In Britain's new defence policy (which was signalled by the 1957 White Paper) reliance on nuclear deterrence seemed a good exchange for dropping conscription and as many imperial defence commitments as possible. It came as the first proposals to limit tests were made, and in this same year the Campaign for Nuclear Disarmament began. An *annus atomicus* if not an *annus mirabilis*!

This chapter has said little about other nations deeply involved in transatlantic nuclear roles, except for Canada and France, which were affected—the former positively and the latter negatively—by the Anglo-American nuclear partnership. I have referred to Britain's atomic debt to the French scientists, without whom she would have had no stake in the plutonium route to a bomb, and to the fact that when the Americans refused to take the wartime Anglo-French plutonium team,

Canada agreed to provide facilities for a joint project which flourished. Canada, then a small nation with very limited scientific resources, became one of the first countries to be involved—and very successfully—in nuclear power. Canada took part in the atomic heads-of-state discussions and was a member of the top policy committees: the atomic story is, as I suggested, an important part of the development of her own power status. As for France, Britain had a heavy atomic obligation to her and the United States had none. Primarily because of the paramountcy of the American connection, Britain treated France badly and de Gaulle never forgot this. When Britain decided that her economic future lay with Europe, her transatlantic atomic role was a powerful obstacle.

My last point concerns one of the deep underlying currents in the adjustment of the transatlantic roles in defence which may seem banal to Americans but was not appreciated in Europe before World War II. This is the supremacy of American science and technology. Europe had long been aware of the sheer size of American agricultural and industrial capacity, for by the end of the nineteenth century the United States led the world in mass production industry based on empirical technology and production engineering. But then the honours in science-based innovation still lay with Europe—notably Germany. It was not realized that behind the American achievements was a dedication to science right from the birth of the Republic and that the land-grant colleges, which spread across the continent after the Civil War, were the framework for the wide diffusion of science—at first applied science—in the population. They, together with great university research institutes, private foundations, and industrial research laboratories, were to make the United States the world leader of science-based industry and the just-beginning capital-intensive scientific research by the time World War II broke out. In the 1930s and 1940s it was often said that the refugees from Europe *made* American physics, but this simply was not true. Between 1933 and 1941, 100 European physicists of very high calibre went to the United States, but in the same period American universities produced 1,500 PhDs in physics. Such delusions—alongside perhaps the old destroyers and rifles which were the first fruits of American help to Britain in the days of her neutrality in 1940—concealed American scientific strength.

If Britain had appreciated this strength, she would have realized, in the autumn of 1941, the brevity of her own atomic lead and would not have rejected the American President's offer of a joint project—another tempting essay in counterfactual history. As it was, the scientific-technological gap between the countries was soon—perhaps for the first time—painfully apparent in the atomic project. The American wartime achievement was phenomenal. The first batch of irradiated plutonium-bearing slugs was discharged from the first American nuclear reactor at Hanford less than two years after Fermi had achieved the world's first self-sustaining chain reaction in the Chicago University squash court in 1942. And despite the urgency, the plant's health and safety achievement was very high. Over the subsequent years this gap has constantly widened. Of course Russian scientific strength was also underestimated but that is another, if related, story. Along with economic strength and political commitment, scientific performance has been, and is, a dominating feature of the adjustment of transatlantic strategic roles.

8

The United States, Britain, and the Defence of Europe

SAMUEL F. WELLS, JR.

THE struggle for Europe in World War II formed the unique character of the 'Special Relationship', and Europe has remained the principal object of Anglo-American concerns since 1945. Discussions between Washington and Whitehall often dealt with questions of nuclear weapons, trade and finance, or territorial issues in what came to be called the Third World, yet the attention of policy-makers ultimately focused on the relationship of the two Anglo-Saxon nations to the states of continental Europe. In crises within the Atlantic alliance until the mid-1960s, the United States and Great Britain frequently co-operated on issues revolving around the role of Germany in Europe and nuclear strategy. But since 1970, and especially since 1981, the United States has often sided with France on questions about the nature of Europe and intervention outside NATO boundaries. The most important shift over the last generation in terms of bilateral ties has been the rise of the United States–West German relationship to be the key determinant of alliance policy. To appreciate fully the complexities of contemporary policy debates, it is essential to know how relationships have evolved over the last forty years on issues of European defence among the United States, Britain, France, and Germany.

NATO AND THE IMPACT OF KOREA

The formation of NATO was an important step in the evolution of Western cohesion. In the eyes of its founders, the Atlantic alliance was established as a security guarantee for the states of Western Europe and as a form of political reassurance at a time of economic and political crisis, not as an operational military alliance. The outbreak of the Korean War changed the way most officials in the West thought about the alliance. Policy-makers in the United States, Britain, and Germany saw the North Korean invasion as Soviet-directed and as a probe of

Western resolve. Thinking that the next challenge might come in Europe, possibly against Germany, the United States in deciding to respond with force to the North Korean invasion allocated a very large proportion of its subsequent military build-up to Western Europe. In the period from 1950 to 1952 the United States dispatched four additional divisions to Europe, revised NATO to become a functioning military alliance, and determined that the Federal Republic of Germany had to be rearmed and integrated into the alliance.

British officials generally agreed with this line of analysis and response, and in Germany Chancellor Konrad Adenauer saw the changes within the alliance as a way to move Germany more rapidly back into European affairs with full independent status. While London and Washington agreed on the means to be used in responding to the Korean challenge, officials in the two capitals thought differently about the nature of the Europe they wanted to develop. American officials of virtually all political persuasions wanted an integrated Europe which would include Great Britain. Most British officials of the day were happy to co-operate with Europe but wanted to remain apart from any integrated political and defence structure on the continent in order to continue their close involvement with the nations of the Commonwealth and to pursue the 'Special Relationship' with the United States.

From the early months of the Korean War, France had a different view of the challenge as well as the shape of Europe. French leaders desired a revived Europe with improved economic co-ordination and a degree of political unity, but they were almost unanimous in wanting this Europe to be French-led. They were divided on the extent to which they felt Britain should be part of the new Europe, and the basis of their division essentially revolved around whether they believed Britain would be needed to help contain the power of an economically revived Germany. As early as January 1949 French ministers began to suggest the concept of a three-power directorate based in Washington, London, and Paris to co-ordinate the political and security future of Europe. After the Korean War broke out this theme was revived again in 1950 and 1951 well before General de Gaulle returned to power.

When the United States as a condition of its reform of NATO and assignment of additional troops to Europe insisted upon the rearmament of Germany, the French resisted. They proposed schemes such as the Pleven Plan of 1950 which would limit any German armed forces to battalion-size units and in other ways constrain the military power of the Federal Republic, and they attempted to resist any other proposals which would have made full use of German military potential. The French were the principal cause of the defeat of the European Defence Community (EDC), the most promising security arrangement developed in the immediate post-war period. After trying to modify the terms of the treaty signed in May 1952 and seeking additional commitments from the British, who had declined to be formal members of the EDC, the French national assembly ultimately killed the treaty in 1954. In the meantime the government of the Federal Republic also had difficulty winning the necessary two-thirds approval, and Chancellor Adenauer withdrew the treaty from the Bundestag. West German armed forces did not form operational units within the alliance until 1957, and the terms of German rearmament and membership in the alliance continued to pose difficulties.[1]

DE GAULLE'S VISION

The return to power in May 1958 of General Charles de Gaulle opened a new era in the relations between the United States and the principal states of Western Europe. De Gaulle shared many of the ideas of other post-war leaders about the need to restore French economic and political power, but he put these in a context of unparalleled ambition for his country and single-mindedness of purpose which had been previously unknown in the politics of democratic France. De Gaulle was less concerned about threats from the Soviet Union than he was about domination by the United States. He worked to make France the principal leader within Europe, and he sought to control Germany through a series of supranational economic and political institutions such as the European Economic Community (EEC) while at the same time forcing West German leaders to choose between French and American policies on security. He was determined to develop an independent French nuclear force and to use this as the centre-piece of his campaign for revived French prestige. He worked hard to develop a special relationship with the Soviet Union which he hoped would produce a special *détente* that would make it easier for France to move independently of American protection. He pursued for a time the previously suggested three-power directorate for the Western alliance, although it is likely that had Washington and London agreed to such a directorate de Gaulle would have developed other requests which they would not have accepted.

But the United States had no intention of sharing its leadership of the

[1] For more detailed information on early questions of European defence see Olav Riste, ed., *Western Security: The Formative Years: European and Atlantic Defence, 1947–1953* (Oslo, 1985), especially the chapters on the United States by Samuel Wells, on West Germany by Norbert Wiggershaus, on Britain by Geoffrey Warner, and on France by Pierre Melandri; Arthur Cyr, *British Foreign Policy and the Atlantic Area: The Techniques of Accommodation* (New York, 1979); and Edward Furdson, *The European Defence Community: A History* (New York, 1980).

Western alliance with France. American leaders believed that the French would have difficulty developing an independent nuclear force, and many were convinced that de Gaulle's policy was a great deal more bluster than reality. One experienced policy-maker contended as late as 1963 that de Gaulle had no interest in pursuing a totally independent policy and, if the United States could keep Germany moving parallel with itself, the French would come back into line. Based on the desire for continued American predominance within the alliance and a clear underestimation of the French general's single-minded pursuit of his objectives, the United States refused to share nuclear secrets or *matériel* with the French and found various reasons to object to a three-power directorate. The American agreement at Nassau in December 1962 to provide Britain with Polaris missiles and the information to construct the submarines and nuclear warheads to go with them simply confirmed de Gaulle's suspicions. There was a unique relationship between the two Anglo-Saxon powers, he contended, which made the United States unreliable in protecting European interests and essentially meant that Britain could never be fully part of Europe.[2]

From the announcement of the Anglo-American agreement at Nassau at the end of 1962, Charles de Gaulle began to put into motion his plan to withdraw France from the military components of NATO. At one of his most carefully staged press conferences on 14 January 1963, de Gaulle announced his rejection of the British application for membership in the European Economic Community as well as his rebuff of the proposal to share nuclear forces jointly with Britain and the United States in the form of a multilateral naval force. He also rejected the American offer of Polaris missiles to France. Within six months he had withdrawn the French Atlantic fleet from NATO, and early in March 1966 France sent a memorandum to its NATO allies announcing plans to withdraw its military forces from the alliance, expel all foreign troops from French soil, and cancel certain bilateral accords which provided for foreign military installations on French territory. A major turn in the development of the Atlantic alliance occurred with the French withdrawal, and only now are we beginning to see French political leaders questioning the magnitude of this step.[3]

ADOPTION OF FLEXIBLE RESPONSE

The impact of the French withdrawal from the military components of

[2] Cyr, *British Foreign Policy and the Atlantic Area*, pp. 133–7; Robert R. Bowie, 'Tensions Within the Alliance', *Foreign Affairs*, 42 (Oct. 1963); Richard Neustadt, *Alliance Politics* (New York, 1970).

[3] Maurice Couve de Murville, *Une politique étrangère française, 1958–1969* (Paris, 1971); Edward A. Kolodziej, *French International Policy under De Gaulle and Pompidou: The Politics of Grandeur* (Ithaca, NY, 1974).

NATO caused a general review of alliance strategy. The problems confronted by Western leaders were quite different in 1967 from those they had faced in 1949. The post-war reconstruction was now completed and the European economies were producing at a high rate. By comparison, the United States was losing the economic hegemony that it had enjoyed since 1945. General de Gaulle's decision to withdraw from the military parts of NATO posed significant problems, but even greater were the complications stemming from the realization that the Soviet Union would achieve nuclear parity by 1970. The prospect of Soviet nuclear parity challenged many of the bases of alliance strategy as it had developed after the Korean War, a strategy in which the West sought to compensate for an inferiority of conventional arms with superiority of nuclear weapons and a commitment to use those weapons first. Further complicating the military problem in the West, the United States was heavily engaged in a war in Vietnam that absorbed many resources and had already led many Europeans to question American judgement and commitment to Europe.

An extensive review of these problems within the alliance led to the Harmel Report and the strategy of Flexible Response. Adopted by the Ministerial meeting of the North Atlantic Council on 14 December 1967, the Harmel Report enunciated the strategic concept of Flexible Response. This decision provided the basis for restructuring the alliance by establishing the principles of military security through defence and deterrence and the pursuit of *détente* through dialogue and arms control. As applied, these principles led to the adoption of a strategy which relied heavily on the first use of nuclear weapons to counter Warsaw Pact superiority in conventional forces and on the initiation of the Mutual and Balanced Force Reduction (MBFR) negotiations to attempt to establish a conventional force balance at lower levels.[4]

The 1970s saw a continued erosion of Western power and unity, and the oil embargo following the 1973 Arab–Israeli War exaggerated many of the issues between the United States and Europe. The oil shock seriously damaged the economies of all non-oil producing countries, and it sharply increased the sense of vulnerability among Europeans. Still reeling from the political debate over Vietnam, the United States demonstrated a loss of confidence in its world role and a clear reduction of support for an active policy. After two attempts ended by French

[4] For changing economic trends through this period, see the chapters on 1945–60 by Robert Pollard and Samuel Wells and since 1961 by David Calleo in William H. Becker and Samuel F. Wells, Jr., eds., *Economics and World Power: An Assessment of American Diplomacy Since 1789* (New York, 1984); Report of the North Atlantic Council, 'The Future Task of the Alliance' (Harmel Report), 14 Dec. 1967, The North Atlantic Treaty Organization, *Facts and Figures* (Brussels, 1984), pp. 289–91.

vetoes, Great Britain finally joined the European Economic Community in 1972. Partly due to its own absorption in other issues and partly because Britain was now formally part of Europe, the United States began a conscious effort to treat Britain as a member of Europe and less as a special partner. Simultaneously, for security and economic reasons a new and increasingly close relationship began to develop between Washington and Bonn. At the same time as these basic changes within the West, the Soviet military build-up continued, and it included the new dimensions of increased naval and power projection capabilities for the Third World and the deployment of powerful SS-20 missiles in the Soviet Union and Eastern Europe.

NATO responded to the Soviet challenge with its dual-track decision of 1979 which called for the deployment of Pershing II and ground-launched cruise missiles in Europe as well as a standing offer to negotiate on intermediate-range nuclear forces (INF) with the Soviet Union. Despite the offer to limit arms through negotiation and despite the election of Ronald Reagan in the United States and Margaret Thatcher somewhat earlier in Britain, large parts of the population in Europe began to question the bases of Western strategy. This posed particular problems in the Federal Republic of Germany which from 1981 to 1984 experienced the most extensive debate on security and defence issues since 1945. Germans are particularly eager to avoid the danger of their country being the scene of either a significant nuclear exchange or a major conventional war, and at the same time they have developed a new and special relationship with the people of the German Democratic Republic which they do not want to see endangered by revived periods of Cold War tension.

CHALLENGES TO WESTERN STRATEGY

During the debate over INF missile deployments, critics have challenged anew many elements of the restructured alliance as being both ineffective and outdated. Foremost among these is the centre-piece of NATO strategy: the first use of nuclear weapons in theatre warfare and the ultimate validity of the American nuclear guarantee. As the German Christian Democrat political leader Kurt Biedenkopf recently declared: 'The basic assumption of NATO has come into doubt: that the US is still willing to risk having a nuclear exchange with the Soviets that could mean trading the destruction of Chicago to save Bonn. To many the American nuclear "umbrella" today seems purely imaginary.' Such questions are all the more serious because opinion leaders in Europe do not agree on the answers, and the broader European public has for the first time in a generation become deeply involved in the security debate.[5]

Germany is at the centre of the problem. Virtually all Germans want to avoid the use of nuclear weapons, but many are also strongly opposed to improved conventional defences. One astute analyst, Josef Joffe, opposes high-technology conventional defence and such variations as Deep Strike and Follow-on Forces Attack, feeling that Flexible Response remains a superior strategy. He contends that 'the system has worked too well to be lightly abandoned in favour of reform-minded conventionalism. Nuclear deterrence in Europe has a track record, conventional has not, and four decades of ultra-stability are an impressive argument for the status quo.'[6] Joffe is also comfortable with present circumstances on broader issues beyond strategy. In an earlier essay, he argued that the German unrest of the early 1980s would soon subside and that the Green Party would disappear as a significant political factor, leaving the Germans satisfied with cheap security supported by the United States and willing to make up in complaints what they have lost in autonomy.[7]

Looking at the same events, Walter Schütze comes to very different conclusions about the stability of the Federal Republic as the centre-piece of the alliance. The battle over the deployment of INF missiles, he believes, left lasting scars in the Federal Republic. It reminded Germans of their high degree of dependence on the United States and their sharply limited autonomy. 'What is even more important,' he argues, 'and might have long-lasting consequences, is the fact that beyond the INF problem, consensus on security policy, and on defence, which lasted for more than twenty years, has broken down.'[8] As evidence of the shifting positions in the Federal Republic, Schütze examines the qualifications introduced by the government in its statements of support for NATO policy, the anti-nuclear defence platform of the Social Democratic Party, and the severe constraints over the next five years on both manpower and finances for the Bundeswehr. He concludes that the Nunn amendment, if intended as a means of pressuring the Germans,

[5] Kurt H. Biedenkopf, 'Policy Implications of Development and the Present Status of U.S.–German Relations: A German Point of View', in James A. Cooney *et al.*, eds., *The Federal Republic of Germany and the United States: Changing Political, Social, and Economic Relations* (Boulder, Colorado, 1984), p. 209.

[6] Josef Joffe, 'Stability and Its Discontent: Should NATO Go Conventional?' *Washington Quarterly*, 7 (Fall 1984), p. 146.

[7] Josef Joffe, 'Squaring Many Circles: West German Security Policy Between Deterrence, Detente, and Alliance', in Cooney *et al.*, *The Federal Republic of Germany and the United States*, pp. 174–203.

[8] Walter Schütze, 'Prospects for Effective Conventional Defense in Europe: The Case of the Federal Republic of Germany: Problems and Trends', Working Paper no. 60, 30 Oct. 1984, International Security Studies Program, The Wilson Center.

will be counterproductive. 'To put it in a simple way,' he argues, 'people in Germany and in Western Europe are beginning to get fed up with being pushed around. By and large Germans are convinced that they do their fair share within the overall western defence effort . . . and that, after all, better security cannot be bought by more armaments but by arms control agreements with the other side. As Chancellor Kohl said in a recent Bundestag debate: "We want peace with less weapons!" '[9]

For the foreseeable future, alliance strategy will remain based upon a strategy of Flexible Response and forward defence. This strategy has the dual advantages of being based upon the fundamental military and political capabilities of the alliance members and having the requisite degree of suppleness to allow frequent refinement. Adjustments can be made in the strategy to improve conventional defence with new technology and increased mobility, but such changes will not remove the need to rely on nuclear weapons to a significant degree in responding to any major Warsaw Pact attack. Given the great emphasis placed upon nuclear weapons in military and popular thinking, the maxim that 'only nuclear weapons can deter or respond to nuclear weapons' has assumed even greater weight in the last five years. 'The most crucial function of battlefield and theatre weapons', Josef Joffe argues, 'is not tactical or strategic but political: as a tangible token of escalation which threatens to engulf both superpowers and might leave no sanctuaries.'[10] NATO will also remain committed to forward defence, because the German public will overwhelmingly reject any other option which calls for accepting a high level of combat on the soil of the Federal Republic.

Much of what passes for strategic debate within the alliance is misnamed. At best it deals with strategic concepts, but mainly alliance discussions revolve around relative contributions, leadership, and tactical changes forced by economic or technological imperatives. As long as the members of the alliance are unwilling to spend a great deal more money on defence or accept a significantly higher level of risk, NATO will have no viable strategic alternatives to current policy.

MITTERRAND'S GERMAN INITIATIVES

A promising series of initiatives to assuage West German insecurity and strengthen the alliance has come from the Socialist government of France under François Mitterrand. Within the first three months after assuming power in May 1981, he developed a consensus within government for several major policy departures. Under Mitterrand, France would be firmer in its relations with the Soviet Union, more

[9] Ibid., p. 25.
[10] Josef Joffe, 'Stability and Its Discontent', *Washington Quarterly*, 7 (Fall 1984), p. 139.

completely supportive of the Federal Republic of Germany, co-operative and friendly with the United States, and committed to pursue the basic Gaullist defence policy. Very early after his first meeting with the German Chancellor, Helmut Schmidt, Mitterrand publicly endorsed the INF deplóyments and offered French support for carrying out this decision. The government also committed itself to giving top priority within the French defence budget to nuclear modernization, increased the range of the new ground-launched tactical missile Hadès by 100 kilometres to a range of 350 kilometres, and began early steps in the creation of a new rapid intervention force for the Central Front of NATO.

The most significant element of Mitterrand's policy was expanded military co-operation with Germany. Motivated by concern over apparent neutralism and indecisiveness within the Federal Republic, French reaction was heightened by the realization that the German response to the imposition of martial law in Poland in December 1981 had been quite weak. Many French analysts took this studied German indifference to the fate of the Poles as an index of their neighbour's anxiety about its own security before the Soviet threat. Regarding the new relationship with Germany which would develop to meet this concern, a senior French diplomat involved in the process declared: 'We are building there something completely new.'[11]

The new relationship with Germany began with French support for the INF deployments. Initiated in the first week that Mitterrand was in the Élysée Palace, it continued through his dramatic and unusual speech before the Bundestag on 20 January 1983, in which he positively endorsed and made a very strong case for the deployment of the Pershing II and cruise missiles in Germany. Other aspects of defence co-operation began after martial law was imposed in Poland and the French realization of the reasons for Germany's mild response. In January of 1982 Paris proposed a new security dialogue building upon the unimplemented strategic co-operation clauses of the 1963 Franco-German Treaty. At the summit meeting of 24–5 February 1982, Schmidt endorsed the French proposal, but it could not be implemented until a new government came into office in Bonn.[12]

The change of chancellors in Germany had no adverse effect on the warmth and quality of the developing Franco-German relationship. Helmut Kohl came to Paris on his first day as chancellor, 4 October

---

[11] This statement and much of the other information in this chapter on French policy come from the author's non-attributable interviews with French political leaders and senior civil servants done for a forthcoming book on 'The International Policies of François Mitterrand'.

[12] Some of these developments are discussed in Bruce George and Jonathan Marcus, 'Change and Continuity in French Defence Policy', *RUSI Journal* (June 1984), pp. 13–19.

1982, and endorsed the new discussions on security co-operation. This relationship functions on three formal levels and in a series of informal channels. Within the structured channels, there are regular meetings at the ministerial level including foreign and defence ministers; there is a Permanent Commission on Security and Defence meeting at the level of departmental under-secretaries; and there are three working groups dealing with issues of arms control, tactical co-operation, and defence procurement. The informal channels include individuals from one side or the other appearing at seminars or small meetings to conduct essentially educational and sensitizing sessions and an innovative meeting which took place around a long weekend at the ski resort of Courchevel in April 1984. The ski weekend included some of the key people from the Permanent Commission, some parliamentarians from each side, and a few consultants and other officials. They had a wide-ranging discussion which, while not resolving any issues, was of a positive and candid nature. The meeting of these formal groups has continued, the procurement working group designed the agreement for the co-production of a combat helicopter that was announced in May 1984 at Rambouillet, while the tactical working group has considered the implications of the creation and deployment of the French *Force d'action rapide*.

The *Force d'action rapide* (FAR) represents the most concrete aspect of Mitterrand's efforts to reassure Germany. It was basically designed to accomplish two missions: provide a rapid intervention force that would signal a commitment of France to a major struggle on the Central Front, and provide forces for regional crisis intervention such as those units recently in Lebanon and Chad. This force of 47,000 men is organized into five divisions, the most innovative of which is the Air Mobile Division. This unit will have 250 helicopters including 90 anti-tank and 30 fire support and protection aircraft, and General Georges Fricaud-Chagnaud, one of the division's creators, estimates that it 'will be capable of effectively counter-attacking a force of about 3 armored divisions at about 250 km from its main operating base'. Use of the FAR has been a point of extensive discussion with the Germans in the formal and informal security groups. They have discussed the elements of how the FAR would intervene in the forward battle, such as logistics, air rights, and its relationship with the First French Army along the Rhine. The Germans have also raised questions about how the FAR would relate to French tactical nuclear doctrine and targeting. The French have discussed in considerable detail the elements of their tactical nuclear doctrine, but they have made it clear at every point that the circumstances under which both the FAR and tactical nuclear weapons would be used remain those for independent French decision. Many issues remain to be resolved, but the French willingness to discuss a larger number of tactical and nuclear issues than at any past point should be seen as promising.[13]

A REVITALIZED WEST EUROPEAN UNION

Another key dimension of French policy toward Germany is the attempt to revitalize the West European Union (WEU). Starting in 1982 the French began looking for a way to broaden their co-operation with Germany, and they soon seized upon the West European Union, an organization that had totally disappeared from the news and was in fact quite moribund. The French chose the WEU for a variety of reasons. They wanted an opportunity to remove the old constraints on German rearmament set up in the original treaty of 1954 creating the West European Union. They wanted to expand their co-operation with Germany to include the other major states of Europe, but not those NATO members frequently referred to as the 'weak sisters', meaning Denmark, Greece, and Turkey. They also wanted to use the WEU as a vehicle for a more active European pillar of the alliance, a pillar which would obviously be French-led and whose accomplishments would redound largely to the benefit of the French. In describing their hopes for a more active WEU, all French officials assert that it will not be in conflict with NATO. 'West European Union', a high defence official asserts, 'will not become for us a NATO-bis!'

The members of the West European Union met for a widely heralded thirtieth anniversary session in Rome at the end of October 1984. The meeting concluded with a commitment for the foreign and defence ministers to meet two times a year and with pledges to deal with the problems of arms standardization and disarmament as well as crises beyond NATO's boundaries. In a closing statement at the WEU meeting, the German Foreign Minister Hans-Dietrich Genscher warmly praised the agreement on 'intensive and in-depth co-operation between the seven member states in security and defence' and said that the revival of the WEU would bring a 'new and important dimension to the process of European unification'. The British put aside their earlier coolness and showed genuine enthusiasm for the new effort. The British Foreign Secretary Sir Geoffrey Howe expressed the hope that the meeting's declaration would be 'translated into effective action'. While the French representatives expressed approval at the results of the meeting, they seemed to have lost some of their enthusiasm as others had

---

[13] Général Georges Fricaud-Chagnaud, 'Origins, Capabilities and Significance of the Force d'Action Rapide', Working Paper no. 61, 30 Oct. 1984, International Security Studies Program, The Wilson Center, p. 9.

gained it. At the time of writing the prospects for a successful revival of the WEU remain unclear, and one must record the sceptical point that each of the members seems interested in using the WEU for different purposes.[14]

ECONOMIC LINKS

Beyond security co-operation, France has sought a high level of economic co-ordination with the Federal Republic of Germany. When Helmut Kohl was elected chancellor in his own right in the national elections of March 1983, he and a number of his principal ministers came to Paris and had a working week of discussions on defence, foreign policy, and economic issues. These talks resulted in a broad tacit set of agreements to pursue, wherever possible, parallel policies. While concrete commitments do not exist, one can find numerous instances since the spring of 1983 when Paris and Bonn have co-operated on monetary and economic issues, on important questions pending before the European Economic Community, and on explorations of the bases for common industrial ventures. Indeed, while he was still Minister of Industry and Research, Laurent Fabius published an article in *Politique étrangère* in which he clearly alluded to the need for France to make its industrial policy European in nature, and his examples and thoughts are clearly focused upon Germany.[15] While the degree of economic co-operation that will emerge is not certain, the ability of France and Germany to pursue parallel, if not common, policies on defence and economics is substantial. When one adds to this the emphasis on European Union as contained in François Mitterrand's speech in Strasburg on 24 May 1984, the basis for a new combination in the centre of Europe clearly exists.

Recent debates in Europe over participation in the Strategic Defense Initiative (SDI) research programmes indicate the potentially disruptive effects of the new American interest in strategic defence. Almost all European specialists are critical of the impact of SDI on strategic doctrine and the credibility of the American nuclear guarantee, and most are sceptical about its technical viability at any affordable cost. Yet they are all interested in improving their research capability in high technology areas and would like any American assistance they can get in

[14] A good discussion of the WEU initiative and defence co-operation generally is contained in James Eberle *et al.*, 'European Security Co-operation and British Interests', *International Affairs*, 60 (Autumn 1984), pp. 557–8; for reports of the WEU meetings in Rome, see *Le Monde*, 30 Oct. 1984, Foreign Broadcast Information Service (FBIS), Daily Report: Western Europe, 30 Oct. 1984, and the *Sunday Times* (London), 28 Oct. 1984.

[15] Laurent Fabius, 'Pour un espace européen scientifique, industriel et social?', *Politique étrangère*, 49 (Spring 1984), pp. 49–56.

this direction. At the Bonn Economic Summit, President Mitterrand announced that France would not participate in SDI research, yet within days there were signs in Paris that this declaration might not prevent nationalized French companies from joining in SDI research. The German government is divided about participation in SDI, with Helmut Kohl and Franz-Josef Strauss wanting to join and many others lukewarm or negative. The Finance Minister Gerhard Stoltenberg opposes participation on financial grounds, while Hans-Dietrich Genscher does not want to do anything that would endanger Bonn's relations with Paris. Recently Kohl has expressed ambivalence, declaring in Stuttgart on 20 May 1985 that 'SDI means opportunity and risk for the North Atlantic Alliance at the same time'. The British are similarly divided but have indicated a strong desire to participate in amply funded research programmes and on 30 October 1985 were the first government to agree in principle to join the SDI research effort. Most knowledgeable Europeans would agree with a senior allied diplomat who recently said that he had serious doubts about the technical feasibility of research co-operation given the scientific problems involved and American policies on technology transfer. 'In the long run it would be a serious error', he declared, 'for the U.S. to offer something it could not deliver.' The debate in Bonn, and to a lesser extent in other capitals, reflects the desire not to choose between European programmes and SDI. Yet as it is presently structured, SDI poses a serious challenge to both alliance cohesion and increased European co-operation.

EURÊKA

The French government took the lead within Europe in responding to SDI. Initially this response took the form of objections to the adverse influence of the American proposals on the strategy of deterrence. These complaints were registered in quiet official exchanges and at meetings of strategic specialists. After the United States Defense Secretary Caspar Weinberger asked on 26 March 1985 for allied participation in SDI research, the Mitterrand government moved to create a programme of European high technology called Eurêka. Asked why it took so long to develop a concrete response to Reagan's proposal of March 1983, a senior French official said: 'We felt it was just a Reagan Sunday speech like those about the evil empire or school prayer. But when we realized that American generals were touring Europe with their checkbooks open ready to sign up our best technology firms, we knew we had to respond in a substantive way.'

The Mitterrand government had already done considerable work to stimulate European co-operation in high technology. As one diplomat put it, 'Eurêka would have happened anyway, but SDI was a stimulus to more rapid action.' At the Versailles Economic Summit of June 1982, the French president had made a series of proposals about technological co-operation and economic growth. In September 1983, the government approved a memorandum on European technological and scientific space which adopted a new flexible approach to European co-operation. Mitterrand returned to these themes during 1984 in speeches in The Hague, Strasburg, and Paris. Early in 1985, the Center for Analysis and Planning of the Ministry of Exterior Relations produced a study which argued that SDI would exacerbate Europe's technological backwardness, because it would draw off top talent and would be likely to constrain or prevent the commercial application in Europe of technologies developed under SDI contracts. The best response to the challenge posed by SDI, the study concluded, was European co-operation in a project of high technology development linked to promising consumer markets.

These arguments combined with earlier government decisions to shape the Eurêka programme announced by the Mitterrand government on 17 April 1985. Designed to create a 'technological Europe', this programme would focus on civilian research and development in six areas. Eurêka is unique in French industrial planning, because it lacks a comprehensive structure, designated sources of funding, and a common framework for all projects. It is an open-ended programme designed to attract the co-operation of corporations from diverse political and economic environments. A project for telecommunications can have a very different form of organization and funding from another in micro-electronics. Generally, the designers of Eurêka wanted to set up a loose organization outside the rigid structure of the European Economic Community that could attract industrial participation and investment on a wide variety of projects with commercial promise. Eurêka contracts will be of two basic types: mid-term projects of 4–5 years using available technologies to produce a product such as a supercomputer with immediate commercial promise, and higher-risk long-term projects of 8–10 years that capture the imagination of Europe's best minds in trying to solve fundamental problems in new fields like genetic engineering. This concept is addressed to the European Community of ten plus Spain and Portugal, as well as to Norway, Sweden, Switzerland, and Austria, and it is shaped to exploit the benefits of a multi-speed Europe in which various combinations of states can move toward closer economic and political co-operation at their own pace.

The initial reactions to Eurêka were cool. The Paris weekly *L'Express* headlined its feature story, 'Eurêka: projet ou gadget?' The proposal was discussed at the West European Union Council of Ministers meeting in Bonn on 22–3 April 1985 without any consensus of commitments developing. At the Bonn Economic Summit of 2–4 May there was a direct clash between SDI and Eurêka, and Chancellor Kohl, having earlier pledged his support to the European programme, seemed to move away to favour SDI.

Yet by the end of June, Eurêka had gained significant momentum. The programme received the official support of West Germany and Great Britain early in the month, and all of the European Community governments were positive in their reactions at the Milan summit of 28 June. Even the Japanese and the Soviets have enquired discreetly about participation. Several industrial agreements were signed under the project by such combinations as Matra and Norsk Data, Thomson–Philips–Siemens–British General Electric, and Matra–Messerschmidt.

In the last half of 1985 Eurêka made significant progress. On 17 July a conference of the original sixteen members plus Finland and Turkey convened in Paris to develop further procedures and projects. During the meeting the French government pledged one billion francs to Eurêka programmes during 1986 largely in the form of guarantees and soft loans, and early in September the Federal Republic announced a commitment of one billion marks for 1986 and a plan to invest up to ten billion marks within the next six years. New contracts announced in the next few weeks included agreements between Bull and Siemens for a supercomputer, between Matra and SGS of Italy for integrated circuits, and between the French electrical giant CGE and ten partners for five different projects. At a subsequent meeting in Hanover, West Germany on 5–6 November, the eighteen participating governments agreed on a charter for the Eurêka programme and approved ten mid-term projects to be funded primarily by the participating companies. These contracts include: a standard microcomputer for educational and home use, a new amorphous silicon computer chip, a high-speed computer, a cloth-cutting laser, membranes for water filtration and desalinization, high-powered lasers, a system to trace air pollutants, a research computer network, a diagnosis kit for sexually transmitted diseases, and advanced optic electronics. Commitments from other governments and corporations must follow promptly if the Europeans are to seize the opportunity to close the high technology gap in time to re-establish economies that can compete successfully with the United States and Japan.

From the start European leaders have sought to avoid choosing between Eurêka and SDI. The Mitterrand government has worked to overcome this attitude by emphasizing that Eurêka is a civilian programme that will not be antagonistic to SDI. Chancellor Kohl described his support for Eurêka to the Bundestag on 5 September 1985 by asserting: 'the common security interests of Europe and the U.S. also demand a comparable state of the respective economic and technological developments. If we want to strengthen the European pillar of the transatlantic bridge, it also presupposes that we must increase the technological and industrial efficiency in Europe.' He later added that 'we can achieve that only if we coordinate and combine the existing national potentials'. In reality, specialists understand that the vast majority of products from both programmes will have dual use in both civilian and military areas and that the real constraints on participation in either effort will be financial resources and scientific talent. A new set of attitudes appears to be crystallizing in support of Eurêka. European officials acknowledge that the state of high-technology research in their countries lags far behind the United States and Japan, but they increasingly appreciate that they have a valuable reservoir of technological expertise and that collectively they allocate as much of their resources for basic reasearch as the United States. The problem is that without collaboration, they get less impact from their research expenditure. More serious is the realization that participation in SDI might drain off their best scientists without allowing Europe to take advantage of civilian applications of research findings under the United States programme. This logic persuades many officials that Europe's first job is to develop, in a co-operative manner, its high-technology base to a competitive state. Then they can explore potential compatibility with SDI from a more equal footing. But many difficult financial and technological problems lie ahead, and it will be a number of years before either Eurêka or SDI develops a range of new products for civilian or military use.

A STRONGER EUROPEAN PILLAR

Confronted with widespread opposition to a defence strategy tied to the use of nuclear weapons and growing uneasiness and self-doubt in Germany, the North Atlantic Alliance faces some difficult decisions. Many Europeans no longer want to respond to another set of initiatives drafted in Washington. Various proposals are circulating for a strengthened European pillar of the alliance in which the Europeans would play a larger and more autonomous role in decisions on strategy, tactical innovation, arms control, and procurement.

France has shown the greatest interest in strengthening European security co-operation. Indeed, the French security analyst Nicole Gnesotto in a feature article in *L'Express* in July 1984 described

European defence as 'a French passion'.[16] Like other political passions, the French plan for improved European defence is somewhat incomplete and opportunistic. In official and private statements the French call for improved co-operation in arms production and procurement, separate European discussions of alliance policies, and increased defence expenditure by the nations that have not met their pledges for three per cent annual growth. While there are minor differences among the political parties, all generally share the commitment for improved European security co-operation. This is seen as a means of reassuring Germany as well as preparing for the day when the United States will eventually apply some of its defence resources now in Europe to other regions of the world.[17]

Despite its pledges of increased co-operation, France faces problems in meeting its commitments. President Mitterrand has serious political difficulties and must prepare for future political challenges when domestic economic issues will be paramount. His own defence budget for 1986 reflects cutbacks, and major weapons systems will be delayed to keep costs down. Mitterrand also has to confront the results of twenty years of Gaullist security and economic policies which left his European colleagues suspicious of French motives. Other Europeans complain regularly about the fact that French independence in earlier years has caused them to lose the capacity to compromise in joint political and industrial ventures. Everyone remembers the long years during which France sought to force its partners to choose between European and Atlanticist policies, and this memory casts a shadow over current proposals from Paris. The challenge for France is to overcome these Gaullist legacies in order to continue the new course and advance European co-operation in arms production and industrial development.

German officials initially responded with caution to proposals for European defence, because they feared this movement might be viewed in Washington as reducing the influence of NATO. But as talks with France progressed, Bonn became more enthusiastic for a broader European role in defence. Chancellor Kohl views co-operation with France as a top priority, as does his Foreign Minister Hans-Dietrich Genscher. The Defence Minister Manfred Wörner stated in Washington that 'Germany has a special political relationship with France, and we try to use German–French co-operation as a motor for European

---

[16] Nicole Gnesotto, 'Défense Européenne: Histoire d'une passion française', *L'Express*, 20 July 1984, pp. 56–62.

[17] Pierre Mauroy, 'France and Western Security', *NATO Review*, 31 (1983), pp. 21–5; see the cluster of eight articles on 'La France et la sécurité de l'Europe', *Politique étrangère*, 48 (Summer 1983), pp. 313–407.

unity. We also have close defense co-operation . . ., but we cannot
substitute a French nuclear guarantee in any way for an American one.'
He went on to emphasize that German–French co-operation including
the proposed revitalization of the WEU were totally within the Federal
Republic's commitment to NATO. Other political leaders have tested
the waters with bold proposals. In April 1984 Jürgen Todenhöfer, a
member of the Bundestag who is one of the CDU–CSU spokesmen on
defence questions, called for the creation of an integrated European
nuclear force including American, French, and British weapons and
managed by an executive group consisting of the United States and all
European members of the alliance including the Federal Republic.
Somewhat to his surprise, Todenhöfer received favourable reactions
from a number of French and German politicians and officials. Since the
spring of 1985, leaders of the Social Democratic Party have expressed a
new interest in Franco-German nuclear co-operation.[18]

On 28 June 1984 Helmut Schmidt delivered an important speech in
the Bundestag. The former chancellor surveyed the world economic
situation and concluded that Europe had to take new steps in order to
remain a vital economic area. Responding to Mitterrand's recent
Strasburg speech, he called for a joint Franco-German industrial
programme and for close co-operation in defence based upon the
expanded use of reserves to strengthen conventional defences to a total of
eighteen German and twelve French divisions after mobilization.
Schmidt proposed that Germany help pay for the expanded conventional armament for France, and he suggested that France consider
extending a nuclear guarantee to cover the territory of the Federal
Republic. Although his speech got little public endorsement in France
or Germany, officials privately acknowledge that it is taken very
seriously and his proposals are being studied. Schmidt reinforced these
themes in an unusual letter to Chancellor Kohl of 23 May 1985. In this
letter, Schmidt argued strongly against German government participation in SDI and called for increased defence and economic co-
operation with France, declaring that 'our close relationship with
France is of extreme importance' and justifies 'considerable German
willingness to compromise' as well as 'large financial expenditures'.[19]

French responses to these German proposals show signs of movement
on nuclear and conventional defence co-operation. At the conclusion of
major Franco-German military manœuvres on 20 June 1985, the

---

[18] Manfred Wörner's speech before the Statesmen's Forum, Center for Strategic and
International Studies, Georgetown University, 12 July 1984; *Le Monde*, 19 Apr. 1984; author's
interview with Jürgen Todenhöfer, Washington, DC, 11 Jan. 1985.

[19] Schmidt speech in the Bundestag, 28 June 1984, FBIS, Daily Report: Western Europe, 6 July
1984; Schmidt letter to Chancellor Kohl, 23 May 1985.

French Defence Minister Charles Hernu made an important statement declaring that the Federal Republic was France's 'closest ally' because the two states had 'security interests that are common'. About a week later, a *Le Monde* poll showed that forty per cent of the French respondents felt that their country's vital interests would be seriously threatened by an attack on West Germany, and that a French nuclear guarantee should be extended to their neighbour. In this poll only twenty-four per cent disagreed, with thirty-six per cent having no opinion. Both the Socialist Party (PS) and the Union for French Democracy (UDF) have issued official statements that endorse extending French nuclear deterrence to Germany. Although these steps are all declaratory and involve no change in strategy or deployments of forces, they are a significant indication of a broad political shift in France toward closer co-operation with Germany.[20]

British reaction to proposals for European defence co-operation has been sceptical until very recently, while to suggestions for an integrated European economy the British response has been hostile. Mrs Thatcher's government faces serious financial pressure in trying to maintain the British Army of the Rhine at its current strength and complete the programme of equipment modernization while also attempting to carry out the schedule for construction of the new Trident nuclear deterrent force. Closer European co-operation could offer benefits in helping meet these difficulties, and since the autumn of 1984 the British show signs of moving toward expanded co-operation with France and Germany. The case for Britain to join European defence co-operation cannot be better put than it is by Admiral Sir James Eberle and his Chatham House 'Gang of Four' in the autumn 1984 issue of *International Affairs* when they argue:

The current German enthusiasm for defence co-operation with France might seem an over-enthusiastic reaction to the return of a prodigal son, neglecting the sustained quiet loyalty of the elder brother; but symbols and rhetoric have their part to play, and a danger exists for Britain, unless it shows more enthusiasm for developing West European defence co-operation, of being relegated to the margins of the debate.[21]

Official American responses show little more warmth than those of the British. The consistent response from senior officials at the Department of State to questions about European defence co-operation is that the United States supports any larger European role in defence so long as it is within NATO. To the consternation of officials in European capitals,

---

[20] Hernu statement at Müsingen, 20 June 1985; *Le Monde*, 28 June 1985.
[21] For a strong co-operative signal, see Sir Geoffrey Howe, 'The European Pillar', *Foreign Affairs*, 63 (Winter 1984–5), pp. 330–43; Eberle *et al.*, 'European Security Co-operation and British Interests', *International Affairs*, 60 (Autumn 1984), p. 552.

the Assistant Secretary of State Richard Burt conveyed this message in unusually direct fashion in April 1985. State Department officials see no need to revitalize the WEU and feel that co-operation in armaments production can best be done through the Eurogroup. Basically, the United States wants the Europeans to pay more of the cost of NATO and to follow policies made in Washington for enhanced conventional defence, completion of the INF deployments, SDI research, and the reduction of battlefield nuclear weapons as scheduled. An isolated positive note comes from a senior American official serving at NATO headquarters in Brussels. In discussing the need for increased armaments co-operation throughout the alliance, he declared that 'the WEU initiative of the French is a helpful factor. The French insist that it will be fully within the NATO framework, and I find no evidence to the contrary. It would be helpful to have an effective group which can move forward on these questions without one or two weak sisters.' This official even goes on to propose the revision of the anti-trust laws in the United States and European actions to improve economic integration, because he is convinced that no European state can develop a sufficiently large market to support its own defence industry.

The movement for European defence co-operation promises to solve some of the long-term problems of the alliance. We cannot know whether it will work, but it is clear that such a movement should not fail for lack of support from the United States. Should that happen, all future efforts at increased defence co-operation would surely be met by pointed reminders of the failure to support this European-initiated effort. The United States should explore in a positive fashion the French proposals for stronger security co-operation among the Europeans. The Anglo-Saxon governments should make it clear to Germany that they welcome strong Franco-German co-operation and would like to help in every way possible. The United States can even provide economic incentives for European arms production which might in the long run offer considerable defence savings for the American taxpayer. Great Britain should support increased arms production by European consortia and should in NATO and in EEC councils endorse proposals for improved industrial co-operation within a multi-speed Europe. Western leaders, and especially those in Washington, should move beyond decisions based on near-term economic and political advantage and respond positively to the opportunity for greater European autonomy within the alliance.

NEW REALITIES

Relationships among the European states are changing, and with these shifts the United States has developed new ties with the principal states of Europe. Elements of the 'Special Relationship' with Britain remain, especially those in nuclear and intelligence matters. But since 1970, the relationship with the Federal Republic has become the most important political and military tie for the United States. Although everyday exchanges may not be as easy and familiar as with Britain, American understandings with Germany are at the core of every element of United States policy for Europe. They permeate political, economic, scientific, and cultural relations with Europe. Americans have been slow to recognize the greatly expanded scope of French relations with Germany, but this is likely to be acknowledged in coming months. With the successful conclusion of the INF crisis and the steady recovery of the German economy since 1983, German–American relations are destined to increase still further in importance.

By placing a high priority on its 'Special Relationship' with America, Britain may well have paid an unreasonably high price in its relations with continental Europe. The delay in applying to join the European Economic Community was costly, and the nuclear relationship with Washington almost certainly determined De Gaulle's two vetoes of subsequent British applications to join. Even after entry into the European Community in 1972, Britain has hesitated to join many EEC projects, has refused to join the European monetary system, has not adapted its marketing strategies to European requirements, and in recent years has brought the EEC to a standstill as a result of Mrs Thatcher's attempts to adjust the annual British contribution to the community budget. All of this comes on top of the problems already discussed of defence organization and production within Europe.

As a result of these new realities and in view of the prospects for further weakening of the British economy compared to that of Germany, many American friends of Britain feel that it is in Great Britain's interest to become more fully and permanently integrated into Europe. The recently signed Anglo-French treaty for a Channel tunnel symbolizes the hope that this decision has now been taken. When completed, the process of Britain's joining fully into Europe will also be in the best long-term interests of the United States.

9

The Military Relationship

ADMIRAL SIR JAMES EBERLE

A FULL account of the post-war Anglo-American military relationship will one day come to be written. That day is likely to be later rather than sooner, because the relationship has been at its closest in fields which carry a high military security value—the development and testing of nuclear weapons, intelligence collection and evaluation, research and development on missile guidance systems, the targeting of nuclear weapons, anti-submarine warfare, and the operation of nuclear submarines—for all of which sources are often highly and continuingly sensitive. Nevertheless, the admirable account of post-war co-operation in nuclear weapon programmes by Margaret Gowing shows well that thorough research into even the limited sources available can produce a clear and coherent picture. This account, however, is not primarily based on research, but on the practical, personal experience of one who is himself a product of that post-war Anglo-American military relationship. It has an inevitable naval bias.

It is, however, not only on matters of high security value that there has been close co-operation. There are very few fields within the whole spectrum of military activity that have not been the subjects of bilateral Anglo-American agreements for the exchange of information or techniques. But it has been co-operation in these highly classified fields that has been one major factor in sustaining a 'special character' for the Anglo-American military relationship.

A second major factor has been the role played by Britain as the 'first military ally' of the United States. This particular role stemmed directly from the close wartime associations in battles in North Africa, Europe, the Atlantic, the Pacific, and South-east Asia. It continued naturally into the post-war period, for Britain had for many years been a global military power, and the United States had just become one. There was thus a natural affinity of interest in the means of deploying military power, even though its political ends, as at Suez, were sometimes in conflict. Such conflicts of regional interest, however, were of secondary importance amongst military men, against the background of their common global enemy, the Soviet Union. Together these factors have led to a relationship which is unique in terms of the mutual confidence and trust that it has inspired between the individual services of the two countries.

Closer examination of the overall defence relationship reveals that there have emerged somewhat different patterns of co-operation between the three individual services, the Navy, the Air Force and the Army. These differences arise both from the particular experiences of the three services in wartime co-operation and from the co-operation and degree of their involvement in the 'high security' fields.

The war in Europe was one in which the co-ordination of military operations at the highest level reached a unique pitch of international co-operation. The Combined Chiefs of Staff, despite deep divisions over priorities between North Africa and continental Europe, and between Europe and the Pacific, provided a coherent framework within which the various theatre commands were able to conduct joint planning, of which the Normandy landing was an outstanding example. But at the fighting level, units of the American and British forces 'co-ordinated' their operations, rather than 'combined' them. There was a great deal of joint planning but few joint operations. At the strategic level in the air, the Royal Air Force continued its night bombing offensive, whilst the US Air Force carried out major daylight raids. On the ground, the British and US Armies operated alongside each other, with units only very rarely (such as at Anzio and in the 'Battle of the Bulge') being placed under command of other than their own national commanders. In tactical air support, US ground attack aircraft were principally involved in the offensive support of US Army formations whilst RAF units provided the equivalent support for British ground forces. At sea, the general picture was not dissimilar. Rather than operating together British and US warships co-ordinated their operations. Their operational organizations were different; they used different tactical procedures; their communication systems often made it difficult for them to speak to each other; and when they did, despite the common language, there were often misunderstandings concerning the message that was being conveyed. The subtlety of the fine, but important, difference of meaning in the Royal Navy's use of the words 'propose' and 'intend' was generally lost to American ears—and the British took a long time to appreciate the usefulness of such American expressions as 'Tuesday through Friday'.

The big change for the Royal Navy came with the formation of the British Pacific Fleet (BPF). Although ships of the BPF were to operate principally within their own self-contained formations, now designated within the USN systems of Task Groups, and with their own supporting 'Fleet Train' to provide logistic support, the BPF put to one side its

British books of signals and operating doctrines and adopted those of the USN. This was not only a large and important practical step towards the ability to carry out fully 'joint' operations, but also an important psychological step. The control of the tactical movements of ships at sea, and particularly during wartime, is at all times of day and night vitally dependent upon the quick, accurate interpretation of brief signalled instructions. These books thus play an all-pervasive part of life on the bridge of a warship at sea. For the British to give up 'their books' and accept the 'American books' was an act of recognition of the dominance of the USN in the Pacific theatre. In anthropological terms, it was perhaps an act of 'submission'. But to the young British officer it was a new and exciting challenge. It was the breath of the novel world of aircraft carriers and 'circular screens' of escorting destroyers. It swept away the cobwebs of the battleship era with its 'bent-line screen' of escorts, an era whose roots go back to Jutland and the Grand Fleet. Here was a new language, a new world, and a demonstration of new techniques for long-range amphibious operations. But the British had much to offer as well as to learn. And in that two-way process were sown the seeds of post-war naval co-operation.

The dropping of the atomic bombs on Hiroshima and Nagasaki brought an unexpectedly early end to the war against Japan—and by early 1946 the British Pacific Fleet was steaming home towards demobilization and the task of rebuilding war-torn Britain. But the presence of a Royal Air Force observer at this, the first and, mercifully, so far the only operational use of nuclear weapons, was a symbolic and practical gesture which was to be an important underpinning for the post-war RAF-USAF relationship.

At the political level, the post-war Anglo-American nuclear relationship was marked by great difficulty following the McMahon Act of 1946. However, non technical collaboration continued and was eventually codified in a *modus vivendi* agreement signed early in 1948. This was followed by the stationing of American nuclear-capable aircraft in the United Kingdom.

The first British atomic test in 1952, and the construction of the V-bomber force, provided further incentive to the United States for nuclear co-operation, including the provision of nuclear weapons to the RAF to be used under a dual-key system, pending the adequate provision of British atomic and later hydrogen bomb weapons. These developments provided a common RAF-USAF concern with a new front line of strategic air power. At last, the two Air Forces had a weapon, that they had lacked during World War II, which could without doubt decisively affect the course of war. These developments were intensified by the deployment in Britain of Thor intermediate-range missiles, with warheads under American control; and by the British decision to pursue its own strategic missile development programme with Blue Streak.

Whilst the deployment of strategic air power, nuclear weapons, and nuclear missiles provided the centre-piece for RAF-USAF co-operation, the development of high performance aircraft, helicopters, long- and short-range air transport, air-to-air, air-to-ground, and ground-to-air missiles, in-flight refuelling, and many other areas of post-war warfare provided fruitful ground for the exchange of technical and operational information to sustain a vigorous and healthy relationship. This relationship was reinforced by the shared experiences of RAF pilot training in the United States, by the Berlin air lift, and by the major deployment of USAF aircraft to bases in the United Kingdom.

For the two armies, there was no equivalent centre-piece upon which the post-war relationship could be built. The regimental system of the British Army has no counterpart in the United States—and whilst common ground could be, and was, established in the fields of combat vehicle development, weapons, and tactical doctrine, the maintenance of close working relationships needed more attention than was the case with the other two services. Nevertheless, the success of the British Army's Malaysian campaign against Communist terrorists served well to remind the US Army that it still had much to learn in order to fulfil the American role as a global power. And subsequently, the necessity for joint planning in the use of American and British tactical nuclear weapons in Europe has ensured that the army-to-army relationship has remained intimate and live.

But there was another field in which very close wartime co-operation was extended into the post-war period: intelligence. The war experience had shown that only the evaluation of all available intelligence sources would yield the reliable information that was needed by the customer. The great increase in radio traffic during the war and the success of certain code-breaking operations had also demonstrated the importance of communications as a potential source of intelligence. Inter-Agency agreements, confirmed by governments, thus covered major areas for the full exchange of both raw and evaluated intelligence. Britain, with her war experience, and with colonial territories that spanned the world to serve as a base for intelligence gathering, had much to offer. The agreements then made were thus on the basis of an equal partnership, a relationship which despite ever increasing disparity in the technical capabilities of the two countries for the collection of intelligence has remained effectively unchanged.

The United Nations' operations in Korea provided renewed opportunities for the British Army and Navy to demonstrate their ability to operate with US forces without difficulty. The British naval forces, operating from the US base at Sasebo in Japan, provided aircraft carrier and naval gunfire support on the west coast, whilst USN forces together with ships of the Canadian navy operated on the east coast. British ground forces, part of the British Commonwealth Force Korea (BCFK), operated from Kure in Japan and took their place in the front line alongside units of the US and Republic of Korea (ROK) armies. The Royal Air Force involvement was confined to the participation of exchange aircrew in USAF squadrons. There were good times and bad times as the war moved from defence to offence and then back to defence, further offence, and finally stalemate. But throughout, the military relationships remained excellent and provided ample proof that wartime memories had not faded.

The years that followed during the 1950s were a time of great technological change. It was the age of the guided missile and the supersonic fighter. It was a period of great urgency as the Western powers sought to develop weapons that would allow the newly formed North Atlantic Treaty Organization to contain the threatened further expansion of the Soviet empire. British officers of all three services crossed the Atlantic by sea to reinforce the Service Staffs in Washington, to undertake courses in the United States on advanced weapon technology, and to participate in American weapon development and testing programmes. Once the established procedures had been completed, there were very few barriers of security—and there was almost total integration of British officers into American units. Harmony abounded—and at the military level was little affected by the events of Suez, and its associated political stresses. Even the entry of a strong element of commercial competition from the defence industries of the two countries, who vied with each other to influence the content of the new NATO Basic Military Requirements so that they would better match existing weapons which they had to sell, did little to disrupt the high degree of agreement between the military professionals on both sides of the Atlantic. They knew and they agreed what it was they were trying to achieve. A 1960 report by a senior Royal Navy aviation specialist, following a visit to the United States, stated that there were no significant differences between the USN's aviation policies and those of the RN. It is unlikely even to have entered that author's head that, bearing in mind the inevitably growing differences in the roles and missions of the two navies, and the widening gap in their available resources, there should have been significant differences. For was not Britain still leading America in naval aviation, with such 'firsts' as the first carrier deck landing in a jet-powered aircraft, the angled deck, and the minor landing sight? Britannia still ruled the waves in the Admiralty in Whitehall.

The collapse of Skybolt and the beginning of a British programme for four Polaris submarines deeply aggravated the inter-service rivalries in Whitehall. A senior civil servant of the Admiralty was heard to remark to a naval colleague, in rejecting arguments for the Navy's contribution to a paper on strategic nuclear deterrence which was to go forward to the Cabinet Defence Committee, 'you have got it wrong. We are not fighting the Russians. We are fighting the Air Force Department.' And in fighting the Air Force Department, the Royal Navy continuously enlisted the direct and indirect support of the USN. Just as surely, the RAF made certain that they were in the closest cahoots with the US Air Force. But the United States had its own inter-service battles to fight too. And thus each of the American services was only too ready to join hands across the Atlantic against a common 'enemy', its sister services. Thus were the Atlantic service links further strengthened.

The advent of the Polaris Programme, and the resulting transfer of the British strategic nuclear task from the Air Force to the Navy, opened a new chapter in the transatlantic naval relationship. The Polaris project extended far beyond the technical challenges of solid-fuelled ICBMs, underwater launch techniques, and the building of nuclear-powered, ballistic-missile-firing submarines. It provided entry into new fields of management techniques, of intelligence, of strategic targeting, of communications, and of nuclear submarine operations. Only the advent of transatlantic air travel could have permitted the RN to adapt at the speed which was required to complete the programme on time.

However, as the Royal Navy's horizons broadened, those of the Royal Air Force tended to narrow as the US Air Force devoted increasing proportions of its resources towards space. This was a route which Britain could afford to do little more than to observe as an envious bystander.

The single-minded determination of the Royal Navy to complete the Polaris Programme successfully, a feat which it achieved with outstanding success, diverted the attention of British submariners from the major developments that were proceeding in parallel in the United States in the use of nuclear-powered submarines for anti-submarine warfare, for intelligence, and for other aspects of open ocean warfare. Furthermore, new passive acoustic techniques, used from fixed installations and from submarines, had opened up a whole new window on the underwater world in which there were originally but two players, the United States and the Soviet Union. By agreements reached between the RN and the USN during the mid-1960s, the Royal Navy with its own increasing force of nuclear-powered attack submarines (SSNs) came to be a third player in this game of underwater 'hide-and-seek', with the game then being played 'two against one'.

As the Polaris Programme provided new horizons for the Royal Navy, so were their horizons yet further expanded by joining the 'SSN club'. Such complex and sensitive operations as those which can be carried out by SSN's demand high-grade intelligence support, sophisticated communication facilities, most carefully co-ordinated planning, and high professional skills in the operation of the submarines. In this latter field, the Royal Navy's excellence was a major factor in the maintenance of mutual confidence between the two navies.

But the benefits of underwater co-operation also extended into the surface fleet, and to the operation of maritime patrol aircraft. Anti-submarine operations are seldom fully successful without the close co-operation of air, surface, and sub-surface units. Thus Britain, by paying an 'SSN subscription', obtained membership to a 'premier league' of naval operations that was not fully available to any other NATO or allied navy.

The intelligence relationship in the communications field between the US National Security Agency (NSA) and Britain's Government Communications Headquarters (GCHQ) was largely confined in the earlier post-war period to matters of strategic intelligence. But technical developments during the 1960s, particularly in satellite capabilities, opened up new opportunities for tactical intelligence. The Royal Navy was again slow to appreciate either what could be done for maritime operations or what was being done in the USN. Fortunately, the message that the US Navy had for some time been trying obliquely to pass to their British counterparts at last fell upon fertile ground and opened yet another chapter in the navy-to-navy relationship. This relationship is now coming to fruition—and in its turn is giving rise to yet further significant developments in the field of Command, Control, Communications, and Intelligence (C^3I) systems.

The Vietnam War, in which Britain played no part, diverted a great deal of American attention away from the Atlantic and European security. Nevertheless, close co-operation between the British and American services across the Atlantic continued. It is difficult, however, to escape the conclusion that there was at least some connection between the relative decline of American military power during the 1970s and the strengthening of Britain's military interests with its European partners. Nevertheless, the evidence of the Falkland Islands War shows that it would be wrong to conclude that the special Anglo-American military relationship had, by the 1980s, weakened to a significant degree.

It would, also, almost certainly be wrong to conclude, as some have done, that the recapture of the Falkland Islands could not have been achieved without the indirect assistance of the United States. Certainly, that assistance was of great value; and without it, the operation would have taken longer and been more difficult and more hazardous. But it was the way in which the assistance was provided that is significant. Stemming from both the United States Secretary for Defense, Mr Weinberger, and the Chairman of the Joint Chiefs of Staff, General David Jones, an attitude of 'What can we do for the British today?' prevailed throughout the American defence establishment. The direct personal contact between Admiral Lewin, the British Chief of Defence, and General Jones reflected not only their own personal good relationship, built up through direct contact in many bilateral and NATO meetings, but the whole post-war history of continuity in the Anglo-American military relationship from the highest levels of command to the day-to-day levels of staff contact.

Not everything, however, is sweetness and light. There remain considerable doctrinal differences between British and American concepts of operations, which stem not only from differences in the size of the forces involved. There are continuing difficulties in rationalization and standardization of equipment and logistic services. There remains intense competition between the arms industries of both countries for sales within NATO and outside it. There is hard bargaining in terms of 'offset' agreements when transatlantic purchases are agreed.

Neverthless, there can be no doubt as to the 'special nature' of the post-war Anglo-American military relationship. This special nature is anchored in the experience of World War II co-operation. It is sustained by the bonds of professionalism that extend in common throughout the armed services of both countries, by a common cultural heritage, and by the unique nature of the military tasks that they, almost alone among Western countries, perform. Both countries are nuclear powers, a status which not only governs their position in terms of military capability but which also extends their influence into the field of arms control. Both countries are powers with global interests and responsibilities. For Britain, the withdrawal from empire has greatly lessened both of these, but nevertheless, the British military establishment still maintains a degree of experience and capability for global operations that is not to be ignored.

Joint understandings for the use of British facilities in Ascension Island, Bermuda, Cyprus, and Diego Garcia, together with formal agreements such as CANUKUS, provide important elements for the worldwide deployment of US military power. Both countries share operational responsibilities in a number of 'special task' areas, such as intelligence and SSN operations. They regularly demonstrate their capability for joint bilateral operations and exercises, not only in the

European theatre, but also in such joint enterprises as UN peacekeeping, the Hormuz Patrols, and the mine clearance operations in the Red Sea. British real estate in the United Kingdom provides important operational and logistic facilities both for the direct defence of the continental United States and for American military operations in the Atlantic and in Europe.

The question with which I leave this brief narrative is 'Will this "special" nature of the relationship continue?' The answer would seem to rest largely upon the continuing involvement of Britain, with something to offer, in such militarily and technologically advanced fields as nuclear warfare, global operations, intelligence, and SSN operations. Were Britain to reduce her capability in these fields, then it seems that the 'Special Relationship' would have little to feed on other than the past. It would then almost inevitably no longer be 'special'. But if Britain, whilst fully acknowledging her commitments to her European allies as a member of a growing European Union, is willing to pay the price of maintaining these advanced military capabilities, then there seems every hope that, with careful political management of the Atlantic Alliance, Britain's continuing special military relationship with the United States can play a major part in the new framework of Atlantic and European security.

10

Defence Relationships: American Perspectives

ERNEST R. MAY AND GREGORY F. TREVERTON

ON 26 July 1956, the British Prime Minister Anthony Eden received a report of the Egyptian seizure of the Suez Canal. At the time he was giving a dinner for the King and the Prime Minister of Iraq. The visiting Iraqis were politely but quickly ushered out. Eden, still in formal dress, moved to the Cabinet Room. He was followed by the Foreign and Defence Secretaries, Selwyn Lloyd and the Marquess of Salisbury. At his invitation, the French ambassador and the American chargé, attending the dinner in the absence of the American ambassador, joined the group. Almost as a matter of course, Eden thus invited a Frenchman and an American to help him decide what *British* policy ought to be.[1]

Though it is hard to imagine a similar scene in Downing Street today, it is even harder to imagine it happening in, say, 1936. A 'Special Relationship' grew out of World War II. The purpose of this essay is to sketch some reasons for its growth, especially in the military sphere, and to explore the question of whether, in any important respects, it persists into the present.

WHY 'SPECIAL'?

There are some obvious reasons why Americans should have felt particularly close to Britons, once their country had accepted the role of global superpower. One is language. Few Americans have a detailed command of any foreign tongue. Most of those who have gone abroad (or travelled the embassy circuit in Washington) have been grateful when able to speak—and be understood—in English. And it has not been all one-sided, for even experienced British diplomats find it easier to discuss sensitive topics with others who share their mother tongue.

Equally obvious is cultural inheritance. Educated Americans recognize allusions to Shakespeare and Milton. Few have comparable familiarity with Corneille and Molière, let alone Goethe or Schiller. Almost all educated Americans over the age of fifty know some English history, for most good American colleges and universities used to require

[1] Roy Fullick and Geoffrey Powell, *Suez: The Double War* (London, 1979), pp. 12–13.

its study. Many younger Americans are similarly equipped because English history remained a popular elective subject even as requirements broadened or disappeared altogether. And, of course, a substantial part of the American ruling class became such by studying the Anglo-American legal tradition and qualifying to practise law. Through all the post-war years, a number of America's political and military leaders have felt an identification with Britain that they have not felt with any other country.

This has been assisted by the good judgement of the executors of the Rhodes Trust. An extraordinary number of former Rhodes Scholars have subsequently become influential in American public life. Many military officers are among them. General Bernard Rogers, the mid-1980s Supreme Allied Commander for Europe, is one example. But a mere tallying of such names would tell only part of the story, for it would miss the influence the Scholars themselves have. Another former Rhodes Scholar was George A. Lincoln. As the chief US Army planner during World War II and afterwards head of the Social Science Department at West Point, Lincoln selected and trained a whole generation of Army and Air Force staff officers. Colonels and generals from this 'Lincoln brigade' were influenced by his Rhodes Scholarship regardless of whether they won scholarships of their own.

And, like language, the tug of history and culture has pulled more than one way. Little by little, British officialdom, especially in the domestic ministries, may have shifted its focus toward Brussels and the European Community. But no government since Edward Heath's has made a determined effort to 'Europeanize' its mandarins, and many in the British Civil Service regard the Heath experiment as excessive. History and culture have helped maintain in Whitehall, and in the British military services, what has been called in other contexts a 'bureaucratic lobby' for continued closeness to Washington.[2]

Like all relationships between governments (and most relationships within governments), the special American–British defence relationship has been grounded more in interest than in sentiment. But its history is misunderstood—and its prospects probably misjudged—if the interests in question are seen exclusively as national interests of the type likely to figure in National Security Council papers or *Foreign Affairs* articles. They have been at least equally the particular interests of individuals and organizations.

For American presidents the value of the 'Special Relationship' has complemented and sometimes perhaps transcended its value for the

[2] This label is borrowed from Robin Edmonds's *Setting the Mould: The United States and Britain 1945–50* (forthcoming).

United States as a whole. Presidents have often been sensitive to British opinion in the way in which they are sensitive to opinion in lower Manhattan or on Madison Avenue or in Hollywood—because it sets a pattern for the broader public opinion which in some degree controls their ability to govern. In the White House, members of the staff seldom start the day with the *President's Daily Brief* or the *National Intelligence Daily*. They give first priority to newspapers. And *The Times* and the *Financial Times* of London are apt to be read soon after the *New York Times*, the *Washington Post*, and the *Wall Street Journal* (and before the *Los Angeles Times*, but that largely because of time zones). Zbigniew Brzezinski, in his memoir of the Carter Administration, quotes only *The Times* and the *Financial Times* when writing of the impact of Carter's first major foreign policy speech.[3] Among weeklies White House members of staff are likely to pay as much attention to *The Economist* as to *Time* or *Newsweek*. And sometimes individual British journalists figure among those closely watched. In the 1960s and 1970s Henry Brandon of the *Sunday Times* was one of these. In *The Best and the Brightest*, David Halberstam brackets Brandon with Joseph Alsop and James Reston as 'almost a part of the high level of government'.[4]

Presidents have shown far more sensitivity to criticism or praise from British sources than from sources in France or Germany or other parts of the world (even, oddly, Canada and Mexico). Questions about nuclear fall-out that had first been raised by the British Campaign for Nuclear Disarmament occupied a large fraction of President Eisenhower's press conference time in the mid-1950s. Questions raised much more vehemently in 1958 by the German *Kampf dem Atomtod* never made such penetration. The special value which presidents attach to British opinion may have been most clearly indicated in 1974 when President Nixon, desperately trying to escape the scaffold, attempted to arrange a state visit to London which would permit him to be televised at Buckingham Palace in company with the Queen. His memoirs contain pathetic quotations from *The Times* of London offered in proof that he had public support even to the end.[5] Presidents have cared about British opinion because it affected their strength at home.

Partly because of this attitude on the part of presidents, good repute in Britain has sometimes been an asset for cabinet officers or other members of the American executive. The reputation of being well thought of by British prime ministers was an advantage to Harry Hopkins and Averell

---

[3] Zbigniew Brzezinski, *Power and Principle: Memoirs of the National Security Adviser, 1977–1981* (New York, 1983), p. 56.

[4] David Halberstam, *The Best and the Brightest* (New York, 1969), pp. 45–6.

[5] *New York Times*, 5 June 1974; Richard M. Nixon, *Memoirs* (2 vols.; New York, 1978), vol. ii, pp. 443–4.

Harriman during World War II and to David Bruce and others in subsequent years. Because of Jimmy Carter's warm feeling for James Callaghan, Callaghan's approval strengthened by a little the position of Zbigniew Brzezinski. (Because of Carter's detestation of Helmut Schmidt, Schmidt's dislike for Brzezinski had the same effect.) High opinion of General Alexander Haig, reported from London during 1980–1, helped him become Secretary of State. Changed opinion, reflecting irritation over his role in the Falklands affair, contributed to his losing that post. In his memoirs, Haig makes the accusation that he fell victim to a clique in the White House which used press leaks as their chief weapons. One of their favoured implements, he indicates, was the Washington correspondent of the *Guardian*.[6] For officials like Haig, as for presidents and the members of their staff, British opinion has mattered for reasons more or less independent of calculations about abstract national interest.

This has not been true at all times or of all Americans. Lyndon Johnson's relations with Harold Wilson were such that most members of his Administration preferred not to have people in London say kind words about them. And on Capitol Hill this has been the rule rather than the exception. Not even the ex-Rhodes Scholar J. William Fulbright wanted his constituents told that he was popular in a foreign country, whatever its language and history. Nevertheless, in general, and to a degree that has no counterpart for any other country except Israel—certainly not the German Federal Republic or Japan—American policy-makers have had reason to be mindful of British perceptions and verbal reactions.

In the defence sphere, the interests of organizations have also played a large part in shaping the American government's policies and behaviour. In the eyes of members of career services, national interests are often functions of departmental interests. For officers of the United States Navy, for example, the overriding interest of the United States is upkeep of the Navy. For the group of officers generally dominant since World War II, the overriding interest has been even more specifically upkeep of large aircraft carriers. For others in the service it has been submarines; for still others, destroyers. In the eyes of Air Force officers, the overriding national interest may have been strategic missiles or bombers or fighter aircraft or even transport capability. And so on. The carrier, the bomber, or the armoured division may be rationalized in terms of larger national purposes or postures—'power projection' or

---

[6] Alexander M. Haig, Jr., *Caveat: Realism, Reagan, and Foreign Policy* (New York, 1984), pp. 301–2.

'deterrence' or 'flexible response'. From the service standpoint they are ends in themselves.

This observation is not cynical or even necessarily critical. We would all look back less happily on World War II had officers of the British and American armed services not then defined national interests in comparably parochial terms. It needs nevertheless to be recognized that, for the services and other organizations in the United States government, the 'Special Relationship' has derived much of whatever value it has from its usefulness to them when justifying or defending their weapons, programmes, or budgets.

During World War II, the relationship had particular value to the Army and Air Force (then the Army Air Forces). George C. Marshall, the Army Chief of Staff, and other American generals often quarrelled with their British opposite numbers. On occasion Marshall said or implied that, if the British did not come to terms, the United States might shift priority to the war against Japan. But the threat, if carried out, would have injured Marshall's service. Concentration on the European theatre and preparation for a cross-Channel attack gave the Army and the Army Air Forces priority for manpower and war production. Even though there was an Army theatre in the Pacific, with Douglas MacArthur in command, the war against Japan was essentially the Navy's war. From the standpoint of Marshall's naval counterpart, Chief of Naval Operations Ernest J. King, Mediterranean and European operations were secondary, and combined Anglo-American planning had the effect of helping the British and the Army divert resources away from the Pacific or, worse yet, to peripheral parts of Asia such as Burma. The wartime 'Special Relationship' linked civilians and ground and air force officers, not naval officers.[7]

After the war, this condition changed. American naval officers found it hard to persuade Congressmen and other civilians of the need to spend billions on modernized aircraft carriers, submarines, and ocean escort forces. The Imperial Japanese Navy no longer existed. The Royal Navy was not a plausible threat. Russia, which seemed the most likely adversary in a future war, had no ocean-going fleet and was largely landlocked.

Together, the Cold War and the 'Special Relationship' rescued the Navy. As early as 1946 naval spokesmen were arguing the vital importance of controlling communications through the Mediterranean. Protection of oil supplies was the initial reason. As relations with the Soviet Union grew worse, the Navy added a contention that, in case of war, the route for direct attack on Russia would run—as in the 1850s—

---

[7] The best account is in Christopher Thorne, *Allies of a Kind: The United States, Britain and the War against Japan, 1941–1945* (New York, 1978).

through the Straits and the Black Sea, into the Crimea. Then in the winter of 1946–7 came the British confession of inability to continue propping up Greece and Turkey and Ernest Bevin's plea that the United States take on this task. From the Navy's standpoint, this appeal was a godsend. No presidential advisers pressed harder for Greek–Turkish aid than did Secretary of the Navy James Forrestal and King's successor, Chief of Naval Operations Chester Nimitz.[8] The ecumenical scope of the consequent 'Truman Doctrine' provided a rationale, otherwise hard to find, for large, balanced naval forces.

The interests of the Navy were served, it is true, by a rather special conception of the 'Special Relationship'. Britain, her dependencies, and her historic zones of influence had to be viewed as important to the United States, but Britain herself had to be viewed as weak. In budget debates, the Navy always had to beat back arguments from the other services that some of its missions could be accomplished by the Royal Navy.[9] After 1950, when Britain had begun to recover economically and both Britain and the United States invested much more heavily in military and naval forces, this became harder. When General Eisenhower became Supreme Allied Commander for Europe, the British government sought to have a British admiral named Supreme Allied Commander for the Atlantic. When the United States Navy categorically refused, the British retreated to proposing that there be a separate Supreme Allied Command for the Mediterranean and that its chief be British. This, too, the United States Navy found intolerable, not least because of its implications for the Navy's bargaining position in Washington. Years of wrangling (and one vote of confidence which the Attlee government barely survived) produced a nearly incomprehensible and doubtfully workable compromise, with American *and* British commanders in the Mediterranean and a United States Mediterranean fleet answerable to neither.[10]

Subsequently, the Navy acquired another reason for interest in the 'Special Relationship'. When the era of accurate, long-range missiles arrived, the Navy's claim to a share in the strategic nuclear mission came to rest on nuclear-powered submarines mounting intermediate-range Polaris A-2 missiles. Because of the range of these missiles, the case for their forming a leg of the 'triad' equal to bombers and longer-range, land-based missiles became stronger if the submarines could operate from forward bases. An Eisenhower–Macmillan agreement of 1960

[8] Robert G. Albion and Robert M. Connery, *Forrestal and the Navy* (New York, 1962), pp. 185–91.
[9] See, for example, Paul Y. Hammond, 'Super Carriers and B-36 Bombers', in Harold Stein, ed., *American Civil-Military Decisions: A Book of Case Studies* (Birmingham Ala., 1963), esp. pp. 493–4.
[10] United States Joint Chiefs of Staff, *The History of the Joint Chiefs of Staff: The Joint Chiefs of Staff and National Policy* (Wilmington, Del., 1979); vol. iv. *1950–1952*, pp. 230–41, 310–18.

provided for the US Navy's use of Holy Loch. Even though the submarines soon had longer-range Polaris A-3 and Poseidon missiles, the existence of this base continued to figure in briefs for spending money on undersea-based strategic forces.

For the Air Force, the 'Special Relationship' became a powerful interest during the surge of rearmament that accompanied the Korean War. The service became autonomous in 1947. By the end of the 1940s it seemed to be effectively dominated by bomber pilots, particularly those grouped in General Curtis LeMay's Strategic Air Command. During that period, though anti-Communist and anti-Soviet feeling ran high, neither the public nor Congress showed enthusiasm for the painful measures required to maintain trained reserves and a mobilization base. The public and Congress did seem willing, however, to spend money for long-range bombers and atomic bombs, and LeMay and SAC were the beneficiaries. At the time, the forces under LeMay's command consisted mostly of medium-range B-29s, and during the Berlin blockade crisis of 1948 B-29s were deployed to bases in Britain. But these arrangements were thought temporary; LeMay's planning looked towards a bomber force based in the United States.

With the Korean War, the Air Force and the other services suddenly found the President and Congress willing, for practical purposes, to buy anything they asked for. The prevailing view, embodied not only in secret documents such as NSC 68 but in public speeches, envisioned a 'year of maximum danger' in 1954, or perhaps earlier, when the Soviets might be tempted to start a war. The services were asked to prepare for it.

LeMay and SAC were not yet in a position to spend large sums on intercontinental bombers. Though they had defended the B-36 against criticism from the Navy, the plane was obviously no prize. It was propeller-driven, stood four stories high on the ground, had a maximum speed of 300 miles an hour, and could barely carry one atomic bomb the distance from North America to Russia. An all-jet B-52 was not yet out of the design stage. In any case, many Air Force technicians had doubts about it. SAC's hopes rested on sketches, not yet even blueprints, for supersonic long-range bombers or for nuclear-powered bombers that could stay aloft indefinitely. (The largest single project of the Atomic Energy Commission during the 1950s was that for a nuclear-powered airplane.)[11]

To make use of the bonanza of the early 1950s, SAC had to order B-47s. These were jet bombers of comparatively high speed with comparatively advantageous fuel-to-payload ratios. Their great disad-

---

[11] Richard G. Hewlett and Francis Duncan, *Atomic Shield, 1947–1952* (vol. ii of *A History of the United States Atomic Energy Commission*) (University Park, Pa., 1969), pp. 419–20.

vantage was limited range. To reach Soviet territory, they had either to be refuelled in the air or to fly from forward bases. SAC did, in fact, procure large numbers of B-47s. By the mid-1950s it had almost 1,500 of them. But, in addition to planes, it also had to acquire base rights. Hence the complicated arrangements which Duncan Campbell details (and protests against) in *The Unsinkable Aircraft Carrier*, allowing the United States use of large numbers of military facilities in the United Kingdom.[12] Similar arrangements were made with Morocco and Libya. The United Kingdom, however, seemed politically more stable. It was certainly preferred by the majority of SAC officers and their families. The preservation of a comfortable American–British 'Special Relationship' thus became an important Air Force interest and, by the same token, a component in Air Force officers' interpretations of United States national interests.

The Korean War rearmament also revivified some of the Army's interest in that relationship. Part of the Army's buildup went to new divisions, four of which were assigned to NATO to augment the two division equivalents still on occupation service. The deployment of these divisions to Europe was originally described as and understood to be temporary, pending the formation of German units and the establishment of a European army. But progress toward a European Defence Community stalled. The Korean War ended. A new economy drive developed in Washington. Arguments against withdrawing American divisions from Germany became crucial to the Army's case for a proportionate share of the shrinking defence budget. One of these arguments was that the British wanted the Americans to remain; another was that the British were demonstrating their own concern by maintaining their forces in Germany. Duncan Sandys's Defence White Paper of 1957, foreshadowing reductions in the British Army of the Rhine, produced more consternation in the United States Army than almost anywhere else. In going public with their criticism of the Eisenhower Administration's parsimony towards the Army, Generals Matthew B. Ridgway and Maxwell Taylor blamed the British move on their own government's policies. The United States, they contended, was not holding up its end of the 'Special Relationship'.[13]

In addition to the fighting services, various elements in the American intelligence community developed parochial reasons for regarding the 'Special Relationship' as an important national interest. During World War II, American and British cryptanalysts worked closely together. After the war, both groups faced lean times. They agreed, in effect, to

[12] Duncan Campbell, *The Unsinkable Aircraft Carrier: American Military Power in Britain* (London, 1984).
[13] Matthew B. Ridgway, *Soldier* (New York, 1956), pp. 323–32.

pool resources. Though it has never been officially acknowledged, there appears to have been a formal United States–United Kingdom–Canada–Australia–New Zealand agreement in 1947 dividing up responsibility for collecting communications intelligence. Each country took a particular portion of the globe. After 1950, when funds for intelligence collection flowed much more freely, particularly in the United States, co-operation continued. The British Government Communications Headquarters (GCHQ) and the American National Security Agency (NSA) exchanged personnel, and the two organizations apparently made common use of facilities not only in the United Kingdom but elsewhere around the globe.

American and British agencies concerned with photographic intelligence also collaborated. The United States Air Force and the Royal Air Force shared the results of slant photography along the borders of the Soviet Union (and probably also the products of their occasional accidental or purposeful penetrations of Soviet air space). When the American Central Intelligence Agency developed the high altitude U-2, its initial flights were from bases in the United Kingdom. This, however, was merely a matter of convenience. When Eden becme nervous about possible effects on British–Soviet relations, the CIA readily transferred its U-2s to bases elsewhere.[14] It was the sharing of photographic takes and interpretive expertise that made, here, for a 'Special Relationship'.

Similarly, in regard to human intelligence, co-operation had little to do with location. There had been some British–American collaboration during the war. Afterwards, the residual intelligence organizations eked out their scarce resources by working together. The British were thought to have more experienced case officers and a more extensive string of agents. The Americans had better relationships with surviving German intelligence officers and better facilities for interrogating refugees and returnees from Eastern Europe. Though the evidence is necessarily fragmentary and dubious (and some of the most plausible appears in novels), it suggests considerable continuing interchange at the station level.[15]

All of these organizational interests have undergone change. The currently projected six-hundred ship Navy, with a 'maritime strategy' for Trafalgar-like direct engagement with the Soviet Navy, no longer needs the position in the Mediterranean that it once did. Trident II submarines carrying D-5 missiles can easily get along without Holy Loch. The Air Force long ago phased out its B-47s. By the 1960s, most

[14] Stephen E. Ambrose, *Eisenhower, the President* (New York, 1984), p. 340.
[15] The insider novels of John LeCarré and Charles McCarry are suggestive. So are such details as we have concerning the Penkovsky affair: see Walter Laqueur, *A World of Secrets: The Uses and Limits of Intelligence* (New York, 1985).

SAC bombers were of intercontinental range. By the 1970s its paramount weapons were intercontinental ballistic missiles. The Army's case for forces in Europe came meanwhile to hinge chiefly on the level of evident German, not British, concern and commitment.

But organizational interests and organizationally shaped definitions of national interests are only partly functions of immediate needs. As a rule, organizations resist changes that are more than marginal. Practical programme and budget interests created command arrangements in the Mediterranean, a network of shared military facilities in the United Kingdom, and a body of rhetoric connecting the American commitment to European defence to a 'Special Relationship' with Britain. The command arrangements may have practical drawbacks. They probably contributed to the failure of the Carter Administration's effort to rescue hostages from Tehran in 1980, and they almost certainly hindered intelligence evaluation, planning, and communications which might have prevented or lessened the effects of the 1984 terrorist attack on the Marine barracks in Lebanon. Yet the American armed services have been consistently hesitant to change command lines, in part, probably, because of institutional memory of the extent to which the original effort seemed to irritate American–British relations. While the original rationale for Air Force bases in the United Kingdom may no longer be valid, the Air Force has the bases. The burden of proof falls on those who would argue for getting rid of them. And so on. In the military services and American intelligence agencies, the maintenance of a 'Special Relationship' with Britain counts as an important national interest for reasons, and because of experiences, only casually related to the current balance of power.

WHAT IS LESS SPECIAL?

Before turning to the question of what remains 'special' about the actual defence relationship, it is worth noting some aspects which never were special.

There has been nothing special about the British connection when it comes to pronouncements about strategy. In that regard, there is, unhappily, an unbroken line of continuity. It did not occur to President Truman to consult the British as he gradually developed the original strategy of nuclear deterrence. NSC 68 and other such documents were products of wide consultation within the United States government but not much outside it. In 1951, after agreements had been reached for basing B-47s in the United Kingdom, Ernest Bevin registered with Dean Acheson a personal complaint about his lack of familiarity with

American strategic plans.[16] This condition did not change during the Eisenhower Administration or during the Kennedy Administration's reappraisal of strategy leading to the Athens speech by the Secretary of Defense, Robert McNamara, in May 1962. It persisted in the Nixon Administration National Security Memorandum 3 exercise and the similar exercise of the Carter Administration yielding Presidential Review Memorandum 10 (which, despite all the fuss, produced no dramatic changes in strategy). And it continued, strikingly, into President Reagan's Strategic Defense Initiative (SDI) of March 1983, though SDI may be a slightly pathological case since the British were no more surprised by the speech than were senior American Defense and State Department officials. Still, the pattern has been consistent. No ally has been engaged, formally or informally, until American strategy has been decided.

The same pattern has held for major decisions about the shape of military forces. While the Air Force may have needed British co-operation for credible deployment of its B-47s, there seems to have been no advance consultation about the decision to order the planes. With similar lack of warning, the Air Force and Army procured intermediate-range Thor and Jupiter ballistic missiles likely also to need British bases. Little wonder, then, that decisions on intercontinental bombers and missiles showed no apparent concern for British opinion, even though those decisions were, if anything, more crucial to allies than had been the earlier ones. American strategic weapons which had to be based in Europe were at least symbols of the unity of the alliance. Weapons based an ocean away from Europe made deterrence *extended deterrence*, and Europe an uncertainly exposed forward area.

Despite the special Anglo-American intelligence connection, a non-special relationship seems to have obtained with regard to judgements about Soviet strategic forces. While there may have been some collaborative estimation in the very early years, there is little evidence of British contribution to intra-agency American debates about the 'bomber gap', the 'missile gap', the doctrine of 'sufficiency', or the 'window of vulnerability'.[17] As with strategies and forces, so with estimates of the major adversary: the American government has not involved the British, or any other ally, in its internal debates.

Nor has any ally, Britain included, had a noteworthy role in American decision-making regarding any security realm outside Europe. The American government may have sought co-operation, but only after decisions had been taken, unilaterally. The Suez crisis

---

[16] United States Department of State, *Foreign Relations of the United States, 1951*, vol. i, pp. 802–3.
[17] Lawrence Freedman in *U.S. Intelligence and the Soviet Strategic Threat* (London, 1977), does not mention a British contribution after the early 'missile gap' debate. See esp. p. 75.

demonstrates that, in earlier days, the favour could be more than returned. The Falklands War of 1982 suggests that those days are not entirely gone. But in different ways the Kennedy Administration's Alliance for Progress, the Kennedy–Johnson–Nixon Administration's war in Vietnam, and the Carter Administration's Camp David accords illustrate standard American practice. Allies were told after the fact of policies upon which Americans had decided. They then had their arms twisted, Britain especially, to support American policies which they had no part in framing and about which they had qualms.

American responses to the Soviet invasion of Afghanistan in 1979 provide another illustration. Prime Minister Thatcher, like Harold Wilson during the Vietnam War, was cajoled into supporting the United States, though in the instance of the Olympic boycott she could not deliver. And the multi-national force, so called, in Lebanon is another, despite its façade. When the US Marine garrison was bombed and the United States decided to withdraw, it did so on its own, leaving the British, French, and Italian units to fend for themselves.

WHAT REMAINS SPECIAL?

If the 'Special Relationship' has not given Britain a voice in American strategy or much say regarding American weaponry or American estimates of the Soviet Union or American policy outside of Europe, it has, nevertheless, given British governments an extraordinary degree of access and leverage in regard to European affairs and other matters of high moment to particular Cabinets at particular times.

This access and leverage has not been contingent on Britain's power, for, relatively speaking, that power has steadily diminished. The extent of change is easily illustrated. For all Bevin's pleas of poverty, Britain had emerged from the war with an advanced technological base in atomic energy, electronics, and aviation. In 1950 its GNP had just ceased to equal that of France and the Federal Republic of Germany combined. As late as 1959, though far behind the United States, Britain had still the second largest GNP in the world. By 1970 it had been overtaken by the Federal Republic and matched by France. By 1985 Britain's GNP per capita was less than that of Italy.

In the military realm, Britain in 1945 had 488,000 soldiers stationed in Germany as compared with 391,000 for the United States.[18] As late as 1959, Britain's total armed forces of about 600,000 were three times those of the German Federal Republic, then rearming. As of the mid-1980s, Britain's armed forces had fallen to 325,000, about two-thirds

[18] Stephen Kirby, 'Britain, NATO and European Security', in John Baylis, ed., *British Defence Policy in a Changing World* (London, 1977), p. 95.

those of either France or the Federal Republic.[19] In 1962, when Britain chose to buy American Polaris missiles, it projected deployment of nuclear warheads totalling about one-sixth those of the leading superpower. Even with Trident II submarines and missiles, it will not have one-sixtieth the nuclear arsenal of either the United States or the Soviet Union.

Yet, despite these diminished capabilities, the British government seems to have undiminished influence in Washington when real British interests are in play. Consider the following three instances:

First the case of intermediate-range nuclear forces (INF). The chain of events that led to the NATO decision of December 1979 to deploy 572 American cruise and Pershing II nuclear missiles in Europe probably did not begin, as usually alleged, with the German Chancellor Helmut Schmidt's celebrated speech in London in October 1977. Rather, it began with a letter from the British Defence Minister, Fred Mulley, to his American counterpart, Harold Brown, in the summer of that year. In May, a gathering of NATO heads of government in London had set in motion a broad programme of alliance-wide defence improvements— the Long-Term Defence Programme. One of the ten task forces under that Programme was to treat NATO's 'theatre nuclear forces' (TNF, in the shorthand of the time). Mulley's letter directed attention to longer-range TNF, later called INF. It made arguments that became the basis for the decision. In the context of Soviet-American nuclear parity and of growing Soviet INF capabilities, most notably its SS-20s, INF was the weakest link in NATO's spectrum of deterrence.

From beginning to end, under a Labour Government and a Conservative one, it was Britain, even more than the Federal Republic, that was the driving force behind the issue. When in April 1979 NATO decided on new deployments in the range of 200 to 600 missiles, Washington waited for some indication from Europeans of exactly what the number ought to be. It was a British official who spoke for the 'Europeans'. At another point in the deliberations, the Federal Republic decided to accept the longer-range Pershings but to scale down the number of cruise missiles to be deployed on its territory. Britain agreed to take an extra wing (36) to compensate, raising its total from 124 to 160. At the eleventh hour, Belgium and the Netherlands were tempted to put off a final decision pending the results of arms control negotiations (the 'negotiate before deploying' option, as it was dubbed). The British Defence Secretary, Francis Pym, agreed with the United States in arguing against this line, his logic being that only clear

[19] Compare the first edition of International Institute for Strategic Studies, *The Military Balance* (London, 1959), with the edition for 1984–5.

NATO movement toward deployment would give Moscow incentive to negotiate.

The British Government was at least an equal partner with the United States in initiating INF deployments and determining their scale and timing. While Mulley's moves at the beginning were of no apparent service to him or to the Callaghan government, the prominence of Pym in subsequent decision-making was of considerable use to Mrs Thatcher in a period when she was defining, for domestic audiences, her attitudes toward the Americans on one side and Europe on the other.

The sale of American Trident missiles to Britain in 1980, revised in 1982 when the United States moved from the C-4 to the D-5 version of Trident, is a second case. The instance of Trident suggests how little had changed in the nuclear area since the Skybolt affair of 1962.[20] The outcome in both cases was the same: the United States agreed to sell Britain its most advanced nuclear system—Polaris in 1962, Trident in 1980. In both cases the British were to develop their own nuclear warheads (though with some American co-operation, including the testing of British warheads in Nevada). In fact, the main difference between the two instances is that in 1962 there was opposition in the Washington machine to selling the British Polaris; in 1980, by contrast, there was hardly a murmur of opposition to selling Trident.

Several aspects of the Trident affair, like the Polaris arrangement earlier, would have been inconceivable had the ally been any save Britain—even Israel. No other ally would have been sold Trident, certainly not cheaply. Britain purchased Polaris at a bargain basement price: the cost of the missiles plus a 5 per cent surcharge as a contribution to American research and development costs. Comparable information is not available on the Trident deal, but still the terms seem generous. Britain's Secretary of State for Defence says it will come 'at the same price as the U.S. Navy's own requirements', with only a small surcharge.[21]

Not only the price but also the form of the Trident deal was special. It was accomplished with a secrecy for which the American government is not renowned, and this is particularly striking, given that it was 1980, with an election in progress and the leak-prone Carter Administration still in office. Moreover, there was no whisper of protest from Congress— a far cry from the day of Britain's greater relative power, when the McMahon Act obstructed even discussion of nuclear matters.

Of course, even bargains can be costly. When in 1981 the United

---

[20] The classic study of the Skybolt affair of 1962 and the subsequent agreement to sell Polaris to Britain is Richard Neustadt, *Alliance Politics* (New York, 1970).

[21] See appendix 12 to John Baylis, *Anglo-American Defense Relations, 1939–1980* (New York, 1981); Ronald T. Pretty, ed., *Jane's Weapons Systems 1982–1983* (London, 1982), p. 10.

States switched from Trident I, with the C-4 missile, to Trident II, with the longer-range, more accurate D-5 missile, Britain was virtually obliged to go along. It did so despite the fact that, for its deterrent needs, the C-4 was quite good enough. But once C-4s were no longer in the US Navy's inventory, spare parts and technical support would have been hard to come by unless Britain reproduced for itself a portion of the American military-industrial base. It was cheaper to shift to the D-5 even though the cost was over a billion dollars.

Nevertheless, if Britain is to have a credible nuclear deterrent force under its own control, it would find it hard to put one into service at a lower cost—certainly not one based at sea. Without the special relationship evident in the comparatively generous terms of the Trident deals, Britain would have great difficulty in remaining a member of the nuclear club.

The war over the Falklands/Malvinas in 1982 is a third example. However much the Argentine Junta may have been misled by overly warm words from various members of the Reagan Administration, there was never much doubt that the United States would side with Britain if fighting actually broke out.[22] That fact does not, however, point to the specialness of the Anglo-American connection, for, in similar circumstances, the United States would probably have sided with any of its European allies.

It is the form and extent of American support for Britain that makes the episode evidence of a relationship without clear parallel. Even before the United States decided, on 30 April, that no further purpose would be served by witholding material assistance to Britain, American tankers and support planes had been arriving secretly at the base on Ascension Island. After 30 April, that help was given openly, and the United States provided a range of other aid: air-to-air and air-to-surface missiles, fuel and ammunition, and back-up planes to free British tankers from NATO duties.

More important, the United States made available a range of signals intelligence and communications facilities. Reportedly, American electronic facilities in southern Chile were used by Britain, with Chile's consent. The extent of military-to-military co-operation is remarkable. On one occasion, the British commander, Sir Terence Lewin, felt compelled to call the Chairman of the US Joint Chiefs of Staff, General David Jones. The latter is said to have responded quickly, 'I know what you're going to ask for, and it's already done.'[23] American assistance stopped short of direct involvement, but only just short. In a war over

---

[22] Haig, *Caveat*, p. 269.
[23] Max Hastings and Simon Jenkins, *The Battle for the Falklands* (New York, 1983), p. 142.

symbols and prestige, not one for survival, no other American ally—not even Israel—could imaginably have obtained support of such extent, given ungrudgingly and with little or no sign of dissent.

WHY THE SPECIAL ACCESS?

Part of the explanation for Britain's special access and leverage in Washington derives from what was said earlier about American interests affected by the 'Special Relationship'. If British ministers or officials want to catch attention at high levels in the American government, they have only to excite their own press or to have a word with someone in the London bureau of a major American newspaper or news magazine. Some elements of the British government take part in American governmental processes. The British Polaris Executive and the American Special Projects Office appear to have worked hand in hand.[24] As Admiral Eberle suggests elsewhere in this volume, the nuclear attack submarine forces of the two countries have been allies not only within NATO but in relations with other elements of their own services and the other services at home. The network of shared military facilities in the United Kingdom gives officers of the Royal Air Force a number of channels into the United States Air Force. Similarly, British Army officers have many links with the American Army. Not the least important place is Germany where there might otherwise have developed more of a special American Army–Bundeswehr relationship. The British Army of the Rhine, at 55,000 (most of which is now in Germany, not in northern Ireland), is still the second largest non-German presence in Germany. And residual four-power occupation rights in Germany give Britain a status in the alliance deliberations it might not otherwise command. The intelligence connection seems to remain special. The British government has a web of contacts, without counterpart anywhere, up and down the American military and intelligence establishments.

In addition, the British 'work' Washington probably better than do any others except, perhaps, the Israelis. Most NATO countries send good ambassadors to Washington, but below the ambassadorial level the British Embassy has consistently been more effective than the others. It has also been, most of the time, better than the American Embassy in London. Moreover, since British officialdom is more disciplined than American, American officers in London find it harder to know what is afoot than do their British counterparts in Washington. Foreign Office officials in London often already know what the American diplomats

---

[24] For a discussion of this connection, see G. M. Dillon, *Dependence and Deterrence* (London, 1983), especially ch. 4.

who come to see them are instructed to say. And that points to another reason for their ease of access: British representatives in Washington are apt to have information about one part of the United States government which another part of that government wants to know.

The quality of the men and women Britain posts to Washington is such that American officials may offer them special access for that reason alone. What Americans can get from clever Britons is an informed but objective view, presented in a language that makes conversation easy. This contributes to making American officials more willing to confide in their British counterparts than in their own colleagues across town. Henry Kissinger put it almost exactly that way in describing his dealings with British officials when he was in the White House: '. . . the British played a seminal part in certain American bilateral negotiations with the Soviet Union—indeed, they helped draft the key document. In my White House incarnation then, I kept the British Foreign Office better informed and more closely engaged than I did the American State department.'[25]

What is true of the American executive is also the case for Congress. At any time, there are likely to be half a dozen former Rhodes Scholars scattered across the Congressional leadership and concentrated in committees dealing with defence and foreign policy. Ease of British access may be even more important in Congress than in the Executive since there are fewer routine points of entry and both language skills and institutional sensitivity to foreign cultures are in shorter supply. And, when they are moved to do so, the British can work the Hill better than any others except, again, the Israelis. That was apparent in regard to Trident. It was also evident during the Falklands War. The then British Ambassador was all over Capitol Hill, talking to anyone who would listen.

HOW SPECIAL IN THE FUTURE?

Most likely, these 'special' links will erode only slowly. Britain will continue to have both special connections—American airbases, missiles, service, and intelligence links—and special access. American officials will get not just a sense of company but also informed, objective views of what is going on inside Europe. That will be all the more important as political—and even defence—co-operation grows within the European Community.

Yet, however slowly, the special connections seem bound to erode. Though Britain's growth rate in the 1980s was healthy, the economy

[25] Henry A. Kissinger, 'Reflections on a Partnership: British and American Attitudes to Postwar Foreign Policy', *International Affairs*, 58. 4 (1982), 577.

remains under strain. The Falklands War stimulated public support for defence, but the effect is bound to pass. In 1985 Britain met its NATO commitment to increase defence spending by 3 per cent. It is unlikely to do so in 1986 and later. At some point even a defence-minded Tory government will face yet another round of major defence cuts. For a Tory government it would again be a choice between the Royal Navy and the British Army of the Rhine. A better would pick the BAOR as the target, for the first time in twenty years. But major reductions in either would cut some of the links between London and Washington.

If the Labour Party came to power, the change might be dramatic, not gradual. According to its current policy, Labour is committed not just to scrapping Trident and not deploying the cruise and Pershing missiles, but also to closing British airbases to all American nuclear weapons.[26] The reality of power might moderate Labour's actions—the Party's 1984 report calls for an 'effective conventional defence of Europe' and recognizes that 'U.S. bases and facilities in Britain have an important role in . . . conventional defence . . .'.[27] Yet it is hard to see how the Party could swallow both the cruise missiles and Trident. If, for example, Trident went, it would mean having wasted a lot of money (since the Conservative Government has put as much of the expenditure as possible in the early years to try to create, as with Polaris, a *fait accompli* for Labour). Trident would surely go down surrounded by blame for the United States.

It is also hard to imagine that any Labour government that would come to power in the next half decade would simply watch the service and intelligence connections with the United States continue as they are. Or if Labour were prepared to do so Washington might not be, either because it regarded the new government as a security risk or in retaliation for, say, British rejection of the cruise missiles.

Even if these dramatic changes do not ensue, Britain is bound to become more 'European' in security policy as well as economics. That was evident during the 1973 Arab–Israeli war. Washington looked to Britain for firm support; it found London tucked safely in the midst of the European consensus. In part, the maladroitness of the American administration's so called 'Year of Europe' spilled over onto inter-allied dealings during the crisis. The American nuclear alert at the height of the crisis, involving forces in Britain, seemed insensitive. Most notably, however, Britain shared the European view that the crisis, even if it had serious repercussions on oil supplies, was at most regional in character and ought to be contained—sentiments that characterized the 'Euro-

---

[26] See the Party's report, 'Defence and Security for Britain', overwhelmingly adopted at the 1984 party conference.

[27] Ibid.

pean' view in the aftermath of the Soviet invasion of Afghanistan six years later.[28]

In the 1973 instance, Britain not only refused to sell Israel ammunition for the Centurion tanks Britain itself had delivered earlier. It also, depending on the account, either refused the United States permission to trans-ship supplies through Britain *en route* to Israel and to stage U-2 overflights of the battle area from Britain and Cyprus, or it made it plain to the United States that it 'should not ask' for such permissions.[29] It may also have broken the communications link between the clandestine intelligence services of the two nations, albeit briefly.[30] The episode prompted Kissinger's famous comment that the allies were acting 'as if the alliance does not exist'. The damage was fairly quickly repaired. By 1976, with Labour once again in power, Kissinger reported himself working in his negotiations over Rhodesia 'from a British draft with British spelling even when I did not fully grasp the distinction between a working paper and a Cabinet-approved draft'.[31]

Still, recent episodes also suggest the more 'European' flavour to British policy. In the 1982 gas pipeline affair, for example, Margaret Thatcher's government was no less staunch than Paris or Bonn in rejecting the American demand that US sanctions against participation in the Soviet pipeline be applied also to European subsidiaries or license-holders of American firms.[32] Typically, perhaps, Britain escaped the brunt of the American opprobrium because it, unlike its continental counterparts, was regarded as reliable on other issues. As a footnote, however, it is worth remembering another pipeline dispute in the alliance, this one in 1962. On that occasion the Soviet pipeline was to carry oil, not gas, but, as two decades later, the United States pressed its European allies not to participate. The German government of Konrad Adenauer had its arm twisted by Washington, but the British position was the same then as Mrs Thatcher's twenty years later.[33]

In the case of the US Strategic Defense Initiative (SDI), Geoffrey Howe staked out the first and clearest 'European' view in his speech in March 1985. Characteristically for a British statesman, the speech was

[28] See, for example, David Owen's discussion of the 1973 instance in his 'Britain and the United States' in William E. Leuchtenburg and others, *Britain and the United States* (London, 1979), p. 74.

[29] Henry A. Kissinger, *Years of Upheaval* (Boston, 1982), p. 709.

[30] Reported in the *New York Times*, 12 Mar. 1979.

[31] Kissinger, 'Reflections on a Partnership', p. 577.

[32] For accounts of the pipeline case, see Angela Stent, *Soviet Energy and Western Europe*, The Washington Papers, 90 (Washington: Georgetown Center for Strategic and International Studies, 1982), pp. 60 ff.; and *NATO Today: The Alliance in Evolution*, Report to the Senate Committee on Foreign Relations, 97 Cong., 2 sess. (Ap. 1982), pp. 29 ff.

[33] Good sources on this earlier episode, similar in most particulars, are Angela Stent, *From Embargo to Ostpolitik: The Political Economy of West German–Soviet Relations 1955–1980* (Cambridge, 1981), pp. 98 ff.; and Robert W. Dean, *West German Trade with the East: The Political Dimension* (New York, 1974).

no broadside against SDI, but its content amounted to a devastating critique:[34] SDI would put too much reliance on technology that might be countered; its cost would rule out other defence improvements that might be more stabilizing; it would undermine arms control by feeding Soviet suspicions that the United States sought nuclear superiority and by threatening the Anti-Ballistic Missile Treaty of 1972; and it would damage alliance confidence by feeding fears that the nuclear balance was unstable and that the United States sought to retreat from its European commitment. For Howe, SDI might be a way to preserve NATO's defence 'into the next century', but it was far from the best way. When, in the autumn of 1985, London signed a formal agreement to permit British firms to participate in SDI research, that, too, was characteristic: Britain stayed close enough to Washington to hope to have influence, but it reversed neither British misgivings about SDI nor the fact that Britain had been out in front of the other Europeans in expressing those misgivings.

The British role in the SDI issue makes an interesting comparison to the attitude of another British government, this one a Labour government headed by James Callaghan, toward the enhanced radiation warheads (ERW), or 'neutron bombs', in 1977–8. Britain did not have any direct stake in ERW, since the system was intended for short-range nuclear launchers deployed only along the Central Front. But Callaghan was steadfast in support of the American position. Moreover, in 1977 the Callaghan government agreed to have the United States double (to 156) the number of its nuclear-capable long-range F-111 aircraft stationed in Britain. The planes simply arrived, and the subsequent announcement of their presence caused little public fuss.[35]

A GOOD THING OR NOT?

In the end, it is worth asking of the 'special' Anglo-American connection in the security realm not just 'Has it existed?' and 'Will it continue?' but also 'Has it been a good thing?' In an article prepared for the 1976 American Bicentennial but published posthumously, Alistair Buchan posed just that hard question that lies behind the fine language of 'Special Relationship':

Has this continuous and pervasive contact . . . damaged or strengthened the two countries? Has the one society been able to prevent the other from making serious mistakes or to contribute to its learning process? Have the two countries lured each other into needless adventures, inspired a false sense of confidence in

---

[34] Speech to the Royal United Services Institute, London, 15 Mar. 1985. See also David S. Yost, 'European Anxieties about Ballistic Missile Defense', *Washington Quarterly*, 7.4 (1984), 7–19.

[35] See Freedman, *Britain and Nuclear Weapons*, p. 125.

each other, distorted the other's perspective; or has the relationship been as benign as much Bicentennial oratory will no doubt maintain?[36]

Our answer, from an American perspective, to the hard question is affirmative. The sense of political company in what has remained 'special' about the relationship in defence has not, to be sure, been an unalloyed blessing. The two allies have at times reinforced each other's delusions, and the pleasure of the status quo may have reinforced the temptation of each not to adapt to changed circumstances. Yet that sense of company has been valuable in two senses. For American officials, it has provided both advice and understanding. It is not the old saw about Britain playing Greece to America's Rome: rather, it is a sense of company in a confusing, unfriendly world.

For citizens, not officials, the connection with Britain has also served to diminish the sense of being alone in a hostile world. It goes without saying that the kind of deep American engagement abroad of the post-war period is unusual in American experience and unpleasant. The Anglo-American link at least has served to check the temptation to disengage from Europe.

A British view might be different, as Buchan hinted his might have been.[37] For both Americans and Britons the answer depends on what the alternatives are, and how realistic. In retrospect, it is easy to argue that British interests, and probably American ones as well, would have been better served in the realm of defence as well as others had Britain opted earlier and more firmly into Europe. It is also easy to argue that the tug of the 'Special Relationship' was one reason why it did not do so. Yet it is much harder to argue that the tug was *decisive* in determining British actions.

By the same token, Britain and Europe, and also America, might be better served over the long run if Britain took the lead in constructing new European defence arrangements much less dependent on the United States. That, however, does not seem in the cards. Britain's capabilities no longer give it easy claim to such a role. A Britain shorn of the 'Special Relationship' in ways that can be imagined—for instance through an electoral victory by an unreconstructed Labour Party—would be more inward-looking and less European, in the short run at least.

More likely, for the foreseeable future there will remain something special about the Anglo-American relationship in the realm of defence.

[36] 'Mothers and Daughters (Or Greeks and Romans)', *Foreign Affairs*, 54.4 (1976), 645.

[37] A notable example is Edmonds, cited above. The argument that the 'Special Relationship' inhibited British adjustment to changed circumstances has been made at various times throughout the post-war period. See, for example, Coral Bell, 'The Special Relationship', in Michael Leifer, ed., *Constraints and Adjustments in British Foreign Policy* (London 1972), p. 103.

Even as Britain becomes more 'European', officials in both Britain and the United States will have specific reasons for sustaining special connections across the Atlantic. Those links will continue to rest on history and shared culture. They will persist through episodes of tension between London and Washington. They will have some costs, for both Britain and America. Yet, on balance, both nations, and especially the United States, will be served by them. So, too, will the broader North Atlantic alliance of which both are a part.

ECONOMIC

11

Sterling–Dollar Diplomacy in Current Perspective

RICHARD N. GARDNER

In Washington Lord Halifax
Once whispered to Lord Keynes:
It's true *they* have the money bags
But *we* have all the brains.

THIS mischievous bit of poetry, written on a yellowing piece of paper left over from the first Anglo-American discussions on the post-war monetary system, stirs memories of one of the great adventures of economic diplomacy in our time. It recalls an effort of creative statesmanship that has seldom been equalled—an effort to construct an international economic order capable of serving the two overriding goals of world peace and the general welfare of nations.

LOOKING BACKWARD: A 'POLITICAL MIRACLE'[1]

From a current perspective, perhaps the most remarkable thing about the birth of the Bretton Woods–GATT (General Agreement on Tariffs and Trade) system was that it was essentially an Anglo-American enterprise. The basic outlines of these institutions were negotiated during the Second World War between the United States and the United Kingdom. The other industrialized countries that today are central players in the game of economic diplomacy were either enemy countries or under enemy occupation. Most of today's developing nations had not achieved independence; those that were already independent played but a small part and only in the final stages of the negotiations (somewhat greater in GATT than for the Bretton Woods institutions). Never before in history—and surely never again—could

---

[1] What follows in this section is a brief distillation of a history set out at length in Gardner, *Sterling–Dollar Diplomacy*, first published in 1956 by the Oxford University Press and republished in 1980 by the Columbia University Press.

an economic order for the world be designed by Britain and the United States alone.

This act of creative statesmanship was the work of a small handful of men in the two countries. Roosevelt and Churchill gave broad political direction to their efforts, but the two leaders were preoccupied with winning the war. The work on the post-war economic system was done by a combination of officials at Cabinet and sub-Cabinet level, by career civil servants, and by distinguished persons seconded from universities for wartime service. The key figures in the Bretton Woods negotiations, of course, were John Maynard Keynes and Harry Dexter White, but the post-war trade and financial institutions were also shaped, on the British side, by men like James Meade, Lionel Robbins, Dennis Robertson, Richard Hopkins, Sir Percivale Liesching, Richard Law, Sir Kingsley Wood, and Sir John Anderson, and on the American side by Cordell Hull, Dean Acheson, Henry Morgenthau, Edward Bernstein, Ansel Luxford, Will Clayton, Harry Hawkins, Winthrop Brown, and Willard Thorp.

It was a relatively small group of men united by a common commitment to practical and constructive internationalism. They conceived of a post-war economic system ruled by law. They wanted it to be a universal system, if possible, including the Soviet Union and Communist countries, but failing that at least a single multilateral system including everyone else, rather than a collection of trading blocs. They wanted permanent international institutions to promote co-operation on monetary, trade, and development problems.

The post-war international economic system created by these men is today in deep crisis. Some of its key elements, such as the system of fixed but adjustable parities, have already been swept away. Other elements, such as the most-favoured-nation principle, are eroding rapidly. In the forty years since the system was born we have discovered fundamental flaws in the original design; and radically altered political and economic circumstances have required major adaptations. Still more changes will be required if the system is to take us safely into the twenty-first century.

Still, before examining the shortcomings of the international institutions created by the 'founding fathers', we ought to acknowledge what their handiwork did make possible. In the first twenty-five years after the war, in the years 1945–70, we had a quarter century of the most dramatic and widely shared economic growth in the history of mankind. World GNP grew in those twenty-five years from $300 billion to about $2,000 billion. World trade grew from $30 billion to over $300 billion. Even allowing for inflation we are talking about a growth of real income of about three times, and a growth of world trade of over four times. The post-war institutions, supplemented by another act of creative statesmanship, the Marshall Plan, made possible an unprecedented period of export-led growth for Europe, North America, Japan, and even for much of the developing world. Although it is often forgotten, the fact is that in the 1950s and 1960s the developing countries as a whole had a faster rate of economic growth than the developed countries, and thus shared very considerably in the benefits of the system.

Although the economic record since 1970 for both developed and developing countries is far less positive, the fault is surely to be found more with the policies of national governments than with the deficiencies of the international agencies. Moreover, it is hard to imagine how we would cope with today's problems—containing protectionist pressures, coping with international indebtedness, and mobilizing resources for economic development—without the international institutions created after the last war.

So the 'founding fathers' must have done something right. I would go so far as to decribe what they achieved as a 'political miracle', because the post-war system they bequeathed to us was in very considerable degree created against the prevailing currents of the time in the United States and Britain. In both countries a large part of the financial, industrial, political, and journalistic establishments were against what they were trying to do. The big problem for the 'founding fathers' on both sides of the Atlantic was not one of resolving divergent economic theories but rather one of coping with divergent political realities in the United Kingdom and the United States in such a way as to accomplish what they were trying to do. Today, when political realities impose severe constraints on new efforts of constructive internationalism, it is worth recalling for a moment how great the obstacles were for our leaders forty years ago.

On the British side, there was deep scepticism throughout the Establishment that a system based on open multilateral trade would be in Britain's interests. The Federation of British Industries and the London Chamber of Commerce were hostile. Many felt that the wave of the future was barter trade, managed markets, discriminatory arrangements, currency controls. Many believed that the United States was destined to go into a deep depression after the war, dragging Britain into the abyss and destroying Britain's post-war commitments to the welfare state and full employment. To these people it was folly to be so closely linked with the United States in an international system based on liberal economic principles. There were also doubts that Britain's post-war balance of payments would be strong enough to permit it to operate successfully without exchange and trade controls. And, of course, there were those on the right who wanted to make Imperial Preference and the sterling area the basis for a post-war order.

Those two pillars of Establishment opinion in Britain, *The Economist* and *The Times*, looked at the post-war planning with deep misgiving. As *The Times* put it:

We must . . . reconcile ourselves once and for all to the view that the days of *laissez-faire* and the unlimited division of labour are over; that every country— including Great Britain—plans and organises its production in the light of social and military needs, and that the regulation of this production by such 'trade barriers' as tariffs, quotas, and subsidies is a necessary and integral part of this policy.[2]

One Member of Parliament warned that acceptance of the American post-war monetary proposals 'will be the end. The end of all our hopes of an expansionist policy, and of social advance. It will be the end of the Beveridge Plan, of improved education, of housing reconstruction, the end of the new Britain we are fighting to rebuild. It will lead again to world depression, to chaos, and, ultimately, to war.'[3]

The United States Ambassador to Britain, John Winant, cabled Washington in 1944 that 'a majority of the directors of the Bank of England are opposed to the Bretton Woods program . . . It is argued by those in opposition that if the plan is adopted financial control will leave London and sterling exchange will be replaced by dollar exchange.'[4]

A leading financial journalist said that in the view of many MPs he had talked to 'it would be preferable to have two international systems, a dollar bloc and a sterling bloc. It is argued that conditions, interests, and mentality within the two groups differ fundamentally, and that for this reason any attempt to lump them together is foredoomed to failure.'[5]

One of the things that inflamed British opinion was the American emphasis on non-discrimination, the insistence that Imperial Preference would have to be eliminated. Lord Croft described this demand as the 'Boston Tea Party in reverse', and an 'interference with the freedom of our own country to manage its affairs that I regard as unparalleled in the history of the world'.[6] On the other end of the political spectrum, Lord Lindsay of Birker was no less incensed: 'When I heard Americans making snooty remarks about that poor little preference of ours, I thought it was the limit, and I still think so.'[7] One MP rose in the House of Commons and solemnly declared: 'If the Government tries to eliminate Empire Preference a number of us will conduct such a nationwide campaign in this country as will light the very beacons on

---

[2] *The Times*, 11 Jan. 1941.

[3] Robert Boothby, 389 H.C. Deb. 702, 12 May 1943.

[4] Telegram from Winant to the Secretary of State, 12 Apr. 1944, included in the Private Papers of Harry Dexter White.

[5] Paul Einzig, *Financial News*, 12 May 1943.

[6] 138 H.L. Deb. 754, 17 Dec. 1945.

[7] Ibid., cols. 838–9.

the hills. We will attack them in the market place, in the towns and the cities, we will rouse this whole country against them in such a crusade as will overcome this Government, because we will not have it.'[8]

The post-war economic plans had no smoother reception on the American side. The *Wall Street Journal* called the Keynes plan 'a machine for the regimentation of the world'.[9] The *New York Times* considered the Bretton Woods propoals unnecessary—it favoured going back to the gold standard, 'the most satisfactory international standard that has ever been devised'.[10] The American Bankers Association said, 'a system of quotas or shares in a pool which gives debtor countries the impression that they have a right to credits up to some amount is unsound in principle, and raises hopes that cannot be realized'.[11] The Guaranty Trust Company, progenitor of the Morgan Guaranty, called both the British and American plans for Bretton Woods 'dangerous' on the grounds that they would 'enable nations to buy merchandise without being able to pay for it'.[12] Senator Robert Taft, leader of the right wing of the Republican Party, denounced the Bretton Woods agreements with the charge that the United States was 'putting all the valuable money into the Fund', and would be 'pouring money down a rat-hole'.[13] A Senator from Utah rose in indignation on the floor of the Senate, brandished a fistful of foreign currencies, and defied any one of his colleagues to 'go downtown in Washington and get his shoes shined with this whole bunch of bills'.[14] And, again, the American Bankers Association objected to the IMF because 'we should be handing over to an international body the power to determine the destination, time, and use of our money', abandoning, without receiving anything in return, a vital part of American bargaining power.[15]

The post-war trade arrangements were also bitterly opposed by many in the United States. In their final form, free traders found them too protectionist and protectionists found them too liberal. When the International Trade Organization was completed in 1948, the US Congress wanted no part of it. The National Foreign Trade Council, the National Association of Manufacturers, and the US Chamber of Commerce were strongly against it. Even GATT, which survived the demise of the ITO as a multilateral trade agreement, lived for years in a kind of political limbo. The Congress was so sceptical of being restrained

---

[8] Beverly Baxter, 425 H.C. Deb. 1639, 19 July 1946.

[9] *Wall Street Journal*, 30 Mar. 1943.

[10] *New York Times*, 30 Mar. 1943.

[11] A.B.A., *The Place of the United States in the Post-war Economy*, Sept. 1943, pp. 14–15.

[12] *The Guaranty Survey*, 23 (1943), p. 4.

[13] 91 *Cong. Rec.* 7573, 16 July 1945.

[14] Senator Elbert Thomas, ibid.

[15] A.B.A., *Practical International Financial Organization*, 1 Feb. 1945.

in the use of its tariff and other foreign commerce powers that in successive renewals of the trade agreements programme it inserted a clause stating that renewal of the legislation 'shall constitute neither approval nor disapproval' of GATT.

It is in the light of such attitudes in the two countries that the creation of the post-war institutions deserves to be called a 'political miracle'. The 'miracle' was only possible because it was accomplished at the end of a war, when public opinion could be mobilized in the hopeful enterprise of building a better world, and because both countries were led by men of vision, surrounded by dedicated internationalists of great intellectual ability. We may well ask ourselves how we can create the conditions for a similar 'miracle' as we face the task of future institutional adjustment without a war in a world where a consensus must be sought among dozens of countries, not just between the United States and Britain.

RESOLVING THREE DILEMMAS— YESTERDAY, TODAY, AND TOMORROW

Anglo-American efforts to create and maintain a co-operative international economic order during the last two generations have sought to grapple with three major dilemmas, none of which has yet been satisfactorily resolved: (1) how to organize an international monetary system reconciling the desire for international stability and the desire for national autonomy; (2) how to organize a reasonably free and non-discriminatory world trading system in which the gains from trade could be realized together with high levels of employment and growth; and (3) how to promote the economic growth of developing countries through adequate capital flows and appropriate policies from the developing countries themselves.

The remainder of this paper looks briefly at how British and American thinking on these questions has evolved since the wartime planning for a post-war economic order. The author's own views on these difficult matters are set forth at more length in a report of the Aspen Institute.[16]

The monetary dilemma

In their early thinking about the post-war monetary order, the British and American governments had a supranational design. The post-war planners saw fluctuating and misaligned exchange rates, completely free capital movements, and completely autonomous national monetary and fiscal policies as incompatible with an open trading system and the

[16] William Eberle, Richard Gardner, and Ann Crittenden, *The Next Four Years: The United States and the World Economy* (Washington 1984).

achievement of high levels of employment and growth. They wanted collective intergovernmental management of the quantum of international liquidity, of international capital flows, and of exchange rates and national adjustment policies. The following statement by the Chancellor of the Exchequer eloquently summarized the original concept shared by both Keynes and White:

We want an orderly and agreed method of determining the value of national currency units, to eliminate unilateral action and the danger which it involves that each nation will seek to restore its competitive position by exchange depreciation. Above all, we want to free the international monetary system from those arbitrary, unpredictable and undesirable influences which have operated in the past as a result of large-scale speculative movements of capital. We want to secure an economic policy agreed between the nations and an international monetary system which will be the instrument of that policy. This means that if any one Government were tempted to move too far either in an inflationary or deflationary direction, it would be subject to the check of consultations with the other Governments, and it would be part of the agreed policy to take measures for correcting tendencies to dis-equilibrium in the balance of payments of each separate country.[17]

But the collective intergovernmental management of money envisaged in the early post-war planning proved impossible to realize. The ambitious Keynes Plan for overdraft facilities in a Clearing Union was set aside for White's more modest conception of a system based on gold and IMF drawing rights. In the post-war world of rapidly growing trade and inflation, neither gold nor IMF quotas could provide sufficient international reserves. The world thus ended up on a dollar standard, in which the quantum of international reserves was determined mainly by the balance of payments deficits of the United States, which is certainly not what Keynes or White or the other post-war planners had in mind.

The creation of Special Drawing Rights in the first amendment of the Fund Articles at the end of the 1960s was meant to signal a return to a truly international reserve system. Yet this has not worked out either. SDRs represent only a tiny fraction of world liquidity today, and although some developing countries continue to press for SDR issues as a form of development aid or as a means of improving the distribution of world liquidity, neither Britain nor the United States, nor any major developed country, now favours moving toward an international reserve system based on SDRs. The idea of a limited form of reserve consolidation, with national holdings of dollars being placed in the Fund in exchange for SDRs, proved non-negotiable during the Carter Administration and has been set aside indefinitely. The interest in London and Washington today is no longer in the collective manage-

[17] Sir Kingsley Wood, 386 H.C. Deb. 826, 2 Feb. 1943.

ment of liquidity but in a more modest and achievable objective—the gradual movement toward a multi-currency reserve system in which the yen, the mark, and perhaps eventually a European currency unit can join the dollar as international reserve assets. Whether such a multi-currency reserve system can be managed to assure the stable growth of international liquidity sought at Bretton Woods is an open question.

The original ideas of the 'founding fathers' for collective international monetary management proved no more feasible for capital movements than for liquidity creation. The IMF articles approved at Bretton Woods provided for freedom from exchange controls only on current transactions; significantly, the post-war planners envisaged that countries would need the latitude (and, in extreme cases, should be required) to control disequilibriating movements of short-term capital. In both London and Washington in those days there was a strong belief that governments would have to protect the system against the uncontrolled activities of private bankers. Secretary of the Treasury Henry Morgenthau went so far as to describe the purpose of the Bretton Woods Conference as 'to drive the usurious money lenders from the temple of international finance'.[18]

It is precisely here, of course, that the world of today contrasts most dramatically with the world envisaged at Bretton Woods. The 'money lenders' are still with us. We have developed a highly sophisticated, twenty-four hours a day, global capital market, which facilitates instantaneous transfers of funds on a scale that the 'founding fathers' could not have imagined. We are now in a world in which capital flows have displaced trade flows as the principal determinant of currency relations; some $20 to $30 trillion in capital now moves through the foreign exchange markets each year compared with about $2 trillion in annual trade in goods and services. As the post-war world evolved, both the British and the American governments came to attach a high priority to freedom from controls on capital as well as current transactions. Moreover, few people have much confidence that international capital movements could be effectively limited, even if we wanted to do so.

All of this brings us to the last respect in which the original design for international monetary management proved inoperable: the international adjustment process. The post-war monetary order was to be based on fixed exchange rates, which could be adjusted to correct a 'fundamental disequilibrium' through a process of international consultation and agreement. In their original versions, the American and

[18] Address of Morgenthau at the final session of the Bretton Woods Conference, 22 July 1944, in US Department of State, *Proceedings and Documents of the United Nations Monetary and Financial Conference, Bretton Woods, New Hampshire, 1–22 July 1944* (Washington 1948), vol. ii, p. 1227.

British currency plans envisaged that such a regime would be made possible by far-reaching international control over the economic policies of deficit and surplus countries.[19] But in the course of the negotiations leading to Bretton Woods it proved impossible for the British and the American negotiators to agree on the appropriate balance between deficit and surplus country responsibilities; references to international oversight of domestic economic policies were watered down to facilitate approval of the IMF by Parliament and Congress. By the time of the Bretton Woods conference and its aftermath, national autonomy was being emphasized instead of supranationality. Keynes went so far as to assure the House of Lords that, under the IMF, the external value of sterling 'would be altered if necessary so as to conform to whatever de facto internal value results from domestic policies, which themselves shall be immune from criticism from the Fund'.[20]

So we went full circle from international oversight to national autonomy while still committed to the maintenance of fixed exchange rates. The IMF became a kind of do-it-yourself kit with rather defective instructions. The system might have functioned if countries could have been relied on to manage their affairs voluntarily with due regard for the requirements of international adjustment in a regime of stable currency relationships. This was to prove an impossible dream. The two great English-speaking democracies themselves set no good example. In the first post-war decade, Britain tried at one and the same time to run a welfare state, maintain a world currency, and continue a world military role, leading both to sterling devaluation and to sluggish domestic growth. More serious for the international system, the United States, in the 1960s, overreached its resources just as Britain had done, refusing to trim the Great Society in the face of the Vietnam War; it thus inaugurated an era of high inflation and huge United States balance of payments deficits, leading to the collapse of the system of fixed currency relations in 1971.

---

[19] Under the first (unpublished) draft of the White Plan, members were obliged 'not to adopt any monetary banking measure promoting either serious inflation or serious deflation without the consent of a majority of member votes of the Fund'. The published version omitted this far-reaching (and politically unrealistic) provision, but authorized the Fund to make recommendations for changes in the economic policy of countries going too far toward deficit or surplus. Moreover, recommendations could be reinforced by sanctions—the denial of the use of Fund resources beyond a certain point for a deficit country, the rationing of the 'scarce currency' in the case of a country in surplus. Under the Keynes plan, the Clearing Union could require a deficit country that drew more than half of its overdraft facilities to deposit collateral, depreciate its currency, control outward capital movements, or surrender liquid reserves in reduction of its debit balance. It could recommend to that country internal economic measures needed to restore equilibrium. It could require a surplus country whose credit balance exceeded half its quota to carry out such measures as the stimulation of domestic demand, the appreciation of its currency, the reduction of import barriers, and the making of international development loans.

[20] 131 H.L. Deb. 845, 23 May, 1944.

Today, the original concept of international oversight of domestic policies exists only in relation to the developing countries, which must seek IMF approval for their adjustment programmes as the price of access to the Fund resources and Fund-approved restructuring of their external debt. For the developed countries, there is no international adjustment process worthy of the name.

The United States trade deficit, $123 billion in 1984, was expected to reach $150 billion in 1985. The richest country in the world is now in the anomalous position of borrowing $100 billion a year from foreigners and has become a net debtor nation for the first time since 1914. The dollar has appreciated 50 per cent on a trade-weighted basis since 1980; it is estimated that the existing dollar exchange rate, if uncorrected, could produce United States current account deficits in excess of $300 billion a year by 1990.[21]

Transatlantic relations are once again troubled by arguments about surplus and deficit country responsibilities. Europe asks the United States to 'put its house in order' by reducing its budget deficits; the United States asks Europe to 'put its house in order' by removing structural rigidities, particularly in labour markets, and by creating an environment in which capital will stay in Europe rather than flow to the United States.

As we enter the second half of the 1980s, the idea of collective international management of money in any of the three respects envisaged by the 'founding fathers'—liquidity, capital movements, exchange rates and adjustment—is rejected in both London and Washington. Indeed, it is doubtful if Margaret Thatcher or Ronald Reagan would have signed the Bretton Woods agreements even in their watered-down form, had they been in office at the time. The emphasis in both countries is on free markets and freedom to pursue domestic agendas through monetary and fiscal policies not influenced significantly by international considerations.[22] Yet the old dilemma on the minds of the 'founding fathers' remains—if you don't manage money, at least in some degree, won't you have to manage trade? With a dollar overvalued by at least 20–30 per cent in trade terms, the Reagan Administration has increasingly compromised its free trade principles; pressures have been rising in Congress for an across-the-board import surcharge as a quick answer to United States fiscal and trade deficits.

With the increased interdependence which exists today, including the high degree of capital mobility among nations unforeseen at Bretton

[21] C. Fred Bergsten, Testimony before the Subcommittee on International Economic Policy and Trade of the House Foreign Affairs Committee, 5 Mar. 1985.

[22] There are still nuances of difference between London and Washington, even today. The Bank of England joined in the co-ordinated intervention of European central banks to check the rise of the dollar in early 1985. Washington largely abstained.

Woods, it is even more essential that countries adjust their domestic economic policies with a view to maintaining a mutually beneficial world economic system. It is simply impossible to have complete national policy autonomy and maintain an open international system of trade and capital flows. If we wish to preserve the latter we shall have to accept some limitation on the former. It is therefore appropriate that both the United States and Britain are participating in the current effort of the Group of Ten to see if some meaningful process of IMF consultation on domestic as well as international policies could bring greater order and rationality into currency relationships. Were Keynes and White still with us, no doubt they would approve.

The trade dilemma

The post-war Anglo-American design for a reasonably free and non-discriminatory world trading system has survived rather better than the original design for a post-war monetary system. Successive rounds of tariff negotiations have brought the average height of tariffs in the industrialized countries of North America, Europe, and Japan down to about 4 per cent. The post-war aim of establishing transparency, stability, and non-discrimination in the use of trade restrictions was at least partially achieved through the General Agreement on Tariffs and Trade, at least for much of the trade of the industrialized democracies. Without GATT, the post-war record of export-led growth would not have been possible. But today, the trading system is under unprecedented stress; indeed, it is rapidly eroding barely forty years after it was first created.

Some of today's problems might have been avoided had the International Trade Organization been set up alongside the Bretton Woods institutions, as originally intended. GATT had a weak institutional underpinning, and the failure to create an ITO provided the excuse for the creation of the United Nations Conference on Trade and Development (UNCTAD), an organization that has worked against the concepts of trade freedom favoured over the years by the United States and Britain. GATT lacks a small and efficient decision-making body of key countries. Its provisional status at the outset encouraged frequent deviations from its rules. There was, and still is, no adequate system to settle trade disputes and assure compliance.

A more fundamental weakness, perhaps, was the narrowness of GATT's original focus. For domestic political reasons, both the British and American governments did not want agricultural protectionism subjected to the same limitations as protectionism on industrial products. Today, both countries are fighting an uphill battle to assert their interests against the negative effects of the European Community's

Common Agricultural Policy. GATT did little at the outset to limit non-tariff barriers. The Tokyo Round codes have helped to correct this shortcoming, but in some cases, as in the subsidies code, the vagueness of the provisions and the limited number of participating countries makes for continuing difficulties. Trade in services and trade-distorting foreign investment requirements have never been covered by GATT. The British and American desire to include these subjects in its new trade round is encountering resistance from developing countries. Finally, GATT focused mainly on barriers to trade constructed at the border; but in today's world a host of domestic government interventions, often called 'industrial policies', can be an equally serious cause of trade distortions.

A major issue in the negotiation of GATT was how to reconcile the principle of non-discrimination with the principle of regional and other special trade arrangements like Imperial Preference. The formation of the European Community, Britain's subsequent entry, the Community's special trade arrangements with Mediterranean and African countries, the current enlargement of the Community to include Spain, Portugal, and Greece—all these steps have served to diminish the benefits of the most-favoured-nation treatment for non-Community members like the United States. The establishment of other regional groupings and of the Generalized System of Preferences further eroded the principle of non-discrimination. Today, for the first time since GATT was created, the United States has begun, perhaps understandably, to look to bilateral and regional arrangements of its own—the Caribbean Basin initiative, the Free Trade Area with Israel, and now discussions with Canada on sectoral free trade. Britain, whose preferential trade arrangements were once the object of American hostility, now feels concern as the United States starts fashioning less than multilateral trade arrangements of its own. We may well be heading for the very regional blocs and Balkanized trading system that the post-war trade plans were supposed to avoid.

Both the British and American governments agreed at the birth of the GATT system on the 'escape clause' principle embodied in GATT Article XIX, permitting temporary derogations from GATT commitments to deal with an increase of imports causing injury to a domestic industry. But as originally conceived, such safeguard measures were to be temporarily applied on a non-discriminatory basis, and with compensation to the affected countries. Instead, we have witnessed the growth of voluntary export restraints, orderly marketing agreements, and other managed trade agreements covering steel, cars, textiles, footwear, and consumer electronics, all undertaken outside the GATT rules. If we take the GATT concept seriously these grey-area arrangements should, at a minimum, be brought into the GATT, and subjected to a process of multilateral discussion and surveillance.

Can the multilateral system be preserved and extended in the face of these and other challenges to its existence? Both the British and American governments have reiterated their commitment to the system and to a new GATT round. A report of a GATT expert group published in 1985 has offered useful recommendations. Yet the economic and political climate is not a favourable one. Britain and the United States no longer have the power they once had to move the world forward to freer and fairer trade arrangements. Challenged first by Germany, then by Japan, and now by the newly industrializing countries, the two great English-speaking democracies have seen a steady decline in their international competitive positions. Both know what trade concessions they seek from others, but both are severely limited in their capacity to offer new trade concessions of their own—Britain, by its high (13 per cent) levels of unemployment, the United States by its overvalued currency, huge trade deficit, and rising protectionist sentiment. The declining capacity of the United States and Britain to exercise trade leadership casts doubts on the capacity of the GATT system to overcome its past problems, much less cope effectively with its new ones.

The development dilemma

A third dilemma that has preoccupied Britain and the United States for most of the post-war period has been how to assist the development of the less developed countries, both through technical aid and capital flows and through encouraging better economic policies in the developing countries themselves. This was not recognized as a major issue in the post-war planning over forty years ago. When, on the eve of Bretton Woods, the negotiators finally focused on the World Bank, they were in a conservative mood—the British did not expect to be beneficiaries, the Americans were afraid of the Congress. The Bank's lending capacity was limited almost entirely to what it could raise by bonds issued on the private capital market. There was simply no conception of the vast needs of the less developed countries and of the role the Bank should play in meeting them. Indeed, the Bank was conceived mainly as an institution for reconstruction. Incredible as it seems today, the word 'development' did not even appear in Harry White's first draft circulated within the United States Treasury Department.

We have come a long way since then. The enormous growth of World Bank lending to developing countries; the creation of its concessional aid affiliate, the International Development Association; the establishment of Regional Development Banks for Latin America, Asia, and Africa; the stimulation of increased and better co-ordinated bilateral aid efforts through the Development Assistance Committee of the Organization for Economic Co-operation and Development (OECD); the new role of the International Monetary Fund in coping with the debt crisis; the growth of multilateral technical assistance from the UN Specialized Agencies; and the establishment of the UN Development Programme, the UN Fund for Population Activities, the UN Environmental Programme—all this adds up to something unprecedented in human history, a massive effort of international co-operation in support of economic development.

To draw an adequate balance sheet in just a few pages on more than a generation of effort in such a vast area is impossible, but perhaps a few brief observations are worth making.

First, despite the best efforts of the Bank, the Fund, and bilateral aid donors, and with the exception of a few success stories like Taiwan, Korea, and more recently India and China, the performance of the developing countries in helping themselves to self-sustaining growth has been disappointing. If present trends continue in sub-Saharan Africa, according to the World Bank, per capita income in the year 2000 will fall below the level of 1960. In the final analysis, the developing countries' futures will depend upon their own policies. As Paul Hoffman remarked at the beginning of the Marshall Plan, 'only the Europeans can save Europe'. The developing countries must get their own economic houses in order, and only their own commitment to wealth-creating strategies, to incentives for industry and agriculture, to realistic foreign exchange and interest rates, to better managed public projects, to less corrupt and more responsive bureaucracies, to limiting population growth, can assure them a decent future—no matter what the United States, Britain, and the industrialized countries do. How to create incentives and institutions to assist the developing countries to do these things remains a major challenge for the international community.

Second, the developed countries have not done enough to provide the capital flows which the developing countries require to meet minimum development goals. The debt crisis which afflicts so many developing countries, particularly in Latin America, is partly the result of excessive reliance during the 1970s on commercial bank lending at variable market-related interest rates instead of official transfers accompanied by conditionality. If the debtor nations are to service their indebtedness, even with the help of debt restructuring, and achieve adequate export and income growth, their current debt, according to World Bank estimates, will have to grow by about $4\frac{1}{2}$ to 5 per cent a year for the foreseeable future. Given the reluctance of private borrowers to increase their exposure indefinitely, this additional $40 billion or more per year will have to come in large part from official transfers, mainly at market rates, but with a certain amount of concessional aid for low-income countries. Yet official development assistance in Britain and the United States is now down to 0.35 and 0.25 per cent of GNP, respectively; both countries recently refused to contribute to the World Bank's special fund for Africa; and neither the Reagan Administration nor the United States Congress have been enthusiastic about supporting substantial increases in the resources of the IMF, the World Bank, or the IDA. Without a change in US attitudes, it is hard to see where the money needed for development is going to come from.

Third, not nearly enough has been done to expand private investment in developing countries and to enlarge Less Developed Countries' (LDC's) exports. Much of the responsibility for these failures rests with the developing countries themselves, whose trade policies have often favoured import substitution instead of export-led growth, and whose hostility to private investment has driven their capital overseas while deterring foreign investment. Now there is welcome evidence, at least in some developing countries, of a new receptivity to market-related growth strategies. A multilateral programme of investment insurance and other initiatives to move from debt to equity financing would thus be timely. But the most difficult part of the development dilemma may rest with the United States, Britain, and other developed countries: are they prepared to maintain the open trade policies that will permit an export-led growth solution for developing countries to succeed? As Prime Minister Thatcher reminded us in her eloquent speech to the Congress on 20 February 1985, 'The developing countries need our markets, as we need theirs. We cannot preach adjustment to them, and refuse to practise it at home.'

A HOPEFUL CONCLUSION?

Looking backward over forty years of history, we can be grateful that, with all their mistakes, the British and American 'founding fathers' created international institutions like the Fund, the Bank, and the GATT, without whose assistance we could not even imagine the solution of our present problems. What we need now is surely not 'a new Bretton Woods conference', for there is no international consensus on how to revise the existing institutions and certainly none on the creation of new ones. The task ahead is less dramatic but no less important: the intelligent evolution and adaptation of the institutions we have through a greater commitment of the major countries, particularly the United States, to the constructive internationalism that animated the post-war planning of two generations ago.

Is this still possible? Many non-Americans, normally sympathetic to the United States, are beginning to have their doubts. The following comments, the first from a Canadian, the second from a German, are worth pondering:

Forty years ago the key initiators of Bretton Woods were the United States and Great Britain. Unfortunately, the current leadership in the Western world, particularly in the United States, is apparently not in the mood for such multilateral initiatives. Indeed, it is not entirely clear that the directions the Reagan administration would set for such a negotiation process, if it were to be involved, would be those that many others would care to follow. Recent U.S. positions on the Law of the Sea treaty, East–West trade, the management of exchange rates, the replenishment of the International Development Association, and the appropriate size and character of World Bank and IMF activities—not to mention its continuing disregard of the international effects of U.S. domestic macroeconomic policies—are profoundly antithetical to the views of the majority of America's own increasingly distressed and embarassed allies.[23]

There was a time when America was a super-power in the true sense: confident not only in its own strength but also in the ability to build, together with others, a world of shared duties and rights, and ready to carry the major burden in this enterprise. None of today's international organizations would have been created without this American readiness. . . . The sad truth is that America has given up the traditions it established after World War II, apparently not only without regrets but with a sigh of relief. Rather than accept the challenge of formulating an international order that promises co-operation and stability for the 1990s, America prefers to pursue its interests alone.[24]

Among Americans there may be some who consider such judgements overstated or unfair. But surely all Americans have an obligation to rethink the direction of United States policy, for constructive leadership in support of a co-operative international economic order will be required of the United States in the future no less than it was required over forty years ago.

[23] G. K. Helleiner, Professor of Economics, University of Toronto, and Chairman of the Commonwealth Study Group, in 'An Agenda for a new Bretton Woods', in *World Policy* (Winter, 1984).
[24] Christoph Bertram, Political Editor of *Die Zeit*, in the *Washington Post*, 25 Nov. 1984.

12

Europe, Britain, and the United States in the World Economy

STEPHEN MARRIS

THE election of Mrs Thatcher in 1979 and Ronald Reagan in 1980 marked the culmination of a radical change in attitudes to the management of the world economy—not only in Britain and America, but also in Germany and Japan, and thus in the heartland of the industrial democracies. The basic tenet of this new attitude is: 'If each country puts its own economic house in order, the world will look after itself.' In other words the world economy should not be 'managed'; it should be left to the free play of market forces.[1]

In 1986, the world economy will be entering the fourth year of a recovery combining a reasonable rate of growth with a much improved inflation record. The debt crisis appears to be receding. And there is a growing sense—particularly in America—that the worst may now be behind us; that we are headed for a new era of sustained recovery that will be a major improvement over the disappointing 1970s.

This chapter is intended to provide the basis for discussion of a number of issues arising from the current situation. First, should we conclude that the new Thatcher–Reagan economic philosophy has proved itself, and that all that is needed is to consolidate and build on it? Or, alternatively, are we living in a temporary fool's paradise? If so, does this mean that, without a return to more explicit co-operative efforts to manage the world economy, we are headed towards a new crisis and a new world-wide recession? And, for those who take the second view, what could or should be done about it?

THE INTERNATIONAL RAMIFICATIONS OF THATCHERISM AND REAGANOMICS

It may be helpful to start by summarizing the main elements of the

---

[1] I have analysed the origin and nature of this remarkable change in conventional wisdom at more length in *Managing the World Economy: Will We Ever Learn?* Princeton Essays in International Finance, 155 (Nov. 1984).

Thatcher–Reagan economic philosophy, especially as it relates to international economic affairs. In doing so, it should be noted that in important respects the change in international philosophy can be regarded as simply the by-product of the change in domestic economic philosophy.

Domestic policies

The starting point for the changed domestic economic philosophy was a common diagnosis. Growth had withered because of the adverse effects of big government on incentives to work, save, and invest. Inflation was accelerating because central banks were printing too much money. The answer was to cut marginal tax rates and the disincentives to work and savings built into the social welfare system, to encourage investment through deregulation, tax incentives, and a tough line against the unions, and to adhere to fixed and declining targets for the rate of growth of the money supply.

There have, of course, been important differences in the application of these common principles. Both Mrs Thatcher and Mr Reagan found it easier to cut marginal tax rates than to reform and cut back on the welfare state. But, whereas the Thatcher government responded by postponing further tax cuts and and raising more revenue, President Reagan stuck tenaciously to the view that the only way to reduce expenditures is to refuse to raise the necessary revenue. In the event, both countries' fiscal policies have been 'anti-Keynesian'—but in diametrically opposite directions. Thatcher, in 1980–2, took action to reduce the structural budget deficit by several percentage points in the middle of a deep recession. Reagan, in 1983–4, accepted a rise in the structural budget deficit of similar magnitude in the middle of an unusually strong cyclical upswing.

On the monetary side, American policy has been more consistently monetarist—although this has been the work of Paul Volcker and has at times had a mixed reception in the White House. In Britain, after a strong monetarist start, monetary policy has become a good deal more pragmatic for reasons discussed further below.

The international ramifications of these policies can be seen in four areas: exchange rates; trade policy; relations with the developing countries; and macropolicy co-ordination.

Exchange rates

More or less inevitably, these domestic policies generated overvalued exchange rates. Initially, at least, this was welcomed. In a Hayekian world of competition between national currencies, a strong currency can be seen as the free market's positive verdict of the soundness of domestic economic policies. Overvalued currencies have also made a major contribution to the improved inflation performance in both countries. There has been, however, some reluctance to make much play out of this latter aspect, since it raises questions about the magnitude and permanence of the progress made in bringing down domestic inflation. Indeed, the transient nature of the gains against inflation made by exporting it through an overvalued exchange have become uncomfortably apparent in Britain following the attacks on sterling in the summer of 1984 and early 1985.

The other side of the exchange-rate coin has been intense foreign competition and rising protectionist pressures. In Britain this led, quite early on, to an implicit departure from the new macropolicy orthodoxy. Indeed, it can be argued that the main reason why the anti-Keynesian fiscal policy of 1980–2 appears to have worked is that it enabled the Bank of England to back away from monetarism behind a smokescreen of multiple monetary targets, and concentrate for a time on bringing the exchange rate down to a more realistic level. The government, however, still stoutly—although increasingly shakily—maintains that it has no target for the exchange rate.

Trade policy

It is at the micro-economic level, however, that overvalued currencies have created the most awkward conflict between free market principles and economic and political realities. To be fair, in a world of sinners, both administrations have *tried* very hard to live up to their principles. But it remains the case that the automobile and steel industries of both countries would be on their knees were it not for extensive trade restrictions and, in the British case, subsidies; that both countries acquiesced in a tightening up of the Multi-Fibre Agreement, a flagrant effort to deny the working of comparative advantage; and that Britain has at times found it convenient to hide behind the more explicitly protectionist views of some of its partners in the European Community.

In fact, what has happened in trade policy is only one example of the rather striking contrast between the boldness with which a new approach has been applied to macro-economic policy and lack of courage in applying more distinctively free market principles at the micro-economic level in such areas as trade policy, industrial policy, and social policy.

The Third World

At least until the debt crisis, the Third World came low in Mrs Thatcher's and Mr Reagan's political agenda. Extrapolating from their domestic economic philosophy, the basic message has been self-help and reliance on market mechanisms. The former justified a frugal attitude to foreign aid. The latter justified allowing new efforts to manage commodity prices via the Common Fund (about which many other industrial countries were also dubious) to run into the sand. This shift in attitudes in the North coincided with a rather similar shift in many parts of the Third World in favour of more market-oriented development policies after the rather encouraging experience of countries that followed such policies in the 1970s. Africa increasingly came to be regarded as a special case.

Europe has, however, not been prepared to carry free-market principles as far into the realm of North–South relations as has the Reagan administration, in such areas as the Law of the Sea, the World Bank energy affiliate, the International Development Association (IDA), and the current American position on population control. At the same time, when it came to the crunch—as in the IDA replenishment fiasco—Europe has not been prepared to take matters into its own hands. And, on the more strictly financial issues, e.g. allocations of Special Drawing Rights and International Monetary Fund quotas, Britain and Germany have been on the—ungenerous—American side of the argument.

The debt crisis brought the problems of the developing countries more sharply into focus. The origins of the crisis were seen by the Thatcher and Reagan Administrations to lie very largely in the inflationary and insufficiently market-oriented policies of the debtor countries themselves, abetted by the inflationary policies of their predecessors in the North. Confirmation of this diagnosis is seen in the way the low inflation, more market-oriented Asian debtors have successfully weathered the storm.

The debt crisis did, nevertheless, provide a vivid demonstration of the reality of economic interdependence, especially for the Reagan Administration. Rather suddenly it became clear that events in Latin America could have serious consequences for the viability of the United States banking system and for US export interests. The response was a laudable effort at global economic management, spearheaded by Mr Volcker and M. de Larosiere, whereby private banks were induced and coerced into behaving in their collective rather than in their individual interest. The Reagan Administration modified its earlier rather hostile attitude to the International Monetary Fund—a shift facilitated by the Managing Director's enthusiastic espousal of the themes of monetary and fiscal discipline and the need for greater reliance on the free market.

Macropolicy co-ordination

This evidence of a more global view of economic interdependence has been much less evident in the area of macro-economic relations *between* the major industrial countries. The natural corollary of the new domestic economic policy was a 'hands off' approach to attempts to co-ordinate monetary and fiscal policies, with each country left alone to get on with putting its own house in order. The slogan became 'convergence'. In essence, this meant that all countries should follow an idealized version of the anti-inflationary supply side policies adopted by the heartland. On the British side 'demand management' was banished from the vocabulary, and, together with the Germans, they took the lead in rejecting calls for 'a temporary fiscal stimulus' right through the worst post-war recession. On the American side, the espousal of monetarism ruled out—and rendered suspect—attempts to co-ordinate monetary policies between the major financial centres designed to dampen the wide swings in exchange rates.

Thus the main thrust of Anglo-American—and for that matter German—international economic policy has been self-discipline. This both provides an example to other countries and subjects them to an external discipline that is good for them. In this *optique* the French Socialist U-turn provided a useful lesson in the new morality. With one major exception, the main actors have studiously avoided criticizing each other's monetary and fiscal policies. Thus, for example, in its dealings with Japan, American policy-makers have not raised the issue of the contribution that Japan's restrictive fiscal policies may have been making to the undervaluation of the yen. Instead they have looked for micro-economic solutions.[2]

The exception is, of course, American fiscal policy. This has been persistently criticized, both in public and in private. It is noteworthy, however, that America's allies were generally not prepared to carry this criticism to the point of jeopardizing their relations with the Reagan Administration. Thus, for example, the British and Germans were reluctant to follow the French lead during the missile crisis by arguing that the United States could not expect unconditional support on security matters if it were not prepared to take into account the economic interests of its allies in the conduct of its monetary and fiscal policies. Equally, the British and Germans were the strongest opponents of proposals for a collective European response to high interest rates and the strong dollar, through, for example, trying to tax or control capital outflows to the United States, or through a programme of co-ordinated fiscal reflation. Instead, they appeared to become resigned to the idea

[2] Including liberalization of Japanese financial markets at a time when the conjunction of macro-economic policies in the world is such that this is most likely to lead to increased capital outflows and downward pressure on the yen, as argued by Jeffrey A. Frankel in *The Yen/Dollar Agreement: Liberalizing Japanese Capital Markets* (Institute for International Economics, 1984).

that nothing much would be done about the US budget deficit until this is forced upon the Administration by market forces. Meanwhile they might as well sit back and enjoy the virtuousness of their own fiscal discipline and the strong demand stimulus they are getting from America's fiscal indiscipline.

TWO VIEWS OF THE FUTURE

The steady-as-we-go scenario

It may be evident by this point that the author has many reservations about the new philosophy. Nevertheless, a good case can be made that, whatever the internal inconsistencies, the results have so far been impressive. It can also be argued that economists do not understand the importance of the much broader psychological and political agenda underlying the Thatcher–Reagan approach. The basic aim is to create a new spirit of self-respect and self-reliance. Inefficient management is being disciplined by market forces. Union members are being forced to question accepted dogmas and the wisdom of their leaders. Both are being made to realize that they will no longer be bailed out by the government or by inflation. Firm and consistent leadership is creating a new sense of national pride and optimism about the future. And, because of these changes, behavioural relationships concerning inflation, productivity, or budget deficits established by economists on the basis of past experience are no longer valid.

Thus, according to this school, far too much fuss is being made about the United States budget deficit. The American recovery will slow down to a sustainable cruising speed. Interest rates will come down to reflect lower inflationary expectations. Unemployment will come down quite quickly to its 'natural' rate, but inflation will not accelerate because labour has learned its lesson. The combination of tax incentives, renewed animal spirits, and the enthusiastic espousal of new technologies will prove to have raised America's non-inflationary growth potential. This higher growth will go a long way to eliminating the budget deficit. The remainder can be dealt with, without raising taxes, and without cutting defence or social security entitlements, by cutting out 'wasteful' public programmes.

On the external side, the dollar will fall at a manageable rate. The pace of recovery in the rest of the world will pick up: the debt crisis will be resolved, and the same reinvigorating forces will make themselves felt in Europe. Together with a lower dollar, this means that the United States current account deficit will begin to decline. It does not have to be eliminated, it is argued, because, as a result of Reaganomics, rates of return in America are now higher than in most of the rest of the world, from which it will continue to attract savings.

The European side of this optimistic scenario is somewhat less rosy—or at least has a rather longer-run time horizon. Taxes cannot be cut until further progress has been made in reducing expenditures. There is still some way to go in removing 'rigidities' that insulate business and labour from economic reality, and in restoring profit margins. Nevertheless, the external environment is favourable. German interest rates have gradually become uncoupled from American rates. If the dollar begins to depreciate against the European currencies, this will help to keep inflation down. Recovery should therefore continue to pick up momentum, and, since it is not based on a Keynesian fiscal stimulus (unlike America!), should prove sustainable.

The sore point is that neither the British nor German authorities, in particular, appear to expect to achieve growth rates which could make any significant dent in depressingly high rates of unemployment. In their view the solution to this problem can only be found in the long term. With changing attitudes in the labour markets, real wages should continue to lag behind productivity, and with labour 'pricing itself back into the markets', growth rates in the range of 2 to 3 per cent should be sufficient to slowly absorb existing high levels of structural unemployment. Meanwhile the adverse social and political consequences of high unemployment will, it is hoped, continue to be manageable.

A digression on Britain

While the steady-as-we-go scenario can clearly be applied to Britain, a digression is perhaps in order, because of her special circumstances. Inflation remains stubbornly higher than in Germany. Interest rates are much less clearly uncoupled from American rates than in Germany, as recent events demonstrate only too clearly. Surging demand from America has provided less of a boost because of Britain's weak competitive position. And the miner's strike has been a painful reminder of how far there is to go before the Labour movement is converted to the 'new realism'—let alone the new optimism. As things stand, therefore, there is the prospect that it might take an agonizingly long time before workers really do price themselves back into jobs. Moreover, recent empirical work confirms what should have been obvious fom the start: a cut in real wages by itself will not have much positive effect on employment because of the negative impact on demand. What is needed is a combination of real wage moderation and fiscal stimulus. But the former is proving very hard to achieve, and the latter is ruled out by the Medium Term Financial Strategy.

One alternative to the steady-as-we-go approach takes as a premiss that the only way that Britain could reverse the inexorable march of economic decline would be to become a 'cheap labour' country for an extended period. If this could be achieved, it is argued that with high domestic rates of return and a strong external competitive position, existing endowments of capital, entrepreneurship, and technology should be sufficient to reinvigorate the British economy and wean it from North Sea oil.

There are two fundamentally different approaches to achieving this happy outcome. The radical conservative approach would be to alter labour market mechanisms, and particularly the operation of unemployment insurance, to greatly increase the incentives to accept work at lower wages, and the penalties for not doing so.[3] This could be coupled with a progressive opening of the coal, steel, automobile, textile and clothing, and consumer electronics industries to the full force of competition at world market prices.

The other alternative would be an incomes policy and devaluation approach. There is a not very encouraging British precedent in 1977–8. For a short while under the Labour government a combination of monetary, fiscal, and incomes policies did manage to bring about a fairly encouraging combination of lower inflation, a realistic real exchange rate, and rising profit margins. All this, however, was thrown away in the run-up to the 1979 election. A contemporary example is provided by Sweden. A deliberately 'excessive' devaluation, coupled with incomes policy, has produced a shift to profit and a significantly improved competitive position. So far the results have been quite promising, but it remains to be seen whether these gains can be maintained on a permanent basis.

The crisis scenario

Returning to the global picture, there is another very different view about what the future holds in store. This school largely discounts the political and psychological atmospherics of Thatcherism and Reaganomics. It is true that progress has been made in bringing down inflationary expectations and restoring profit margins, but it is too soon to say how permanent this will prove. Nevertheless, with the oil problem behind us, we should be able to look forward to some improvement over the poor performance of the 1970s were it not for the uncoordinated and internationally inconsistent monetary and fiscal policies being pursued by the major industrialized countries.[4]

According to this school the strength of the American recovery can be

---

[3] A striking difference between the United States and Europe is that unemployment benefits are not normally available in America for more than 26 weeks, and that as many as half of the unemployed also, in time, lose their health insurance.

[4] The following draws heavily on my book *Deficits and the Dollar: the World Economy at Risk* (Institute for International Economics, 1985).

explained very largely in conventional terms. The 1981 budget provided a strong fiscal stimulus. A very restrictive monetary policy was abruptly eased after August 1982 and has subsequently been broadly neutral. In addition, investment responded strongly to the tax changes in the Economic Recovery and Tax Act of 1981 which raised the after-tax rate of return on investment by several percentage points.

The weakness of the recovery in the rest of the world can be explained in similar terms. In striking contrast to the United States, the other industrialized countries have, since 1979, been reducing their structural deficits by an amount which, for the industrialized countries area as a whole, has just about offset the fiscal stimulus in America. This is primarily the case for Britain, Germany, and Japan, who, according to figures from the Organization for Economic Co-operation and Development (OECD), will have improved their structural budget balances by an amount equivalent to 4 per cent of their GNP between 1979 and 1985, with both Britain and Germany moving into a structural budget surplus already in 1983.

Some observers would argue, moreover, that although the demand effects of fiscal expansion and contraction in different parts of the OECD area have been roughly offsetting in effect, large budget deficits in the United States have exerted a net upward influence on world interest rates because of the dominant role of the dollar in world financial markets.

Against this, the rest of the world has been enjoying a strong demand stimulus from the deteriorating US current account deficit which, allowing for multipliers, may have accounted for one-third to one-half of the growth the rest of the OECD area achieved in 1983 and 1984. Finally, the extremely unbalanced nature of the world recovery has been accentuated by the debt crisis which has led to sharp fiscal and monetary restraint and dramatic reductions in imports in many developing countries.

According to this school, the remarkable combination of prosperity and low inflation in America achieved in 1983–5 cannot be taken as evidence that Reaganomics has produced a radical change for the better in the performance of the American economy. It can be explained rather in terms of this historically unusual concatenation of policies and events in the world economy as a whole. These have made it possible for America to finance its recovery to an important extent by sucking in savings from the rest of the world,[5] and at the same time to hold down its inflation by sucking in cheap goods in large quantities.[6]

[5] Over the two years to the first quarter of 1985 the share of investment in US GNP rose by 4.3 percentage points. Three-fifths of this rise was financed by borrowing from abroad.

[6] It is usually suggested that the rise in the dollar has reduced American inflation by 1.5 percentage points a year in 1981–5. Some observers believe that this may be an underestimate.

It can also be argued that Europe's poor showing so far in this recovery can be largely explained in terms of global macro-economics rather than in its much discussed structural weaknesses and overgenerous welfare statism. The benefits from its anti-inflationary policies have accrued disproportionately to the United States. Thus, for example, while the dollar price of oil declined by nearly 20 per cent over the four years to late 1984, the ECU (European Currency Unit) price *rose* by over 20 per cent because of the appreciation of the dollar. At the same time, the failure to enjoy an American miracle of job creation and strongly rising investment can by plausibly explained by the fact that domestic demand in Europe, under the influence of restrictive fiscal policies, rose by only 6 per cent over the first two years of the recovery, compared with a phenomenal 15 per cent in America. These same facts can also help to explain why the cloud of despondency about loss of dynamism and technological leadership evident in America only a year or two earlier seemed to have largely evaporated, while it still hung like a pall over Europe.

To those who hold these views, we are clearly headed towards a major international crisis which will probably lead to a new—unnecessary—world recession. The inevitability of such a crisis, unless policies are changed, can be demonstrated by a few statistics:

—If the dollar were to stay at its early 1985 level, then, on the basis of some basically favourable assumptions, the United States' current account deficit would rise to around $300 billion, or over five per cent of GNP, by 1990.

—This would mean that America, which probably became a net debtor nation in early 1985, would by some time in 1986 be the world's biggest debtor, and by 1990 would have a net external debt of over one trillion dollars.

This obviously will not happen because foreigners, who are now putting a substantial fraction of their savings into America, will lose their nerve. So, equally obviously, the dollar will not stay at its early 1985 level. But it would take a decline of the dollar of 25 per cent over the next three years simply to stop the current deficit from rising further, and of as much as 35 per cent (taking it back to its 1979–80 trough) to stop America going further into debt. However, once the dollar starts declining at a rate of over ten per cent a year a bandwagon will develop against the dollar. Foreigners' willingness to invest savings in America will dry up faster than America's need for these savings: there will be a 'crunch' in the financial markets, and the long-predicted 'crowding out' of private investment will begin with a vengeance.

The Federal Reserve Board will be then faced by a very unpleasant dilemma. If it tries to resist the strong upward pressure on interest rates by a faster rate of monetary expansion it will be accused of abandoning its anti-inflationary stance, with disastrous consequences for confidence in the financial and foreign exchange markets. If it does not, the economy will be pushed into a recession. On the fiscal side, it may well turn out that in the end confidence can only be restored by indulging in the kind of anti-Keynesian fiscal overkill which became necessary in Britain in 1981, Belgium in 1982, and Mexico in 1983.

What then happens to the rest of the world? The expansionary stimulus it has been enjoying from the deterioration in the US trade balance will stop and go into reverse. On unchanged policies the recession would spread to Japan and Europe. And with a recession in the North, and high dollar interest rates, there would be a new debt crisis in the South.

WHAT SHOULD OR COULD BE DONE?

The right answer

It is relatively easy to set out what *should* be done to prevent such a crisis.

The United States should immediately take convincing action to cut the budget deficit to around zero by 1990. This would no doubt involve cuts in defence spending and social security entitlements, but taxes would also have to be raised. A good start would be to phase in a fairly heavy tax on oil and gasoline, yielding something in the range of $50 to $100 billion.[7] The Federal Reserve Board should stick to its present monetary targets. Until the financial and foreign exchange markets become convinced that the necessary domestic and external adjustments are 'manageable', it should be very careful to avoid any impression that it is willing to ease up; at a somewhat later stage, however, some easing up might become possible and desirable.

Europe and Japan should realize that the joy-ride is over. As the dollar comes under strong downward pressure they should be prepared to let their interest rates come down to quite low levels. This would not, however, be nearly enough, under the changed external circumstances, to provide the necessary stimulus to domestic demand. They should therefore take a leaf out of the Reagan book and cut taxes (or, where appropriate, increase infrastructure investment) by an amount equivalent to, say, 3 per cent of GNP. But they should not make the same mistake as the Reagan administration. These tax cuts and/or expenditure increases should be structured in such a way that they would be reversed once a strong recovery in private investment got under way.

Paradoxically, Reaganomics has created the potential for a Reagan

[7] This would still leave the after-tax price of gasoline lower than in Europe and Japan.

miracle in Europe and Japan. So far the unbalanced mix of fiscal and monetary policies in the United States has affected them in three ways: with weak currencies (*a*) inflation has been higher than it would otherwise have been, (*b*) interest rates have been higher than they would otherwise have been, and (*c*) external demand has been stronger than it would otherwise have been. As the dollar goes down the reverse will be true in all three areas. Europe and Japan could thus then do what Reagan did. They could give themselves a fairly strong dose of fiscal expansion, and set off a strong rise in domestic demand, while inflation would be held down because their currencies were appreciating, and budget deficits would not crowd out private investment because their savings would be flowing back from America.

These changes in fiscal policy should be accompanied by an explicit agreement between the Federal Reserve Board and the other major central banks to work together to manage an orderly decline in the dollar. In the first phase they would need to demonstrate their determination to bring the dollar down to a more reasonable level.[8] In the second stage—which could develop quite quickly—they would need to show that they were equally determined to prevent the dollar from overshooting downwards. Monetary policy should be the main instrument used in these attempts to manage the decline in the dollar (e.g. if it goes too fast the Fed should be prepared to tighten up temporarily and the others to ease up). But co-ordinated intervention on substantial scale in the exchange markets could also be extremely useful, especially as it would demonstrate that the central banks were prepared to take on the exchange rate risks (and enjoy the profits!) involved in betting against the markets.

What if things go on as they are?

The likelihood of the above policies being adopted in time to stave off the crisis appears slim. For one thing everybody is reasonably happy with the situation as it is—for as long as it lasts. More fundamentally, adoption of such policies would involve a repudiation of the new conventional wisdom that each country should do its own thing, and a return to explicit international co-ordination of fiscal and monetary policies and the management of exchange rates of an earlier, discredited, age.

If this is simply not in the cards, what should Europe do? As a defensive measure Britain could join the European Monetary System, which has clearly helped to shelter France and Italy through difficult

---

[8] This was written before the meeting of the Group of Five in New York on 22 Sept. 1985, at which a significant move was taken in the right direction.

periods of internal and external fragility. One question, however, is whether sterling could enter at a low enough level *vis-à-vis* the other members to make Britain the kind of cheap labour country it needs to be, if it is ever to restore its industrial base, even with a lower dollar. Many observers seem to think sterling has come down far enough. I have my doubts.

On a more aggressive note, there is perhaps one thing Europe (and Japan) could do to burst the bubble. Once again, it would involve taking a leaf out of Reaganomics. It is now clear that the supply-side tax changes in the 1981 United States budget achieved only one of their two intended objectives: they raised America's propensity to invest, but not its propensity to save. The result was to raise American interest rates, without inhibiting American investment demand, and at the same time the savings necessary to finance a consequent investment boom were attracted from abroad.

Europe and Japan could perhaps play the same trick. The most simple way would be to allow companies, over the next two or three years, to write off all new investment for tax purposes in the first year. This would in effect be a substantial subsidy to all those who decide to invest their savings in private productive domestic assets. As such, the record suggests that it would be a far more powerful means of keeping savings at home than tax on capital outflows, which would be both complicated and too easy to evade. The impact on market psychology would no doubt be enhanced if action along these lines was taken together by the European Community and presented as a deliberate attempt to protect themselves against high American interest rates.

Making constructive use of a crisis

Again, none of the above seems likely to happen. If that is so, we are indeed headed for a crisis. This need not necessarily, however, be a pessimistic conclusion. History shows that genuine reform—or simply change—in the untidy and amorphous entity which constitutes 'the international monetary system' has generally only taken place as the result of a crisis, and has then sometimes happened surprisingly quickly. So, to be realistic, perhaps the most important issue is how we might try to make constructive use of the oncoming crisis.

In this context, a first question is who is likely to lose their nerve first: America or its allies? By about a year after the crisis begins the situation will have become distinctly unpleasant for the American authorities. Inflation will be accelerating, interest rates will be high, the economy will probably be weak, and stories about the falling dollar will, after it has gone beyond a certain point, be very damaging to the image of an 'American renaissance'. The record shows clearly that it is under these conditions, when America's external economic position is weak (the 1960s, 1977–9) that it turns away from 'benign neglect' and becomes more enthusiastic about co-ordinating monetary and fiscal policies and deliberate attempts to 'manage' the exchange-rate system.

Post-war history, however, also teaches us another lesson. If the situation deteriorates far enough, then, because of the weight of the United States and the dollar in the world economy, it may be America's allies who lose their nerve first. In an uncoordinated and unconditional way they may start intervening in the exchange markets on a significant scale to slow down the appreciation of the dollar. For the same reasons, and partly as the direct result of such intervention, their monetary authorities may begin to tolerate faster rates of monetary expansion. Indeed, the uncomfortable fact is that periods of US balance of payments weakness (under fixed rates) or a falling dollar (under flexible rates) have almost always been associated with excessive rates of monetary expansion in the world, and to a subsequent acceleration of inflation. Perhaps the most important thing that Europe and Japan should realize, as the crisis unfolds, is that ultimately the worst possible outcome would be for them to end up printing the money needed to finance the United States' budget and current account deficits.

What we must hope is that at some point America becomes sufficiently worried about the situation to *want* to co-operate, while America's allies are still sufficiently unworried about the situation to be able to respond constructively and *collectively* to America's requests for help. If such an opportunity were to develop (which it may not), how should America's allies respond?

First, they should be ready, under appropriate circumstances, to help in a big way. At some point, it may well be desirable to indicate to the markets that the central banks are prepared to commit large amounts of money in exchange market intervention—measured in tens of billions of dollars—and stand ready to deviate temporarily from their domestic monetary objectives, in order to prevent the dollar going down too far. In this endeavour the central banks should realize that the first essential step in halting the unwholesome way in which the flexible-rate regime has been evolving since 1973 would be a successful collective effort to prevent the dollar overshooting downwards the next time the wheel turns.

Second, such help to the United States should be conditional—although political skills will be needed to camouflage this as much as possible. In the first instance this conditionality would be of a short term nature:

—action to cut the US budget deficit to around zero by 1990

—a continuing commitment by the Federal Reserve Board not to monetize the internal and external deficits.

Third, as discussed earlier, Europe and Japan should stand ready to take over the locomotive role in the world economy from America through an appropriate dose of fiscal expansion. Since, however, this would also clearly be in their own interests, it is hard to see how it could be used as a bargaining counter.

But the most interesting question is whether, somewhere along the road, such short-term conditionality might lead to longer-term American commitments, paving the way to systemic change.

One approach would be to work for new rules, or at least new guidelines. Among the most relevant would be:

—An agreement to set up target zones for the dollar, the yen, and the Deutschmark (or the ECU).
—An agreement between the major central banks to be prepared to systematically diverge, in opposite directions, from the central points of their targets for monetary expansion, as exchange rates move towards the outer limits of their target ranges.

However, this could well prove to be too ambitious an approach, at least initially. If so, an alternative might be to try to use the crisis to bring about a significant strengthening of the procedural and institutional processes for macro-economic policy co-operation.

In the first instance it seems inevitable that attempts to manage the crisis will be concentrated in the Group of Five and the Summit. But one would like to think that America's allies will not lose sight of the fact that, over the last few years, this relatively new institutional structure has proved singularly incapable of exerting effective collective pressure on the United States to follow more internationally consistent policies. In the author's (admittedly biased) view, this is at least in part due to the fact that a process of co-operation which only involves *national* officials and ministers has an inherent tendency to keep away from the really central and difficult issues because, for political reasons, everybody wants to be nice to one another. And this natural tendency is a particular weakness when one of the partners, the United States, is so disproportionately powerful.

In my view, therefore, one aspect of making constructive use of the crisis would be to try to bring the process of macropolicy co-operation between the major powers more firmly back into the framework of the multilateral institutions that were created for precisely this purpose. For this to happen it would be necessary for these institutions, and particularly for the International Monetary Fund, to show foresight and initiative as the crisis unfolds. This has not so far been as evident as one would have liked. But there is perhaps still time.

There are various aspects of these procedural and institutional questions which deserve more study. If large-scale co-operative intervention in the exchange markets becomes necessary, under what institutional framework should it be organized? Should it lead to some kind of formal concordat between the Federal Reserve Board and the other central banks? Should the central banks of the major European countries participate individually or through some European Community vehicle? Should the Bank of International Settlements (BIS) play a centralizing and operational role? Where would the IMF come in? Should America be pushed by her allies into making a drawing from the Fund, or would this be a time-consuming diversion, and perhaps also politically inept?

Suppose that, along the road to the crisis, America resorts to an import surcharge; or that we go several steps further down the road of a 'savings war' with Europe and/or Japan following the advice given above and retaliating against the American tax changes which have helped to suck their savings across the Atlantic and Pacific. Should somebody then not take the initiative to suggest that if we are going to continue with a flexible rate system, albeit a better managed one, we are probably going to need new rules, or new guidelines, and quite possibly also new institutional arrangements, to bring such resort to measures affecting either trade or capital flows arising from, or contributing to, prolonged periods of currency misalignment, under a greater degree of collective surveillance?

All this may well sound Utopian. But it is perhaps worth noting that the emphasis in the recent report on the functioning of the system by the Group of Ten was, in fact, on how to strengthen 'multilateral surveillance'. They did not get very far. But then there is nothing like a crisis to concentrate the mind.

13

Anglo-American Economic Relations
and the World Trading System

SIR ARTHUR KNIGHT*

INTRODUCTORY

THIS essay argues that national economies must be looked upon as the extension of a global and integrated system with a logic of its own, and explores some implications which might affect policy-making in the next five years or so.[1] No aspect of economic policy is irrelevant, but the emphasis here is primarily on trade issues.

Some appear to ascribe the unprecedented growth of the period from 1945 to 1970 wholly to the good functioning of the multilateral system which was set up immediately after the war. Its beneficial consequences are not to be understated, in particular the once-and-for-all impetus to trade which was imparted following the relative stagnation of the 1930s. But the multilateral system also helped the wider exploitation of other influences positive to growth in the period.

The long period of relatively slow growth from 1970 onwards must be ascribed to the interaction of a series of developments which demonstrate that there is indeed a global and integrated system. New factors in the 1970s included the OPEC price rises which exerted a world-wide deflationary influence; and the way in which petrodollars were recycled through the private banking system which, though beneficial on balance, gave rise to some unsustainable debt situations leading in due course to crises, so far handled to avoid major disasters.

An increase in protectionist measures must be seen (in large part if not wholly) as a consequence of these developments, but international trade flows have continued at levels which have been quite high in relation to levels of output. Indeed, the share of manufactures in world trade represented an increasing proportion of their output from 1960 up to 1981, though the trend was reversed in 1982 and 1983, only to be

* Thanks are due to all those whose comments helped in the writing, in particular Raymond Appleyard, Miriam Camps, Fred Knickerbocker, Roger Louis, David Mayes, and Tom Wilson.

[1] Albert Bressand, 'Mastering the World Economy', *Foreign Affairs*, 61 (1983).

restored in 1984.[2] There has been no clear evidence so far that protectionism is imparting its own independent impetus to the decline in manufacturing, but there must be a substantial risk that this will happen.

The immediate debate for the purpose of this essay concerns the proposal for a new round of negotiations within the GATT. Writing in mid-1985 in the context of a wider examination of Anglo-American relations and of a general concern about the state of the economic system of which they form part, it seems necessary first to consider whether there is now any particular reason for emphasis on the relations between these two members of the global system rather than upon other relationships. There was a limited period in which the United States and the United Kingdom (despite the acknowledged disparities in their power) were able together to influence events, but both now necessarily see themselves as increasingly constrained by the policies of others in pursuing their economic interests.

Changing Anglo-American relationships

They were not so constrained when the post-war international institutions were being formed. The Americans set the pace. The British were quite clear that the American approach reflected a powerful sense of what would best suit their interests, and there was a hankering on the British side after some alternative, more independent line; but the realities of the power relationships of the time prevailed, and led to the much-told tale of the close technical collaboration between a few key individuals on both sides. In the event, compromises were made which proved for a long time to serve the participants well, even the British. Despite continuing relative decline the improvement in British national income in the 1945–70 period was more rapid than in any previous period. But the story of close personal working relationships has not been wholly one of working out ways of giving effect to a perceived common interest, and a continuing uneasiness has characterized Anglo-American trade relationships.[3]

The bilateral relationship must appear now as of secondary importance in the context of British membership of the European Economic Community, and a present perspective on Anglo-American relations must recognize the role of the EEC as the formal channel for negotiations in trade matters. But though the EEC has the formal role in trade matters its institutions still leave individual governments with

[2] Calculations are derived from Table 6 in *National Institute Economic Review*, 108 (1984).

[3] See as one example Douglas E. Rosenthal and William Knighton, *National Laws and International Commerce* (Royal Institute of International Affairs, 1982) for an examination of problems arising from the extraterritorial reach of US legislation.

considerable power to influence policy and to take their own initiatives, such as the negotiation bilaterally with non-EEC suppliers of 'voluntary restraints' on sales into domestic markets. The United States therefore needs relationships with individual members.

More than intergovernment relationships are involved. The British have long been particularly encouraging to inward investment as a means of gaining access to foreign technology and management skills. By 1981 inward investment accounted for 18.6 per cent of British net output and 25.5 per cent of net capital expenditure; and by 1983 direct investment in the United Kingdom accounted for 39 per cent of all such American foreign investment. American-controlled firms in Britain have generally performed well in comparison with British ones. The large volume of transatlantic trade which reflects the strategies of multinational corporations is sometimes seen as worrying because it reduces the ability of governments to influence what happens through conventional methods. Investment relationships are particularly important to those for whom Britain is an American Trojan Horse in Europe.

Whatever may have happened in the past, a primary emphasis on Anglo-American relationships must now appear inadequate to the purpose in hand; but Hugh Seton-Watson expresses a historian's sense of what is still valid in this quotation from the 1985 Martin Wight Memorial Lecture (which he had prepared before his death in Washington in December 1984):

What has remained a reality is the English-speaking world, consisting of the United States, Britain and the three Old Dominions. When de Gaulle inveighed against 'les anglo-saxons', he was speaking of something real. I do not see how any citizen of this country, who knows something of international affairs and is concerned for the future of Britain can doubt that Britain belongs both to Europe and to the English-speaking world. For my own part, I know that my roots are in both, that I cannot give up either, that I cannot cut my mind or brain in two. The task that has lain before the British for the last three decades, and which regrettably their rulers have not discharged, is to be a strong binding force between the two, not to stand shivering on the brink of the Channel and the Atlantic, sneering in turn at those on each of the opposite shores, indulging alternately in self-reproach and self-pity, doomed to the fate of the donkey which could not decide from which pile of hay to eat, ending up as prey for carrion-feeders.[4]

Among the policy prescriptions for those British who recognize the risk of that fate, and would seek to avoid it, there must surely be included, so far as economic policies are concerned, an objective view of the global system with the United States, Japan, and the EEC as its three power centres; of where British interests might coincide or conflict

[4] Published under the title 'What is Europe, Where is Europe?' *Encounter*, 45 (1985).

with those of others in the EEC and the United States in particular; and (in the present context) of the relationship with the United States which will need to be managed. The theme of this essay can thus be more sharply focused.

The common Anglo-American objective

A continuing and more successfully developing multinational trading and financial system can be presumed to be a common objective which the British and the Americans share with others. It is difficult to think of any within the system who might seek, as a deliberate policy, to withdraw from it; though all will seek to further their own interests and, in so doing, may put the system itself at risk.

Trade in manufactures between the Organization for Economic Co-operation and Development (OECD) members still accounts for 70 per cent of world trade and probably for at least as much of the trade in services. If we accept a multilateral trading system as having been and being likely to remain a major factor in general economic prosperity and growth, the collective importance of OECD members does not need emphasizing. Moreover, the OECD has a secretariat which analyses and influences policy-making in a unique fashion, capable of further useful development.

The OECD is losing its dominant position, however. In the past decade the decline in its members' share of trade in manufactures has been due to the growth of newly industrializing countries, such as Brazil and Korea. A GATT panel in 1985 pointed out that only 50 of every 1,000 people in the next twenty years will be living in developed countries. But the OECD remains the primary focus within the time-horizon of this survey.

In this essay the needs and interests of the less developed and of the newly industrializing countries are hardly mentioned. This does not arise from any sense of their being unimportant, but rather from a belief that, unless the OECD members can find improved ways of handling their trade and financial relationships, it is difficult to imagine any way in which there could be useful discussion about improved policies in relation to non-OECD members. The high levels of growth in the 1945–70 period were, of course, the result of a unique conjunction of favourable influences. They may have given rise to expectations which it will be difficult to satisfy. The limitations of what can be achieved through deliberate policy-making need more emphasis throughout the global system than they often receive.

I. PERSPECTIVES ON THE ACTORS

If the OECD is viewed as a useful encompassing analytical unit within which to develop perspectives on Anglo-American economic relationships, it is helpful at this stage in the argument to look briefly at some perceptions of the chief economic agents within it—individual firms, governments and their interventions, and policy stances with regard to Japan, the United States, and the EEC.

The key role of individual firms

The widening application and development of new technologies and of those already commercially established has been one outstanding characteristic of the post-1945 period. Growth is not continuous and some firms grow at the expense of others; there are many failures; investors pass through crises of confidence and fears of vast miscalculation. The business historian might see it all as a process of sorting out what the products are going to be and the scale-factors which will determine industry structure.

Within the developed countries a relatively few large manufacturing firms account for a high proportion of output. About half of the largest disappear from the list in a twenty-year period, and are replaced by others. There seems sometimes to be a correlation between these changes and the growth and decline of technologies. Scale-factors relating to a particular technology can be a major factor in accounting for growth. In Europe generally the large firms collectively do not show an impressive performance,[5] and some of the causes have been examined: the search for 'national champions', preferred public procurement which absolves the management from developing a proper sales organization, market fragmentation which drastically reduces the demand available to each producer, and high regulatory costs.[6] But the linkage in some situations between size and competitiveness is undeniable.

Multinationals now account for a high proportion of international trade in manufactures. An OECD study of 1984 quotes estimates from various sources to indicate the magnitude of intra-group trade: for the United States in 1977, 39 per cent of imports and 36 per cent of exports; for UK exports, an increase from 29 per cent of the total in 1976 to 31 per cent in 1980.[7] Statistics about trade in services are less reliable, but patterns of specialization (such as in data flows) indicate the possibility that, here too, scale-factors will favour those who first achieve success in their chosen field and become large.

The logic of the global system includes those limitations on sover-

---

[5] Paul Geroski and Alexis Jaquemin, *Large Firms in the European Corporate Economy: Public Policy and Corporate Strategy*, ed. Alexis Jaquemin (Oxford, 1984).

[6] See his article in the *Financial Times*, 26 June 1985.

[7] See *Restrictive Business Practices of Multinational Enterprises* (OECD, 1977) and *Competition and Trade Policies: Their Interaction* (OECD, 1984).

eignty which find expression in intergovernment agreements and in willingness to co-operate through international institutions. But more important particularly for the present argument is the industrial logic which stimulates the growth of multinational corporations. Their activities to a great extent escape from the rules and the scrutinies which are the essence of the GATT system. What rules and what scrutinies might be appropriate for them? Would those for the OECD members be different from those for others, and would they be easier or more difficult to formulate and administer?

The Japanese phenomenon

The failure elsewhere in the OECD to match Japan's competitiveness calls for a comment on the characteristics of their achievement which appear relevant. Governmental supports have at times gone well beyond the intelligent deployment of those interventions which are an inevitable part of a developed government, and have included subsidized finance and protection, selectively and for the limited periods necessary to reach international competitiveness. There have been more successes than failures and the overall results demonstrate how effective this government-industry partnership has been.

For interventions to be successful the pre-conditions have to be right, and here are two ways in which the Japanese case illustrates this point. Any study of the reasons for Japanese success in the post-1945 period must take account of the continuity in government attitudes: each government could survive only with the acquiescence, at the least, of big business. Furthermore, the Japanese have an educational system which consumes a high proportion of resources and produces people well prepared for an industrial economy. Thus in the 1978–82 period British universities produced 10,000 more scientists than the Japanese; but the Japanese produced 250,000 more engineers.[8]

The Japanese may well find it difficult to maintain their previous level of success. They are, for example, finding themselves drawn more closely into the international financial system. Will Japanese investors continue to be satisfied with the modest interest rates paid to them in the past? And whereas bigness makes firms malleable, success makes them less so.[9] Nor may there be continued easy access to technology developed elsewhere and awaiting exploitation in Japan. With the greater uncertainty which this brings the tensions between interventionists and free-traders will not necessarily so often be resolved in favour of the interventionists. However, the strengths remain formidable.

---

[8] H. Peter Jost, Manchester Technology Diamond Jubilee Presidential Address, 1984.
[9] Andrew Shonfield, *In Defence of The Mixed Economy*, ed. Zuzanna Shonfield (Oxford, 1984).

The United States

The British student learns that the Americans see government as a process of rule by law rather than as the rule of men, but is nevertheless struck by the way that principle works when applied to issues such as those concerning industry and trade. Pragmatic adjustments to the rules are made to accommodate changing perceptions of where the public interest lies. In the field of competition policy, however, the change in thinking did not develop soon enough to accept steel mergers in the 1950s when these could have been one element in an American response to the increasing competitiveness of Japanese producers of carbon steel. When government action has proved a failure some find comfort in this demonstration of the validity of fundamental principles.

The aversion to sectoral policies is political and ideological. Its consequence has been an emphasis on trade-policy measures alone as the means for bringing about the adjustments which are required to meet changing competitive conditions. Three strands of development are identified by American students. Firstly, in the period until 1974 a shift of power from the legislative to the executive branch insulated policy-makers from protectionist pressures. But the Trade Reform Act of that year reasserted the role of congressional oversight and thus gave greater weight to the demands of domestic interests sensitive to competition from imports. The dispersed activities of the various executive agencies concerned have made for disjointed responses. The Office of the United States Trade Representative, which was designed to co-ordinate in this field, can only do so with strong presidential endorsement, which has been lacking, at least up to 1983.

Second is the fact that trade policy has always served two masters: domestic economic prosperity on the one side, and international trade and national security goals on the other. A relative decline in American power internationally, it is argued, has increased the attractiveness of trade policy in its bearing on more limited domestic goals. A decline in the influence on trade policy of the State Department, matched by an increase in that of the Agriculture and Commerce Departments, was apparent to the non-voting foreign constituents of United States trade policy and influenced them towards less accommodating responses.

Third is the effect of the 1974 Trade Act, which contains defences against foreign trade practices seen as unfair, and the 1979 amendments to it which gave domestic firms a stronger role.

The overall effect of these developments has been that the United States has responded to external competitive pressures primarily with protectionist actions. The United States government appears to have had one policy option. The free-trade versus protection dichotomy is consonant with a political structure and ideology which abhors direct intervention.[10]

The European Community and British attitudes

A European must share some of the American sense of frustration and accept some of the criticisms, for example about the rigidity of some of the institutions and about the limited talents deployed to the study of European issues. All can recognize the institutional weakness of the EEC which makes it difficult to find a common front.

In the transatlantic dialogue about trade questions some Europeans refer to irritations rather than to tensions; tensions are seen to characterize the American dialogue with Japan. But although the matter is not always seen in this light in Washington, it is difficult for a European to feel any sense of guilt when looking at the level of American agricultural subsidies, or at protection in carbon steel, or in textiles, or in arms procurement. Neither is it possible to feel that any particular guilt attaches to the use of different policy instruments which arises from differing constitutional practices when it is recalled that in carbon steel, for example, both the EEC and the United States have failed to meet Japanese competition; and this should surely be the main concern.

There seems little prospect that the Europeans will move towards a generally more protectionist position by design. There is too much at stake for them in the multilateral system. The French, in 1983, pressed the notion of new selective protection in high technology activities but were rebuffed by the British. It is possible to argue a case for new protection in some circumstances, but the pre-conditions for success are not present in Europe; for example, there is generally an acute shortage of people with suitable training in the skills required in information technology. To protect (even if it takes the limited form of a European preference) might well make a bad position worse.

II. TOWARDS AN AGENDA

Although for some analytical purposes it is useful to think of the OECD as a unit, it becomes necessary to extend the horizon when considering the policy agenda.

Managed trade or managed money?

Because protectionist pressures in the United States have been so much a

---

[10] These four paragraphs draw heavily upon John Zysman and Laura Tyson's chapter in *American Industry in International Competition*, which they edited, and from James C. Millstein's essay in that volume, with the use also of comments by George C. Lodge and J. David Richardson in their contributions to the Kansas City Bank Symposium published as *Industrial Change and Public Policy*.

consequence of an overvalued dollar, many have argued the need for giving prior attention to some new arrangements about exchange rates and the factors which influence them, fearing that new negotiations about trade must have a doubtful prospect of success while trade patterns are so distorted by more transitory monetary influences. Gardner's essay poses the dilemma as follows: if you don't manage money, or at least in some degree, won't you have to manage trade? Padoa-Schioppa puts it more comprehensively as the 'inconsistent quartet': a group of independent countries cannot simultaneously have free trade, capital mobility, fixed exchange rates and autonomy in national economic policies.[11]

The American authorities have now stated their intention to work towards a gradual realignment of the overvalued dollar and are seeking massively to reduce the budget deficit which is so widely seen as necessary if that end is to be achieved. Whether there will be the crisis, of which Marris writes, will depend in part upon the responses of non-Americans who will be affected. It will become clearer whether capital movements into the United States have been mainly a response to the prospects there for long-term investment or to the prospect of short-term gains, and the consequent magnitude and manageability of the fall in the exchange value of the dollar will influence the extent of the domestic disruption and protectionist pressures on other governments in the face of the increased competitiveness of American exports. With so much that is uncertain it is difficult to imagine any great readiness to agree to new international arrangements for a co-ordination of policies; but it is possible to imagine that the growing realization, especially in the United States, of the link between trade and other economic issues might generate pressures for some international discussion, despite any misgivings on the part of those responsible for having to decide what can be achieved thereby.

Economic performance: the intellectual framework

In the context of a policy agenda it is possible to debate whether trade or financial issues come first. For the present purpose trade flows (in the widest sense) will be the main focus of attention. The intellectual basis for a belief in the merits of a multilateral trading system derives from a particular conceptualization which leads to the conclusion that if people allocate their resources solely in response to market signals, there is no change (in the way in which people allocate the resources which they have) which could be to anyone's advantage.[12] This is reinforced by

---

[11] Tommasso Padoa-Schioppa, 'Squaring the circle, or the conundrum of international monetary reform', *Catalyst* (Spring 1985).

[12] Economists will recognize this attempt to define Pareto optimality and, it is hoped, accept it as adequate for its purpose.

pragmatic considerations. Governments which interfere with the market process get involved in decisions with consequences which they have but limited competence to assess, and with the risk of provoking retaliation by other governments. Moreover they may become captive to internal political pressures, not just in the given case but also in other cases which their prior action must encourage.

But governments do get involved for all kinds of reasons, some of which are generally accepted as an inevitable consequence of their role and some of which are controversial, either because of doubts about whether they serve the domestic public interest or because of their external effects. All developed countries have policies which influence business performance in a selective manner; they relate to trade, to competition, and to defence procurement. In their effects the interactions between them can be quite close, much more so than is usual in their administration. Some governments go further in their selective actions than is normally embraced within these conventional categories. The historical evidence, and not just that for post-1945 Japan, demonstrates that such interventions can be associated with successful performance and that an absence of intervention can be associated with relative decline. The historical evidence also shows that interventions can be associated with repeated failure: witness the post-1945 record in the United Kingdom.

The economic concepts expressed in discussions of policy, whether about trade or about competition, appear at times to be inadequate for the requirements of industrial competitiveness. Though the existing rules are adequate for many purposes, they are not completely sufficient, in part because there is no well-established theory about the dynamics of economic growth, nor as yet any sufficient empirical understanding to permit the formulation of rules or codes capable of being applied.

A new GATT round

In the management of international trade, a system of rules is necessarily imposed because there is no overriding administrative authority and there are too many participants for every issue to be settled through a case-by-case treatment. But there has been no important extension of the multilateral trading regime since the successful reduction of the major tariff barriers. In the Tokyo round of these talks the United States and Europe sought and failed to establish an operational set of rules to govern the use of non-tariff barriers, especially relating to subsidies, public procurement, and selective safeguards.

A new GATT round must now be the most important item on the agenda, even if one suspects that the Americans would not insist on it so much were it not for protectionist pressures which a realignment of the dollar would do much to moderate. Uncompleted programmes from the previous round, and little sign of sufficiently well-prepared new initiatives, evoke the fear that there will be no more than the repetition of old formulas, which lead to disappointment, frustration, and an atmosphere in which new protectionism will flourish. A study, a GATT panel report, and a subsequent lecture by I. G. Patel, one of that panel's members, indicate the hopes of those who attach particular importance to the GATT system. The agenda which the panel puts forward is a good starting point. Patel makes it clear that the issues are so complex and muddled already that negotiations will be protracted and indeed spread over years. He expresses the hope that in the meanwhile there would be sufficient change in the objective situation to make co-operation in the monetary and financial field more urgent as well as more feasible. There is no suggestion that everyone should be in on the trade discussions or negotiations from the beginning to the end: 'something like a multi-ring circus'. He and his colleagues see the initial move as coming from the developed countries, because as the largest traders they bear the largest responsibility for the functioning of the system. They make important proposals on which it is not proposed to comment here.[13] The discussion here is about the initiatives which are or might be launched, and the questions about bilateralism and regional arrangements to which they give rise.

American threats of bilateral negotiations if others are not ready for multilateral ones suggest that they have well-prepared initiatives. There is a well-publicized intention aggressively to improve the American share of the trade in agricultural products. As to manufactures, the scope for multilateral tariff negotiations must surely be fairly limited because of the substantial tariff reductions which have resulted from previous negotiating rounds. The problems here arise from non-tariff barriers of all kinds: quantitative limitations which have been agreed bilaterally, national subsidy and other visible supports for particular sectors, and those more opaque situations such as are prevalent in Japan or in the German insurance industry, where those who believe themselves to be competitive nevertheless find themselves frustrated. The Americans have made no secret of bilateral negotiations with Japan relating to four sectors, one outcome of which has been the signing (in May 1985) of an agreement about telecommunications equipment. The Americans have argued, with some justification, that the tactics they have employed have required the involvement of people in numbers and

---

[13] See Miriam Camps and William Diebold, Jr., *The new multilateralism: can the world trading systems be saved?* (Council on Foreign Relations, 1983), *Trade policies for a better future: proposals for action* (GATT, Mar. 1985), and I. G. Patel, *Next steps in international economic cooperation* (LSE Society Lecture, London, 16 May 1985).

with skills which the Europeans are quite unable to match. But even those most involved have seemed to doubt how much real progress could be expected, and the press has carried articles about the limited capacity of the Japanese authorities actually to influence events; and the risks seem considerable. Will Congress be appeased if all this effort produces little result? Will those in Congress who initiated the proposed import surcharge as a demonstration of seriousness find themselves committed to go through with it?

It seems odd, if the outcome is so doubtful, that so great an effort is being made. It is doubtless true that the increasing Japanese trade surplus can be related in large part to the growing US trade deficit, but the circumstances suggest exchange rate disparities rather than sectoral factors as the cause.

Bilateralism, 1985-style, appears also in American negotiations about free-trade area agreements, involving Canada, the Caribbean, and Israel. It has been suggested that the GATT rule which permits such regional groups was ill-considered, and it has been pointed out that they breach the non-discrimination principle. Whether that principle can now be seen as having great practical significance is doubtful, unless there is some rapid progress in defining and giving effect to GATT rules which apply to non-tariff barriers. It is difficult too for EEC members to discover a great issue of principle here, provided the Americans accept the same rules as did the Europeans—that all trade within the area must flow freely and that the new groupings must give rise to no increase in external protection. Moreover, one strand in the discussion is that national sovereignty is now becoming a major barrier to efficient economic organization. Since free-trade areas involve an abandonment of sovereignty in the trade field, surely they can be seen as moves in the right direction?

Bilateral approaches might perhaps also be envisaged in negotiation with newly industrializing or developing countries in need of external financing. It is possible to imagine bargains which link the offer of finance and market access (for shoes or textiles, perhaps) in exchange for wider access for manufacturers and services from the developed countries. To the extent that finance might be the making of some bilateral bargains, the Japanese and individual European companies and governments might also be active. The present American Administration appears to see itself as the only member of GATT with the power at least to make an attempt at ensuring the survival of the multilateral system. But the problems and the dangers of its present bilateral programme are all too clear.

A European initiative?

Bilateral approaches create the risk of a proliferation which would disrupt the development of the the multinational system. A network of interconnected bilateral relationships might be created which would be far more difficult to unravel than the existing single-product quantitative restrictions. The Europeans in particular have reason for concern. What is needed is a European initiative which offers the prospect of opening up new trade possibilities. It could embrace agriculture, textiles, carbon steel, defence supplies, and telematics (the joining together in technology and in markets of telecommunications and data transmission).

Agriculture is, of course, a major source of tension. For the Europeans to offer a substantial revision of the existing Common Agricultural Policy offering improved prospects for American agricultural exports might appear as no more than a hollow gesture, since the Americans show signs of aggressive intent and all the cards are in their hands. But the psychological impact would be considerable.

Carbon steel problems on both sides of the Atlantic reflect a common failure to meet Japanese competitiveness. If both sides were to agree to a gradual (four to five years) removal of existing support a powerful bargaining counter would be created for negotiations with the Japanese.

The British have already announced their intention to move towards the first stage in the elimination of the present protection for their textile industry. The United States has hitherto had a more effective lobby than the British, but if the British, together with others in Europe, are now ready to give undertakings about the removal of existing protection over a period of years, a powerful bargaining counter with newly industrializing countries (NICs) and developing countries would be created.

The Americans' protection of their defence industries is notorious. It is difficult to think of any bargain the Europeans might offer to gain greater access: access to the European telecommunications market, perhaps? A further problem is that, despite its formal role in trade negotiations, the EEC appears so far to have been unable to find the administrative route towards even a common consideration of questions of armament supply. Will the American threat of bilateral action be a sufficient spur in this and in other fields to lead the Europeans quickly enough to a common position?

Telematics is another field in which the lack of a common European position will prejudice the prospect of a worthwhile dialogue with the United States. It is a field in which high research and development costs encourage a trend towards global market and production strategies.

There are close links in this field between the regulatory framework and product markets. As a result of the way in which the United States regulatory system has developed, the American domestic market is relatively open, and there is a broad consensus that American policy should aim at a progressive liberalization of international markets in this field, in which American suppliers have an overall competitive advantage.

In the EEC generally, however, there has been no corresponding liberalization. The separate national authorities retain their monopolies, and the markets for equipment remain fragmented; though the British have been rather more liberal than others in the EEC, as for example in the denationalization of British Telecom. This situation provides one more source of transatlantic tension, but it is difficult to imagine a common European negotiating position until there has been much more progress towards agreement on the conditions for a common European market. As with defence supplies there must be great doubt as to whether the Europeans can organize themselves quickly enough to forestall the consequences for the international trading system of past failures.

A bilateral two-year EEC–American programme with an undertaking to report at the end of it to GATT might have the advantage of buying time for improvements to occur in macro-economic concertation and exchange rate alignments, while at the same time diminishing pressures in the United States for new protection. It would also give time to assess the results of American efforts with Japan. To take on all the vested interests in the EEC and the United States at one fell swoop (each individual aspect of the programme would require its own separate negotiation) might be more effective than taking them one by one. The magnitude of the resistance would arouse those whose interests would be furthered but who might otherwise be silent. External commitments are, besides, often a useful weapon in countering internal pressures.

Such an initiative, leading to bilateral discussion between the EEC and the United States would play its part in preparing the agenda for the wider GATT forum, the prospects for which would be vastly improved if there were a common EEC–American position on some important issues. It would offer an alternative to the apparently rather desperate aggressiveness of some American actions, and if the results of these appeared to be disappointing it would diminish the risks of the protectionist reactions on the part of other countries or of Congress. It might also be helpful as a preliminary to any EEC–American dialogue to seek objectivity by assessing (to the extent technically possible) the tariff or subsidy equivalents of the supports given on the two sides over the whole range of the relevant trade sectors.

Whether Patel's multi-ring circus turns into the bilateral deals which could lead to spheres of influence and beggar-my-neighbour discrimination or into more generalized GATT rules (applied more widely and with credible safeguards) could depend upon whether the EEC and the USA act together to promote multilateralism. Too much is at risk to rely upon the hope that the United States is strong enough to do it alone.

The multinationals: a twin-track approach?

There is a further strand of thought: the creation of an integrated investment-technology-trade complex with the prospect even of a return to unrestricted trade, but against the background of a large area of managed international trade relationships with corporate executives as the strategists and planners.

The possibilities of the twin-track approach with an emphasis on the multinationals are as valid for the Europeans as for the Americans. It is difficult, however, to see the basis for any useful further discussion about multinationals in the GATT framework until more progress has been made in examining whether it is possible or desirable to consider the rules which should govern their global strategies. The 1984 OECD study considered the interrelation between competition and trade policies and the need for concertation between those involved in managing them, and has made a step towards bringing the relevant issues further onto the international agenda. But the OECD emphasis is on the conventional criteria of anti-competitive behaviour; the dynamic impact of global strategies is reflected only in such phrases as 'reasonable co-ordination of activities and allocation of tasks' as a source of efficiency necessary 'to maximize performance of the group as a whole'. These phrases suggest a limited awareness of the full and potentially beneficial aspects of global strategies. If governments were to see the encouragement of such corporations as one part of a twin-track approach to managing the trading system, the other issues with which the OECD report is concerned will not lose their importance. For policy-makers the aggressive market strategies of global corporations will become a primary concern, going well beyond generally established ideas about competition policy and a liberal international trade policy. Such thoughts might be congenial to those in the United States who resist suggestions about government intervention in industrial decision-making and to those in the EEC who recognize the weakness of EEC institutions and their limited capacity for effective action, even when intervention is seen as desirable.

III. THE ANGLO-AMERICAN FACTOR

Anglo-American economic relations now appear to depend more than they did in the past upon the way in which the EEC–American relationship develops. Trade relationships form only one part of the integrated system, but the EEC is not yet established as the channel for handling all trade matters, and there is a continuing national involvement in the handling of those matters for which the Commission is formally responsible. There is thus a substantial range of issues on which British and US perceptions of where their interests lie will give rise to bilateral relationships.

It is now convenient to pull the threads together. In the context of a discussion about trade, other economic policies find their most important expression in exchange rates. The debate about trade policy cannot have any satisfactory outcome if exchange rates are widely out of alignment, and in 1985 the emphasis is on the overvalued dollar; but the adjustments needed do not relate only to American policies. The proper management of the European Currency Unit (ECU), with all that this involves in handling fluctuations in its value and in compatible macroeconomic policies within the EEC, could be one element in the adjustment process, potentially more powerful than the management of the mark alone; but this potential cannot be fully realized until the British have decided to join the European Monetary System (EMS) exchange rate mechanism; and this must be an issue of interest in the Anglo-American relationship. The setting up of an EMS reserve fund would be a desirable further development in the good management of the ECU, and one from which the British, with their extensive international financial network, might hope especially to benefit; and that network is now one in which American interests are firmly established in the United Kingdom.

Defence procurement issues arise in relation to NATO. The NATO discussion relates in part to American protectionism and in part to a European inability so far to manage to good effect the supply arrangements with respect to disbursements in Europe. That the Americans are protectionist is acknowledged. But the failure of the Europeans effectively to organize their own internal arms supply arrangements must be seen as more worrying, since it has adverse consequences for economic and military performance within Europe as well as for sales in external markets. The outside observer is indeed given cause for concern when Lord Carrington, as Secretary-General of NATO, refers in this context to the complacency and chauvinism of the British.[14] Here surely is a case in which close Anglo-American relationships in their present form may be prejudicial to the long-term interests of both sides.

The Strategic Defense Initiative (SDI), put forward by the Ameri-

[14] *Financial Times*, 12 June 1985.

cans in a defence context, is seen in Europe as particularly important for the ways in which this massive research and development programme might provide the basis for new industrial applications yet to be identified. The French Eurêka project was devised as a European counterpart to SDI but with an emphasis on the potential industrial applications, and its principle was adopted by others, including the British. But, Janus-like as ever, the British have also been more positive than others about direct involvement in SDI. Here again, therefore, there will be continuing Anglo-American relationships.

In trade matters generally the inability of the EEC to formulate a common position for discussion with the United States stems in large part from the failure so far to make sufficient progress in achieving an integrated internal common market. Within the Commission the programme put forward by the recently appointed Commissioner, Lord Cockfield, is widely acknowledged as offering a realistic prospect that internal barriers will be well on the way to being removed by 1992; and in the discussion between member governments the British argue that their proposals for widening the scope for majority voting would bring about more rapid progress than could be expected from a more fundamental debate about a revision of the Treaty. Here is an issue on which the American authorities might be expected to feel the need for some Anglo-American exploration of the ways in which integration of the EEC market can be achieved rapidly and in ways which would strengthen an EEC–American partnership in the search for wider multilateralism.

In the trade in telecommunications equipment the British have been more liberal than others. The telematics field is one in which a case for selective intervention, including protection, can be argued, but the British did not support French proposals for this. A reinforcement of this stance might be seen in the subsequent privatization of British Telecom, its unique position in this respect in Europe, and its first moves towards an international procurement policy and towards international investment. It is to be expected that the scope for Anglo-American co-operation will be considerable, between firms as well as between governments.

In textiles the British have declared an intention to remove some of the existing Multi-fibre Arrangement (MFA) protection; and they are less wedded than either the Germans or the French to the full scope of the present Common Agricultural Policy.

If there is an advantage in an EEC initiative it might thus be hoped that the British would be the first to identify it and to prepare it. It would be wrong to see this as clutching at the straws of whatever past special relationships there may have been, or as playing the role of American

Trojan Horse in Europe. Any such action should be seen rather as a hard-headed assessment of where British and other European interests lie. In the context of the trade issues which have been the theme of this essay, there can be little doubt about the kind of Anglo-American dialogue which is necessary at government level. Neither can there be doubt about the British interest in fostering the further development of investment relationships (in finance, in other services, and in manufacturing), in particular—for the reasons argued above—those of the multinational corporations where a pattern has now been set which it would now be difficult and counter-productive to change.

A consideration of present Anglo-American economic relations can thus conclude with an expression of hope: that within the relationship there will be a sufficient weight of informed opinion on both sides to see a common interest in helping the British to avoid the fate of Hugh Seton-Watson's donkey.

14

Finance, Trade, and Development: Issues in Transatlantic Co-operation

RICHARD PORTES*

DESPITE current economic problems and conflicts—or perhaps as their cause—the concordance of policies among the major industrial countries in the first half of the 1980s in dealing with finance, trade, and development is at a peak. This has been the result not so much of co-operation or co-ordination as of the more or less independent adoption of common policies. The policies are similar not because they are imposed by a dominant, hegemonic power or an international institution, nor by imitation, but because governments have chosen similar approaches to their common problems. It is nevertheless possible that the alliance between the United States and Britain has played a significant role in getting others to follow them, through some influence of Britain in the EEC as well as the force of the American example.

In economics as in other domains, that alliance is much less important now than it was forty years ago. The high point in economic relations between the United States and Britain came in 1944, when together they built the foundations for the monetary and commercial policy institutions that were to guide the international economy in the post-war period and beyond. The setting up of the IMF and the World Bank at Bretton Woods in 1944 and, to a lesser extent, of the GATT at Geneva in 1947 were largely the result of US–British efforts. At Bretton Woods the chief negotiators for the two countries, Harry Dexter White and John Maynard Keynes, each advanced a plan for international monetary reform. These had much in common. Their differences reflected divergent national interests, particularly between a surplus and a deficit country. The Bretton Woods agreement incorporated a compromise between these differences that leaned towards the Ameri-

* This essay arose out of reflections on the papers and discussions of the Conference at Ditchley in April 1985. This explains its discursive and summary character as well as the absence of the scholarly apparatus which would have to accompany a more analytical or empirical piece. That may make it easier, however, to draw the main issues together and bring out some relations among them. I am grateful to Joan Pearce for comments.

can position. That Britain was in effect, with the United States, the joint author of the Bretton Woods agreement was due more to its being the sole surviving ally in Europe and to the personal and intellectual authority of Keynes than to its standing in the international economy.

Although in some respects this partnership was perpetuated, for example, in the IMF by the fact that initially the quotas of the USA and the UK together amounted to more than half the total, it was clear that Britain no longer had the economic weight appropriate to leadership. A particularly telling demonstration of this came in 1947 when the restoration of sterling convertibility led rapidly to a substantial devaluation. Increasingly the most special feature of the relationship was the link between the nation that had once been the dominant power in the international economy and the one that now filled that role. By the 1970s American economic dominance was declining, and the 1980s saw a retreat from multilateralism, though recently there have been signs that this is ending. Britain, for its part, has been increasingly drawn into the European Community. Both countries are among the small number which participate in the Group of Five and the economic summits—perhaps the two most influential groups on the international economic scene—but their bilateral relationship has ceased to be central.

Common perceived interests have been a necessary but not sufficient condition for the recent similarities between economic policies. Governments could have chosen alternative means to similar ends had their political perspectives differed greatly. One may reasonably doubt, therefore, whether the concordance of policies will endure beyond the current political conjuncture in the United States and Britain. But the current administrations do represent a continuity of development from previous medium-term trends, and German and Japanese policies are also similar.

After a general introduction, I shall consider successively the problem areas of finance, trade, and development. The objectives of policy are the same throughout: stable non-inflationary growth at high levels of employment, equitably distributed within and among countries. The record in meeting these objectives of the policies followed under the Bretton Woods system as it operated until the early 1970s is ambiguous. The greatest sustained economic expansion in history could be seen as obscuring a secular rise in the natural rate of unemployment and of inflation rates, as well as the accumulation of many structural rigidities, punctuated by 'stop-go' macro-economic policies responding to balance-of-payments crises, all accompanied by disappointing economic performance of Less Developed Countries (LDCs). The post-war boom might be interpreted as the result not of the happy functioning of the Bretton Woods system until it was disrupted by external events, but rather as the consequence of falling commodity prices and the utilization of a backlog of unexploited technological progress. It is less disputable, however, that fixed exchange rates did force some co-ordination of economic policies, and that this in itself was important and useful. But the economic summitry of the floating-rate period has also brought some results, notably at the first Bonn economic summit in 1978.

There are clear linkages among the three main problem areas I shall cover. Some go so far as to claim that managing international money is necessary to permit unmanaged international trade. Money first, trade second, might be not only a logical but also a necessary temporal sequence. Progress on macro-economic and exchange-rate policies is a prerequisite, if only politically, for progress on commercial policies, even if some actions in the trade field might be mutually beneficial economically, regardless of the macro-economic environment. The sequence can be taken further in the proposition that open and growing export markets are the essential condition for broad-based growth of the LDCs and avoidance of a debt crisis, which would in turn put intolerable strains on the management of international money.

It is perhaps surprising that despite these strong linkages between the major issues, there is little support on either side of the Atlantic for a new Bretton Woods, or even unanimity on the desirability of an early GATT round. Although there is some nostalgia for the era of institutionalized co-operation, one certainly finds less internationalism now in both America and Britain. More attention to trade and capital flows has brought some knowledge of the rest of the world, but no greater commitment to any international system. How should we explain the decline of internationalism? Perhaps in the link between economic and security issues, as a response to the lessening of the perception of external threat which originally stimulated the co-operation of the first two post-war decades. Whatever the reason, any revival of internationalism now might in practice come down to better economic summitry rather than more formal international institution-making or even rule-making.

A historical perspective brings out major changes in the roles of the United States and Britain in the post-war economic world. Those changes might be best interpreted in the light of a question: would we see more or less international economic policy co-operation now if the two countries were as dominant as when the Bretton Woods regime was constructed? The genuineness of that co-operation might itself be doubted: was it not even then the United States imposing its will, somewhat modified by clever British manipulation? And it might be maintained that the United States still is very much the dominant economic power, because of the size and strength of the American economy, the role of the dollar in international finance and capital markets, and American power in the international economic institutions. Moreover, the official policies of both countries are still sceptical of formal economic co-operation. In the American case, this might arise not only from economic arguments but also from a popular shift to a less internationally minded attitude. For its part, Britain is in the EEC but still in some respects not of it, notably in regard to the exchange-rate mechanism of the European Monetary System (EMS). It is not clear what would be the net effect on international economic co-operation if Britain were to gain more influence in the EEC relative to France and Germany.

The current British and American administrations clearly share common attitudes towards economic policies: against discretionary macro-economic management ('fine tuning'); for micro-economic, structural, 'supply-side' policies rather than macro-economic measures in any case; and overall, for the view that if each country can put its own economic house in order, there should be little need for co-ordination or the explicit management of the world economy. There are some immediate qualifications to these propositions—for example, the United States budget deficit is a glaring example of not putting one's own economic house in order, while on the other side, even the Reagan Administration has found it necessary to get international co-operation in dealing with the debt problem and lately with the exchange rate of the dollar. It is nevertheless doubtful whether Mrs Thatcher and Mr Reagan would have signed the Bretton Woods agreement.

Even though this particular set of domestic policy attitudes might not prove adequate to the needs of the international economy, it may be argued that the problem is not systemic but rather due to the absence of consensus on some other set of domestic economic policies which would be more appropriate (e.g., expansion with incomes policies and industrial policies). Three views of this linkage between internal and external policies attract support. The first is that international economic management, particularly intervention into foreign exchange markets, could not be successful without changes in current fundamental domestic economic policies. This hypothesis will now be tested, unless the Gramm–Rudman law is actually effective in reducing the United States deficit. A second position holds that a stronger international system, especially for exchange rates, is needed to force some coherence among domestic policies, and indeed to guide the choice of domestic policy stance. Taking these two jointly produces the third proposition, that the harmonization of domestic economic policies is both necessary and sufficient for exchange-rate stability and for an international economic environment conducive to healthy trade and economic development.

The fundamental theme of 'management' versus 'hands-off' can be pursued further. Management might be day to day in the form of a system, institutions, and rules. Alternatively, it could be seen as the kind of 'deal' which might come out of a summit, involving a package of domestic and international economic policy changes by each of the major countries. What might such a package look like? Judging by recent experience, any workable deal would have to be played out in 'no-trumps', with domestic and international policies, macro-economic and commercial policies all being traded off among each other. Some believe that the nature of such trade-offs inevitably involves a conflict between domestic and international objectives. If so, it would be necessary to persuade governments to act in the interests of the world economy, a laudable but unattainable objective. Others argue, with some support from empirical models, that there are packages which would make all countries better off. The floating-rate system and its consequences may have obscured the fundamentally co-operative character of the international economy; countries are not playing a zero-sum game, so that co-operation and international-mindedness may be good domestic policy as well.

Consideration of the operation of the international financial system naturally divides into two principal areas: the structural weaknesses and failures of the mechanism as it currently operates, and the conjunctural problems arising from the various national policy stances assumed by the major countries in recent years, particularly by the United States.

There is wide-ranging agreement that the current system (or non-system) has a chronic tendency to produce exchange-rate misalignments; and that their nature and effects should be distinguished from those of exchange-rate volatility. The foreign exchange markets have developed in their futures and swap markets a sophisticated means of 'locking in' current rates and protecting against currency exposures. The difficulties created by misalignments, however, cannot be mitigated in this way. News affects asset markets and generates speculative capital flows that drive exchange rates far from any reasonable measure of their true or 'equilibrium' level. The consequent trade flows and patterns of adjustment are economically inefficient for all participants. This proclivity of the system to produce misalignments is considerably greater than under Bretton Woods. Distorted industrial development, the destruction of capacities, debt service problems, the growth of protectionism, are all actual or potential by-products of these misalignments.

Some argue that exchange-rate misalignments are generated by domestic economic policies, and that the problem is how to run domestic policies if you do want exchange-rate stability. Even then, however, the system itself might amplify exchange-rate movements resulting from domestic policy shifts. The floating- rate system can also be defended on the grounds that shocks to the world economy or to individual national economies must be accommodated somewhere, and it may be preferable that the impacts should be taken primarily by exchange-rate movements rather than by other unanticipated changes of economic variables or policies.

Nevertheless, there is a widespread conviction that the floating exchange rate system has not worked; that there are persistent misalignments which can be identified; that their degree can be assessed; and that something can be done about them, although not necessarily by official intervention in the foreign exchange markets. A popular course is a strengthening of the *de facto* (if unpublished) system of exchange-rate targets. The Europeans have the EMS; exchange-rate targetry is not foreign to the Japanese; the British now take the exchange rate into account in the formulation of monetary policy; and there are clear signs of movement from the United States on this issue, in the effort to bring the dollar down and thereby weaken protectionist pressures. An alternative would be wide margins under fixed parities, with the Americans, Europeans, and Japanese adopting overt ranges of movement for their currencies. Criticism of all such half-way houses can be met by the response that it is the pure systems—whether pegged rates or free floating—which have demonstrably failed.

Both proposed systems would need some form of multilateral surveillance of national economic policies. And a principal obstacle to launching such a target zone or wide-margin system would be to reach agreement over the actual targets, given today's structure of rates. Such agreement presupposes, of course, that governments would have a better idea of the correct rates than today's markets, a premiss which does not command universal agreement. Yet dispute over the chances of success or the merits of any particular scheme should not obscure the wider agreement that if some kind of mechanism could be found to reduce misalignments it should be pursued, and that such a mechanism would necessarily require more international collaboration than currently exists, especially on the part of the United States.

Either of the proposed systems would provide considerable impact on the psychology of market traders, in convincing them that position-taking need not be a one-way ride. Manipulation of market sentiment is as significant as actual intervention by central banks. Exchange controls have relatively few advocates, but in some circumstances might be an appropriate policy of last resort. If any such initiative were taken, it might best take the form of tax surcharges or the withdrawal of tax privileges. The same effect on capital movements would thereby be produced, without recourse to the direct controls which have proved difficult to operate so often in the past. Real interest equalization taxes might be more effective, as well as more efficient, than capital controls in limiting the scope for short-run capital flows to shift exchange rates. British entry into the exchange-rate mechanism of the EMS might stimulate further consideration of such policy tools.

An overvalued dollar, high real interest rates, and a severe trade imbalance between Japan and the United States have been the major conjunctural problems of the past few years. All may be seen as directly linked to the United States budget deficit, with some reservations. A credible deficit reduction package would not solve all the world's economic problems and might create others, such as cutting American demand for LDC exports. The Europeans want a reduction in the American deficit; the Americans want fiscal stimulus and structural reforms from Europe and a rapid reduction in their trade imbalance with Japan. These might be the basis for a deal, but no major country is willing to make significant concessions (Japan's recent liberalization moves are not likely to affect trade flows greatly). This bodes ill for prospects of international co-operation, even at the level of dealing with exchange-rate misalignments. Given the severity of the pressures on developing countries, prospects for any solution to the evidently grave debt service difficulties of some major debtors appear very poor.

The system is clearly under pressure, but it would take a crisis to trigger any major change of policies or institutions. Yet the limited willingness of the United States for international co-operation might diminish further if the economy slows down, and the basic policy stance in both Britain and America is to resist change even if (or the more so as) the going gets tough.

Even now, most discussions on trade are conducted within the framework of a shared assumption that the multilateral system must be preserved. Co-ordinated reduction of barriers to trade should be encouraged, and pressure now mounting for increased protection should be forestalled. It is clear, however, that democratic political frameworks make this much more complex than the assertion of abstract principle and require a better understanding of the many forces that shape trade policies. The urgency of coming to grips with these tensions is enhanced by changes in the relative importance of particular trading nations and by the major technological changes that have occurred since the GATT approach to trade practices was initially formulated.

Even from an Anglo-American perspective, the EEC and not Britain must be the focus of attention on the European side, except perhaps in so far as Britain and the United States have a special common position as major suppliers of financial services. Trade has never been the warmest area of Anglo-American relations. There is a long-standing American view of Britain as protectionist (Imperial or Commonwealth Preference) and now, although the two countries may have closer views on the main issues than ever before, Britain is severely constrained by its EEC membership. Views of GATT differ significantly: the United States sees it in a legalistic manner, the Europeans as a framework for consensual negotiations. Multilateral trade negotiations are themselves now more difficult than in the past because they are necessarily more complex than previous discussions about the percentage by which tariffs should be cut across the board. Indeed, 'trade rounds' may have become obsolete, to be replaced by 'trade-offs' between commercial and other policies.

The role of GATT is complex, even if we look at it only as a forum for further discussion of troublesome issues. There are potential benefits, notably the buying of time during which domestic pressures for increased protection can be resisted; and potential costs, such as damage to the GATT system if expectations for successful negotiations are disappointed. The observation that the last GATT round has not been properly implemented might suggest some scepticism for another and for its likely success. That is accentuated by the continuing heated discussion of whether a more or less precise agenda is needed before a commitment to a new GATT round, or whether we could move towards useful negotiations without one. The monetary and macro-economic uncertainties appear so important that some wish there were no pressures for a new GATT round until the exchange-rate system could be sorted out, which leads to the minimal position that any agenda should simply be a list of issues which need further discussion.

There appear to be tensions between the macro-economic and trade policy-makers within each government. Those responsible for trade policy want their macro-economic counterparts to do something about exchange-rate misalignments and other macro-economic problems so as to permit progress on the trade side. Those on the macro-economic side argue from the principle of comparative advantage that progress in commercial policy is possible even if there are exchange-rate misalignments. Many Americans feel a sense of urgency, because they believe that the GATT system itself is at risk, that we must have a new GATT round producing results over a four- to five-year period or the system will break up. Yet is this possible without American leadership, and can the United States lead as long as its current account is so heavily in deficit?

For the United States, an alternative to GATT might be the promotion of regional 'free trade areas' (e.g., United States–Canada, United States–Pacific basin) with external trade barriers kept to a minimum. There are serious fissiparous tendencies inherent in such a move, perhaps the break-up of GATT; but it is difficult for the Europeans to tell the United States not to do what they have done themselves.

A third possibility is the adoption of a unilateral position by the United States to link access to American markets with reciprocal access to those countries currently practising restrictionist policies. This may be seen as a technique for widening the scope for the free play of market forces generally, perhaps an alternative to case-by-case bargaining on specific issues. The recent American approach to Japan is a case in point.

Several further outstanding issues merit particular attention. Notably, these concern the position of the Newly Industrializing Countries (NICs) in the international trading system. Future expansion in the volume of world trade might well depend on enlarging their role as importers. This seems an unlikely prospect, in view of their highly restrictive practices; in turn, these are partly a response to their debt servicing difficulties. To counter this, it might be desirable to reformulate trade practice rules in order to separate the NICs from the poorer countries in the Group of 77 and to co-ordinate the procedures of GATT and IMF so as to link the provision of finance to the NICs with trade liberalization by those countries.

Looking broadly at Anglo-American relations on trade policies, the issues in contention (e.g., subsidized steel and agricultural exports, defence procurement policies, strategic export limitations) appear to be largely irritants, so that no new mechanisms are required to cope with them. It would nevertheless be worth while seeking long-run agreements to restrain their sources in all these areas. The term 'industrial policy' is much abused and should probably be avoided (the new American phrase, 'targeting the process', is certainly no improvement); but we do need deeper understanding on both sides of the ways in which the system works as a basis for progress towards removing some existing forms of market-distorting supports. The policy argument has rested hitherto on simple competitive equilibrium models, and advances towards more realism in economic theory have brought new and intellectually more defensible cases for protection, intervention, and industrial policies. The analysis of policy alternatives must in future take more account of these arguments for 'strategic' trade policy, even if they prove in practice limited to special cases.

In both countries, the government will continue to be involved in industrial restructuring. Its ultimate objective should be not to protect declining industries but to encourage the growth of new ones which will not require protection. This is essential for co-operative trade policies. Whereas the multilateral system was developed and sustained by the United States, its future will depend upon American–EEC co-operation, in which Britain can play a significant positive role. With common sense and some luck, muddling through may be a feasible outcome.

Development problems, too, must be seen in an international and systemic context. Necessary conditions for the economic development of LDCs are that there be a source of capital flows to them, a way of converting those flows to long-run loans, a source of supply of capital goods, and a power enforcing international contracts. Since the 1970s, these functions have been fragmented. Effort should now be directed towards seeking a system which would co-ordinate them in a pluralistic way. Except for sub-Saharan Africa, developing countries are better off now than two decades ago. On the other hand, the impact of actions by developed countries on the performance of the LDCs seems on balance to have been slight.

Development aid policy is a continuing source of controversy. The United States and Britain have transferred significant amounts of resources to LDCs for a variety of political, commercial, and ethical reasons. The results have varied across different recipient countries and projects, but the overall effects have been marginal. This might be attributed more to the misuse of the aid given than to the policy of development aid itself.

There is now some divergence between British and American aid policies. The multilateral component of British aid has risen, chiefly because the total has been limited and multilateral contributions are 'demand-led'. British aid has shifted away from big projects and towards programmes (interpreted as seeking to ensure that things work). There is more emphasis on developing natural resources and some trend towards gifts for very poor countries with loans for richer ones. Britain has also become tougher in insisting on action to control population growth. Almost one-fifth of British aid is channelled through EEC funds. Britain is generally well disposed to increasing the World Bank's capital, but it sees no need to press this since at present the World Bank does not require it. This is perhaps more a cause for concern and criticism of current policies than for complacency.

American aid policy is subject to pressure from Congress, but as in other areas, this can easily be used by the executive as an excuse for policy stances which it finds desirable in any case. The United States resists any increase in the multilateral component of aid. It has declined to increase its contribution to the International Development Association (IDA) partly because of budget constraints, but also because the IDA's funds go to large public-sector projects which the United States considers inefficient, preferring small, private-sector projects in countries of its own choosing. Aid is being focused on humanitarian relief (food). The Administration's philosophy of self-help means that more is given to countries that appear to be 'helping themselves', i.e., the better off. The United States is withholding support from organizations which seek to control population growth, and it is firmly opposed to increasing the World Bank's capital. Both United States and Britain have tied aid extensively, but the United States has been more virtuous in the use of mixed credits. Britain does support American efforts in the Organization for Economic Co-operation and Development (OECD) to achieve more transparency and more discipline in this regard, and it is maintaining this view in the EEC (especially *vis-à-vis* France) as well.

Collaboration between Britain and the United States in dealing with problem debtor countries has been excellent, however, even though high American interest rates have exacerbated both economic and political pressures in this area. Britain has in particular supported multi-year debt rescheduling. For the future, both countries agree on the need for increased private investment to offset the decline in bank lending and to reverse the trend towards developing countries becoming net capital exporters. The debt problem is not merely conjunctural, but will continue as a long-run structural difficulty in the world economy. Even if interest rates do come down and the world economy grows rapidly, there will still be 'hard-core' debt service problems.

A major thing that the United States, Britain, and other developed countries could do for the LDCs would be to reduce import barriers against their manufactured goods. Such barriers have led to a general deterioration of the competitive system as other countries have imitated and countered them, and any serious supply-side policies would put the highest priority on eliminating them. On the other hand, the free-trade underpinnings of GATT might be inappropriate for LDCs; and even if trade liberalization would be good for both the NICs and LDCs, balance-of-payments constraints (debt servicing difficulties) will continue to impede it. Britain's membership of the EEC has affected its agricultural trade policies in ways which are detrimental to the LDCs.

We should encourage LDCs to provide proper incentives for development, and we can contribute to this through education and training; but self-help is not easy, and it is difficult for developed countries to exert leverage in that process. We should refrain from imposing preferences as between public and private sector, centralization and decentralization, large scale and small scale, but rather should encourage the LDCs to get the best from each. This view is decidedly in opposition to current American policy, which takes a hard line on privatization and other such issues. We must hope this policy will change. Conditionality might have more justification in principle and in practice coming from an international organization like the IMF, but that too has disadvantages: it is politically suspect, it appears to encourage LDC internal bureaucracies, and the combination of restrictive policies for many individual countries produces a global deflationary bias.

Although there may be agreement in principle that the 'rules of the game' in the current international economic system are less favourable to LDCs than we might like, in practice there is long-standing deep resistance to pressure for a 'New International Economic Order'. British and American responses could include sympathy towards providing more liquidity to LDCs in the context of international monetary reform, facilitating trade among LDCs (arranging credit, encouraging complementarity) and prompting technological innovation and indigenous technological development.

There is great diversity among developing countries. It might be easier to deal with their problems if they did not act as a group. Countries like Brazil and India do naturally seek to organize them, however, and it would in any case be counterproductive for industrial countries to aim to break them up. Britain and the United States should nevertheless in their own policies seek to distinguish between countries and problems. Major common problems will still continue to characterize relations between the developed and developing worlds for many years to come, such as the collaborative management of debt and corresponding LDC needs for open, growing export markets in the developed countries. Even sustained rapid growth in the industrial countries would not solve all the problems of development, however, and might even bring hidden ones to the fore (brain drain, raw material shortages, capital hunger).

Might there be a paradox or at least an inconsistency in the dominant views taken separately on the three major themes discussed above? In trade and development, despite the serious problems confronting the system and individual countries and policies, there are few voices of doom, few prophecies of catastrophe or even of crisis. In money and finance, however, it is often suggested that crisis is most likely, and perhaps the only source of necessary change. Yet there is some agreement that the macro-economic–money–finance nexus is primary; that progress there on both the systemic issues and the conjunctural imbalances is necessary for progress on trade and (hence) development; and that without such progress the debt problem could itself become the crisis we fear for the international monetary system and domestic financial systems.

THE NON-EUROPEAN WORLD

15

The End of the British Empire and the Assumption of World-wide Commitments by the United States

LORD BELOFF

To judge from the rhetoric of political leaders and the thrust of scholarship, Americans today tend to the view that nearly all the problems they confront outside Europe are the result of the pressure of Soviet expansionism or of subversion brought about through the Soviet-inspired propagation of Marxist doctrine. A British view might be that, without denying the importance of these factors or downgrading the contribution of Soviet malevolence to world instability, there is another way of looking at these problems. What we are witnessing—not merely instability but deprivation, famine, civil and tribal war, and even genocide—is the direct result of what one might style the catastrophe of decolonization. The downfall of the British, French, Dutch, Belgian, and Portuguese Empires has created a political void, or series of voids, which have in turn produced the time of troubles which Toynbee observed as the sequel to Empire in a great variety of historical instances. And it might further be observed that, despite its enormous economic and military potential, the United States has not been able to find a way of bringing this time of troubles to an end. The *Pax Britannica* has disappeared; the *Pax Americana* has yet to be made manifest.

For the historian there are two questions to be answered. First, how far did the United States either wilfully or through inadvertence contribute to the dissolution of these Empires and, since our subject is a confined one, to the dissolution of the British Empire in particular?[1] Second, what have been the impediments in the way of the United States filling a successor role as a guarantor of world order? Have the failures been those of the intellect or of the will?

It has often been pointed out that the Americans, whose national existence was the product of a successful revolution against an imperial

---

[1] The subject is illuminated from a variety of angles in D. Cameron Watt, *Succeeding John Bull: America in Britain's Place, 1900–1975* (Cambridge, 1984).

system, have a strong tradition of anti-colonialism. And the arguments about the undesirability of colonial possessions familiar in Britain in mid-Victorian times were echoed in the United States at the time when the United States was acquiring its first overseas possessions.[2] Indeed later on after the Second World War when the United States was seeking to win the plaudits of newly independent nations an eminent American sociologist, S. M. Lipset, wrote a work entitled *The First New Nation*, in which he endeavoured to demonstrate that the United States' own revolutionary experience entitled it to be regarded as part of the anti-imperialist camp.[3]

For obvious reasons of size and contiguity, the British Empire was the most frequent object of American attack on anti-colonialist grounds, and its dissolution in favour of independent republics a recurrent ambition of American policy-makers, and one increasingly fuelled by arguments of an economic nature as American trade and enterprise sought new horizons beyond the borders of the United States itself. A minority of Americans have from time to time taken a different point of view, being less certain of the stability of different parts of the globe if the imperial constraints were removed, and admiring the constructive work of Britain's proconsuls and their agents in the field. First among such Americans was the most intellectual and broadly educated of America's twentieth-century presidents, Theodore Roosevelt.[4]

The importance of American attitudes to the handling of Britain's imperial policy was made manifest when the First World War led to major changes in the balance of world politics and gave the United States a new role as an industrial, financial, and naval power with the proven capacity to mobilize great military strength. It became an axiom of British policy to try to maintain good relations with the United States as a minimum, and to hope, as a maximum, that it would see American interests as involved in supporting the now rapidly evolving Empire and Commonwealth. The United States for its part, while often seeing eye to eye with the British on matters affecting the stability of Europe and the balance of power in the Far East, never looked at the British or other European empires as positive factors even though its own role for the most part remained a passive one.[5]

It might have been expected, and clearly was expected for instance by

[2] See e.g. Max Beloff, 'Anti-Colonialism in American Foreign Policy', *Commentary* (1957) reprinted in Max Beloff, *The Great Powers* (London, 1959).

[3] S. M. Lipset, *The First New Nation* (London, 1964).

[4] See Max Beloff, 'Theodore Roosevelt and the British Empire' a centennial lecture, in Max Beloff, *The Great Powers*.

[5] See Max Beloff, 'The Special Relationship: An Anglo-American Myth', first published in Martin Gilbert, ed., *A Century of Conflict* (London, 1967) and reprinted in Max Beloff, *The Intellectual in Politics and other Essays* (London, 1970).

the Irish, that Woodrow Wilson's commitment to national self-determination would extend to the subject nationalities of the British Empire. But Wilson's concerns were Eurocentric and given the nature and ramifications of the conflict, only the former Ottoman Empire provided serious non-European issues of a political kind. Here the United States could only have prevented its British and French allies or a renascent Turkey from establishing a successor order if the Americans had been willing to take on mandatory responsibilities themselves. For such direct involvement neither Wilson nor the American public was prepared.[6]

For the most part the United States was not directly involved with the changes in Britain's imperial relationships in the inter-war period. Its interest was only aroused when an attempt was made to deal with the impact upon Britain of the world depression by a preferential tightening up of the economic ties between Britain and the self-governing Dominions as well as the colonial territories properly speaking. Such policies ran against the doctrine of non-discrimination which seemed likely to be more beneficial to the American economy and was an essential part of the American approach to world problems.

The development of the Anglo-American wartime relationship after 1939 helped to illuminate the differences of approach between the two countries. The British, concerned with husbanding their resources and conscious of the precariousness of their hold over their world system, were averse to constitutional experiments while the Empire-Commonwealth was at war; the Americans were fortified in their view that self-government was everywhere, and in all circumstances, preferable to alien rule by the rapid collapse of the European empires in South-east Asia under the impact of the Japanese onslaught. The interventions of President Roosevelt's agents in India brought these differences into the open.[7] At the same time, in Latin America and the Middle East in particular, divergences in economic interest were difficult to ignore and played some part in the developing discussion of the proper shape for the post-war world to take.[8] To some extent these divergences were counterbalanced by the feeling in some British as well as American quarters that if the British imperial system were to be written off there

---

[6] The matters are dealt with in Max Beloff, *Imperial Sunset*, vol. i. *Britain's Liberal Empire* (London, 1969; New York, 1970), chs. 6 and 7. On the involvement of the United States in the post-war settlement of the Near East, see in particular, H. N. Howard, *The King-Crane Commission* (Beirut, 1963).

[7] These issues have been magisterially handled in Christopher Thorne, *Allies of a Kind: The United States, Britain and the War against Japan, 1941–1945* (London, 1978).

[8] No study of the general United States attitude to the British Empire in the war years has yet come from a British historian but much of the story is available from an American standpoint in Wm. Roger Louis, *Imperialism at Bay 1941–1945: The United States and the Decolonization of the British Empire* (Oxford, 1977).

would be strategic consequences, since the United States would have to develop its own power to fill the vacuum created.

In his review of the second quarter of 1944, the British Ambassador wrote: 'Attacks on the Empire reveal conflicting tendencies. On the one hand there has been an increased realization of America's own interest in the perpetuation of the Empire for strategic reasons . . . On the other hand from the economic standpoint the belief has gained strength that British and American interests conflict all along the line.' There was, the dispatch noted, a tendency to view the United States, Russia, and China as the Great Powers of the future and an unspoken assumption that the British Empire was falling apart. It also noted that the traditional attacks on colonialism and imperialism from liberal circles, which had been muted in the interests of allied unity, were now again coming to the fore.[9]

At this time and subsequently the words 'imperialism' and 'colonialism' were used by Americans even in high places in a very loose sense to encompass not merely colonial rule but also any apparent use of superior power to achieve economic ends. In a note of a conversation with President Roosevelt on 17 February 1945, Secretary of State Stettinius wrote: 'The President then got on to the subject of the British and the Argentines. He said the British were imperialistic and worse than the Argentines . . . It is very apparent that he distrusts the British and dislikes them immensely.'[10] Yet this analysis was not applied to the American position being established in Saudi Arabia which was becoming a classic instance of the maintenance of economic and political influence without any impairment of a country's legal sovereignty.

It is perhaps not to be wondered at that, when the Americans were seeing a vast expansion of their areas of concern and the need to decide upon new policies in almost every quarter of the globe, they should, except in very expert circles, tend to fall back upon the traditional simplicities of a less complex past. And as the image of a world dominated by the Great Powers in which the United States and the Soviet Union would find common purposes and common language receded—and it did so before the war ended—this unwillingness to face the complexities in the choices to be made was the source of much anxiety to America's British partners.

'They either wish', wrote Harold Macmillan in his diary for the period 21–3 May 1944, 'to revert to isolation combined with suspicion of

---

[9] T. E. Hackey, *Confidential Despatches: Analysis of America by the British Ambassador, 1939–1945* (Evanston, 1974).

[10] *The Diaries of Edward R. Stettinius, Jr., 1943–1946,* ed. T. M. Campbell and G. C. Herring (New York, 1975), p. 26.

British imperialism, or to invervene in a pathetic desire to solve in a few months problems which have baffled statesmen for many centuries. Somewhere between these two extremes we have got to guide them both for their own advantage and ours and for that of the future peace of the world'.[11] What Macmillan had immediately in mind was not an imperial problem but the affairs of south-eastern Europe, but he was clearly influenced by the United States' handling of North African questions as he had seen it from his Algiers vantage point. Nor indeed can President Roosevelt's cavalier assumption that the French Empire could be treated as a thing of the past have failed to worry those looking to the way in which the British Empire was to chart its future course.

For it must be remembered that, while the British certainly expected a continuation and indeed acceleration of the evolution of the Empire-Commonwealth with economic and social objectives added to the constitutional ones, they did not for the most part envisage its dissolution. And although the growing intimacy of Canada and the United States in the pre-war years and the shift to a policy oriented towards the United States on the part of Australia and New Zealand during the war itself had suggested that political independence was not a sufficient guarantee of future co-operation in all respects, there was more optimism about the future of the British world system than appears reasonable in retrospect. And although the need for American sympathy and support was widely recognized, it was not thought possible or desirable that the United States should take Britain's place in crucial areas of British concern.

For a variety of reasons, the original testing of Britain's ability to hold her own in a part of the world where the United States had major interests was, as after the First World War, in the Middle East. Indeed American intervention in the Palestine question, which was only the focal point of a much wider area of divergent interests and perceptions, overshadowed the more far-reaching implications of what was happening in South Asia.[12] In 1945 the British Chiefs of Staff were still arguing against abandoning the Palestine mandate: 'The abandonment in favour of the Americans of our present position in Palestine will adversely affect our position, not in this country only but throughout the Moslem world . . . this area will remain of prime importance to the British Empire and we should become dependent to a considerable extent on another country for an area in which we have the major interest'.[13]

[11] Harold Macmillan, *War Diaries: Politics and War in the Mediterranean, 1943–1946* (London, 1984).
[12] See Wm. Roger Louis, *The British Empire in the Middle East, 1945–1951: Arab Nationalism, the United States and Post-War Imperialism* (Oxford, 1984).
[13] Quoted in Michael J. Cohen, *Palestine and the Great Powers* (Princeton, 1982), p. 16.

Two years later, with India and Pakistan independent and with a much better realization of the limitations upon Britain's military, economic, and psychological reserves, such sentiments were to seem outdated. Yet it was again the Middle East—during the Suez crisis—that produced the biggest rift between the two countries during the whole post-war period and that also gave rise to the most explicit and sometimes virulent explosion of anti-colonial sentiment in the United States. It was true enough that an appreciation of the two countries' common interest in resisting Soviet expansion enabled the quarrel to be transcended and relations restored to a better footing. It is also true that some leading Americans were conscious that the standard American view of British imperialism was outdated. But this was a minority view that found difficulty in obtaining a hearing. When in a lecture at Oxford on 24 May 1957, Adlai Stevenson defended Britain's record in leading imperial possessions towards independence, his words received much notice in the British press but were not widely reported in the United States. There are, wrote Stevenson later in the year, 'too many people expounding emphatic views about colonialism and imperialism who haven't travelled in the ex-colonial world in my opinion'.[14]

It would of course be wrong to overlook the fact that the attitude of the United States to the dismantling of the British imperial system was always a subordinate issue to what became between 1945 and 1947, and thereafter remained, the preoccupation with the resistance to the expansion of Communist power, Soviet throughout the subsequent years and Chinese for much of the time. In Europe the issues seemed to be clear-cut and the mutual interests of the partners to the Atlantic Alliance a sufficient guide to measures of defence and deterrence. It was not so in the rest of the world where difficult choices had to be made between sustaining existing imperial structures and seeking for a new clientele among the newly independent successor states. Since the American tradition was against a permanent commitment of power outside the United States, the latter course seemed the preferable one. It is not therefore surprising that, as was noted at the time, the anti-colonialist chorus at the time of Suez was conducted by political figures in the old isolationist tradition and that President Eisenhower was already on record as regarding the United States and Russia as being 'free from the stigma of colonial empire building by force'.[15]

The pursuit of understandings with newly emancipated nations was not without its own perils for American policy-makers. While the older

[14] Adlai E. Stevenson to John Fischer, 14 Aug. 1957, *The Papers of Adlai E. Stevenson*, ed. Walter Johnson (Boston, 1977), vol. vi, p. 49.
[15] See Lionel Gelber, *America in Britain's Place: The Leadership of the West and Anglo-American Unity* (London, 1961), pp. 263–5.

members of the Commonwealth could be relied upon to see world events in ways conformable with American preferences, the newer ones tended to take a more neutralist line and were in some cases much more amenable to the Soviet point of view, as 'non-alignment' proved to have a generally anti-Western bias. Furthermore it became necessary to realize that the new states, whether in the Middle East or Asia, were more closely concerned with local issues than with the so-called East–West struggle. The combination of circumstances that produced the general lack of sympathy between India and the United States and the contrastingly close relationship between the United States and Pakistan affords the most vivid illustration of the point, the more striking in the light of past American sympathies for the Indian nationalist movement. And these problems in turn reacted upon the Anglo-American relationship itself, since it often appeared to Americans that the British attached more importance to keeping the Commonwealth as a going concern than to the actual policies of its individual members.

Nevertheless, it would be true to say that until the last phase in the process of imperial withdrawal, signalled by Harold Macmillan's 'wind of change' speech in 1960, the United States itself—outside the Middle East—played a very minor part in the process.[16] It could indeed be said that in that speech Macmillan accepted what had been fundamentally the American view, namely that 'the great issue in this second half of the twentieth century' was 'whether the uncommitted peoples of Asia and Africa would swing to the East or to the West', and that the only hope for the West lay in accepting the force of local nationalism and seeking to combine it with a respect for racial equality and to embody it in institutions based upon this principle.[17]

By the early 1960s indeed, most of the process of 'decolonization' had been completed and it was clear that the two large remaining areas of British rule—Central and East Africa—would follow the same route, though in Rhodesia for a time to the advantage of local settler rule. But what Britain still retained in the Mediterranean and on the rim of Asia were strong points from which sea and air power could still be exerted for the benefit of the West as a whole. And it was when the United States found itself embroiled in South-east Asia in a post-colonial situation through intervention against Communist aggression in Vietnam that the Americans began to worry that the pressures on Britain of her economic weakness might lead to a premature abandonment of her 'East of Suez' role.[18]

[16] For a useful summary see H. Field Haviland Jr. and Arnold A. Offner, 'The United States and the Commonwealth', in W. B. Hamilton, Kenneth Robinson, and C. D. W. Goodwin, eds., *A Decade of the Commonwealth, 1955–1964* (Durham NC, 1966).

[17] For the main passages of the speech itself, see Nicholas Mansergh, ed., *Documents and Speeches on Commonwealth Affairs, 1952–1962* (London, 1963), pp. 347ff.

[18] See H. G. Nicholas, *The United States and Britain* (London and Chicago, 1975), p. 169.

A British diplomat has recorded this aspect of the visit made to Washington in 1964 by the new Labour Prime Minister, Harold Wilson, and his foreign secretary, Patrick Gordon-Walker:

The US ministers made moving appeals to their British colleagues not to abandon their role in the Far East. Concerned over Britain's balance of payments difficulties, they were afraid that the Labour Government would suddenly do in the Far East what they had done in Greece, pull out and leave the burden of resisting the spread of Communism entirely to the USA. Rusk said with some eloquence and evident sincerity that the US did not want to be left alone with the task of maintaining peace in the Far East, and that they were convinced that Britain still had an important role there. I had the impression that this appeal had an effect, unacknowledged at the time, which endured until economic difficulties became still more acute a few years later.[19]

Whether or not the delay in withdrawing from east of Suez was due to pressure exercised by the United States, the Vietnam War, itself so important for its impact upon American thinking, was also revealing of the differences of attitude within the Commonwealth to the United States role; and the various and unsuccessful efforts by Commonwealth governments to see a mediated end to hostilities are best understood in light of the desire of the British and others to minimize their impact upon the unity of the Commonwealth.[20]

By the early 1970s, the United States appeared to have achieved its principal objectives and desires. Britain had become a member of the European Communities which the United States had always insisted was its correct role.[21] It had also freed itself from what the Americans had regarded as the inhibiting burden of colonialism. Such territories as it retained were retained almost without exception by the wish of their inhabitants, or like the US trust territories in the Pacific were strategic outposts too small to be thought of as serious exceptions to the general principle of self-determination. The Commonwealth itself, with which the United States had found it difficult to come to terms, was of decreasing significance in Britain's affairs in almost every respect. It may be that it played its last important role in providing a mechanism through which negotiations could take place by which Britain with the minimum loss of face allowed Rhodesia to begin the process of becoming a normal African one-party state. It should perhaps be added that the emotional, as opposed to the practical, aspect of the Commonwealth can still be evoked when it suits a British government, as in relation to the United States' successful intervention in Grenada.

---

[19] Nicholas Henderson, *The Private Office* (London, 1984).

[20] See J. D. B. Miller, *Survey of Commonwealth Affairs: Problems of Expansion and Attrition, 1953–1969* (London, 1974), ch. 6, 'The Commonwealth and Southeast Asia'.

[21] See Max Beloff, *The United States and the Unity of Europe* (Washington, DC, 1963).

The only direct intervention of the United States in recent years in dealing with the legacy of colonialism—again leaving the Middle East on one side—has been with respect to Namibia, where a basic hostility to the South African presence has been influenced by the connection of the Namibia problem with the role of the Cubans in Angola, that is to say with the extension to the African continent of the world-wide struggle against Communism which remains the inevitable core of American policy. And this struggle has also tended to align British and American policy in relation to South Africa, where alienation of Third World opinion has been balanced by concern over the strategic interests of the West—a balance made more difficult to hold because of the very different analysis of the situation embraced by the majority of white South Africans. But South Africa's absence from the Commonwealth for a quarter of a century makes the connection with British decolonization a rather remote one.

From the point of view of the Soviet bloc and much of the Third World it is the United States rather than Britain that represents imperialism, since its power is greater and more obvious. Nor, if one uses the word—as is not usually done—in a neutral sense, is this view without foundation. If it is true that on the political side in the sense of a direct claim to or exercise of sovereignty, the American 'Empire' is much smaller than the European empires that have now all but disappeared, its informal empire, that is to say the propping up of states and regimes through advice and assistance and in the last resort military guarantees, is a considerable one, and in the debatable areas on the Soviet periphery, covert activities of various kinds remind one of the 'great game' in central Asia in the last century. The difference between the United States today and the old imperial powers—and indeed the Soviet Union with its own specific form of imperialism—is that while they had conscious or unconscious philosophies which to their ruling élites, and at times to wider strata of society, seemed to justify their status and activities, the United States is clearly still reluctant to accept its imperial role as anything but an expedient resorted to in self-defence. The ignorance and lack of expertise that Macmillan noted in the war years may have disappeared; many Americans are clearly well-equipped to understand the particularities of individual situations, but domestic political considerations make it unlikely that such insights will always be used.

In dealing with the Third World the United States has also passed through a learning experience in which the former colonial rulers could give little help. It was only in the last years of the British Empire that positive programmes of economic and social development began to be undertaken, and these were largely superseded by the coming of independence at a pace unforeseen when these programmes were embarked upon.[22] British action was throughout empirical in nature, and limited by the paucity of available finance. The United States, in dealing with these countries after independence and in the context of aid, was for a time much influenced by development economics which had as its basis a belief that the mere liberation of national energies would suffice, with a little technical assistance and financial pump-priming, to put such countries on an upward path; all that was needed for flight was 'take-off'. What was lacking was the perception of how much many of these countries owed to externally imposed constraints upon internecine conflict, and the degree to which even a subsistence economy, let alone one integrated with world markets, depends upon the ability of government to sustain a minimal apparatus of law and order.[23] When on top of the new governments' inability to offer these services was imposed their propensity to economic policies of the most counter-productive kind, the results were inevitable—poverty, falling living standards, famine.

Yet because of the overriding desire to keep these countries 'non-aligned', and perhaps because it was felt that colonial guilt had to be expiated, there was a long period during which such observations in international agencies on the part of Western representatives were considered very bad form. The United States thus found itself in the position (shared with other Western countries) of being denounced by the partisans of the 'new economic order' at the same time as being threatened with further troubles if it did not accept these governments' views about the rightfulness of their claims for ever-increasing assistance on their own terms. It could be argued that the American contribution to the disappearance of the European overseas empires was at most a marginal one—perhaps least important in the British case. What is correct is that the events themselves have produced a situation which was never desired by the United States and with which neither its history nor its institutions are very helpful in enabling it to cope.

In more recent years a greater sense of realism has made itself felt in American policy and the fact that the United States preceded the United Kingdom in giving notice of leaving UNESCO—a symbolic as well as a practical gesture—might even suggest that in their basic attitudes towards the Third World the paths of the two governments have converged.

When one looks at the effect of the whole of this history upon relations between the United States and the United Kingdom, one must keep in

---

[22] D. J. Morgan, *The Official History of Colonial Development*, 5 vols. (London, 1980).
[23] See Max Beloff, 'The Third World and the Conflict of Ideologies', in W. Scott Thompson, ed., *The Third World: Premises of US Policy* (Revised edn., San Francisco, 1983).

mind the fact rightly emphasized by Professor D. Cameron Watt that it is not only governments and their policies that are relevant to this subject. And this is equally true of both countries. In the United States there has been a shift in the general balance of power between regions and ethnic groups, bringing to the fore new élites particularly in Congress. But the relevance of this development to British decolonization has been only intermittent. Only Palestine attracted much domestic political attention. Black Americans were too preoccupied with their own struggles to show much consistent concern with decolonization in Africa or the Caribbean although they may contribute to the pressures for a harder line in relation to the unresolved problems of southern Africa.

More important as a source of possible friction has been the ability of the Irish-Americans to persuade themselves and others of their fellow-countrymen that Northern Ireland presents a colonial situation in the modern sense and could be resolved by 'decolonization' in defiance of the wishes of the majority of its inhabitants.

On the British side, the problem requires a rather different analysis, since the left-right polarization of British party politics and the existence of powerful pressure groups particularly on the extreme left have had some impact upon relations with the United States. Almost until the coming of the Second World War, a friendly attitude towards the United States was characteristic of the left rather than the right in British politics. But with the post-war polarization of the world between the two superpowers, elements on the British scene fundamentally more favourable to the Soviet Union than to the United States have been active in trying to shift the policies of successive British governments in an anti-American direction. Most of the issues that have been raised did not relate to decolonization or the Third World—issues of strategy and above all arms control and disarmament were more important. But the strong anti-colonialism of the extreme left has been mobilized against the United States at the time of the war in Vietnam and more recently over Grenada and Central America. A minority of such people have defended Soviet behaviour even in Afghanistan, but on the whole anti-Americanism has proved a more widely acceptable stance than a generalized support for the Soviet Union. An enthusiasm for aid programmes and an unwillingness to countenance criticism of the governments aided goes alongside criticism of the United States for doing too little to assist in promoting improvements in the standards of living of the Third World and in giving it a share of the guilt for the 'neo-colonialism' which is held to be to blame for the economic difficulties that Third World countries encounter.

So far anti-Americanism of this kind, whether adumbrated in respect of decolonization or Third World issues or not, has been ineffective in terms of policy—such pressures have been resisted by both Conservative and Labour governments. What the growth of anti-American predispositions in the Labour and Liberal parties portends for the future is another matter. But it is not easy to see the specific issues with which this paper has been concerned playing a more than marginal role in whatever difficulties and disagreements may lie ahead.

The conclusion must be that while the United States has directly or indirectly played a major role in replacing the world dominated by the European Empires with the quite different international environment with which the United Kingdom and her European partners find themselves confronted today, the immediate and concrete manifestations of this process have been overshadowed by ideological conflict and superpower rivalry and the technological revolution that has fuelled both.

16

American Anti-Colonialism and the Dissolution of the British Empire

WM. ROGER LOUIS

In the previous chapter Lord Beloff has argued—in what has become known as the 'Beloff thesis'—that the United States has failed to fill the political void left by the downfall of the British Empire. Despite the 'Special Relationship' with the British, and the opportunity to learn from them the lessons of management of world affairs, the Americans continue to rely on antiquated doctrines of the American revolution that amount to little more than the patently unsatisfactory proposition (in Lord Beloff's view) that good government is no substitute for self-government. The United States, having helped to bring about the collapse of the British Empire, has not replaced Britain as a guarantor of world order. The *Pax Britannica* has disappeared; the *Pax Americana* has yet to emerge. Have the failures of the United States, he asks, been those of the intellect or the will? A further and perhaps more fundamental question might be asked. Was it ever the intention to create a *Pax Americana*?

This chapter will pursue the question of American motive as well as strength of purpose, and will link the themes of the Anglo-American 'Special Relationship' to the issue of anti-colonialism by examining certain long-term themes and specific cases: India during the Roosevelt period; Libya during the Truman years; and Suez under Eisenhower.

It is useful to bear in mind British suspicions. In 1954 the British Ambassador in Washington, Sir Roger Makins (now Lord Sherfield), like Lord Beloff, raised the question of motive:

There is on our side a very understandable suspicion that the Americans are out to take our place in the Middle East. Their influence has greatly expanded there since the end of the second World War, and they are now firmly established as the paramount foreign influence in Turkey and in Saudi Arabia. They are gaining a similar ascendancy in Persia, and it now seems that Pakistan may to some extent be drawn into their orbit. . . . Are the Americans consciously trying to substitute their influence for ours in the Middle East?[1]

[1] Memorandum by Makins, 25 Jan. 1954, CAB 129/66. All references to British records refer to documents at the Public Record Office, London. An expanded version of this chapter has appeared in *International Affairs*, 61.2 (1985). My thanks to John Roper and Lucy Seton-Watson.

Makins also asked whether the political influence of the United States in such places as the Middle East was an 'inevitable' consequence of America's growing military and economic power. His enquiry retains historical interest. Americans of the post-war era were certainly aware of their economic, political, and military strength. Whether or not they believed themselves to be the heirs of the British Empire is more problematical. Whether or not they became latter day imperialists because of the nature of the world economic system is even more debatable. Of those who guided American policy, one thing can be said with certainty: they were determined not to repeat the mistakes of the inter-war period. In 1945, just as in 1919, they attempted to apply broad principles to complex colonial problems.

One of those principles was the idea of self-determination. Franklin Delano Roosevelt no less than Woodrow Wilson embraced the concept. Both were gradualists. Both held that colonial peoples would and should eventually determine their own future, but neither foresaw the abrupt end of the European colonial system. The speed of the liquidation is a key point, as will be seen, in the question of responsibility for the aftermath. F.D.R. was a rogue Wilsonian. He believed in the same goals as Wilson, or so it seemed because of his frequent reiteration of some of Wilson's principles. He used Wilsonian rhetoric, but his aim was different. He wished to reshape the League of Nations and make it an effective force to preserve the peace. Yet his scheme of the 'Four Policemen' (the United States, Britain, the Soviet Union, and China) resembled the old spheres of influence which Wilson had hoped to abolish. On the issue of security Roosevelt went in the opposite direction from Wilson. Never again would nations such as Germany and Japan be allowed to menace the peace of the world. Disarmament had proved to be a broken reed. Regional security would be the foundation of the future. In the Pacific the United States would administer the Marianas, Marshalls, and Carolines as a trust territory of the United Nations but would remain free to fortify them or use them as testing sites. The ideology of trusteeship was easily forged into a weapon of American defence. Ideology serves self-interest. American anti-colonialism, if not the principle of self-determination, was always reconciled with the needs of security.

The ideology of 'free trade' served a similar function for the expanding American economy. Robinson and Gallagher's Victorians would have recognized the methods of the post-Second World War Americans. Leopold Amery, whose involvement in the affairs of the British Empire extended from the Boer War through the Second World War, once said that he would prefer Hitler's 'New Order' to Cordell Hull's 'Free Trade'. By 1945 Amery believed that American economic expansion represented an attempt to reduce Britain to the status of a satellite state. What type of economic order were the two countries in fact attempting to create? There was a great divergence of aims in fields such as international trade and finance as well as civil aviation. In economic affairs as in colonial matters, self-interest, rather than the clichés of 'free trade' or 'independence', helps to explain the course of events after 1945.

As Donald Watt has perceptively written, Anglo-American relations can be understood only by comprehending the nature of the élites in both countries, by studying their misperceptions and fixations, and by examining their unspoken assumptions.[2] By the end of the Second World War, the British view about the men of 'our race' ruling America was no longer true, and it is still less true today. Yet there are certain continuities. In 1945, as previously and still today, most Americans admired the British for their civility and their belief in the rule of law and parliamentary democracy.[3] It would be a grave mistake to underestimate the genuine admiration felt by most Americans for English values, or for that matter Scottish, Welsh, and Irish values. The same cannot be said for the creed of the British Empire. With the exception of some fanatical Anglophiles of the English Speaking Union, and the romanticists of the 'White Man's burden' (and perhaps a further, more rational minority who regarded British rule as an instrument of progress), Americans did not admire British imperialism. Perhaps the best example of one organ of the press catching the collective sentiment of the American public was the 'Open Letter to the People of England' published by *Life* magazine in October 1942 at the time of the 'Quit India' movement:

One thing we are sure we are *not* fighting for is to hold the British Empire together. We don't like to put the matter so bluntly, but we don't want you to have any illusions. If your strategists are planning a war to hold the British Empire together they will sooner or later find themselves strategizing all alone. . . . In the light of what you are doing in India, how do you expect us to talk about 'principles' and look our soldiers in the eye?[4]

The ideology of the American anti-colonial campaign was more than a reflection of self-interest. It was a force in itself which helped to shape the

[2] D. Cameron Watt, *Succeeding John Bull: America in Britain's Place* (Cambridge, 1984).

[3] It should be noted however that some Americans with longstanding connections with Britain regarded the Labour victory of 1945 as a turn for the worse. 'I feel that the trouble [with post-war Britain]' commented Judge Joseph Hutcheson (the American Chairman of the Anglo-American Committee of Inquiry on Palestine), 'is that the British have abandoned their ancient traditions and feeling for England as England in exchange for a sorry mess of pottage, a socialist theory and a labor government.' Hutcheson to James G. McDonald, 9 June 1947, McDonald Papers (Columbia University).

[4] Quoted in W. R. Louis, *Imperialism at Bay* (Oxford, 1977), p. 198.

substance of defence, economic, and foreign policy. It was a set of principles that most Americans upheld. The essence of it was the belief that colonial subjects had the inherent right to become independent and to rule themselves.

INDIA

It would be unjust to the protagonists of the Second World War era, American as well as British, to assume that they were unaware of the potential as well as the limits of their ideological assumptions, or the danger of conceding political principles. 'Our war aims . . . [are] practical weapons', Wendell Willkie once said privately.[5] When Churchill and Roosevelt (and their respective advisers Sir Alexander Cadogan and Sumner Welles) penned Article III of the Atlantic Charter in August 1941, each party in the transaction knew precisely how far these weapons could be employed within the context of the Anglo-American alliance. The Americans were insistent on a statement that the war was being fought to uphold the right of self-determination. Churchill acquiesced, but the ambiguity of the phrasing allowed him to argue afterwards that the aims of restoring self-government applied only to those countries subjugated by the Nazis. The principle of self-determination was a double-edged sword. In Churchill's hands it proved to be a suitable weapon for defending, negatively, the British Empire and the status quo. If the doctrine were applied to the Middle East, Churchill stated, the Arabs might claim by majority that 'they could expel the Jews from Palestine'.[6]

Within the American government the key official who dealt with colonial affairs was the Under Secretary of State, Sumner Welles. He harboured a deep-seated animosity towards what he believed to be the malignant forces of British imperialism. It is now clear from the historical records that his influence extended beyond official circles into behind-the-scenes manœuvres designed to weaken the British presence throughout the world. Welles is thus a good example of Lord Beloff's point about a concerted American effort to undermine the British Empire. He was pro-Zionist as well as anti-British. After he resigned as Under Secretary in 1943 he carried his campaign against the British Empire into the public arenas of newspaper controversy and, later, into the politics of the United Nations. At first sight it might therefore seem surprising that, at the time of the signing of the Atlantic Charter, Welles did not attempt to seize the initiative by insisting on the universal

[5] In an interview with Louis Fischer, 13 Aug. 1942, Louis Fischer Papers, Franklin D. Roosevelt Library, Hyde Park, NY.

[6] Winston S. Churchill, *The Hinge of Fate* (Boston, 1950), p. 890.

applicability of the self-determination principle as a means of breaking up the British Empire by, for example, liberating India. Welles's attitude in fact was identical with Roosevelt's. It was a question of priorities. The war was being fought against Germany and Japan. He judged that the war effort as a whole might be disrupted by the discord injected into the the Anglo-American alliance by an anti-colonial crusade.[7]

The American Secretary of State, Cordell Hull, believed that guarantees of political 'independence' should be accompanied by a reform of the international economic system. Of all the ideologues in the American government, Hull epitomized, to the British, the cliché of the 'open door' whereby world trade would be 'opened' to the Americans at the expense of the British. Hull of course resented the British interpretation of his doctrine and his motives, but Amery (who served as Secretary of State for India during the war) was not far off the mark when he described Hull's philosophy as dating back 'to somewhere round 1860' if not the eighteenth century. Hull for his part accurately identified Leo Amery, Lord Linlithgow (the Viceroy), and Churchill as the arch-opponents of any attempt to break up the system of Imperial Preference or to extend the principles of the Atlantic Charter to India and the colonial dependencies. Like Roosevelt and Welles, Hull never lost sight of the colonial issue, and he also realistically attached a higher importance to the Anglo-American alliance and the winning of the war. 'The difficulty is that when the other party is immovable we cannot interfere', Hull said about the British in 1942. 'It is just as if some foreign country tried to tell us how to implement the Monroe Doctrine.' Hull's comments reveal the American frustration at this stage of the war with the Indian crisis as well as the whole colonial issue: 'while the President is not missing any opportunities, we cannot do much while the British are immovable. The other fellow may dig his toes in and say, "There I stand even if everything else goes to pieces." '[8] As far as Churchill, Amery, and Linlithgow were concerned, that was an accurate perception.

Roosevelt did not miss any opportunities to press for economic advantage (though he too subordinated economic as well as colonial

[7] The conclusion is dramatically different, though not contradictory, if drawn from an Indian rather than Anglo-American perspective. A leading Indian historian has written: 'To win the war as speedily as possible was the President's overriding objective. He and his closest associates showed no disposition to reflect on the currents and forces unleashed by the war itself and [the] proclaimed Allied commitment to democracy and the right of peoples to determine their own destiny. America's elite groups remained unresponsive to the Indian demand during India's year [i.e. 1942] of travails. But a relatively small number of Americans [e.g. Wendell Willkie] refused to remain silent and fervently argued that India was a test case of the sincerity of Allied intentions. These men were the salt of the American earth.' M. S. Venkataramani and B. K. Shrivastava, *Quit India: The American Response to the 1942 Struggle* (New Delhi, 1979), p. 335.

[8] Quoted in a note by Louis Fischer, 27 Aug. 1942, Fischer Papers.

issues to the higher purpose of winning the war). Nor did Churchill miss
any chance to strengthen the Anglo-American alliance while simultaneously he attempted to check American ambitions on the British
Empire. In the short run Churchill had the better part of the game. The
principal reason why American anti-colonialism during the Second
World War proved to be an ineffective force was that Churchill, Amery,
Linlithgow, and, it should be added, Oliver Stanley (Colonial Secretary
1942–5) managed to contain it in the limited yet symbolic area of
international trusteeship affairs. But it should not be forgotten that the
game was being played for the highest stakes. One cannot read the files
of the Presidential correspondence at the Roosevelt Library without
recognizing that Roosevelt and his advisers in 1942 were apprehensive
of revolution in India. From a Tory point of view Linlithgow's robust
response in jailing the Indian nationalist leaders in 1942 was necessary,
decisive, and admirable. The Americans were given no opportunity to
meddle in what was, as Cordell Hull was forced to acknowledge, an
internal affair.

The British managed to hold their own. They were uneasily aware
that if they failed to keep their grip on India, then others, the Americans
if not the Japanese, would intervene. The Americans might protest that
India would be an unwelcome burden, but they would eventually
attempt to mobilize the Indians against the Japanese, and to launch
India on a new course. The American 'scare' of 1942 lingered on in
Anglo-American relations casting a shadow over the colonial world. At
the time the lesson was clear, above all to Amery, who believed that the
British Empire would have to be integrated into a more effective and
self-contained economic and political unity because of the danger of an
American take-over. 'In spite of Atlantic Charters and all that sort of
stuff', Amery wrote, 'it looks as if the world were moving steadily
towards more intensive national organisation and if so, our Empire may
have to follow suit or fall into the hands of others.'[9]

Amery was fully aware of the danger, from the British point of view, of
the economic implications of Article VII of the Lend-Lease agreement,
which obligated the British to eliminate 'discrimination', in other words,
Imperial Preference. He wrote in January 1942: 'We, in our anxiety to
secure Lease-Lend and bring America in [to the war], have never had
the courage to say straight out that Imperial Preference is not merely a
matter of economic policy but a natural political right of the British
Commonwealth.'[10] The British faced the predicament not only of
becoming economically dependent on the United States but also of

---

[9] Amery to Linlithgow, 30 Jan. 1942, in Nicholas Mansergh *et al.*, eds., *The Transfer of Power
1942–7* (London, 1970–83), i, pp. 94–5.
[10] Amery to Linlithgow, 5 Jan. 1942, ibid., i, p. 8.

falling into debt to India and certain other countries in the British imperial system, such as Egypt and Iraq. 'The British nation is quite unaware of what is taking place', Churchill wrote in September 1942, 'and no one dreams that if the war goes on until 1944 or 1945 we may owe India seven or eight hundred million sterling . . .'[11] It was not a bad guess. At the close of the war India held favourable sterling balances of £1,100 million. And after the termination of Lend-Lease in August 1945 the British were compelled to accept a loan of $3.75 billion from the United States. Amery's nightmare of economic dependence on America had come true. The vital issue now was whether the United States would support the British Empire in defence arrangements, underwrite economic development in the colonial world, and allow the British to maintain the sterling area, thereby allowing them to endure as a 'world power'.

The Americans were willing to yield on economic issues (as will be seen in the minor but illuminating case of Libya) if the British would help to meet American strategic requirements and make political concessions. In the political domain 'federalism' was an American preoccupation. In one of the most famous but also most misunderstood episodes of the war, Roosevelt in 1942 exhorted Churchill to learn the lessons of the American revolution and to follow the precedents of American constitutional development. Churchill retorted that the wartime crisis was hardly a time for constitutional experiments. He was refusing to listen. Roosevelt was making a point of substance. Though he was hardly aware of it, F.D.R. was vaguely grasping at the elements of the India Act of 1935, which Churchill had opposed and the Viceroy, Linlithgow, had championed (Roosevelt would have had a more exacting dialogue had he been speaking to Linlithgow).

Roosevelt was not merely insisting that the Indians be given a right to frame their own constitution. He was also searching for a federal solution in which 'checks and balances' would stabilize the Indian political system and afford guarantees for the minorities. The State Department later watched with approval the attempt at federal constitution-making in Malaya, Nigeria, the Central African Federation, and the West Indies. In American eyes the supreme test had been India in 1947, when British willingness to transfer power had proved to American satisfaction that the dissolution of the old British Empire and the creation of the new multiracial Commonwealth would provide the basis of a new order of stability and progress. By conceding independence to India and Pakistan the British helped to create an Anglo-American alliance in the affairs of the colonial world—the 'Third World' as it was later known.

[11] Churchill to Linlithgow, 24 Sept. 1942, ibid., iii, p. 37.

To most Americans in 1947, the granting of Indian independence was
one of Britain's finest hours.

Did the Americans foresee the replacement of the British Raj by
American political and economic influence? They certainly drove hard
bargains at British expense. They knew that the expansion of American
power during the war would enable them to play a greater part in world
affairs. But the reduction of Britain, still less India, to satellite status was
a British suspicion, not an American motive. The emergence of the
United States as one of the two superpowers, and the eclipse of British
power, was a result of the Second World War. If the post-war period can
be described as a *Pax Americana* (a dubious assumption at best), it
certainly was not modelled after the *Pax Britannica*.

LIBYA

The post-war Libyan state, which became independent in 1951, was a
British creation within the context of Anglo-American collaboration
and United Nations sponsorship. It used to be assumed that Libyan
independence was the result of the lead taken by certain officials at the
United Nations with the support of the United States government.
There was a mythology of Libyan independence as the first post-war
triumph of the idealism of the United Nations. The historical evidence
now reveals the establishment of a British client state with the active
collaboration of the secretariat of the United Nations and the diplomatic
and military branches of the United States government. Thus Libya is a
good test of the proposition that there was a failure of the will on the part
of the United States in measuring up to post-war 'imperial' responsibilities.

Libya is the fourth largest state in Africa, two and a half times the size
of Texas. But it is ninety-five per cent desert. In 1945 it had a population
of 880,000, eighty-six per cent of whom were Muslim and some five per
cent Italian—a remnant of Italy's colonial rule. During the Second
World War the Italians had been driven out of the eastern province of
Cyrenaica and the Italian community of 40,000 was concentrated in
Tripolitania.

Until 1949 British policy under Ernest Bevin had essentially pursued
the 'bridgehead' tactic of partitioning Libya among the British
(Cyrenaica), the French (the Fezzan), and the Italians (Tripolitania).
In 1949 in response to riots in Tripolitania and protests from the Arab
states, British policy shifted towards the creation of a single Libyan state.
The British were anticipating the eventual evacuation of Suez. Cyrenaica would be the alternative, the new linchpin of British security in
the eastern Mediterranean. From beginning to end the British were

willing to pay a large price for this base, by withdrawing from the other former Italian colonies under British military occupation, Eritrea and Somalia, or even by making concessions to the Russians. Libya was to become no less than the Singapore of the Mediterranean. That plan was quickly overtaken by events, but it is important to bear it in mind in order to comprehend both the importance the British attached to Libya in the post-war period and the significance of it in the debate about American motives.

There was a reassertion of the American anti-colonial attitude in 1949 during the controversy about the fate of Libya. The American reaction can be explained in part by the denunciation of 'imperialism' during the riots in Tripoli and by the remorse of guilt by association with the British. By giving reluctant support to the British plan for Italian, French, and British trusteeship administrations, the Americans had lost, in the judgement of the State Department official responsible for Libyan affairs, 'a large amount of the reserve of good will which we enjoy among the Asiatics as the result of our treatment of the Philippines.'[12] It appeared to the British that the same naïve panacea for the troubles of the colonial world had now resurfaced with a vengeance. For now the Americans made no secret that 'independence' beginning in Libya would eventually sweep through all of north-west Africa. In the American view these developments would be 'inevitable'. 'The Americans will welcome and press for early independence in Libya', wrote the head of the African Department of the Foreign Office, 'not merely as the only practicable solution, but also because they realise its effects on the French position in Tunisia, Algeria, and Morocco. The State Department have made no effort to conceal this from us.'[13]

Hector McNeil (Ernest Bevin's chief lieutenant in these matters at the Foreign Office) thought that regardless of Libya's status, independent or not, it was essential for Libya to become a British client state. The Americans would have to be drawn in to support the British, perhaps by stationing troops in Libya. McNeil summed up the tactics to be used with the Americans: 'Our need is great: our case is not good. We must therefore be as naive as possible.'[14] Such was the political façade of British imperialism.

The military dimension of the Libyan problem is clear in the assessments by the British Chiefs of Staff. They regarded Libya as the future 'pillar of British strategy'. The United Nations' plans for Libya, they believed, had nothing to do with the well-being of the inhabitants

[12] Memorandum by Joseph Palmer, 27 May 1949, State Department 865.014/5-2749 Box 770 (National Archives, Washington, DC).

[13] Minute by G. L. Clutton, 29 May 1949, FO 371/73880.

[14] Minute by McNeil, 28 July 1949, FO 371/73838.

or the peace of the world, except negatively. The enemies of the British
Commonwealth and Empire at the United Nations aimed, indirectly at
least, at altering the political and strategic balance of power in northern
Africa and the Mediterranean. The Chiefs of Staff therefore wished to
make it unequivocally clear how Britain's position as a 'world power'
might be affected:

> Today, we are still a world power, shouldering many and heavy responsibilities.
> We believe the privileged position that we, in contrast to the other European
> nations, enjoy with the United States and the attention which she now pays to
> our strategic and other opinions, and to our requirements, is directly due to our
> hold on the Middle East and all that this involves.
>
> If we surrendered that hold and the responsibilities which it entails, we would
> automatically surrender our position as a world power, with the inevitable
> strategic and economic consequences. We should join the ranks of the other
> European powers and be treated as such by the United States.[15]

It would be up to the British to hold the Middle East in the event of war
with the Soviet Union. The United States would continue to respect
Britain as a 'world power' only as long as the British could defend the
Middle East alone, at least initially. 'We must find a way of holding the
Middle East at the beginning of a war with our own resources and of
developing offensive action against Russia from that area. We believe
this can be done. It must be done.'[16] Such views of the Chiefs of Staff
provide massive substantiation for the argument that in the early 1950s
the British not only believed that they were still a great 'world power'
but were also determined to remain one. To do so they needed the
military as well as the political support of the United States.

American involvement in building the Libyan state was deliberately
kept as low-key as possible. 'I think we must be extremely careful', wrote
Andrew Lynch, the Consul General in Tripoli, not to give the
impression 'of coming into Libya in a high-powered manner'.[17] Support
for the British indirectly bolstered the American position. Like the
British, the Americans were wary of the possibility of a unitary state
which might fall under extremist or Egyptian influence (which by 1949
was already a cause for alarm to the British and Americans as well as the
French). The plan therefore was a federal state—the theme of
'federalism' persists—which might however work out less well in this
case for the Americans than for the British. If the federation collapsed,
then the Americans in Tripolitania would be left to face radical

---

[15] Chiefs of Staff, 'Strategic Implications of an Independent and United Libya,' COS (49) 381,
10 Nov. 1949, DEFE 5/18.
[16] Ibid.
[17] Lynch to Acheson, 20 July 1951, *Foreign Relations of the United States 1951*, vol. v, p. 1332.

nationalism in that part of Libya where anti-Western sentiment was the most severe.

The two allies were making separate calculations in secret. What the Americans did not know was that the British military planners now regarded Tripolitania as well as Cyrenaica as a desirable place for military installations: the barracks built by the Italians in Tripolitania seemed more and more attractive because of the expense involved in building new ones in Cyrenaica. What the British did not know was the projected scope of the American military commitment. 'Wheelus Field' might eventually include seven additional air fields, a US Navy communications facility, supply and service centres, 500 square miles for an amphibious training area for the Army and Marine Corps, and bombing rights in the desert. Wheelus Field had the potential to become an American military area or 'base' in Libya comparable to the British 'base' at Suez. It would be smaller in scale but almost as complex. This was a delicate issue. With their historic tradition of anti-colonialism, the Americans were apprehensive that these plans might be misunderstood. Even the existing installation at Wheelus evoked nationalist protest. 'We are being accused of being new imperialists who plan to take over all of Libya', Andrew Lynch ruefully reported from Libya.[18]

The British and Americans were assisted in their military and political plans by the Dutchman Adrian Pelt, the United Nations Commissioner for Libyan Affairs. Pelt's part in the birth of the Libyan state later assumed almost mythological dimensions because of his own monumental account, *Libyan Independence and the United Nations: A Case of Planned Decolonization*.[19] As in most cases the legend is larger than the historical figure, though Pelt has good claim to be described as one of the fathers of the Libyan state. There was inevitable tension between him and the British because of the anti-colonial sentiment at the United Nations. But there emerges from the British archives a theme which is quite subdued in Pelt's book. He knew from the beginning that, if his mission were to be a success, he would have to work closely with the British on all points of detail as well as principle, strategic as well as financial. 'Collaboration' is an apt word to describe the working relationship between him and the Americans as well as the British.

The critical constitutional issue upon which the British and Pelt were agreed was that Libya should have a federal rather than a unitary government. 'The immediate problem', wrote the British Permanent Under-Secretary at the Foreign Office, would be to establish 'a simple form of government, not a centralised type, but of a federal type.'[20] The

---

[18] Lynch to Acheson, 30 Oct. 1951, ibid., p. 1358.
[19] New Haven, 1970.
[20] Memorandum by Sir William Strang, 20 Feb. 1950, FO 371/89015.

greater the autonomy in Cyrenaica, the greater would be the British influence in the area most critical to them. As Pelt later pointed out in his book, the problem of federation versus unitarism ran like a leitmotiv from beginning to end through the years 1950–1. It was the British–United Nations (i.e. Pelt) combination that proved to be effective in defeating the aim of the Arab states and the radical nationalists who wished to create a highly centralized state that might have been less receptive to British influence. The Anglo-American point of view was that a federal state might be split up, if necessary, with the British, Americans, and French continuing to exert influence in their respective areas of Cyrenaica, Tripolitania, and the Fezzan.

The American contribution was, above all, financial. Pelt knew that the only way the new state could be self-supporting was by leasing bases to the British and the Americans. He assumed from the outset that the British and the Americans would subsidize the Libyan state in return for strategic facilities. This was the key to the 'special' relationship. During a visit to Washington in June 1951 Pelt learned that an annual $1.5 million would be available for economic assistance and that the pending legislation for the mutual security programme would greatly ease the problem of the Libyan budget. This was the origin of the United States–Libyan agreement of 1954 that provided $42 million over the period 1954–71 (which in fact amounted to a vastly larger figure if indirect subsidies such as grain shipments are taken into account). The British figure in comparison was £2.75 million per annum, which was about the same as the annual British subsidy to Jordan.

The tension in this quite special relationship between the British, Americans, and the United Nations arose in the question of Libya and the sterling area. This was one of the principal concerns of the head of the African Department of the British Foreign Office, Roger Allen, when he visited Libya in the spring of 1951 at the time when all the vital issues about impending independence came to a head. Allen heard Andrew Lynch pronounce a representative American view when he spoke of the 'dead hand of the sterling area'. Allen replied in kind by denouncing Lynch as an 'imperialist' of a well-known American type who wished to take over the British Empire by economic means. Pelt despondently observed that the British had persuaded the Libyans themselves of the virtues of sterling. He knew that the British were in dead earnest. Britain's status as a 'world power' depended on holding the Middle East, but this position could be sustained only by economic recovery, and this in turn meant the protection of the sterling area. The British as the occupying military authority therefore put the screws on the Libyans, who made it clear to the Americans, and the United Nations, that Libya would join the sterling area. At one stage Allen noted that if Pelt attempted to block Libya's entry into the sterling area then the British would 'run him down'.[21] Both the United States and the United Nations acquiesced in Libya's entry into the sterling area. To the British it was a crucial issue, to which the other parties were willing to yield in order to achieve their own aims. The solution, Libyan independence in 1951, received the endorsement of the British Cabinet and the American President without ever becoming a divisive issue either between or within the two governments. For the 'Special Relationship', the Libyan case can thus be described as an example of compatible institutionalized inter-relationships between the State Department and the Foreign Office, and between the branches of the military services, with harmonious rather than dissonant resonance at higher levels.

With British armour in Libya, the way was clear for the withdrawal from Suez. Before passing on to the origins of the Suez crisis, however, it might be as well to summarize the argument of this chapter in regard to American anti-colonialism, British imperialism, and Middle Eastern nationalism. American anti-colonialism was a sentiment easily reconciled with defence requirements and economic opportunities. It was always subordinate to the more urgent problem of anti-Communism. Yet anti-colonialism could not be dismissed merely as a self-serving or shallow slogan. It was a genuine sentiment amounting to an article of faith on the part of the American people, who believed that 'independence' should be the end result of colonial rule. So long as the British genuinely seemed to be making progress towards 'colonial independence', then the colonial issue was relatively unimportant in Anglo-American relations. In 1954 the British evacuation of Suez signalled a major effort to accommodate Egyptian nationalism. For the Americans the 1956 crisis represented a return to the old imperialism that should have died with the Second World War. Here there was indeed a question of the 'act of will'—the question of whose will would prevail in Britain, and whose will would prevail between Britain and America. The Suez crisis itself helps to explain the final decline of the *Pax Britannica*, and it also indicates some of the reasons why a *Pax Americana* of the same order has not arisen to take its place.

SUEZ

So complex are the issues, and so tantalizing the unresolved parts of the Suez puzzle, that almost any brief comment on it is bound to seem simplistic and incomplete. Nevertheless this chapter will continue to focus on American anti-colonialism by discussing it as part of the Suez

[21] Memorandum by Allen, 14 June 1951, FO 371/90363.

crisis. Sometimes a single line helps to keep bearings on a landscape that seems so remote yet so close to the present.

The collision of 1956 with the United States was precisely what the British had attempted to avoid since 1945. The British of course were aware that in Egypt as elsewhere their success depended on American support. One of the shrewdest officials at the British Foreign Office, Sir Pierson Dixon, wrote in 1952:

Thinking over our difficulties in Egypt, it seems to me that the essential difficulty arises from the very obvious fact that we lack power. The Egyptians know this, and that accounts for their intransigence. . . . Power, of course, is not to be measured in terms alone of money and troops: a third ingredient is prestige, or in other words what the rest of the world thinks of us.

Here the dilemma arises. We are not physically strong enough to carry out policies needed if we are to retain our position in the world; if we show weakness our position in the world diminishes with repercussions on our world wide position.

The broadest conclusion I am driven to is therefore that we ought to make every conceivable effort to avoid a policy of surrender or near surrender. Ideally we should persuade the Americans of the disaster which such a policy would entail for us and for them, and seek their backing, moral, financial, and, if possible, military, in carrying out a strong policy in Egypt.[22]

There was an unspoken psychological dimension to the problem of power. Rationally the British might acknowledge that they were powerless without American support, and they might genuinely attempt to create an 'equal partnership' with the Egyptians. Yet they still regarded themselves as masters of the Middle East. The underlying purpose was to sustain themselves as a great 'world power'. This was still true in 1956, and here lies the principal significance of the crisis: Dixon wrote later that the main result of the Suez fiasco was that Britain at one stroke had been reduced 'from a 1st class power to a 3rd class power.'[23]

Two general developments need to be emphasized briefly, as background to the crisis itself. The first is the revolution of July 1952 that overthrew the Egyptian monarchy. The British now faced a revolutionary regime committed to social reform and, at the same time, the extinction of British imperialism. One official wrote: 'No amount of concession or evacuation on our part will evoke the slightest gratitude in return. Whoever Egypt may want in the future as an ally, it will not be us'.[24] That was an astute analysis. In a sense it illuminates the logic of the agreement concluded in 1954 for British withdrawal from the Canal

---

[22] Minute by Dixon, 23 Jan. 1952, FO 371/96920.

[23] Piers Dixon, *Double Diploma: The Life of Sir Pierson Dixon* (London, 1968), p. 278.

[24] Memorandum by John Hamilton (British Embassy in Cairo), 15 Feb. 1953, FO 371/102764.

Zone. The British had to accept the best terms they could get. They could not expect any Egyptian nationalist to be pro-British.

An understanding of the British predicament leads to some of the principal unanswered questions about the 1956 expedition. What was the ultimate aim? A more friendly Nasser? A return to another stooge regime that had produced unsatisfactory results in the past? Perhaps the ultimate aim was unclear? Perhaps Eden's plans might have led to another British occupation of Egypt?

The other development was the revolution in nuclear warfare signified by the American and Russian explosion of hydrogen bombs in November 1952 and August 1953. No longer could the nuclear bomb be regarded, as the British tended to view it, as an extension of conventional warfare. Now the Canal Zone could be destroyed almost at one blow. According to the Permanent Under-Secretary at the British Foreign Office in 1954:

I do not believe that in this atomic age we shall have either the wish or the ability to reactivate the base. We will be sufficiently occupied struggling for survival. And in . . . time the power and the numbers of these frightful weapons will be so great that the chance of our wanting to conduct a campaign in the Middle East will be less than it is to-day.[25]

The author of that minute was Sir Ivone Kirkpatrick, accurately identified in American documents in 1956 as the key man behind the scenes in the Suez emergency. Like Eden, he believed Nasser to be a Hitler of the Middle East who had to be stopped. Kirkpatrick had been posted to Germany in 1933. 'Humiliation' was a word that frequently appeared in his minutes. 'If we seek to hang on', he once wrote in regard to the Sudan, 'we may end by being expelled, and that would be humiliating.'[26] On Egypt as well as on general issues of defence, Kirkpatrick saw eye to eye with Eden.

The 1954 agreement between Britain and Egypt, which provided for Britain's right of re-entry into the Canal Zone in the event of an attack on an Arab state or Turkey, was the culmination of British policy since the Second World War. It represented the Middle Eastern equivalent of the transfer of power in India. In Albert Hourani's words, it was 'the greatest change that had occurred in the Middle Eastern balance of power since 1923' when the former Ottoman Empire has been reduced to a rump Turkish state.[27] As Sir Harold Beeley has written in another chapter in this volume, it signified the triumph of Bevin's Middle Eastern policy by recognizing the Egyptians as equals. It could be

[25] Minute by Sir Ivone Kirkpatrick, 26 July 1954, FO 371/108424.
[26] Minute by Kirkpatrick, 14 June 1954, FO 371/108378.
[27] Albert Hourani, 'The Anglo-Egyptian Agreement: Some Causes and Implications', *Middle East Journal*, 9 (1955).

argued that the Middle East today would be a very different place if the 1954 agreement had remained the foundation of Anglo-Egyptian relations and had not been destroyed by the aberration of the Suez adventure.

The complete story of the Suez crisis remains to be told. The British archives are closed after 1954. The historian is therefore left with only a partial record. Even so it indicates an element of Lord Beloff's argument about the 'act of will'. Eden could not do it alone. He needed the support not only of the Cabinet and Parliament but also of the Ministry of Defence and the Foreign Office. The Foreign Office was a delicate problem because the members of the African Department almost to a man supported the 1954 solution and doubted whether toppling Nasser would lead to anything other than another British occupation of Egypt. It was Kirkpatrick who effectively sealed off the usual channels of Foreign Office telegram traffic, at all levels, to conduct an ultra-secret operation. He was not only highly intelligent and efficient but he also had fixed ideas and a will of iron. He would not crack. This must surely have been one of Eden's calculations, as the records already indicate. It is also important, especially in the context of Anglo-American relations, to take account of one further quotation in order to establish how even the pre-1955 records reveal the origins of the disaster: 'We must be careful', Churchill had written in December 1953 of American aid to Egypt, 'not to give the impression of deceiving the Americans.'[28] Churchill's warning, as will be seen, was not heeded.

In his memoirs, Selwyn Lloyd, the Foreign Secretary who served as Eden's stalwart lieutenant during the crisis, comments that the American response was a combination of 'anti-colonialism and hard-headed oil tycoonery'.[29] That was a shrewd if misguided assessment. The Americans contemplated curtailing the oil supplies in order to bring the British and French to heel, not to make a short-term profit. Nevertheless the crisis revealed that anti-colonialism and long-range economic self-interest are easily reconciled, and also that the mixture of those elements with another powerful ingredient, anti-Communism, can lead to deadly results. In this case the combination proved to be almost fatal for the British. This argument can be tested against the American records, which, unlike the British, remain only partly closed. The Eisenhower and Dulles Papers at the Eisenhower Library will be drawn upon here briefly for concluding evidence about the 'Special Relationship' and anti-colonialism.

'For many years now', John Foster Dulles stated to the National Security Council on 1 November 1956, in one of the first full discussions

<hr/>

[28] Minute by Churchill, 28 Dec. 1953, FO 371/108413.
[29] Selwyn Lloyd, *Suez 1956* (London, 1978), p. 78.

about the Anglo-French-Israeli invasion, 'the United States has been walking a tightrope between the effort to maintain our old and valued relations with our British and French allies on the one hand, and on the other trying to assure ourselves of the friendship and understanding of the newly independent countries who have escaped from colonialism.' The United States, according to the Secretary of State, now faced overwhelming pressure from former 'colonial' peoples throughout the world. The Eisenhower administration therefore confronted a challenge, which Dulles posed in emotional and highly moralistic language:

Unless we now assert and maintain this leadership all of these newly independent countries will turn from us to the USSR. We will be looked upon as forever tied to British and French colonialist policies.

In short, the United States would survive or go down on the basis of the fate of colonialism if the United States supports the French and the British on the colonial issues. Win or lose, we will share the fate of Britain and France.

Dulles was distressed that world opinion was diverted from the Hungarian uprising against Soviet domination by this reassertion of 'colonial' control 'by force' over the Middle East:

It is no less than tragic that at this very time, when we are on the point of winning an immense and long-hoped-for victory over Soviet colonialism in Eastern Europe, we should be forced to choose between following in the footsteps of Anglo-French colonialism in Asia and Africa, or splitting our course away from their course.[30]

At that point Eisenhower attempted, according to the minutes of the meeting, to break the 'tension' in the meeting, but Dulles later returned 'with great warmth' to the subject of colonialism: '[W]hat the British and French had done was nothing but the straight old-fashioned variety of colonialism of the most obvious sort. . . .' Unless the United States championed the cause of the 'lesser-developed nations' at the United Nations, then the initiative would be lost to the Soviet Union.

In many ways those statements reveal vintage Dulles: the same Dulles who, with a missionary twist, had withdrawn economic assistance for the Aswan dam a few months earlier after he refused to be 'blackmailed' by Nasser's threat to turn to the Russians. He clearly had not anticipated Nasser's response of nationalizing the Suez Canal Company on 26 July 1956, nor had be foreseen that the British and the French

[30] National Security Council, 302 Meeting, 1 Nov. 1956, Eisenhower Papers, Whitman File. For Anglo-American relations at the time of Suez see especially Herman Finer, *Dulles over Suez* (Chicago, 1964); and Townsend Hoopes, *The Devil and John Foster Dulles* (Boston, 1973). Both books were written before the opening of the collections at the Eisenhower Library. The best general account is Donald Neff, *Warriors at Suez* (New York, 1981). The most important recent analysis, based in large part on documents made accessible by the Freedom of Information Act, is William J. Burns, *Economic Aid and American Policy 1955–1981* (State University of New York Press, 1985).

might bomb the airfields around Cairo and invade the Canal Zone. The element of surprise was critical, for both Dulles and Eisenhower. And in this regard it is for the President, much more than for his Secretary of State, that the Eisenhower Papers change the nuance of historical interpretation.

As Stephen Ambrose's recent biography makes clear, the fatal British miscalculation was that Dulles controlled American policy and that both Dulles and Eisenhower would co-operate in the overthrow of Nasser.[31] Those assumptions are of utmost importance for an understanding of the 'Special Relationship' then and thereafter. As had been the case in Palestine, presidential involvement in a 'colonial' issue can make a decisive difference. In the case of Suez the British were not merely wrong about Dulles. They were also wrong about Eisenhower. Eisenhower, not Dulles, controlled foreign policy. Dulles gave it a certain legal and moralistic tone that made it all the more objectionable to the British, but ultimately it was Eisenhower who dominated. Unlike some other American presidents (even compared with F.D.R.), Eisenhower studied the problems of foreign affairs until he had mastered the essentials. He gave latitude to his subordinates, but he himself set the direction and substance of policy. In the case of Suez he proved to be just as anti-colonialist as his Secretary of State.

Eisenhower's years before the war had been spent in the Philippines. He did not have profound insight into Filipino politics or history, but he was convinced that the United States had governed the Philippines both wisely and well by preparing them for independence and, almost as important, by setting a timetable for independence. By granting independence, Eisenhower once said, the United States had enabled the Filipinos to achieve a 'fierce pride'.[32] He believed that the British should be following the American example. During his first term in office he had written about Churchill clinging to office as Prime Minister: 'He talks [in January 1953] very animatedly about certain . . . international problems, especially Egypt and its future. But so far as I can see, he has developed an almost childlike faith that all of the answers are to be found merely in British–American partnership.'[33] Eisenhower had little use for the 'Special Relationship' in this connection. He believed that the United States was the natural leader of the newly independent countries of the post-war era. Thus he erupted in anger—'barrack room language' is the euphemism repeated in the documents—when he learned of the Anglo-French-Israeli attack at Suez. Indignation in turn became mixed

[31] Stephen E. Ambrose, *Eisenhower: The President* (New York, 1984), ch. 15. See also Robert A. Divine, *Eisenhower and the Cold War* (New York, 1981), ch. 3.

[32] Ambrose, *Eisenhower*, p. 378.

[33] Robert H. Ferrell, *The Eisenhower Diaries* (New York, 1981), p. 223.

with sorrow. His reproaches to Eden conveyed anger as well as a genuine lament for the lost partnership.

We will not know the details until the British records have been opened, but it is possible that Eden and his colleagues calculated that, by keeping the United States in the dark, they might succeed in gaining Dulles's acquiescence because of his antipathy towards Nasser. Eisenhower might not intervene either because of his sympathy for long-range British plans or possibly because of the impending presidential election. If so, those miscalculations have to be recorded as among the ranks of memorable blunders of modern history. 'Anthony, have you gone out of your mind?' Eisenhower asked in a transatlantic telephone call: '. . . You've deceived me.'[34] That was the ultimate miscalculation, even insult. Eden had offended Eisenhower's personal code of honour by not keeping him informed. The ruthless crushing of the British by the denial of emergency oil supplies, and the refusal of financial support, has to be explained at least in part by Eisenhower's sense of betrayal. According to a transcript of a meeting at the White House on 29 October 1956:

The President thought that the British are calculating that we must go along with them (he thought they were not banking too heavily on our being tied up in the election, but are thinking in longer range terms). He thought we should let them know at once of our position, telling them that we recognize that much is on their side in the dispute with the Egyptians, but that nothing justifies double-crossing us.[35]

The British had 'double-crossed' the Americans not merely by the secret attack. It is clear from the records that Eisenhower no less than Dulles believed that the British and the French were now demonstrating a brutal type of 'colonialism' comparable to Russian methods in Hungary. This was surely the low ebb of the 'Special Relationship'.

THE 'SPECIAL RELATIONSHIP' AND THE END OF THE BRITISH EMPIRE

'The British Empire is pre-eminently a great Naval, Indian and Colonial Power', according to a celebrated statement that illuminates

---

[34] Elizabeth Monroe, *Britain's Moment in the Middle East* (London, 1981 edn.), p. 209. Apparently this was Eisenhower's first telephone call to Eden, which was mistakenly put through to William Clark, the press officer at 10 Downing Street (according to Monroe, based on Clark's testimony). The President thus spoke those words before he realized that he had the wrong person on the line. This may explain part of the conflicting stories about what Eisenhower actually said or did not say initially to Eden. For critical assessment of Eden and the crisis see especially David Carlton, *Anthony Eden* (London, 1981), ch. 11. Anthony Nutting, *No End of a Lesson* (New York, 1967) remains indispensable in understanding the crisis within the British government.

[35] Memorandum of Conference with the President, 29 Oct. 1956, Dulles Papers, Eisenhower Library.

the nature of the *Pax Britannica*.[36] In the racy logic of Robinson and Gallagher, the United States can today perhaps be regarded as a 'colonial' power in the sense of exercising indirect political control and dominance throughout much of the world. But there has never been the American equivalent of British India, and we may hope that there never will be. The United States is a great naval and military power, but the bipolar rivalry and the existence of nuclear weapons make the world of the twentieth century quite different from the one of the nineteenth century when the Maxim gun had proved to be an effective weapon in keeping the peace as well as making the conquest.

From F.D.R. to Eisenhower, the Americans attempted to impress upon the British the lessons, psychological as well as technological, to be drawn from the confrontation between European imperialism and indigenous nationalism. In 1882 the British had succeeded in occupying Egypt. By the end of the Second World War they faced a nationalist movement that even sophisticated weapons could not indefinitely suppress. By the early 1950s the Americans apprehended Communist revolution throughout the Middle East. In Dean Acheson's blunt words to Churchill and Eden in 1952:

The Middle East presented a picture that might have been drawn by Karl Marx himself—with the masses a disinherited and poverty-stricken proletariat, no middle class, a small and corrupt ruling class pushed about by foreigners who sought to exploit priceless resources, whether oil or canal. Was there ever such an opportunity to invoke inherent xenophobia to destroy the foreigner and his system and substitute the Communist solution? Anglo-American solidarity on a policy of sitting tight offered no solution, but was like a couple locked in warm embrace in a rowboat about to go over Niagara Falls. It was high time to break the embrace and take to the oars.[37]

Behind Acheson stood a whole generation of Americans who held similar views—the '[George] McGhees', as Selwyn Lloyd bitterly remarked.[38]

McGhee had been Assistant Secretary for Near Eastern, South Asian, and African Affairs, 1949–51, and then Ambassador to Turkey. He was one of the most outspoken yet friendly critics of British 'colonialism'. The trouble was, as he frequently explained, the British continued to think in 'nineteenth-century' terms. Unless they changed their ways and accepted Asian and African nationalism as the prevailing force, then the consequences would be catastrophic for both the British and Americans. This attitude did not make McGhee popular among the British, but it

[36] First report of the Committee of Imperial Defence (1904), quoted in Lord Hankey, *The Supreme Command 1914–1918* (London, 1961), i, p. 46.

[37] Dean Acheson, *Present at the Creation* (New York, 1969), p. 600.

[38] Lloyd, *Suez 1956*, p. 78. See George McGhee, *Envoy to the Middle World* (New York, 1983).

expressed a quintessential American point. The *Pax Britannica* was dead. Nothing comparable would arise to take its place. The Americans would have to do the best they could in a volatile world. The difficult nature of the task, perhaps even more its unpopularity, may explain why no one gets up enthusiasm singing, 'March on Americans, march on in the world', or, indeed, 'Arise, *Pax Americana*'.[39] Perhaps the most basic reason of all was the doubt that there *should* be a *Pax Americana*, which after all implies world dominance as well as order and stability.

Did the Americans, wittingly or by accident, help to bring about the post-war world of Balkanization and unrest by dismembering the British Empire? The American influence on its dissolution is difficult to measure, but it must have been small. Through the trusteeship system at the United Nations, the United States may have helped to advance the dates of independence for some trusteeship territories, for example, by setting a ten-year goal in the horn of Africa so that Somalia became independent in 1960. But it would require an imaginative leap to conclude that international influences precipitated the wave of African independence of the 1960s. The British were responding to the full current of African nationalism and were making their own calculations about the financial and moral cost of holding colonial dependencies against both overseas and domestic sentiment. In 1985 David Fieldhouse completed a study in which he concludes that the dependencies in Africa in the late 1950s were no longer as important to the British economy as they had been in the period of economic recovery. The British had their own reasons for precipitous decolonization, hoping to retain economic and political influence in return for a quick transfer of power.[40] If this analysis is correct, then the British as much as the Americans are responsible for the aftermath, in Lord Beloff's indictment, of instability and deprivation, civil and tribal war, famine, and even genocide.

Has the failure to replace the *Pax Britannica* by a *Pax Americana* been caused by infirmity of the 'will'? In some of the American as well as British literature dealing with the post-war economic crisis and its consequences there runs the theme that the decline of British power might have been prevented if there had been greater determination on the part of the British, or more resolute support of Britain by the United States. The failure of this 'act of will' is an alluring interpretation to those seeking the reasons for the decline and fall of the British Empire.

---

[39] The Permanent Under-Secretary at the British Foreign Office wrote in 1952: 'The Americans ... cannot bring themselves to believe that people do not like them.' Eden noted, 'True'. Minutes by Strang and Eden, 5 Feb. 1952, FO 371/96922.

[40] D. K. Fieldhouse, 'Economic Decolonization in British Africa', paper presented at a conference on 'The Transfers of Power in Africa', University of Zimbabwe, 8–11 Jan. 1985.

Here is an example of the way in which an American writer, Theodore H. White, brings this idea to bear on the devaluation crisis of September 1949. He relates a conversation with Sir Edmund Hall-Patch, one of the principal economic authorities at the British Foreign Office:

[H]is task humiliated him. Begging for the American buck was not his style . . . [he] was talking from the heart. America must move to save and take over the British economy . . . or Britain would fade from power. . . . He doubted whether England had the stomach to go the rough road it must go if it went alone—to cut the Empire adrift, to repudiate its distant and inner obligations, to hold on only to military command of the oil resources of the Middle East. . . .

    It scarcely occurred to me then . . . that, ultimately we would drive the British from the Middle East . . . and leave all of America's economy and civilization in debt to, and uncertainly dependent on, the oil of the Middle East sheikhs and strong men, whom the British had previously policed for us.[41]

A sense of lost opportunity is thus fused with self-recrimination for failure to rescue the British Empire. This is a grotesque lament. In the post-war period there was precious little sentimentality, in official American circles at least, about the British failure to solve their own colonial problems, especially at the time of Suez.

Is it no less reasonable to ask whether there was a failure of 'will' on the British side during the Suez crisis? Even within Britain some held, then as now, that Anthony Eden should have persisted. Others believed in Ernest Bevin's maxim that it requires just as great an act of will not to intervene in the affairs of small nations, or, in this case, to exercise restraint, as it does to impose a peace by bayonets.

No doubt the comparable point in American history was the loss of confidence during the Vietnam War. Then too there was a division of national sentiment and a question of national purpose. Yet in a sense the Suez crisis was a watershed for the Americans as well as for the British because many of the world's problems today can be directly traced to the policies pursued by the Eisenhower Administration. Americans might take pride in Eisenhower's robust anti-colonialist stance at the time of Suez, but, as Michael Howard has written recently, there was a dark side to the Eisenhower era.[42] Eisenhower did not hesitate to employ the subversive capabilities of the Central Intelligence Agency (CIA) in the holy war against Communism, few holds barred. The greater the frustrating restraint of nuclear weapons, the more tempting the use of covert methods. Eisenhower used the CIA to help topple Musaddiq in Iran (as well as Arbenz in Guatemala). In the days of Lord Curzon there had been a popular saying, 'Lift a mullah's beard and you

---

[41] Quoted, with comment in a Middle Eastern context, in W. R. Louis, *The British Empire in the Middle East* (Oxford, 1984), p. 14.

[42] Michael Howard, 'Keeping the Team Together', *Times Literary Supplement*, 8 Feb. 1985.

will find the Union Jack'. Eisenhower's policy of external interference, pursued by his successors, almost certainly contributed to the later Iranian revolution and led to the replacement of Britain by the United States as the 'great Satan'. The global reputation of the British Empire as a satanic force may have ebbed, but the United States as a diabolical and ubiquitous influence is a popular perception throughout much of the world today.

Much to his credit, Eisenhower stopped short of political assassination. There is little evidence that he was involved in the attempt to assassinate Castro, still less Lumumba. The historical record suggests the contrary. Eisenhower was in fact as on guard against possible excesses of the CIA as he was against those of the American military. His wariness remains a warning for the present and the future. Nevertheless the amoral and clandestine operations of the CIA and other American agencies in Iran and Guatemala were endorsed by the Eisenhower Administration. The President himself was perhaps under the impression that a *Pax Americana* of sorts could be created and sustained by such methods. If so there must have been a delicate balance between hoping that the United States could preserve freedom by subversive means (or 'ruling indirectly', American-style) and believing that small nations have the right to conduct their own affairs. In any case, Eisenhower's attitude gives support to the view that, in the competition in the American mind between the 'Special Relationship', 'anti-colonialism', and 'anti-Communism', the last always prevails. As for the more precise connection between the 'Special Relationship' and 'anti-colonialism', Dean Acheson perhaps best expressed the consistent American attitude: 'As we saw our role . . . it was to help toward solving the colonial-nationalist conflict in a way that would satisfy nationalist aims and minimize the strain on our Western European allies'.[43]

---

[43] Acheson, *Present at the Creation*, p. 671.

17

The Middle East

SIR HAROLD BEELEY

Two statements, made at an interval of 77 years, illustrate at once the continuity of certain Middle Eastern problems and a transfer of responsibility, or at any rate of the sense of responsibility, for dealing with them.[1] Lord Lansdowne, speaking as Foreign Secretary in the House of Lords in 1903, said that

we should regard the establishment of a naval base, or of a fortified port, in the Persian Gulf by any Power as a very grave menace to British interests, and we should certainly resist it with all the means at our disposal.[2]

The second statement was made by President Carter in January 1980:

An attempt by any outside force to gain control of the Persian Gulf region will be regarded as an assault on the vital interests of the United States of America. And such an assault will be repelled by any means necessary, including military force.[3]

As the Second World War drew to a close, the primacy of British power in the Middle East seemed to be unimpaired, perhaps even to have reached its zenith. Retrospectively we can now see that it was already in both absolute and relative decline. It might have been possible, as had happened in the history of earlier empires, for this decline to remain incompletely perceived for a longer period if its reality had not been nakedly exposed by the failure of the disastrous Suez

[1] The essential sources for the early post-war years are the British Cabinet and Foreign Office papers in the Public Record Office at Kew, and the admirable selection from the parallel American documents printed in the series *Foreign Relations of the United States*. Two works of major importance are: Alan Bullock, *Ernest Bevin: Foreign Secretary, 1945–51* (London, 1983), and Henry Kissinger's two volumes, *White House Years* (Boston, 1979) and *Years of Upheaval* (Boston, 1982). I have also been particularly indebted to Wm. Roger Louis, *The British Empire in the Middle East, 1945–1951* (Oxford, 1984). On more limited subjects, in addition ot the books mentioned in the text above, Michael J. Cohen, *Palestine: Retreat from the Mandate; The Making of British Policy, 1936–1945* (New York, 1978) is valuable, as are two British memoirs on the Suez affair: Anthony Nutting, *No End of a Lesson: The Story of Suez* (New York, 1967) and Selwyn Lloyd, *Suez, 1956: A Personal Account* (London, 1978).

[2] Address by Lord Lansdowne to the House of Lords on 5 May 1903, *Parliamentary Debates*, col. 1348.

[3] State of the Union address delivered before a joint session of the 96th Congress, 23 Jan. 1980, *Public Papers of the Presidents of the United States, Jimmy Carter 1980–1981* (3 vols.), vol. i. *January 1 to May 23, 1980* (Washington, DC, 1981), p. 197.

adventure of 1956. In the three years 1956–8 it became evident that the Middle East had become so deeply involved in the global contest between the United States and the Soviet Union that in the future Britain would have a secondary and diminishing role. It was in this brief period, 1945–58, that the critical transformation took place.

The defeat of Germany and Japan left the Western alliance preoccupied with the containment of Soviet and Communist pressures in the borderlands of central Europe, the western Pacific, and the Middle East. It was clear even before the formation of NATO in 1949 that the protection of the convalescent states of continental western Europe would be a primary responsibility of the United States, and in the Far Eastern theatre the same conclusion was self-evident. In the Middle East, however, the necessity for some division of labour and the survival of substantial British assets seemed clearly to indicate that the United Kingdom should take the lead. Even here it soon became apparent that the range of British action would be severely limited. It had not been anticipated before 1947 that Turkey and Greece would have to be included in the area of primary American responsibility.

From this beginning was developed six years later, by John Foster Dulles, the concept of the 'northern tier', a barrier of friendly non-Arab States—Turkey, Iran, Pakistan—creating at least a geographical separation between the Soviet Union and the Arab heartland of the Middle East with which British policy was primarily concerned.

In fact Britain and the United States, despite differing priorities and occasional conflicts of interest, developed a system of exceptionally close co-operation on the affairs of the region with the overriding aim of excluding Soviet influence to the greatest possible extent. There were however two massive deviations from this common purpose. The first was the decisive support given by the United States to the implantation of an alien state in the heart of the Arab world; the second was the unsuccessful attempt by the United Kingdom in association with France to perpetuate an alien control over Egypt's principal economic and strategic asset. Each of these provided the Soviet Union with predictable opportunities for exploiting anti-Western Arab reactions.

It fell to Ernest Bevin to pick up the threads of Britain's pre-war and wartime policy in Palestine. His attitude towards it was an integral part of a coherent Middle Eastern policy, the central feature of which was to be the maintenance, in changed circumstances and with modified instruments, of the pre-war alliances with Iraq and Egypt. He sought to revise the treaties, of 1930 and 1936 respectively, on a basis of at least terminological equality. In both cases he succeeded in negotiating an agreement with the government concerned, only to see it frustrated by popular hostility, intensified in the case of Iraq by anti-Zionist fervour.

Bevin was acutely aware of this relationship, and in his prolonged wrestling with the problem of Palestine its Jewish and Arab communities played a smaller part than the independent Arab States on the one hand and the Truman Administration on the other. Their conflicting pressures set limits to the mandatory power's freedom of action and imposed on it a measure of neutrality which owed less to the merits of the case than to calculation of the balance of external forces. The effort in London not to act in Palestine in such a way as to alienate the Arab world should have been, in the context of the increasingly evident Soviet threat to Western interests, as much an American as a British requirement. It was indeed seen in this light by many of the officials of the State Department, notably by the wise and experienced Director of the Office of Near Eastern and African Affairs, Loy Henderson. There is no evidence, however, that President Truman was impressed by this consideration. Neither, it must immediately be added, was Truman emotionally or intellectually committed to the Zionist cause. His attitude is well summarized in the remark he once made that it would help if both the Mufti of Jerusalem and Rabbi Silver were thrown into the Red Sea. Intrinsically the question of Palestine does not seem seriously to have engaged his interest. He had a genuine sympathy for the recent tragedy and the current plight of the Jews in Eastern and Central Europe, which inclined him to accept without much questioning the solution proposed by the highly organized Zionist lobby, deeply entrenched as it was in the Democratic Party and occupying key positions in the White House. In his book, *Decision on Palestine*, the late Evan Wilson writes:

I began this study with the opinion, which I had held since my days on the Palestine desk, that Truman's principal motivation had been humanitarian, but after examining all the evidence, including data that were not available to us in the State Department at the time, I have been forced reluctantly to the conclusion that on certain key occasions (October 1947 and May 1948) he was more influenced by domestic political considerations than by humanitarian ideals.[4]

When, in the United Nations General Assembly in 1947, the Soviet delegation aligned itself with the majority in favour of partition and the creation of a Jewish state, and when in the next year Soviet followed quickly upon American recognition of that state, it seemed to some optimistic observers that Bevin's fears had been exaggerated. But already one Soviet objective had been attained with the withdrawal of British forces from Palestine, thus removing a link in the defence of the eastern Mediterranean and the Suez Canal. And the inevitably hostile

---

[4] Evan M. Wilson, *Decision on Palestine: How the United States Came to Recognize Israel* (Stanford, CA, 1979), p. 149.

relations of Israel and her neighbours were soon to provide opportunities for Moscow to emerge as a champion of the Arab cause. This effect would have been more immediate and more dangerous if Attlee and Bevin had not adamantly refused to play any positive part whatsoever in the partitioning of Palestine, causing Dean Acheson to observe that 'Attlee had deftly exchanged the United States for Britain as the most disliked Power in the Middle East', but at the same time enabling Britain to retain, if somewhat less confidently, much of her influence in the region.

The Russian breakthrough came in 1955, a critical year for Middle Eastern relationships. It took the form of the first military aid agreement between the Soviet Union and the new Egyptian regime, followed by indications from Moscow of readiness to offer financial support for that regime's major domestic project, the High Dam at Aswan. The United States and Britain, in association with the World Bank, made their counter-move at the end of the year in a joint offer of substantial finance for the dam. When this failed to divert Nasser from his pursuit of non-alignment, which he underlined in May 1956 by recognizing Communist China, the Western offer was withdrawn.

It has sometimes been alleged that the decision to withdraw was taken in Washington and accepted only reluctantly in London. This is a misrepresentation. There was British criticism of the somewhat abrasive terms in which Dulles conveyed the American decision to the Egyptian Ambassador, but there was no official dissent from its substance. I have a distinct memory of a meeting of British officials in Whitehall which decided with near unanimity to recommend to the Cabinet that the British offer should be withdrawn. As I wrote a dissenting opinion on the same day, I have been interested to read in Dr William Burns's recent book, *Economic Aid and American Policy toward Egypt, 1955–1981*, that both Henry Byroade from the American Embassy in Cairo and Eugene Black at the World Bank were arguing in the same sense.[5] I must add with regret that I did not foresee the risk to the Suez Canal Company that withdrawal would involve. Nor, so far as is shown by Dr Burns, did either Black or Byroade. I suppose our excuse is that the revenues of Suez were a manifestly inadequate basis for financing so vast a project. The seizure of the Canal was therefore not an alternative to the danger, on which our attention was fixed, that the Soviet Union would step in to replace the Western guarantees.

Nasser's coup had an electrifying effect in the Western capitals. The three months which separated the nationalization of the Canal Company on 26 July 1956 from the outbreak of hostilities on 29 October

---

[5] William J. Burns, *Economic Aid and American Policy toward Egypt, 1955–1981* (Albany, 1985), pp. 62–3.

were a period of intense diplomatic activity, during which the three Western powers, while acting in apparent harmony, were pursuing divergent aims. For the French, who had the most substantial interest in the Suez Canal Company, there was a larger issue in the background. They were confronting rebellion in Algeria, and they probably exaggerated the importance of Egypt's moral and material support for the rebels. The idea took root that the Algerian War might be won by bringing down Nasser. This was not far from Eden's view, as he expressed it to President Eisenhower, that 'we cannot afford to allow Nasser to seize control of the Canal in this way . . . My colleagues and I are convinced that we must be ready, in the last resort, to use force to bring Nasser to his senses.'[6] Concerted Anglo-French military planning, and the assembly of forces in the Mediterranean, flowed naturally from these reactions. The British, however, were equally concerned with the American factor. An entry in Macmillan's diary on 1 August probably represents the view of the Cabinet as a whole at the time: 'We must keep the Americans really frightened. They must not be allowed any illusion. Then they will help us to get what we want without the necessity for force'.[7]

Eisenhower and Dulles however had a different priority and a wider preoccupation. For them the essential objective was to prevent the Suez crisis from resulting in the expansion of Soviet influence. Thus, though they did act as Macmillan had predicted up to a point, notably with the invention of the Suez Canal Users' Association, they refused to concur in a degree of pressure on Egypt which would either have led to a diplomatic victory over Nasser or more probably to a situation in which the United States would have been obliged to condone the eventual Anglo-French action.

That action was triggered on 29 October by Israel, and perhaps the most remarkable feature of the American response was that it was in no way modified by the association of Israel with the Franco-British plans. When the Security Council met on the morning after the Israeli invasion of Sinai, it was an American resolution which condemned the aggressor and which was vetoed by France and Britain. This uniquely uncompromising condemnation of Israel by a United States administration— the more striking because it occurred exactly a week before the end of Eisenhower's re-election campaign—was certainly made easier by Israel's alliance with the powers classified as 'colonial'. Vice-President Nixon made much of this association in a campaign speech on 2 November:

[6] Sir Anthony Eden, *The Memoirs of Anthony Eden: Full Circle* (Boston, 1960), pp. 476–7.
[7] Harold Macmillan, *Riding the Storm: 1956–1959* (New York, 1971), p. 106.

In the past the nations of Asia and Africa have always felt we would, when the pressure was on, side with the policies of the British and French Governments in relation to the once colonial areas. For the first time in history we have shown independence of Anglo-French policies towards Asia and Africa which seemed to us to reflect the colonial tradition. That declaration of independence has had an electrifying effect throughout the world.[8]

The Suez enterprise came to an abrupt end. The Israelis halted their operations on 4 November. On the 5th and 6th French and British troops landed, but their advance down the Canal was halted by a cease-fire at midnight on the 6th, resulting from American pressure (largely though not exclusively financial) on the British Government.

By this time Dulles was in hospital, stricken by the first attack of the disease which was to kill him. On the day before his withdrawal he had expressed in its simplest terms the conviction which had determined his own course and would continue to determine that of the President. He argued that 'if the United States did not lead, the Soviet Union would— and the Russians would gain a political and psychological foothold in the Middle East from which they might not be dislodged for genera-tions'. In fact both policies, that of the United States as well as that of Britain and France, failed to gain their objectives. Nasser was neither toppled from power nor forced to disgorge the Canal Company, but equally the Soviet Union was not prevented from establishing a powerful influence in Egypt for the next fifteen years.

The penalty of failure fell most harshly on Britain. Belief in her capacity for effective military action, which had been the unspoken basis of her influence in the region, was shown to be no longer tenable. There were to be minor interventions, in Jordan in 1958 and Kuwait in 1961, and the special relationships in the Gulf continued for another decade. But the event which more than any other symbolized the end of an era was the death at the hands of the Baghdad mob in July 1958 of Nuri Said, the adroit and far-sighted leader for whom association with Britain had been axiomatic throughout his long career.

The revolution in Iraq also underlined the dependence of the Western defence system on the character of the internal political order in Middle Eastern states. In the case of Egypt it had taken three years for the revolutionary regime to bring about a realignment of the country's international relationships. Iraq's defection from the system was more precipitate, and it conveyed a dual warning. Not only did it remove a not unimportant element in the defensive barrier; it also had a bearing on what can conveniently be described as the alienation effect of the issue of Palestine. Since 1945 there had been a notable contrast between

---

[8] *New York Times*, 3 Nov. 1956, p. 19.

the vehemence and unanimity of the Arab condemnation of Western relations with Israel on the one hand, and on the other the maintenance by a majority of Arab States of friendly and constructive relations with the Western powers. This was in part a reflection of the Arab world's kaleidoscopic disunity. More importantly it resulted from the desire of more or less conservative Arab regimes for some guarantee of protection against Soviet expansion.

The most striking attempt to resolve this conflict between the cherished pan-Arab ambition to rescue Palestine, and the prudent consideration of national self-interest was made by Anwar Sadat, eventually in collaboration with Henry Kissinger, in the war of 1973. Egypt and Syria were fighting with Russian equipment, while Israel was supplied by the United States. On the other hand President Sadat had already embarked on the diplomatic revolution which was to take Egypt out of the Soviet and into the American camp. Sadat's object in launching an offensive against the Bar-Lev line was not primarily a military victory. The military objective, achieved immediately and locally, could not conceivably have been expected to lead to the defeat of Israel on a sufficient scale to solve the political problem. That solution would require superpower, or in realistic terms American, intervention, and the primary aim of the Egyptian attack was to shatter Washington's complacent acceptance of what was from the Egyptian point of view an intolerable status quo. From this point of view it was not illogical that hostilities should finally be terminated as a result of American pressure on Israel.

Kissinger thus removed the danger of Soviet intervention. By the decisive part he played in negotiating the Sinai disengagement agreements, he created an exclusive mediatory role for the United States which continued through the succeeding Carter Administration. By the time of President Sadat's death in 1981 Egypt had moved unambiguously into the American orbit, and was being granted economic and military aid on a scale far exceeding all other recipients with the sole exception of Israel.

The recovery of Egypt gave a new geopolitical solidity to the American position in the Middle East which had been to a large extent based on Saudi Arabia and Iran. With the fall of the Shah the United States lost a heavy moral and material investment. The Soviet Union, however, made no corresponding gain, and it is still by no means clear which if either of the superpowers will benefit from the profound revolution (unique in the Middle East) through which Iran is passing.

In addition to Israel and Egypt, the third regional foundation for American and Western defences in the Middle East is the Kingdom of Saudi Arabia. President Carter's statement quoted previously on the

Gulf as an area of vital interest to the United States was made after the revolution in Iran, and must consequently have reflected a confident belief in the stability of the Saudi regime. There is certainly a great difference between the position of the House of Saud and that of the Iranian monarchy before the revolution. It is firmly integrated in Arabian society and, being closely identified with the conservative religious establishment, is immunized against the Islamic fanaticism which destroyed the imperial system in Iran and struck down President Sadat in Cairo. There is a considerable Egyptian and Palestinian labour force, but the regime has been careful to limit this potentially disturbing influence by taking immigrant workers increasingly from South-east Asia. Nevertheless this and other precautions indicate that it does not take its own invulnerability for granted, and its intimate association with Washington has coexisted uneasily with its pretension to leadership of the Arab-Islamic reaction against the creation and subsequent expansion of Israel.

In the evolution of American policy since 1971 Britain has played little active part. This period, moreover, has seen her entry into the European Economic Community and consequently her participation in the rather tentative movement towards Euro-Arab co-operation, economic in the first instance but necessarily involving also a political dialogue. In 1980 the Foreign Ministers of the then nine member-states of the EEC considered it to be in their interest to issue a collective statement of their attitude to the Arab–Israel situation, a statement which has come to be known as the Venice Declaration and which was reaffirmed two years later by the heads of government. It represents a significant divergence of the Western European attitude from that, so far as it is known, of the United States Government.

In the first place it asserts that 'the Palestinian people . . . must be placed in a position . . . to exercise fully their right to self-determination', and that 'the PLO will have to be associated with the negotiations'. More specifically, 'the nine stress that they will not accept any unilateral initiative designed to change the status of Jerusalem', and 'they are deeply convinced that the Jewish settlements constitute a serious obstacle to the peace process' and 'are illegal under international law'.[9]

It may reasonably be objected that Europe's almost total lack of capacity to exert direct influence on any of the parties more directly concerned deprives the Declaration of practical significance. The point of view which it represents does nevertheless give rise to certain reflections. The Declaration testifies to the continuing relevance of the international consensus which was embodied in the Security Council's

---

[9] 'Venice—From the European Council to the Western Summit', in *Bulletin of the European Council* (June 1980), p. 10, 1.1.6.6.–1.1.6.9.

resolution No. 242 of 1967. It is an encouragement for moderate elements in the Arab States and the Palestinian movement to seek a political settlement with Israel. And its rejection would expose fragilities in the foundations of Western influence in the Middle East, tending to undermine both the willingness and the ability of Egypt and Saudi Arabia to continue on their present course.

18

Britain, the United States, and South Asia

LORD SAINT BRIDES

I

DURING the 1950s and 1960s the British and American governments attached high importance to their relations with India and Pakistan, and to the maintenance of their influence in both countries.

To Britain at that time India and Pakistan were the show-pieces of the post-war Commonwealth. But the Commonwealth in which we 'kept' India and Pakistan was radically and swiftly changed by the fact of India's membership, and by the terms on which it was confirmed in 1949–1950, namely the adoption by India of a non-aligned position in international affairs, and of a republican constitution. In both respects India's example was followed by most other British ex-colonies as they successively emerged at independence into fully sovereign status. As a result the Commonwealth ceased to be the tacit, quasi-military, political, and economic alliance and instrument of British world power which it had formerly been. Instead it developed into the Third-World-oriented forum for discussion of world issues which it is today. British policy throughout was not to challenge this evolutionary process, but to accept it with a good grace whilst seeking to maintain (as with Canada in NATO) close military collaboration with those few other Commonwealth countries which still wanted it. It was also British policy not to take sides in the case of a dispute between any two other Commonwealth countries, even when one of them was a military ally of Britain's, as Pakistan became in SEATO (South-East Asia Treaty Organization) and Cento (Central Treaty Organization), and the other, as India was, non-aligned.

Since the United States was not a member of the Commonwealth it did not suffer from this particular inhibition. Nevertheless, whilst building up Pakistan as a military ally it tried hard to maintain good relations in India also, more especially through the grant to India of generous government-to-government aid.

Despite the surprising measure of goodwill which was generated for Britain in India and Pakistan by the Attlee government's voluntary surrender of power, and (in India) by the brisk and zealous manner in which Mountbatten carried it through, American suspicion of British colonialism died hard. The early dealings of American diplomats—and sometimes of Canadian and Australian ones too—with the new independent governments of India and Pakistan showed an understandable desire to distance themselves from the British, whose influence as the former colonial power should in theory have suffered heavily from past frictions. In fact British influence suffered less than had been expected. Until the late 1960s, when Britain's economic difficulties finally compelled the abandonment of its former role as global power, it was evident that Britain still had an important, even if not a crucial, role to play in South Asia.

Fairly soon, therefore, after 1947 Washington began to reappraise the potential value to America of British collaboration in advancing Western interests in the South Asian subcontinent. Some of the policies and events described in this paper were the result.

The United States and the United Kingdom saw themselves as competing not so much with each other as with the Soviet Union in India and—in the 1960s—with the People's Republic of China in Pakistan. They came to believe that their relations both with India and Pakistan were prone to fluctuate according to how well India and Pakistan got on with each other; the worse the Indo-Pakistani relationship became, the more difficult the Western position got in both countries. This led Britain and America into a continuing endeavour to help improve and stabilize Indo-Pakistani relations. It was evident that only if the Kashmir dispute, and other problems between them, could be resolved, would a lasting improvement be achieved. Accordingly it became both an American and a British objective to help promote such an outcome, and with this in mind successive British governments and American administrations came to believe—especially during the years 1961–5—that they would be more successful if they combined their efforts than if each of them operated alone.

II

The Pakistan government's outlook was shaped from the outset by its preoccupation with India and by its desire to find some outside friend or patron who would help Pakistan stand up to its larger and more powerful neighbour.

In the 1950s US geopolitical thinking was dominated by the need, as Washington saw it, to contain the two Communist giants, the Soviet Union and China, behind a cordon sanitaire of countries which would pool their strength, under the American aegis, so as to provide a system of common defence. NATO and later SEATO and Cento were the fruits of this policy.

First the Pakistani military, led by the Army Chief of Staff, General Mohammad Ayub Khan, and later civilian leaders such as Mohammed Ali of Bogra, sought to persuade Washington that if it were given the necessary logistical backing Pakistan could and would play its part in this system of regional alliances. The result was the Mutual Assistance Pact of May 1954 between Pakistan and the United States. During the years that followed large amounts of modern American weaponry were supplied free of charge to the Pakistani Army, Air Force, and Navy. In return Pakistan soon afterwards joined SEATO and also the Baghdad Pact (later to be renamed Cento), and agreed that a United States intelligence-gathering facility should be set up at Badaber, near Peshawar. (It continued to operate there until 1968.)

There were the seeds of future trouble in these arrangements. Moreover the Pakistani leaders' underlying motive in joining the Pacts had been the threat which they perceived from India, not from the USSR or China. Their hope was that the United States, Britain, and other Pact members would collectively underwrite the defence of Pakistan against Indian attack; but this had never been part of the Pacts' purposes as seen in London, Washington, or the other Pact capitals.

The Indians became thoroughly alarmed at the extent to which the power of the Pakistani military had been increased, and Pakistani ambitions whetted, by American arms aid. They believed that henceforth Pakistan would see itself as a rival to India and could well be tempted to follow adventurist courses in an attempt to settle one or other of its differences with India. Of these the main and most intractable one was the dispute over Kashmir.

Jammu and Kashmir was one of the very few princely states of former India that had resisted Mountbatten's urgings to join one or other of the two new Dominions at Partition. Since the ruling dynasty was Hindu the natural choice from one point of view would have been India. But since the state was mostly contiguous with what was to become Pakistani territory, and most of the population was Muslim, Pakistan was the natural choice from another. For weeks after Partition the Maharaja dithered between the two; but when Kashmir was invaded by bands of Pathan tribesmen from across Pakistani territory he acceded to India. India accepted the Maharaja's accession subject to the Kashmiri people's wishes being ascertained at a later stage. Fighting followed between the Indian Army and forces which the Pakistanis later admitted to be theirs. It ended in a *de facto* division of the state along a cease-fire line which left most of the mountainous northern part in

Pakistani hands whilst Ladakh and the two most populous areas (the Vale and Jammu) were left with India. As time went by the cease-fire line acquired the definitiveness (though not the status) of an international frontier.

Successive efforts were made by the Security Council to find a solution agreeable to both sides. But as time went on India's position over Kashmir hardened to the point of declaring that conditions in the state had changed irreversibly and that Kashmir's accession to India was full and final. Pakistan claimed that Kashmir's accession to India was invalid, and that if India would not agree to a plebiscite it was because, if held, it would go against India. Thus the stated positions of the two sides were irreconcilable. Much to India's resentment the United States and the United Kingdom declined to treat the Kashmir issue as closed. By voting in the Security Council in a way that left the matter open and alive they were guilty—in Indian eyes—of partisanship for Pakistan. (By contrast, the Soviet Union by consistently supporting India's case earned lasting gratitude.) The Pakistanis for their part accused their Western partners of not trying hard enough at the United Nations to get the matter settled to Pakistan's liking.

III

The political *dégringolade* in Pakistan which set in after Jinnah died in 1948 was arrested ten years later when Iskander Mirza, President of Pakistan under the 1956 Constitution, swept away all existing political institutions, only to be displaced almost immediately as Head of State in a *coup d'état* by his Army Chief of Staff, Ayub. As President, Ayub sought to make a fresh start in relations with India, but was rebuffed by Nehru both over Kashmir and over a tentative proposal which Ayub made for the joint defence of the subcontinent. 'Against whom?' was Nehru's dismissive reply.

Thereafter Ayub began a cautious *rapprochement* with the People's Republic of China, under urging from Zulfiqar Ali Bhutto, his young and plausible foreign affairs adviser, and later Foreign Minister. From 1961 onward Pakistan no longer opposed (as it had hitherto done in support of the United States) the seating of the People's Republic of China at the United Nations. In the same year Pakistan proposed to the Chinese, who agreed, that the two governments should try to settle by negotiation their differences over the border between Sinkiang and the Pakistani-held segment of Kashmir.

In India meanwhile Nehru was at the height of his power and authority. In all aspects of foreign affairs his views and outlook automatically prevailed. Nehru's philosophy was simple. It was unthinkable that any two nations which had escaped from bondage (of whatever kind) to the West, and now eschewed politico-military alignment with Moscow or Washington, should ever fight each other.

Accordingly Nehru's India befriended from the outset the new Communist government in China—'the other Asian revolution'—and worked hard to help it get established as a respectable member of international society. Nehru endorsed China's occupation of Tibet in 1950, and was quick to surrender the special position there which free India had inherited from the British. Only in 1959 when the Tibetans revolted and were crushed, and the Dalai Lama fled to India and was given political asylum as a refugee, did the underlying dispute between the two countries surface. It sprang from differences over the location of the Indo-Tibetan border, and was pursued with persistence and increasing acrimony by both sides, though the Indians framed their actions on the assumption that the Chinese would never respond by force. India adopted the so-called forward policy of setting up military posts well within Chinese-claimed areas, but with instructions not to provoke a clash. This was a variant of the non-violent technique which had worked so well against the British. But the Chinese had none of the qualms of conscience which had made the British vulnerable. They decided to put an end once and for all to Indian nibbling into what they considered their territory. They attacked with strong forces both in the north-west and the north-east and in one month (October–November 1962) drove back the ill-prepared Indian Army from its mountain positions on the north-east frontier into the plains of Assam. Having done so the Chinese declared a unilateral cease-fire, and withdrew to positions twenty kilometers behind the line of actual control, calling on the Indians to act correspondingly.

The effect on India was seismic. Nehru had plainly miscalculated. The main assumption on which his and India's attitude to world politics had hitherto been based had been proved false. Indian troops had been routed in battles for which they were ill-trained and ill-equipped. Nehru was obliged to offer up the head of Krishna Menon, his scheming and anti-Western Defence Minister, in order to save his own. To India's disappointment the Soviet Union took up a neutral stance between India and China; so did India's partners in the non-aligned movement. Nehru and his government turned for help to the United States and Britain, who responded by an immediate airlift of weapons, intended to replace some of those which India had lost in the fighting, and an offer of further arms aid in the longer term.

IV

In this sudden crisis Anglo-American consultation and co-ordination of policy on politico-military matters in the South Asian subcontinent became closer than it had ever been before. British and American officials met during November to compare notes and agree on objectives. They were at one in believing that the Chinese meant to teach India a lesson and damage its prestige, not to conquer territory which China recognized as Indian. They agreed that the Indian Army should be enabled to stand its ground in the positions now reached. The Indian parliamentary system must not be jeopardized, and India's non-alignment policy must not be impaired. The Indians should be persuaded to try to resolve their disputes with the Pakistanis, who for their part must be persuaded separately that the Western arms now to be supplied to India would not be used against them.

At the end of November the British and American governments sent missions to New Delhi which were led respectively by Duncan Sandys and Averell Harriman. One of their main purposes was to discuss with the Indians what new equipment would be needed to restore Indian strength in the mountainous border areas where the Chinese had attacked. Another was to visit Rawalpindi and there seek to reassure the Pakistanis about the purpose and extent of Western arms aid to India. A third was—if possible—to get bilateral talks started between India and Pakistan with a view to resolving their differences, especially over Kashmir.

President Kennedy and the British and Australian Prime Ministers had written to Ayub soon after the Chinese attacks on India began, urging him to promise Nehru that he could count on Pakistan taking no action along the Indo-Pakistani frontiers to assist the Chinese. But Ayub replied that India's intentions toward Pakistan were far from peaceful. In this situation how could Pakistanis be expected to show their friendship for India? Weapons now given to India for use against the Chinese would be turned against Pakistan at the first opportunity. Only a settlement of the Kashmir problem would allay each country's fears about the other.[1]

Kennedy asked Harriman to explain to Ayub[2] that owing to the Chinese attack the South Asian subcontinent had become a new area of major confrontation between the Free World and the Communists. Ayub should examine dispassionately the great opportunity which he and Nehru now had to resolve Indo-Pakistani differences in the cause of solidarity against the Chinese. The US government believed that it might be able to assist both parties to reach a reasonable compromise.

Sandys and Harriman together persuaded Nehru and Ayub to meet

---

[1] Mohammad Ayub Khan, *Friends not Masters* (New York, 1967), pp. 141–6.
[2] State Department telegram no. 2329 to New Delhi of 25 Nov. 1962, John F. Kennedy Memorial Library, Boston. (Hereafter referred to as JFKL.)

with each other in an attempt to resolve the difficulties attending Kashmir and other related matters. Their meeting was to be preceded by a series of bilateral discussions between Indian and Pakistani Ministers. An agreement to this effect was announced simultaneously in New Delhi and Rawalpindi on 29 November 1962.

Kennedy wrote to Nehru soon afterward to tell him that 'a full commitment' of India's resources could be reached 'if the issues which divide India and Pakistan, the most important of which is Kashmir' could be settled.[3]

Macmillan and Kennedy met at Nassau in the Bahamas on 20 December 1962. They agreed that the United States and Britain should together make available on a grant basis to India the special equipment needed to produce six mountain divisions from existing infantry divisions of the Indian Army, with supporting units; that measures should be put in hand to make existing combat aircraft effective; that some airlift assistance should be made available; and that a joint Anglo-American-Commonwealth air defence team should visit India at an appropriate time.

It was emphasized to Ayub, when he was told of these decisions, that the military aid being supplied to India by Britain and the United States was for the specific purpose of helping to meet the threat from the People's Republic of China. He replied by complaining that the two Western governments had not made the supply of this aid contingent on a Kashmir settlement. In his autobiography Ayub says that once the United States and other Western countries had decided that they would not link arms aid to India with a resolution of the Kashmir dispute the Indians were under no compulsion to enter into any serious discussion with Pakistan: the Kashmir talks 'which had never held much promise' inevitably 'got bogged down in procedural wrangles and academic inanities'.[4]

The British and American governments were able at this time to harmonize their policies for managing the South Asian situation to a surprisingly complete extent. In part this was due to the personal rapport which existed between Kennedy and Macmillan, and between Kennedy and Ormsby-Gore (later Lord Harlech) who was British Ambassador in Washington. It was made possible also by the close working relationship which Phillips Talbot in the State Department and Cyril Pickard in the Commonwealth Relations Office built up with each other. It was believed in Washington that Britain's influence in New Delhi and Rawalpindi could be put to good use in helping to resolve Indo-Pakistani differences. Moreover British (and if possible Canadian

[3] State Department telegram no. 2583 to New Delhi of 6 Dec. 1962, JFKL.
[4] Mohammad Ayub Khan, op. cit., pp. 150 and 152.

and Australian) involvement in providing arms aid to India would help to make that enterprise appear as in part a Commonwealth operation, not merely a Cold War one, with correspondingly less likelihood of provoking a riposte by the Soviets. Thus at a meeting at the White House on 19 November 1962, which was chaired by President Kennedy, Secretary of State Dean Rusk said he 'preferred to see the U.K. take the lead . . . the more we got in front, the more we would push Moscow toward Peking'.[5] J. K. Galbraith, then US Ambassador in India, was less sanguine. In a cable to Washington at this time he declared with characteristic astringency that 'there are only two and one-half cities where the Commonwealth is taken seriously: London, Washington and Canberra'.[6]

The ministerial Indo-Pakistani talks about Kashmir were held alternately in the two countries. They lasted six months. Britain and America took no direct part, but at each round of talks an Anglo-American team consisting of the respective US Ambassador and British High Commissioner (Galbraith and Gore-Booth in India and McConaughy and myself in Pakistan) hovered watchfully in the wings. London and Washington carefully concerted their instructions to their representatives; but though they had helped to bring the talks about, the two Western nations could not supply a will to agree where none existed. Between the fourth and fifth rounds the British and Americans tried to help by producing ideas designed to block in the area of Kashmir—the Vale—where it was clear that a solution had to be sought. Kennedy put a determined oar in by urging Nehru, in a letter dated 9 March 1963, to 'make proposals which will be proof positive to the Pakistanis that you genuinely seek a settlement by signalling a willingness to give Pakistan a substantial position in the Vale'.[7] This appeal fell on deaf ears. Nehru's reaction was expressed a few months later in a talk to Chester Bowles, who succeeded Galbraith in July 1963. Why (asked Nehru) did the United States attempt to use India's difficulties with China as a lever to force him to make concessions to Pakistan on Kashmir? The Americans had tried to force him to make compromises which the Indian people and Parliament could not possibly accept, and which no Indian Prime Minister could accept without being voted out of office.[8] The bilateral talks ended in failure and there was no Nehru–Ayub summit.

V

In March 1963 the Pakistanis and the Chinese signed and published a

[5] Memorandum by R. W. Komer of Presidential Meeting on 19 Nov. 1962.

[6] J. K. Galbraith, *Ambassador's Journal* (Boston, 1969), p. 443.

[7] State Department telegram no. 3366 to New Delhi of 9 Mar. 1963, Lyndon Baines Johnson Memorial Library, Austin, Texas.

[8] Chester Bowles, *Promises to Keep* (New York, 1971), p. 473.

border agreement. It followed a Trade Agreement signed in January. Ayub was at pains to assure McConaughy and myself that these two agreements were limited and practical in scope and that no further agreements with the Chinese were in prospect. When Zhou Enlai visited Karachi in February 1964 Bhutto made it clear to the press that Pakistan had no intention of entering into military collaboration with China. However, there was other evidence of *rapprochement*, for example the signing of a Cultural Agreement, and in March 1965 Ayub paid a visit to China where he was given a carefully staged tumultuous welcome. In Washington disenchantment grew steadily with Pakistan's tepid performance as an ally and with what came increasingly to be seen as Pakistan's *liaison de convenance* with the People's Republic. In April 1965 President Johnson unilaterally postponed a visit which Ayub was shortly to have paid to Washington. (He similarly postponed one by Prime Minister Shastri of India, to the latter's great annoyance.) By so doing he meant to convey, particularly to the Pakistanis, that US friendship must not be taken for granted. In June Johnson further decided that the United States would not take part in the pledging meeting among donor governments of aid to Pakistan which was due to be held on 27 July. The meeting was rescheduled for 23 September, but no indication was given in Washington as to whether or not an American pledge would be forthcoming at that meeting either. It was implied that until certain issues could be discussed with satisfactory results between the United States and Pakistan no further aid would be forthcoming. In the wake of all this a considerable chill developed in American-Pakistani relations.

Meanwhile an Indo-Pakistani border skirmish had occurred in the Rann of Kutch, an uninhabited salt-marsh whose ownership was disputed between the two nations, lying to the south of the Pakistan province of Sind. The skirmish rapidly escalated into localized fighting between the two armies, from which (for topographical reasons) the Indians came off second best. As an old India hand, now representing Britain in Pakistan, I asked London if I might visit New Delhi to see if I could find some common ground on which to base a British attempt at mediation. Both governments offered a cease-fire. Under skilful orchestration from London my colleague in India (John Freeman) and I after two months succeeded in getting a document agreed on by the Indians and Pakistanis which provided for settlement of the ownership dispute by an international tribunal (which in the end found for Pakistan). The Americans were content to see the British take the lead in this way and gave us all the diplomatic support in their power, both in Rawalpindi and New Delhi.

Ayub was grateful to the British for getting Pakistan a better deal over the Rann than they could ever have negotiated with India for themselves. It was decided between London and Washington that this extra Pakistani goodwill for Britain should be expended for the benefit of the United States. I was recalled from leave with my family in France to fly back as soon as possible to Rawalpindi, where I arrived in late August. My instructions were to explain confidentially to Ayub, speaking as a friend both of Pakistan and the United States, that the impression had been created in Washington that Pakistan had thrown down the gauntlet, and that President Johnson thought it essential to have a talk with President Ayub before going ahead on aid. The British government for its part hoped that the two countries could resolve their differences in time for the United States to make a pledge at the postponed aid-donors' meeting on 23 September.

However, before I could carry out these instructions the whole situation had changed. A group of senior Pakistani officials, including Bhutto, and some of the military, persuaded Ayub that if an uprising could be provoked in the Indian-held part of Kashmir, another and more serious armed confrontation would arise with India which would cause the Western powers to intervene with a view to enforcing a Kashmir settlement. It was apparent that the Kashmiris would not, or could not, be persuaded to rebel of their own accord. So a force of several thousand armed infiltrators was secretly prepared on the Pakistani side of the cease-fire line, and on the night of 5–6 August launched into action. Their task was to create the chaos and disruption which would facilitate an insurrection by the Kashmiris. They would cut telephone lines, blow up bridges, and ambush military convoys, and attack patrols, fuel dumps, and unit and sub-unit headquarters. But no general uprising occurred. With some difficulty the Indians rounded up the infiltrators. In order to block further infiltration the Indians advanced across the cease-fire line at three points. This brought them into armed combat with the Pakistanis (whose government had meanwhile blandly disclaimed all knowledge of or responsibility for the infiltrators). The Pakistani Army then attacked toward Jammu in the south of the state, a communications centre through which passed the only road between India, the Vale of Kashmir, and Ladakh where Indian troops were facing the Chinese. In order to force the Pakistanis to halt this potentially very damaging thrust the Indians then attacked across the international frontier toward two important Pakistani cities, Lahore and Sialkot.

At this point the British Prime Minister, Harold Wilson, sent messages to Ayub and Shastri deploring the extension of the conflict. His message to Shastri said that the attack by Indian forces across the common international frontier was most regrettable and that it had helped to create a most dangerous situation which could have the gravest consequences not only for India and Pakistan but also for the peace of the world. The Indian government and public bitterly resented what they considered to be the pro-Pakistani bias of this message, since it placed on Indian shoulders blame which should properly have been laid at Pakistan's door. In this way Britain—at an inopportune moment—forfeited in India its reputation for impartiality.

In Rawalpindi two weeks later McConaughy and I—working once again very closely together—were able to persuade Ayub to accept the Security Council's appeal for a cease-fire. But by then there could be no question of Britain's playing its former role of accepted peacemaker between Rawalpindi and New Delhi. This role was taken over by the Russians, who (with tacit American encouragement) called the two sides together at Tashkent in January 1966. They wrangled long and bitterly but in the end both Ayub and Shastri accepted a Declaration in which the two countries reaffirmed their obligation under the UN Charter not to have recourse to force. The only reference to Kashmir was in the preamble which touched on Kashmir in passing as a subject on which the two sides 'had put forth their respective positions'. Pakistanis in general saw this as a most disappointing outcome and Ayub lost prestige and popularity accordingly. His readiness to accept the Tashkent Declaration was doubtless the greater after President Johnson's statement to him in Washington in December 1965 that nothing the United States could say or do would induce India to part with Kashmir.[9]

In these circumstances joint mediatory efforts by the British and American governments in the South Asian subcontinent came to an end, and their collaboration in this particular enterprise lapsed, not to be renewed. Other preoccupations (Vietnam in Washington, Rhodesia in London) pressed in on them both. In the end their successive interventions in Indo-Pakistani relations had proved unproductive. It was time to draw a line under the past and switch efforts elsewhere.

VI

During the two decades that have followed some political landmarks of the 1950s and 1960s have disappeared. Others have remained or reappeared.

Today's diminished Pakistan still lacks any serious defence-industrial capacity of its own. India exploded a nuclear device in 1974, but says that it has not produced any nuclear weapons. Pakistan seems to be acquiring a nuclear weapons capability, perhaps to pre-empt and offset

[9] See p. 100 of the Pakistan Government's White Paper on Kashmir of Jan. 1977.

possible similar action by India. Neither country bases its defence strategy on using nuclear weapons against the other; it seems likely that mutual deterrence will prevent this. In overall military terms Pakistan is nowadays much inferior to India.

On Pakistan's northern border a new threat now stems from the Soviet Union's war of conquest in Afghanistan. America has sought to help the Pakistanis meet this threat by its $3.2 billion package of military and economic aid. Just as in the past, India reacted angrily to these new transfers of American arms to Pakistan, and in reply has sought new and up-to-date hardware (especially aircraft and tanks) from the Soviet Union, which (in the absence of any serious intention on America's part to play a competing role) has long since become India's largest supplier of high-technology weapons.

Neither superpower has obtained exclusive strategic facilities in the South Asian subcontinent as the price of its aid, military or otherwise. Cento and SEATO are dead. The Pakistanis value highly their new membership of the non-aligned movement. The United States government says it has no wish to disturb this, and that American interests are best served when South Asian nations are stable, resilient, strong, capable of preventing outside powers from intruding in their regional affairs.

In India the Soviets have built up a situation of considerable political and economic strength. They have done so by careful cultivation of the ruling élite, by a major propaganda effort aimed at virtually the whole literate population, by trade agreements which have brought India substantial economic advantages, by the supply of modern arms on highly favourable financial terms, and by political support of India on the international scene, especially in the United Nations and its agencies. India has repaid some of this support in similar coin, but (despite the Treaty of Friendship which the two countries signed in 1971) has stopped short of granting the Soviet Navy the use of Vizagapatnam on the Bay of Bengal, which the Soviets would no doubt dearly like to enjoy, much as they have already been granted by their other friends, the Vietnamese, the exclusive use of Danang and Camranh Bay on the South China Sea.

Even if—by the strong wish of its inhabitants—the South Asian subcontinent itself is not the scene of inter-superpower strategic rivalry, this certainly cannot be said of the Indian Ocean, where this rivalry is a strong and continuing factor. It is fuelled by Soviet and American moves and counter-moves, such as the development of Aden by the USSR as an important naval base, and of Diego Garcia in the same way by the Americans, with the agreement of the British to whom that island belongs. (Incidentally, it is a measure of India's wilful lack of objectivity in its dealings with the two superpowers that Diego Garcia, and never Aden, is always quoted in Delhi as the cause of strategic tension in the area.)

China and India are once again on speaking terms. But they are no nearer now than they were then to solving the border dispute which led to the fighting between them in 1962. However, the two sides have been careful to avoid repeating their former armed clashes along the frontier. With Pakistan China's friendship has prospered, within the limits of what is feasible between two such different societies. During the 1971 Indo-Pakistani War China once again refrained from intervening militarily on Pakistan's side, perhaps because Peking realized the virtual certainty that the Pakistan Army, in what was to become Bangladesh, must speedily be defeated once battle was joined with the Indians, and was in any case fighting in a bad and lost cause; and perhaps too because following its 1962 débâcle the Indian Army had been given a new and significant capability for mountain warfare.

Britain's military and strategic role outside the NATO area was swiftly and sharply reduced from 1968 onwards. The Wilson Government's sudden and destabilizing decision to remove British troops from the Persian Gulf was greeted in Washington with shock and dismay. Here—like the Anglo-French Suez misadventure of 1956, or the American invasion of Grenada in 1984—was a case where the Anglo-American 'Special Relationship' was very little in evidence.

This voluntary retreat by the United Kingdom from its former global role into the narrower existence of a middle-sized European and Atlantic nation coincided with a protracted series of economic difficulties in Britain. Until Mrs Thatcher and the Conservative Party came to power in 1979 no British government seemed able to master them. These developments were seen by those connoisseurs of power and the will to greatness, the Indian and Pakistani educated élites, as evidence of a decline which meant that in the future Britain would count for significantly less in world and South Asian affairs. As a leading partner in NATO and (later) the EEC, and a permanent member of the Security Council, Britain's future usefulness (particularly as a bridge between the Asian members of the Commonwealth and the EEC) would still on occasion be measurable and significant. But Britain's aura of all-round practical success, which had impressed the world so deeply for so long, had at last faded. Future British reputation and influence internationally would have to be earned anew by the quality of British statecraft (as shown in the final Zimbabwe settlement in 1980) and of British leadership and resource (as shown in the risky naval-cum-military *tour de force* which recaptured the Falkland Islands from Argentina in 1983).

I owe to Ambassador Robert F. Goheen (formerly United States Ambassador to India) the reminder that American bilateral economic assistance to India (including food aid) between 1951 and 1971 amounted to over $10 billion, and provided over 36 per cent of all foreign assistance received by India in those two decades. Allowing for the disproportion in available wealth between Britain and America, the British contribution to the growth of both the Indian and Pakistani economies has also been notable, and has been more steadily and consistently sustained over the years than America's. Aid from our two countries, and from such other nations as West Germany, France, the Soviet Union, and Canada, has helped India to achieve today's resounding double success of feeding its ever-growing population and of developing a sizeable new and diverse industrial potential. Here, incidentally, is a striking refutation of the controversial claim that European decolonization has everywhere been a catastrophe; in India, and to a lesser extent Pakistan, it has proved a signal success. Admittedly in much of Africa the arrival of the European powers was hurried, their stay brief, and their departure precipitate. The results are not pretty. But this leads only to the undramatic conclusion that in some cases decolonization has worked less well than in others. What else was to be expected among so vast and heterogeneous a mass of mankind as that which is so often given nowadays the misleading description of the Third World?

I believe to be ill-founded and untenable the thesis that America has in some way failed in a duty to replace Britain as a guarantor of world order, and (by implication) general enforcer of peace and stability in areas that are today disastrously poor and ill-governed. Britain's then unchallengeable naval supremacy (to which there is no equivalent today, nor—for technical reasons—could be) made possible a British mercantile thalassocracy during the nineteenth century; but even then, within much of the world's landmass (especially in Europe) Britain's writ never ran. Moreover, as the history of the last forty years amply shows, to ensure peace and stability in someone else's country it is necessary to rule it, or in other words to assert hegemony by brute and visible force, as the Soviets did in Hungary and Czechoslovakia. And it is also an empirical fact of our time that recently freed peoples, having thrown off the yoke of one foreign power, are simply not disposed to submit tamely to rule by another. Should America have set about conquering all over again the territories which Britain and other European powers had freed? Obviously not.

VII

As the balance of wealth and military strength has shifted over the years to America's advantage, and against Britain, so prospects have diminished of the two governments working again as they once did in double harness, in South Asia or elsewhere, in pursuit of some single specific and difficult goal. Diminished, but not disappeared; it depends on circumstances. As Richard H. Ullman says in his contribution to the present volume: 'British views are always welcome in Washington, but so are German or Israeli or Japanese views. They are given weight when they concern issues in which the government involved has either an obvious stake or recognized special knowledge.' Mr Goheen generously notes that since 1966 British diplomats in South Asia have continued to be active and able, and consultation between them and their American colleagues has almost always been close and fruitful. As he says, American and British politico-military objectives in the subcontinent have been highly congruent. This satisfactory situation is reflected in the exchange of information and assessment which the British and Americans continue to share, with each side contributing to the other's thinking from its own close but not identical point of view. I can testify from my own thirteen years' experience as a British diplomat in the Indo-Pakistani subcontinent how stimulating and rewarding these confidential Anglo-American exchanges always were. I have no doubt that they are so still. Naturally the possibility of sharp divergences of assessment and policy between our two countries must always exist, as notably happened in 1971 at the time of President Nixon's—as Britain saw it—misguided and aberrant 'tilt' toward President Yahya Khan's gravely compromised regime in Pakistan, when both ethical and practical considerations pointed elsewhere. But what is truly remarkable is not the odd occasion on which the American and British governments have disagreed, but the much greater frequency with which they have come independently to the same, or a similar, conclusion and acted accordingly.

The China Problem in Anglo-American Relations

RODERICK MACFARQUHAR

DURING the first three decades of the post-war era, tensions periodically arose between London and Washington over East Asia. Only during the last decade have such tensions apparently been almost totally absent. The change has of course been due to the gradual decline of British involvement (with the exception of Hong Kong) but above all to the relationship between the United States and China that has developed since the early 1970s, for policy toward the People's Republic has been the most frequent bone of contention between the Americans and the British in East Asia in the past forty years. This paper will focus on that central issue.

BACKGROUND

The origins of the earlier tensions lay in differing roles in China and, as a consequence, differing reactions to the Chinese revolution. In the nineteenth century, Britain had been the first Western imperialist power to break down forcibly the barriers of Chinese isolation, and not surprisingly it was afterward seen as the principal architect of China's century of humiliation. While Americans partook of the benefits of extra-territoriality, Washington seems to have perceived itself as a benevolent protector of Chinese interests and its open-door policy as a restraint upon the grosser depredations of other foreign powers. Chinese expectations of America grew. President Wilson's failure at the Versailles peace conference to prevent the transfer of German concessions to Japan was disillusioning, but the United States remained the only Western power to which patriotic Chinese might look with some hope of sympathy.

The Kuomintang (KMT) government set up in 1928 was passionately nationalistic, and when it looked westward for advice and help, it was to the United States (and Germany for military assistance) that Chiang Kai-shek turned rather than the detested British. Although

Japan had emerged as a major threat to Chinese territorial integrity as early as 1895, Britain remained a focus of Chinese hostility through the 1930s, especially as the British Government maintained a studiously correct attitude toward its one-time Japanese ally even, for a time, after the outbreak of the Sino-Japanese War in 1937.

When the Sino-Japanese War was transformed into the Pacific theatre of World War II, President Roosevelt made every effort to build China's role into that of a great power, with Chiang Kai-shek treated as one of the Big Four at the Cairo conference in 1943. China was promised a permanent seat in the Security Council of the post-war United Nations. In 1943, too, and again at F.D.R.'s instance, extra-territoriality was abandoned, and had the American President survived the war, he would doubtless have tried to obtain the return of Hong Kong to China.

Thus, when the Chinese civil war broke out in the late 1940s, Washington and London viewed it in different lights. Although there had been wartime collaboration against Japan, Britain had not enjoyed the same close ties with the KMT as the Americans. Nor had Britain been wholly sympathetic to F.D.R.'s efforts to transform China into a world power. Whereas the United States devoted itself to achieving some kind of compromise settlement in China and thereafter to assisting the KMT, Britain maintained neutrality, asserting that it was for the Chinese themselves to settle their internal disputes. Disillusion with the corruption and ineptitude of the dying KMT regime was common to both London and Washington, but it was tinged with resignation in Whitehall, anguish in the White House.

The proclamation of an anti-Western People's Republic of China (PRC) on 1 October 1949 was seen by Americans as a humiliating rejection of decades of friendship and care for Chinese interests. 'Who lost China?' became a massively divisive political issue. Returning missionaries helped to transform affection for China into hatred of 'Godless Communism'. In Britain, where commerce had been from the beginning the motivation for involvement in China, businessmen counted for more than clerics, and speedy recognition of the new regime was seen as the only way to preserve a trading tie. London was influenced, too, by the views of the newly independent Asian members of the Commonwealth, notably India, which favoured the immediate establishment of diplomatic relations. The clash between units of the People's Liberation Army and HMS *Amethyst* on the Yangtze River during the final months of the civil war had brought it home to Britain that the era of gunboat diplomacy was over. Realism demanded recognition of the new order, for the Communist government clearly controlled the national territory.

The Truman Administration may have considered the haste of British action in this regard somewhat unseemly, but there was no major confrontation between the two allies. For America, equally realistically, was simultaneously washing its hands of the KMT by declaring Taiwan, whence Chiang Kai-shek had fled, outside its defensive perimeter. Conciliation of China, though it did from time to time cause difficulties between London and Washington, was never as contentious as hostility toward China. This first became apparent during the Korean War.[1]

THE KOREAN WAR

British support for American resistance to the North Korean invasion of South Korea was immediately forthcoming in June 1950. But the British Cabinet was alarmed at the decision to interpose the American fleet in the Taiwan strait, and regarded as 'ham-fisted' Truman's reference to 'centrally directed Communist Imperialism'. While Bevin, the Foreign Secretary, was anxious not to discourage Truman from assisting Britain in fighting Communism in Malaya, a majority of the Cabinet was against reference to Communist encroachments elsewhere in Asia. At this time, only Aneurin Bevan appears to have been agitated about Truman's failure to consult his ally in advance, though this did become an issue in subsequent crises.

The first major rift between the allies occurred after the intervention of the Chinese People's Volunteers in the Korean War in October 1950. As a foreign affairs debate in the House of Commons at the end of November revealed, both the Labour Government and the Conservative opposition were concerned that Truman, or possibly General MacArthur, would drag his allies into a general war with China, in which the Americans might resort to atomic weapons. A fundamental divergence of approach which had existed from the beginning of the war surfaced when the Prime Minster, Attlee, flew to Washington shortly after the debate.

In their discussions, Truman stated his belief that the Chinese were 'Russian satellites', and enunciated the domino theory: that if Korea went, it would then be the turn of Indo-China, then Hong Kong, and then Malaya. For his part Attlee rejected the monolithic Communism thesis, asserting: 'I think that all of us should try to keep the Chinese from thinking that Russia is their only friend. I want the Chinese to part company with Russia. I want them to become a counterpoise to Russia in the Far East.'

---

[1] James MacGregor Burns, *Roosevelt, the Soldier of Freedom, 1940–1945* (New York, 1970), pp. 204–5, 374–8, 403–5, 575; Evan Luard, *Britain and China*, (London, 1962), pp. 19–82; Roderick MacFarquhar, *Sino-American Relations, 1949–1971* (New York, 1972), pp. 59–77.

This early suggestion of playing a China card was rejected by Truman and Acheson, who were smarting from recent defeats at the hands of the Chinese People's Volunteers. Attlee's proposal for admitting the PRC to the UN was also turned down as smacking of appeasement. Acheson argued pointedly that it would be difficult to obtain public support for a robust policy in Europe if the United States did not behave in a comparable manner in Asia. The Americans were equally resistant to Attlee's probing about abandoning Taiwan and Chiang Kai-shek. Reassured that Truman had no intention of expanding the war to Chinese territory, with or without atomic weapons, Attlee evidently felt it was best to evince public solidarity with an ally bearing the brunt of the fighting at a time of great mutual peril. The subsequent dismissal of MacArthur confirmed the correctness of his decision. At a later stage of the war, Attlee agreed in principle that bombing of Chinese airfields might take place—after consultation with London—if they became a serious threat to the UN forces, a decision endorsed by Churchill when he took over as Prime Minister.

Yet fundamental differences of approach continued to bedevil Anglo-American relations on East Asia. As Foreign Secretary in the dying months of the Labour Government, Herbert Morrison had agreed with Dulles, then in charge of negotiating the peace treaty with Japan, that neither London nor Washington would bring any pressure to bear on Tokyo as to which 'China' the post-occupation government should recognize. When Anthony Eden replaced him, he reaffirmed this policy as the official British position to Acheson and Dulles during a visit to Washington. He was disagreeably surprised a few days later when the American and Japanese governments simultaneously published Prime Minister Yoshida's letter revealing Japan's intention of recognizing the Republic of China on Taiwan. Eden's memoirs indicate that he had been told of the existence of the letter and probably its import, though he was not shown its text. His embarrassment was over the timing, which suggested he had agreed to the manœuvre designed to prevent pro-Taiwan senators from voting against the peace treaty. Morrison was far angrier, feeling he had been double-crossed, and wrote to Eden warning him against Dulles. Doubtless Eden remembered the warning at the time of Suez.[2]

THE OFFSHORE ISLANDS CRISIS

If London and Washington were at loggerheads over China policy even

[2] Dean Acheson, *Present at the Creation: My Years in the State Department* (New York, 1969), pp. 478–85; Alan Bullock, *Ernest Bevin: Foreign Secretary* (New York, 1983), pp. 790–802, 811–16, 820–8; Bernard Donoghue and G. W. Jones, *Herbert Morrison* (London, 1973), p. 500; Robert J. Donovan, *Tumultuous Years, The Presidency of Harry S. Truman, 1949–1953* (New York, 1982), pp. 187–362; Sir Anthony Eden, *The Memoirs of Anthony Eden: Full Circle* (London, 1960), pp. 19–20; Kenneth Harris, *Attlee* (London, 1982), pp. 461–7; MacFarquhar, *Sino-American Relations* pp. 78–100.

when the forces of both nations were fighting the troops of the PRC, it is hardly surprising that the differences persisted when wartime exigencies of solidarity disappeared. The Korean War brought a revival of the alliance between the United States and the rump KMT regime on Taiwan. Chiang Kai-shek rebuilt his forces with American aid, and placed a substantial portion of them on the offshore islands only a mile or two off the mainland coast. Though the Eisenhower Administration accepted Premier Zhou Enlai's offer in 1955 to initiate ambassadorial talks, its policy toward the PRC was informed by the unbending hostility of Secretary of State Dulles.

By contrast, Britain's relations with China improved, apparently as a result of the mutually favourable impressions which Eden and Zhou formed of each other during difficult negotiations at the 1954 Geneva conference. Diplomatic relations were put on a firmer footing, although ambassadors were not to be exchanged for another eighteen years. British businessmen were irritated by American reluctance to reduce the restraints imposed on trade with China to the level of those effective for trade with the Soviet Union. But major tension between London and Washington over relations with China did not occur until the second offshore islands crisis, in 1958.

In mid-July 1958, America and Britain had responded to the overthrow of the pro-Western Iraqi government by sending their forces respectively into Lebanon and Jordan. Despite sharp disagreements over Suez little more than eighteen months earlier, the two powers appeared agreed on the necessity for a show of firmness in the Middle East to prevent any more dominoes falling. Incensed at Khrushchev's failure to counter the move by dispatching Soviet troops into the area, the Chinese decided to teach him how Communists should stand up to imperialists. On 23 August a massive bombardment was unleashed on the offshore island of Quemoy, and local radio broadcasts threatened imminent invasion.

Eisenhower was as determined to prevent dominoes falling in the Far East as in the Middle East. He believed that the loss of the offshore islands would lead to the loss of Taiwan, which in turn would threaten the security of Japan, the Philippines, Thailand, Vietnam, and 'even Okinawa', where America had a major base. He strengthened the Seventh Fleet, and authorized it to escort KMT supply ships, ignoring the Chinese claim of a twelve-mile limit of territorial sea made after the crisis began, but respecting the traditional three-mile limit. Though he rejected Dulles's advice at an early stage to authorize the use of tactical nuclear weapons, he indicated privately that he would be prepared to employ them against mainland air bases if an attack on the offshore islands was actually launched. But 'since we do not want to outrage world opinion, perhaps we had better reserve this'.

Eisenhower's assessment of world opinion was accurate, and the British Government was as concerned as Washington's other NATO allies over the possibility that World War III might be started by a struggle over tiny pieces of rock which should unquestionably be under the control of the Peking Government. The memoirs of the then Premier, Harold Macmillan, pinpoint some of the enduring problems that bedevilled Anglo-American relations over China.

Sketching the historical background, Macmillan commented that the

emotion felt in Washington and shared by the whole American people about the course of recent history in China seemed to most foreign observers unnatural and strained . . . Indeed during the Second World War many of us felt that President Roosevelt had made himself something of a nuisance about the Chinese. Their representatives were brought in great state to the Cairo Conference in 1943, where they arrived too early and stayed too late. The President insisted on elevating China, then largely in the hands of Chiang Kai-shek and his supporters, into a world power . . . But when Mao Tse-tung, the Communist leader, utterly destroyed the forces of Chiang Kai-shek and drove his armies out of the mainland, this was a grievous blow not merely to those Americans who took an interest in strategical and military appreciations, but to all Americans, from the most sophisticated to the humblest home.[3]

Macmillan's biting comments were probably an accurate mirror of informed British opinion about the origins of the American obsession over China. But there were more important problems between London and Washington in those tense days of late August and early September 1958. The British Premier seems to have been kept badly informed by the American President. Macmillan relates that he only learned of the initial Chinese bombardment four days later. Though this failure must be partly attributed to the Foreign Office, clearly the State Department should have alerted their principal Western ally in Asia to the significance of the latest crisis in the Far East.

On 3 September, Macmillan wrote to Eisenhower, stressing his desire for a common front despite differing views about the legal and practical considerations concerning the offshore islands, and concluding somewhat plaintively: 'I should therefore very much value a private message from you or Foster [Dulles] giving me some indication of the way your minds are working.' When two days later Macmillan received Dulles's response via the British Embassy in Washington, it was apparently the first he had heard about the 'domino theory', the first he had heard that there were 80,000 Nationalist troops on the offshore islands, and the first he knew about US logistical support to the garrisons there. He felt obliged to reply immediately, pointing out that no one in Britain or the Commonwealth would support the American position wholeheartedly

[3] Harold Macmillan, *Riding the Storm, 1956–1959* (New York, 1972), pp. 139–41.

and that the British Government was on record as asserting that the offshore islands and Taiwan were 'in different juridical categories'.

Macmillan's retrospective account suggests that all along he was confident that, despite Dulles's apparent bellicosity, Eisenhower was too sensible to jump over the brink by using tactical nuclear weapons in the Taiwan strait. But he was clearly under no illusions that his own suggested solutions carried any weight in Washington, and even toward the end of the crisis he was apparently receiving no private explanation of American public positions. His reaction to Eisenhower's and Dulles's press statements was: 'Even to me their meaning was obscure.'

In fact, the crisis had already been effectively defused by Zhou Enlai's agreement on 6 September to resume Sino-American ambassadorial talks, but the Chinese bombardment continued and most of America's allies were aghast at Eisenhower's television assertion that there would be no appeasement. So violent was the reaction—Ike himself estimated the opposition as embracing two-thirds of the world and fifty per cent of American opinion—that Dulles feared that NATO and possibly SEATO were beginning to fall apart. (Mao Zedong, obliged to justify to his colleagues the failure to face down the United States, drew comfort from America's isolation, claiming that only South Korea and perhaps the Philippines had really supported Washington.) Under the circumstances, it was fortunate for Anglo-American relations that the crisis occurred during the summer holidays. The unflappable Macmillan was able to handle the London end without having to face an uneasy parliament or worry about the press panicking public opinion.[4]

CHINA'S UN SEAT

The prospect of a Sino-American war would have been a cause for concern in Whitehall at any time, but on the few occasions when this seemed a real possibility Anglo-American relations were made more difficult, as Macmillan's memoirs underline, by Washington's failure to inform, let alone consult, London. Recalling the Attlee mission in his memoirs, Acheson said that the 'first purpose of the British group was to find out what was going on and why in North Korea', a sad testimony to the lack of collaboration between allies fighting a war. During the 1950s and 1960s, the State Department regularly stationed a middle-rank diplomat at the London embassy to liaise with the Foreign Office on Far Eastern affairs, and there was useful collaboration. But there is no indication that this channel was effective when matters of high policy

---

[4] Stephen E. Ambrose, *Eisenhower*, vol. ii, *The President* (New York, 1984), pp. 482–5; MacFarquhar, *Sino-American Relations*, pp. 101–81; Macmillan, *Riding the Storm, 1956–1959*, pp. 538–56.

were involved, as during the 1958 offshore islands crisis. More recently, Heath was not warned by Nixon about Kissinger's secret trip to China in July 1971 and the prospective breakthrough in Sino-American relations which it presaged. Britain was of course treated no differently from any other ally, but there was considerable unhappiness among Foreign Office ministers and officials engaged at that time in negotiating the establishment of full diplomatic relations with Peking. The announcement of the projected Nixon visit totally changed the diplomatic climate, undercutting the British negotiating position and forcing London to settle on less favourable terms.

The Nixon *démarche* was possibly one reason why Britain, along with all the other NATO allies, deserted the United States in Washington's vain attempt to preserve a position for Taiwan in the UN later that year. Another was Britain's lack of commitment to the Taiwan regime. More importantly, after years of loyal adherence to the American position on the UN China seat, Britain was finally bringing *realpolitik* into line with rhetoric. Hitherto, London had proclaimed its acceptance of the communists as the rulers of China, but failed to follow through by unequivocal support for the transfer of the China seat from Taiwan to the PRC. Instead, the British UN delegate had habitually backed the American device for side-stepping the issue by voting for it to be considered an 'important question', requiring a two-thirds majority to be passed. In the light of the announcement of the Nixon visit, London no longer saw any purpose in sacrificing its burgeoning relationship with Peking on the altar of America's historical entanglement with the KMT.[5]

POTENTIAL PROBLEMS

The normalization of Sino-American relations by the Carter Administration, the acceptance of the new ties between Washington and Peking by a right-wing Reagan Administration, and the settlement of the Hong Kong issue would seem to have removed most major sources of friction between China and the United States and China and the United Kingdom. This should in turn lessen the likelihood of friction between London and Washington over East Asian affairs. The potential for conflict remains, arising out of the historic differences between America and the PRC over Taiwan and the Sino-Soviet relationship.

The Taiwan problem has been finessed but not solved. The passing of Deng Xiaoping in Peking may bring to power leaders who would place

[5] Henry Kissinger, *White House Years* (Boston, 1979), pp. 684–787, 1049–96; MacFarquhar, *Sino-American Relations*, pp. 241–57; Richard Nixon, *RN: the Memoirs of Richard Nixon* (New York, 1978), pp. 544–80.

the island's reunification with the motherland higher on the national agenda, whether for reasons of genuine nationalism or domestic politicking. The passing of Chiang Ching-kuo in Taipei may bring to power leaders who would want to foreclose permanently any possibility of reunification with the motherland, by renouncing claims to be the rightful government of China in favour of becoming a new international entity, Taiwan. This possibility, sometimes known as the 'one China, two Singapores' scenario, would be a diplomatic nightmare for Washington, but it would also pose moral problems for London, especially if a Taiwanese 'UDI' were buttressed by a proper referendum or free elections.

The Sino-Soviet relationship may improve in the years ahead, despite the current differences. A revival of the 1950s alliance is virtually unthinkable, but state-to-state ties could be normalized giving Peking greater manœuvrability *vis-à-vis* Washington. Would such a development be seen by a right-wing administration as destroying the fundamental motivation for cultivating China— building up an anti-Soviet coalition—or is the whole spectrum of American politicians now committed to good Sino-American relations for their own sake? If there were an 'agonizing reappraisal' in Washington, it could well spark new disagreements with London.

No adequate provision can be made for such eventualities. Much will depend on the complexion of the governments in Washington and London. Joint policy planning and regular consultation with ministers involved (conspicuously lacking in the past) could at least minimize potential damage to the Anglo-American relationship. But it could also be argued that Britain's sense of responsibility for and involvement in the geopolitics of East Asia is now so minimal, and America's conception of its vital ties in the Pacific arena has altered so radically, that the likelihood is that there will be even less co-ordination than in the past, but that it will not matter.

20

Africa in Anglo-American Relations

JAMES MAYALL

GOVERNMENTS, it is widely held, have an obligation to defend the national interest, whatever that elusive aggregate is deemed to be. The governments of Great Powers often see themselves, in addition, as shouldering an extra obligation, namely to contribute to the balance of power and to underwrite the values and institutions of international society in the interest of stability. Of course, these values and institutions must operate to the advantage of the Great Power, but since they are regarded as public goods the benefits of which cannot be monopolized, it is only fair, or at least inevitable, that he who pays the piper shall call the tune.

Such, very roughly, was the attitude of British governments in their relations with the rest of the world during the period of British pre-eminence, say from the defeat of Napoleon to the end of the First World War. Throughout this period, the latent tensions between a narrowly defined conception of national interest, the maintenance of the British Empire on which British pre-eminence partly rested, and the general practices and conventions of international society may have been recognized by some of the more far-sighted politicians but they were never publicly acknowledged.[1] The proposition that what was good for Britain was good for the Empire and good for the world was as firmly held (and with considerably less public embarrassment) as the notorious view of Charles Wilson, Secretary for Defense, that what was good for General Motors was good for the United States. It provided the broad framework of a self-confident foreign policy.

By historical standards the process by which Britain yielded leadership to the United States was relatively free from conflict. The United States was not an enemy but Britain's principal ally; nevertheless, the transfer was not everywhere achieved with the smoothness of a boardroom take-over. The major strain in Anglo-American relations arose over the liquidation of the British Empire, although even on this

---

[1] For example, Disraeli speaking in 1852 about Britain's remaining colonial presence in North America: 'These wretched colonies will all be independent in a few years and are a millstone round our neck.'

issue sub-Saharan Africa was never an important source of discord. For the most part, the Commonwealth African countries were the beneficiaries of Britain's 'defeat' over the Suez Crisis in 1956. That episode did indeed place enormous strain on Anglo-American relations, and it can be argued that it finally exposed the fiction of the 'Special Relationship' between London and Washington. Judging by the speed with which Britain's African empire was abandoned, it seems clear that after 1956 the British government finally accepted the logic of its decision to grant India independence in 1947, namely that in the post-war world there was no intellectual defence for the continued maintenance of the empire. Consequently, although there were occasional differences across the Atlantic over the timing and manner of decolonization, most notably over American support for UN action in the Congo, and continued British impatience with the rhetoric of American anti-colonialism whenever it resurfaced, there was no conflict of principle.

Even when they resented American intrusion, the British knew that their world role, such as it was, now depended on American support. British pre-eminence, never in any case as secure as it can be made to look in the afterglow of nostalgia, has long departed the scene and with it has gone the self-confident foreign policy. It was not a Marxist but the late Iain Macleod, one of the most percipient of post-war Conservatives, who noted that the attitudes and policies of British pre-eminence had never been self-sustaining. They rested on three material advantages: on the fact that the British had pioneered industrial capitalism; on the existence of the British Empire which had provided a large, open market for British manufactures and had significantly augmented the country's diplomatic and military strength; and on the Royal Navy.[2]

Overtaken by her industrial competitors, stripped of her Empire by an alliance between nationalism abroad and liberalism at home, and with no permanent naval presence east of Suez since the late 1960s, the contemporary problem for British governments in their relations with the non-European world can be fairly accurately, if somewhat negatively, described as damage limitation. In this regard Britain is not so different from the other industrial democracies, including the United States: they all wish to co-operate with Third World countries in ways which will do as little as possible to undermine the existing distribution of power and influence within international society.

For the United States, as leader of the Western Alliance, this general problem poses a dilemma of political strategy, namely how to combine sensitivity to local political conditions with the need to contain Soviet influence. Relieved of this responsibility, the British have sometimes felt that American policy has underrated the power of African nationalism

[2] Ian MacLeod, 'Reports of Britain's Death', *Foreign Affairs*, 45 (1966), 89–97.

and given too much weight to anti-Communism; but this is no doubt because for British governments the dilemma has a sharper utilitarian focus: how, in an uncomfortably competitive world, to transform the legacies of pre-eminence and Empire from liabilities into assets.

In no part of the world has this problem presented British governments with greater difficulties than in their relations with Africa. The broad strategy for effecting the transformation—decolonization within the Commonwealth—was announced to the world with the granting of independence to Ghana in 1957. But what exactly were the British up to? Nkrumah, the first legatee of the old order south of the Sahara, feared that they had embarked on a process of cosmetic change in order to maintain the reality of power: neocolonialism, he warned, was the worst kind of imperialism because, unlike the real thing, it constituted the exercise of power without responsibility.

But if that was their main purpose—to keep the old imperial show on the road—at the time most British would probably have denied it; in their view they were reacting, as always, pragmatically and as they saw it honourably, to the challenge of the moment. For some time they resisted the argument of General Assembly Resolution 1514 which held that lack of preparation for self-government should not be used to delay independence, but not so much out of opposition to the principle (principles have seldom been debated in Britain in the abstract), as because the presence of settler communities with entrenched political privileges, as in the Central African Federation, created practical obstacles to disengagement. Thus between 1960 and 1962 the Conservative government supported British financial interests in the Northern Rhodesian copper belt, which were linked with Belgian interests in Katanga, in resisting American support for the United Nations campaign to end Katangan secession from the Congo.[3] In other cases, they also resisted rapid decolonization because the concept of a politically independent state, still dependent from its birth on budgetary assistance, was anathema to those trained in the principles of sound administration and Treasury control.

By the mid-1960s, however, it was clear that any such doubts had been suppressed; the British government (first under the Conservatives and then Labour) had decided to seek the country's fortune in Europe as and when the French would permit them to do so; the Commonwealth sentimentalists on the left and far right had been brushed aside, and what remained of the Empire was to be scuttled as decently, but also as quickly, as possible. The Central African Federation was broken up in deference to the wishes of the United Independence Party of Northern Rhodesia and the Nyasaland Congress Party. Grants in aid were

[3] See Stephen R. Weissman, *American Foreign Policy in the Congo, 1960–64* (Ithaca and London, 1974).

accepted as a reasonable price for disengagement in Malawi, Sierra Leone, the former High Commission Territories in Southern Africa; and even Gambia was finally allowed to acquire independence with no more than a theatrical nod in the direction of an economically viable Senegambian Federation.

During the final twilight period of Britain's African empire, there was little to disturb the normal course of Anglo-American relations. Indeed, now that the colonial question no longer divided the allies, the major American concern was with 'burden-sharing' within the Western Alliance. The Kennedy Administration had tried to distance itself from its predecessor, partly by its enthusiastic support for African independence, and by its willingness to provide financial aid to even those new states such as Ghana whose governments paraded their non-alignment in the Cold War. But by late 1962 the President was in such trouble with the Congress over the aid bill that he was forced to appoint a bipartisan committee under General Lucius Clay to mobilize support for his Third World policy as a whole. The tactic worked and the aid budget was approved, but at a price; the Clay Report emphasized that with regard to both development and internal security, Africa was an area 'where the Western European countries should logically bear most of the necessary aid burdens'.[4]

Whatever their views on burden-sharing elsewhere, in Africa the Committee's conclusions fitted well with British efforts to maintain their influence in their former possessions. Only the anomalous constitutional status of Rhodesia frustrated the strategy of translating liabilities into assets and constantly interfered with attempts to create a network of low-key, but still special, relationships between Britain and her former colonies. Although the British eventually responded to Ian Smith's Unilateral Declaration of Independence in 1965 by imposing sanctions against the rebel regime, some African states for a time broke off relations with Britain in protest against its failure to crush the rebellion, and they continued to be suspicious of British intentions thereafter. With one exception, however, the United States supported the Rhodesian policy of Harold Wilson's government and those that followed it. That exception was in 1971 when Nixon endorsed the Byrd amendment exempting chrome from the United Nations embargo. By this time, however, the British, who were aware that their own oil companies were also evading the embargo, were more concerned with appearances in their sanctions policy than with their bite.[5] In any event, there is no

---

[4] *Report to the President of the United States from the Committee to Strengthen the Security of the Free World: The Scope and Distribution of the United States Military and Economic Assistance Programmes*, Department of State, Washington, DC, 20 Mar. 1963.

[5] See T. H. Bingham and S. M. Gray, *Report on the Supply of Petroleum and Petroleum Products to Rhodesia* (London, 1978).

evidence of a major Anglo-American disagreement during any stage of the long Rhodesian crisis.

The final ending of the rebellion in 1979 owed much to Anglo-American co-operation. Admittedly, when a combination of pressures on the major parties in the dispute (i.e. the Zimbabwe Nationalists, the Rhodesian whites, and the governments of the Front Line States) unexpectedly provided a new Conservative administration with the diplomatic opportunity to secure the settlement that had eluded its predecessors, the Americans were noticeably relieved to be cast in a supporting role. Nevertheless, it had been American intervention in 1976, when Henry Kissinger had persuaded Ian Smith to commit himself to majority rule within two years and to release the Nationalist leaders from detention, that set the stage for Britain's later diplomacy.

With the implementation of the Lancaster House Agreement, British sovereignty was finally removed from the African continent. Whatever the future problems of British–African relations, there are no residual imperial commitments, such as those that exist in the Falkland Islands, which might lead to the projection into Africa of British military power. In these circumstances, there is little potential for a major Anglo-American conflict of political (as distinct from economic) interest. In the economic sphere such potential exists, if only because British and American businesses often compete for the same contracts, and it is their commercial stake to which the British now attach most importance in their African relations.

In the contemporary international order, with its emphasis on territorial integrity and anti-colonial self-determination, liquidation of imperial commitments is a necessary but insufficient step in the transformation of liabilities into assets. Once the major assumption of imperial pre-eminence had been abandoned—that British and African interests were the same—the establishment of a framework for post-colonial relations required, in addition, the identification of mutual interests between Britain and the successor states. In the remainder of this chapter, I shall concentrate on three broad areas within which this search for mutuality has been conducted. These are the organization and management of the international economy; bilateral relations, primarily economic in character which occur within this framework; and the overall political organization of international society. In all three areas, particularly in the last, which is overshadowed by the unresolved conflicts of Southern Africa, the legacies of British global pre-eminence and imperial involvement have created problems and opportunities that distinguish Britain's African policies from those of the United States.

THE ORGANIZATION OF THE INTERNATIONAL ECONOMY

Africa's impact on Anglo-American relations emerges most clearly in the field of international economic organization. The pattern is made up of two repeating motifs: the first is a broad strategic convergence; the second, tactical divergence and conflicts of interest over particular issues.

If we look first at the strategic convergence, the obvious contrast is between Britain, and subsequently the United States, on the one side, and France and Germany on the other. During the colonial period, all three European countries hoped that their overseas possessions would contribute to their overall economic and political strength, but the economic philosophies on which they based their policies led them to pursue this common aim in different ways. As the first industrial nation, Britain was the first country to champion the doctrines of economic liberalism as not only being in her own interests but also in the interests of the international community generally and of world peace, the position subsequently adopted by the United States after 1945.[6] Trade and investment, of course, still followed or rather accompanied the flag, but so long as she remained the workshop of the world, Britain was for the most part able to rely on indirect methods for preserving imperial markets and sources of supply.

Had the Third World then existed it would have begun on the Potamac or the Rhine: the United States and Germany were the first countries to insist on their sovereign right of protection as an instrument of development and as a means of closing the 'gap' with industrial Britain. It was not the liberal economy that they challenged so much as the proposition that it knew no frontiers. In France, the mercantilist tradition of economic statecraft and the government's willingness to protect the economy for political and cultural ends had never been broken. In any event, French colonial economies were bound to the metropolis with hoops of iron: colonial agricultural products were subsidized and guaranteed a market; France in turn monopolized the colonial markets and guaranteed, i.e. controlled, the CFA (Communauté Financière d'Afrique) franc, a service which it still performs. When France signed the Treaty of Rome it was on the condition that its partners shared the cost of supporting francophone Africa in return for the partial and largely theoretical opening up of their markets to the other five members of the EEC.

It would have been logical for Britain and the United States to have been united in their opposition to Part IV of the Rome Treaty (under

---

[6] Peter Cain, 'Capitalism, War and Internationalism in the Thought of Richard Cobden', *British Journal of International Studies*, 5. 3 (1979), 229–47.

which French and Belgian colonies were associated with the EEC), the former out of direct calculation of its own interests and those of its Commonwealth partners, the latter primarily from consideration for principle. After all, from the signing of the Atlantic Charter onward, the Americans had sought the abolition of the preferential trading systems which had been developed during the inter-war period. On this occasion, however, London and Washington were divided over African policy. Thus, it was Britain, and its Commonwealth African partners, which took its stand on principle, challenging the legitimacy of Part IV of the Treaty within the General Agreement on Tariffs and Trade (GATT) on the grounds that the Agreement permitted the creation of Customs Unions but not of new preferences, and the United States which decided to subordinate its doctrinal position to pragmatic considerations of what was required to strengthen the Alliance and the process of European unification.

In reality, of course, the British appeal to GATT was no less tinged with self-interest than the American willingness to relax its traditional policy: in London it was believed that both Britain and Commonwealth Africa stood to lose from the creation of a privileged trading relationship between francophone Africa and the European Six, just as the view from Washington was that a united Western Europe would be more able to play a full part in the Alliance and shoulder a higher proportion of the costs of Western defence than an economically divided continent. The American view prevailed; the Afro-British Alliance was defeated. First the East African countries and then Nigeria, which had led the attack in the GATT on the Association concept, negotiated their own arrangements with the EEC to protect their interests.[7]

Once the EEC issue had been resolved, the broad Anglo-American convergence re-emerged, with both governments tending to take similar positions on Third World issues which were often initially in opposition to those of the EEC and the Associated African states. It is probably fair to claim that, in their general approach to institutional questions, Britain, the United States, and Commonwealth Africa remained broadly in agreement. All three were initially in favour of a global regime to cover the relationship between the industrial and developing worlds,[8] although by 1964, when the United Nations Conference on Trade and Development (UNCTAD) was established, the British and American positions on preferences had again diverged. The British now

---

[7] The Nigerian agreement was a victim of the Civil War and was never implemented, largely, it has been claimed, because the French deliberately delayed ratification.

[8] For example, the British supported the Commonwealth argument about non-reciprocity as the appropriate basis for North–South relations as opposed to the contrary position adopted under the first two Yaoundé Agreements.

argued strongly for a General System of Preferences for developing countries on the grounds that this would require the other industrial countries to match the existing Commonwealth system, while the Americans, who by now were thoroughly alarmed at the proliferation of special trading relationships that had been spawned by the EEC, were the most reluctant of all the Western powers to breach GATT's no new preference rule.

Only after its bid to join the European Community was successful did the British position on the institutional issue finally change, and even then, typically, the conversion was not to the principle of special trading relationships. On the contrary, left to itself, no British government would have chosen to assert that the Euro-African community of interest in which it was now involved was intrinsically different and stronger than the mutual interest shared with other parts of the new Commonwealth, in particular the countries of South Asia. British support for the Lomé Convention, which linked the EEC with 46 African, Carribean, and Pacific countries in a preferential aid and trade agreement, was for practical reasons: it provided a solution to the problem of the residual Commonwealth preferences, which, in the absence of a Convention, would have lapsed following British accession. Since the Americans were strongly in favour of British accession to the Community, they have tended to support the Lomé Convention for political reasons, that is, as the necessary price of West European integration. From Washington's point of view the magnetic attraction of Lomé for African states also has advantages in the context of East–West rivalry: for example, the accession of Mozambique and Ethiopia, both of which have signed treaties with the Soviet Union, is welcome as a means of limiting Soviet influence.

African demands for structural reform of the international economic system have for the most part been resisted by both the United States and Britain, although British governments have sometimes tried to make their policies seem more accommodating. From the British point of view, so long as it was a case of tinkering with the liberal market system there was no real problem. Indeed, to begin with, Britain had tinkered with it itself as a way of dealing with the costs which arose when she yielded her position of pre-eminence to the United States. The Americans had initially sought the abolition not only of the Commonwealth preference system but also of the sterling area. These demands were resisted; preferences were frozen but not abolished and for a time the sterling area was actually strengthened, as the British attempted to deal pragmatically with the post-war dollar shortage. But these policies were tactical, essentially a means of playing for time rather than a credible attempt to influence the long-run structure of the international economy; and in time they fell apart and were abandoned in response to pressures from within Africa itself and from outside.[9]

In the early post-war period the British not only developed sectors of the East African economies to meet British needs but also developed the system of common services on which the East African Community was subsequently based. British investors, particularly those in Kenya, and British exporters stood to gain from regional integration. But when new and often more powerful multinational corporations, many of which were incorporated in the United States, began to compete with the British, they often found it advantageous to deal with national governments rather than community institutions, thus reinforcing the already strong centrifugal forces within the region.

The close monetary relations between Britain and Commonwealth Africa similarly suffered with the demise of the sterling area. Unlike France, Britain had, in any case, never attempted to extend the control of the Bank of England over Commonwealth African economies. With the approach of independence, one after the other, Britain's African colonies established independent central banks as essential supports of sovereign statehood.[10] Even before the final liquidation of the sterling area, most Commonwealth African countries had prudently diversified their reserve holdings away from a total dependence on sterling.

Such relatively gradual shifts in economic power and diplomatic orientation—toward Europe in the British case, away from Britain in the African—were only to be expected within the open market order. The British might regret the weakening of their privileged position in Africa, but they had no grounds upon which to complain. The Africans on the other hand complained vociferously—they after all had never been consulted about the desirability of an open trading system. Following the Algerian lead in the Group of 77 in 1974, they increasingly pressed for a radical restructuring of the international economy to give them a greater say in its management, to transfer resources from rich to poor according to a criterion of need, and to enhance the prices of raw materials, on which most of them depended, through indexing, compensatory finance, and the creation of a financially independent and politically powerful Common Fund for commodities. As the least developed group of countries within the Group of 77, the Africans were the most insistent on the creation of an institution that would not merely stabilize commodity prices (a move

[9] See Arthur Kilgore and James Mayall, 'The Residual Legatee: Economic Relations in the Contemporary Commonwealth', in John Groom and Paul Taylor, eds. *The Contemporary Commonwealth* (London, 1984).

[10] Y. Bangura, *Britain and Commonwealth Africa: The Politics of Economic Relations, 1951–1975* (Manchester, 1983).

which the British were more willing than the Americans to concede) but increase the flow of resources to themselves.[11]

In advancing these demands, Third World governments were proposing a system of positive income redistribution, analogous to that carried out by some Western governments within their own societies since 1945. Indeed, President Nyerere has suggested that the creation of such a system is essentially a matter of will, and that there is no essential difference in this regard between the domestic and the international context. There is a body of opinion in Britain as in the other industrial countries which endorses the redistributive thesis of the New International Economic Order (NIEO) campaign—it forms, for example, the broad orientation of the original Brandt Commission report—but it is not a view shared by the current British government or any of its predecessors. On the contrary, British no less than Americans have repeatedly made it clear that they believe the analogy between the Welfare State and the international community to be false.

Although the London-based Commonwealth Secretariat has established for itself a useful role in mediating between the two sides on North–South issues, the British government itself does not stand out from the other members of the Organization for Economic Co-operation and Development (OECD) as more accommodating to African interests. Britain remains a 'satisfied' power, despite the decline of its political and economic influence on the continent, while the African Commonwealth countries are revisionists despite the fact that many of them are ruled by a political class that personally benefits from its association with foreign capital and despite the growing economic disparities between the Commonwealth African countries themselves.

BILATERAL RELATIONS

If over the years American anti-colonialism has become subordinated to geopolitical considerations arising from confrontation with the Soviet Union and concern about burden-sharing within the Alliance, the nature of Anglo-American relations as well as of Britain's relations with independent Africa has constrained the manner in which Britain has responded to this change of emphasis. The contrast between British and French colonial policies is again instructive. The special relationship between Paris and the francophone African countries, although subject to some dilution, continues to be guaranteed by a series of bilateral political and military as well as economic treaties. Since the abrogation of the British Nigerian Defence Pact in 1962 and of the Simonstown base

[11] See Geoffrey Goodwin and James Mayall, eds., *A New International Commodity Regime* (London, 1979).

agreement with South Africa two years later, there has been no British equivalent. The Commonwealth represents an English-language, post-imperial association, but although from its creation in 1966 Britain has remained the largest contributor to the Secretariat, the emphasis has been deliberately placed on the multilateral character of the organization; and so far as Africa and Asia are concerned, it has been most active, and arguably most effective, as an informal lobby on general North–South issues, rather than as a channel through which Britain can maintain a privileged position in its former colonies. In any event, its commitments toward the Commonwealth are both less precise, and almost certainly ultimately more dispensable, than its commitments toward either the EEC or the Atlantic Alliance.

There is a further difference between Britain and France which throws light on the British problem of translating imperial liabilities into post-colonial assets. France remains the centre of a powerful (even if in a global sense a minority) cultural area based on the French language. This common culture is not merely a question of shared intellectual habits and life-style, although both of these are important; it also provides France with a comparative advantage in the securing of contracts, as any analysis of the European Development Fund will quickly demonstrate. By contrast Britain not only surrendered its global pre-eminence but surrendered it to another English-speaking nation whose traditional anti-colonialism was perfectly compatible with economic and cultural competition with Britain for influence in Commonwealth Africa. Since at independence all former British colonies set about diversifying their external relations, and since the United States has greater resources at its disposal, it quickly established in educational as well as economic and political matters a rival, and in some cases a stronger, magnetic field of attraction to the former metropolitan power.

One should not make too much of Britain's decline *vis-à-vis* the United States. In the overall conception of the *Pax Americana*, Africa has low priority. As we have seen, once the rigidities of the Cold War had been established, the Americans were generally content to leave the policing of peripheral areas to their allies who were familiar with the terrain. Nevertheless, except in matters which came before the Security Council, which I will discuss in the final section of this chapter, Britain increasingly returned to its original shopkeeping role. Its primary concerns, in other words, were the protection of trade and investment and the provision of aid both as an inducement to African governments to stay within the liberal market order and as a more direct buttress to British exports.

Let us take first the question of aid. In broad terms the British aid record fairly accurately reflects the country's economic standing amongst other members of the OECD. Britain is the fifth largest donor overall, after the United States, France, West Germany, and Japan, although when expressed as a percentage of GNP (0.35 per cent in 1980) the British performance is better than that of the United States (0.27 per cent) and Japan (0.32 per cent) but considerably worse than that of France (0.64 per cent) and Germany (0.44 per cent).[12] About a third of Britain's bilateral financial disbursements (£1326 million in 1980) have traditionally gone to Africa, although when technical assistance is included the continent accounts for about half the total aid effort. In addition, about 30 per cent of British aid (£526 million in 1980) is channelled through multilateral agencies, a significant proportion of which, of course, ultimately goes to Africa.

What criteria govern the British aid programme in Africa? Obviously it is intended to lubricate Anglo-African relations, but it would be misleading to interpret its growth and pattern according to a deliberately preconceived economic or political strategy. On the contrary, the programme continues to bear the imprint of particular problems which arose in the context of decolonization. For example, despite a deliberate government policy of diversification, particularly since Britain's accession to the EEC, in 1983 over 75% of British bilateral economic aid to sub-Saharan Africa still went to the Commonwealth African countries.[13] American aid, by contrast, has been increasingly determined according to strategic criteria: in 1983, 62% of projected United States economic and security aid was to go to six countries, Sudan, Kenya, Somalia, Zimbabwe, Liberia, and Zaire, the first three of which provide the United States with facilities for its Rapid Deployment Force taking pride of place.[14]

In Britain, policy has generally followed some distance behind changes of view and fashion within the professional community of Western aid experts. For example, the Labour government which held office between 1974 and 1979 was converted to the philosophy of basic needs, echoing a similar change or orientation by the World Bank under the leadership of Robert McNamara,[15] while Mrs Thatcher's government, which has been in the vanguard of the Western monetarist revolt, has not only reduced aid overall, in line with the general cut-back of

[12] 'Development Cooperation', *1982 Review* (Paris: OECD, 1982), 204–5.

[13] *British Overseas Aid, 1983* (Central Office of Information for the Overseas Development Administration), p. 73.

[14] Statement before the Subcommittee on Foreign Operations of the House Appropriations Committee on 25 Mar. 1982 by Assistant Secretary of State for Africa, Chester Crocker. *Department of State Bulletin* (July 1982), 61–3.

[15] The new British policy was set out in a White Paper published in 1975 under the title *More Help for the Poorest*. For a critical discussion of this policy, see Guy Arnold, *Aid in Africa* (London, 1979), pp. 45–50.

government expenditures, but has also increased the Aid Trade Provision (ATP), i.e. that proportion of the Aid budget which is earmarked to meet specific requests for export assistance by British industry which might otherwise fall foul of GATT and OECD rules on export subsidies.[16] Such changes of direction are more a question of degree than of kind: although the British aid programme has never given rise to the degree of controversy within parliament as has customarily greeted the American programme with Congress, its supporters have always had to argue that it is not merely right to provide concessionary finance but that there are also material returns to Britain from doing so. It was a Labour government that accompanied its basic needs strategy with the introduction of the ATP which its Conservative successors have sought to strengthen.

Although British firms have done well in securing contracts not only from bilateral aid but under loans made by multilateral agencies,[17] it is the activities of the major industrial corporations, such as Lonrho, ICI, and the oil companies, together with British banks and financial institutions, that dictate the pattern of trade and investment. As with aid, this pattern is a product of Britain's colonial involvement in Africa: despite a rapid growth in the immediate post-colonial period, in the mid-1970s about 70 per cent of private investment and about 60 per cent of British trade with independent Africa was still within the Commonwealth.[18]

In this case, however, the legacy of the past revealed an uncomfortable paradox: while government-to-government aid relations gave rise to relatively few political problems,[19] the steady expansion of private sector links over which the government has only the most indirect control (through Commonwealth and now EEC preferential arrangements, the support provided to British exports by the Exports Credit Guarantee Department (ECGD) and through Commonwealth Development Finance Corporation (CDFC) investment funds) has increasingly exposed them to criticism.

The reason is well known. Both aid and private investment are

[16] David Nelson, 'Pounds of Flesh', *Far Eastern Economic Review*, 19–25 Nov. 1982.
[17] Of all World Bank loans to developing countries in 1980, the UK share of procurement was just over 6 per cent but in East Africa it was 16.4 per cent and in West Africa 9 per cent. The British share was even higher in soft-loan credits (IDA) to East Africa, 17.5 per cent compared with an overall share of procurement in developing countries generally of 12 per cent. See Vince Cable, 'British Interests and Third World Development', in Robert Cassen, Richard Jolly, John Sewell, and Robert Wood, eds., *Rich Country Interests and Third World Development* (London, 1983), p. 194.
[18] British Information Services, Central Office of Information, *Britain and the Developing Countries, Africa* (London, 1977), p. 7.
[19] Two exceptions were the disputes between the British and Tanzanian governments in the mid-1960s over the latter's refusal to pay colonial Civil Service pensions and with Idi Amin's regime to Uganda over the mass expulsion of Asians and abuse of fundamental human rights. Both disputes led to a suspension of British aid.

heavily concentrated in two countries, the Federation of Nigeria and the Republic of South Africa. With its emergence as a major oil exporter, and hence as a major importer of capital and manufactured goods, Nigeria jumped to being Britain's twelfth largest market in the world and its fifth outside Europe.[20] Simultaneously, it became a more important market than South Africa which had traditionally enjoyed pride of place in Britain's economic relations with Africa and thereby assured itself of British protection at the United Nations whenever the African countries demanded the imposition of economic sanctions against the Republic. When Britain's stake in the rest of the continent is added to its stake in Nigeria, it is possible to argue that there has been a massive shift in the balance of British interests and that as a consequence the African countries, acting under the leadership of the Nigerian government, are now in a position to face Britain with the necessity of a historic choice between white and black Africa.

The theoretical availability of economic pressure on Britain is attractive to the Nigerian government since the fact that most of its oil is sold to the United States does not carry the same weight in Washington. The African view is certainly that change in South Africa requires American pressure, but that the most promising line of attack is to apply pressure indirectly via the allies whose economies are more vulnerable. The reason is that although the United States is now South Africa's most important trading partner and has a total investment stake of over $15 billion, including a sizeable share of the oil, computer, and automobile industries, in global terms South Africa is not a high priority area for American industry.

That Britain has so far been able to avoid the choice between white and black Africa is also well known. The explanation lies in Africa as much as in Britain. Not only is it as difficult in Africa as anywhere else to persuade countries to engage in collective economic sanctions when they would have to bear the cost of imposing them themselves, but the African countries generally need the industrial world more than they are needed. For a time, Nigeria's oil wealth seemed to exclude that country from this general rule, and indeed gave a certain plausibility to the idea of counter-sanctions; but the world-wide recession and the development by Britain of North Sea oil, which is in direct competition with the Nigerian product, suggests that its exemption is more apparent than real. In any event, while there have been token expropriations of British interests—i.e. Barclays Bank and British Petroleum—which have been defended as warnings to Britain over its Southern African policies, these have been isolated incidents and have made no serious impact on Britain's £500 million investment in the Nigerian economy.

[20] Alec Parrett, 'Trade Patterns, the Two-way Pull', *Africa*, 73 (1977), 97–8.

The links between British and American policies in South Africa have more to do with shared governmental perceptions of the dangers of violent revolution in the Republic and, as Richard Ullman notes elsewhere in this book, with the similar intellectual resources on which the two societies draw, than with African pressure. Within both countries there are well-organized pressure groups which regularly campaign for an embargo on trade with South Africa and for disinvestment and which in Britain are supported, at least in principle, by influential sections of the Labour and Liberal Parties and by the Trades Unions. No British Government can afford to ignore such opinion completely, particularly now that it is possible to argue that Britain's historical entanglement with South Africa is putting at risk other, potentially more important, British interests. As a result of such pressure, indeed, the Government was persuaded in the mid-1970s to strengthen its alternative strategy of 'positive engagement' by devising a code of conduct for British investors, the forerunner of the EEC code of conduct and the set of principles which the Reverend Leon Sullivan, a member of the Board of General Motors, successfully persuaded a majority of American corporations with South African interests to adopt.

Pressure on successive British governments for disengagement from South Africa has predictably engendered a counter-pressure in the form of the well-organized, and well-financed, activities of the United Kingdom–South Africa Trade Association (UKSATA). This Association, which claims to have the backing of most of the 'British companies with significant investment and trading interests in or commercial dealings with the Republic of South Africa and many of the medium and smaller British companies'[21] and is supported by a small but vocal group of MPs, regularly disseminates information on such matters as the value of British trade and investment (in 1982 £3,480 million and £11,000 million respectively); the impact on British employment from a policy of disengagement (an estimated addition of 250,000 to the unemployment figures); and the fact that access to South African metals and minerals (i.e. platinum, chrome, vernadium, and manganese) is as necessary to the industrial West as access to Middle East oil.

Similar arguments are deployed in the United States by business interests and generally supported by the Department of Commerce in inter-agency debates about policy toward South Africa.[22] Nevertheless, there remains a difference of emphasis in the way the two governments have responded to them. In the British case no government can afford to

---

[21] UKSATA, *British Trade with South Africa: A Question of National Interest* (London, 1982).
[22] Crawford Young, 'United States Policy Toward Africa: Silver Anniversary Reflections', *African Studies Review*, 27. 3 (1984), 1–17.

ignore such pressure, and indeed although Labour administrations have been generally more eager to disassociate themselves from South Africa politically and in sporting and cultural affairs—for example it was not until 1964 when Harold Wilson first became Prime Minister that Britain joined the United States in imposing a unilateral arms embargo—in power they have been as adamant as their Conservative opponents in resisting both domestic and international pressure for the imposition of economic sanctions.

In the United States, as Crawford Young has pointed out, the commitment against the use of sanctions may not be so secure.[23] This is partly because there is not the same reluctance to resort to economic sanctions in general as exists in Britain. But it also reflects the more direct impact of public opinion on foreign policy in the United States. In addition the slow growth of the Congressional Black caucus, now numbering twenty-one, in alliance with a small but active group of liberal Representatives, has begun to exert an influence on policy. Moreover, while the executive has usually been able to rely on the Senate to veto proposals it did not like, the Reagan Administration has found its support for 'constructive engagement' and opposition to sanctions slipping away even in the Senate. The explanation probably lies in a combination of political horse-trading on the legislative programme between domestic and foreign policy interests and partly in the discovery on the ideological wing of the Republican party that South Africa is a state run on interventionist rather than open-market lines.

Despite such differences, both governments vetoed demands for United Nations sanctions in July 1985 as a response to the South African declaration of a state of emergency, and distanced themselves not only from the Afro-Asian states but from France and some of the other EEC member-states that also favoured a stronger Western response to the escalating state violence in South Africa. Since the economic as well as diplomatic isolation of South Africa is official OAU (Organization of African Unity) policy, it is inevitable that South Africa should continue to cast a shadow over the relation of both countries with the rest of the continent. For its part, it is largely because South Africa constitutes a general problem for the international order in the outcome of which it has a historic interest that Britain remains politically embroiled in African affairs. Other considerations apart, among the 40 per cent of South African whites who are of British descent, a substantial though undisclosed number still hold British passports.

[23] Ibid.

SOUTH AFRICA AND INTERNATIONAL ORDER

In the period between 1945 and 1950, the political map of the post-war international system was drawn; it was not to be altered in any fundamental way until the early 1970s and much of it survives to the present day.[24] There were two versions of this map and some of the most intractable contemporary international problems—including the problem of South Africa—arise from the inconsistencies between them.

The first map, that of the United Nations, established, so to say, the new constitutional order for international society. As with the new economic order its form mirrored the values of its most powerful members, the liberal democracies, and particularly those of the United States. The major concession to realism in the shape of the Security Council and the power of veto which was granted to its five permanent members ensured that the interests of the old imperial powers could not be lightly brushed aside. At the same time, the commitments in the Charter to the right of national self-determination and fundamental human rights, when combined with the anti-colonial rhetoric of the two emergent superpowers, was sufficient to guarantee that the parliamentary procedures of the world body would be used to maintain relentless pressure on the imperial powers to dismantle their colonial systems.

Within this first constitutional map only two kinds of state were envisaged, those which were already independent and whose domestic arrangements were consequently immune from scrutiny, and those which were to be created by decolonization. South Africa, an independent state since 1910, was not immune, however: its traditional policy of racial segregation, even before the National Party reinforced it by the introduction of full-scale apartheid after 1948, was too blatantly at variance with the principles of majority rule under which first Asian and then African nationalists successfully demanded independence. As a result, from 1946, when the Indian government first raised the question of South African discrimination against the Asian community in Natal, South Africa's racial policies have been the subject of annual debate and censure at the United Nations. The simultaneous refusal by the South Africans to place the mandated territory of South West Africa under the UN Trusteeship Council created another issue of contention: not only was South Africa an anomalous state in the eyes of the new Afro-Asian bloc, it had committed the cardinal sin against the new constitutional order by refusing to prepare for independence those whose destiny had been placed in their hands by the mandate 'as a sacred trust'.

In the early post-war period, the British Labour government

[24] For a discussion of this process see the Introduction to James Mayall and Cornelia Navari, eds., *The End of the Postwar Era: Documents on Great Power Relations, 1968–75* (Cambridge, 1981).

repeatedly refused to associate itself with this international campaign against South Africa, arguing that its racial policies were not a proper subject for UN debate. This British attitude was partly determined by their desire to have neither the principle nor the pace of decolonization dictated from outside (except to a limited extent in respect of the Trusteeship territories) but partly also by considerations of a more immediate strategic and political character.

The second map of the post-war world, that of the Cold War, has determined the major international alignments from the late 1940s to the present day. But as we have already noted, initially the common Western stand against what was perceived as an imminent threat of Communist expansion concealed a more friendly rivalry between the United States and the residual force of British imperialism. This placed the British Government in a difficult position: inasmuch as they feared Soviet designs against their global interests, they needed to enlist American support beyond Europe as well as in the North Atlantic area, but in so far as this would require the Americans to lend formal support to British imperial arrangements, proposals for an extension of the Western Alliance, e.g. into the South Atlantic, stood no chance of gaining Congressional support. As Ritchie Ovendale has shown, it was in this context that the Labour government formulated the basic policy toward South Africa which, with relatively minor fluctuations, has been followed ever since.[25]

The basic problem faced by the British had three aspects. The first was strategic. So long as the Americans were unprepared to commit themselves to the defence of British and Western interests in the Middle East, the British would need all the support they could muster within the Commonwealth. As a professed anti-Communist power, South Africa stood ready and willing to help (despite their hostility to the United Nations, the South Africans had sent an air force unit to Korea). The fact that after 1948 the South African government contained men who were deeply hostile to Britain persuaded the Attlee government of the importance of doing nothing that would jeopardize the strategic relationship between the two countries.

The second aspect was economic. Besides being the source of many of Britain's strategic raw materials, in the immediate post-war period South Africa was one of the few countries with which Britain had a favourable balance of trade, a consideration which gave it access to South African gold production to provide much needed backing for sterling area reserves.

The third aspect was political. It was deeply embarrassing for the

[25] Ritchie Ovendale, 'The South African Policy of the British Labour Government, 1947–51', *International Affairs*, 59. 1 (1982–3), 41–58.

government which had both initiated Britain's imperial withdrawal from India and introduced the Welfare State at home to find itself bound by interest rather than sentiment to a government most of whose policies it deeply abhorred.

The solution, which the Labour Party devised and which all British governments have adhered to ever since, was to make the best of a bad job. On the one hand there was no alternative to co-operation; on the other, any latent South African expansionism should be checked, in the first instance by refusing to incorporate the High Commission territories in the Union, as had originally been envisaged in 1910, and then by constructing a bloc of pro-British territories to the north. In presenting the paper which outlined this policy to the Cabinet, the Commonwealth Secretary, Patrick Gordon-Walker, explained the situation in the following way:

Britain should be ready to develop those relations with the Union that bind her to us and make her unwilling to risk a break with us . . . these relations are also in our direct interest. Chief amongst them come cooperation in defence and economic matters. Also important is to give the Union what help and guidance it decently can at the United Nations. Those who argue that because we dislike the Union's Native policy we should ostracise her and have nothing to do with her completely fail to understand the realities of the situation. Such a policy would not only gravely harm us in the defence and economic fields, it would also weaken our power to deter South Africa from foolhardy acts from fear of breaking with us. It would immediately and directly reduce our chances of holding the Territories, which form a vital part in any policy of containing and confining the Union's influence and territorial expansion in Southern Africa.[26]

It may seem far-fetched to claim that this policy has survived the events of the past thirty years, including the withdrawal of South Africa from the Commonwealth, the collapse of the Central African Federation, fourteen years of rebel government in Rhodesia, and the disintegration of the sterling area. Reflection, however, will I believe support its essential validity. The changes that have occurred in Southern Africa have been despite British policy rather than because of it. At the United Nations British governments have fought a long rearguard action against the African campaign to turn South Africa into a pariah state, only joining the majority in criticizing apartheid in the General Assembly once the British Empire itself had been effectively liquidated, and even then drawing a sharp distinction between criticism and action. Whenever there is a demand for sanctions under Chapter 7 of the Charter, the British government, together with the United States and often France, can be relied on to veto it, using whatever arguments are ready to hand to justify their action.

[26] Quoted ibid., p. 57.

It can be plausibly argued, of course, that the threat of sanctions rather than their imposition is what matters, and that their ultimate uncertainty about continued Western support has persuaded the South African government to undertake even such cautious and half-hearted reforms as it has embarked upon. Maybe. On the other hand, the current stalemate in the Namibian negotiations suggests very strongly that, whatever the situation in the past, the South Africans believe that they have successfully called the West's bluff. Britain has now ceded leadership to the United States in designing the containment policy, but, whatever differences there may be between the two governments over the line to be pursued within the Contact Group of Western countries which was set up in 1977 as a diplomatic pander between the South Africans and the Nambian nationalists, it seems unlikely that they are fundamental.

These days both the British and American governments try to have it both ways, to co-operate and contain simultaneously. Formal defence co-operation, it is true, has been abandoned (it is very doubtful whether this has been extended to the contact between the intelligence services) but economic co-operation remains and both governments foster relations at all levels of South African society, for example, by sponsoring visits by *verligte* Members of Parliament and in other ways seeking to encourage domestic reform. Writing in 1985 after eighteen months of violent upheaval in South Africa's black townships, it would be a brave person who could claim that these efforts were accompanied by much hope. The collapse of the Central African Federation was the biggest blow to the early containment policy, but with the independence of Zimbabwe and the establishment of the Southern African Development Co-operation Conference (SADCC) it has, arguably, been revived. Whether, in the face of African opposition to white rule from within the country and outside, Britain and the United States can continue to have it both ways is uncertain. Probably, in the long run, they cannot. But for as long as the two maps of the international system cannot be reconciled, both governments are likely to conclude, as in the past, that the only option open to them is to make the best of a bad job.

21

The 'Unspecial Relationship' in Latin America

WILLIAM D. ROGERS

In the 1970s Latin America commanded considerably less attention in London and Washington than other areas of the Third World and scarcely impinged at all on the Anglo-American relationship. The international community was obsessed with South-east Asia, the Middle East, and *détente* and its aftermath; Britain was as distracted by Rhodesia as the United States, post-Vietnam, by its own introspection. And, with the exception of the Panama Canal, relations between Latin America and the rest of the West were benign and unchallenging.

In the 1980s, this came to an abrupt end. By a remarkable irony, the beginning of Ronald Reagan's term coincided with the explosion of two major crises in the region which had grave systemic significance for the West: the conflict in Central America, and the near-bankruptcy of several of the large Latin countries. In addition, the Reagan years have witnessed several Latin American incidents of commanding if short-term consequence, which have tested the nature of how the two nations perceive the world. So it is relevant to inquire how the 'Special Relationship' has been manifest in Latin American affairs in the turbulent first five years of Ronald Reagan. The answer is, not very.

But there is far more common ground than recent events suggest. The revolutionary eruptions in Central America have tended lately to dominate the American attention to the affairs of their own hemisphere and American and British views have not been very harmonious on that subject. It is the debt crisis, however, that poses the greater threat and the greater opportunity to the West. It is also in the debt crisis that British and American interests in Latin America will most closely intersect in the years to come, with each other and with the broad interests of the Alliance.

ASYMMETRIES AT THE MARGIN: THE FALKLANDS AND GRENADA

Latin America probably yields less evidence of a unique relationship between the United States and the United Kingdom than any other part of the world. This is not surprising: there is no part of the world where the interests of the two nations are so divergent. Washington's sense of the importance of the region, and its almost proprietary engagement there, is captured by President Reagan's unhappy habit of referring to it as America's 'backyard'. No other major grouping of developing countries is so dominated by an economic and military superpower as Latin America is by the United States. No other region of the world has for a century and a half been subject to the exclusive pretentions of a Monroe Doctrine.

Britain's last remaining defence commitment on the mainland of the hemisphere is Belize, and this is strictly marginal in Washington's scheme of things. America's concern is for the nurturing of the tender shoots of democracy in Guatemala, the restraint of its military, and the enhancement of development in that last firebreak between a Central American conflagration and Mexico. So the festering problem of Belize has been an irritant and a side-show as far as American strategy in Central America is concerned for years. For London, on the other hand, it is an obligation involving considerable financial burden with no apparent benefits, to be sustained only as long as absolutely necessary and liquidated as soon as possible.

The Falklands Islands War was another textbook case of the asymmetries between the two nations' interests. The Islands had traditionally been a matter of tertiary concern for American policy-makers. Assistant Secretaries of State usually regarded the dispute as a bore and a distraction from other, larger issues. So when a real war broke out, and people were actually killed, it came as a distinct shock to Washington, upsetting carefully designed priorities and plans and posing the awkward necessity of choosing between one of two 'special' relationships. The Reagan Administration responded to the Argentine invasion with what it hoped the world—and London—would see as even-handedness. Diplomatic prizes are rarely won for even-handed-ness, particularly where morality was as one-sided as in the contest between Britain and Argentina. So by the end of the affair the United States was inevitably forced to identify itself with the British side.

The consequences of the balancing act have been far more serious in the United Kingdom than in Latin America. In spite of the contemporary warnings of Ambassador Jeane Kirkpatrick and others who argued that the United States would pay a permanent price in the hemisphere for its willingness to support the British effort, there is not much resentment today in Latin America. Even in Argentina itself, the very military leadership which the Latin Americanists in the State Department wanted to appease have been sentenced to severe punishment for violations of human rights during the 'dirty war' against the internal subversives in the late 1970s. All of the military commanders of the Falklands campaign stand accused and are awaiting trial for their conduct. The nationalist irrationality which launched the Falklands invasion is discredited in Argentina. It is nowhere evident in the contemporary political life of the country, at least not on the surface, in part because of the trauma of the defeat. The behaviour of the United States over the Falklands War is now forgotten. Argentina's own sense of guilt and humiliation about the nation's behaviour, the universal concern over the financial crisis, and an increasing appreciation that Washington's future willingness to support Argentina's efforts to cope with that crisis, particularly since President Alfonsin initiated the high-risk–high-gain strategy of defeating inflation by shock treatment with his Plan Austral, mean that future relations are considerably more important to Argentina than the United States' past role in the Falklands conflict.

The Falklands issue is not dead in Argentina. It still rankles in the Argentine psyche, and could conceivably one day burst into flame again. But, as that nation's willingness to resolve the Beagle Island dispute with Chile demonstrates, the Argentina of 1985 is not the Argentina of 1981; it has other priorities and other vexations. This has transformed the Buenos Aires–Washington relationship.

On the other hand, at least on the eastern side of the Atlantic, the then Secretary of State Alexander Haig's diplomacy is seen as tilted toward the Latin American side. In fact, the United States did provide assistance which was significant if not decisive in the conflict— intelligence, equipment, and spare parts and the assumption of some British naval roles in the North Atlantic. This was a dramatic reassertion of the 'Special Relationship'. It is impossible to conceive that the United States would go so far for any other nation. Yet one senses that the common view in Britain is that the American effort was less supportive than Britain's real interests, and the moral and legal issues in the conflict, should have suggested. Even Washington's late but unequivocal support failed, one gathers, to dissipate entirely British disappointment.

Sir Nicholas Henderson has suggested that the British reaction tends to underscore a European readiness to criticize the United States for whatever it does in its 'backyard', but an equally automatic expectation of American support when European interests are threatened. Certainly the experience demonstrated the tension for the United States in maintaining its interests by preserving its relationships in Latin America on the one hand, and the development of a common and congenial view of hemispheric political and security issues with Britain on the other.

The Falklands conflict made clear that on those issues there is no automatic identity of policy or behaviour.

Grenada was a parallel example of the non-coincidence of interest. Here the shoe was on the other foot: the United States was looking for support for its use of force. The international legal issues were also reversed. In the case of the Falklands, Britain was responding to a clear violation of Article 2.4 of the United Nations Charter, which prohibits the use of force by any nation against the territorial integrity or political independence of another. Argentina's invasion was clearly labelled as violation of the principle by the Security Council.[1] Even the Organization of American States (OAS) could not bring itself to cast a veil of legitimacy over it.[2]

The American invasion of Grenada was a different matter. America could not claim to be responding to an invasion of foreign troops. The justification for the action rested on three arguments: that the American citizen students at the St George's Medical School should be rescued; that the invasion was legitimated by the joint action of the Eastern Caribbean Federation; and that the only remaining constituted authority on the island, the Governor General, had requested outside support.[3] The international legal community had been almost unanimous in condemning Argentina's action in the Falklands and in upholding the legality of Britain's response.[4] Many analysts of the Grenada action, on the other hand, raised questions about the international legal validity of what the United States had done there.[5]

Nevertheless, the Administration hoped for a warm endorsement from London. Instead, the Prime Minister made her uneasiness quite public. The rest of the Tory contingent in Parliament was not quite as distressed as she by the American action in Grenada. Indeed, the currents of understanding and sympathy were strong in some quarters. Nevertheless, Washington's reaction to the PM's complaints were quick—and scarcely charitable. British policy-makers complained that there had been no consultation. State Department officials answered testily that they could not be trusted to keep a secret. This is not exactly a basis for a 'special relationship'. The memories of Grenada may shape Washington's attentions to future British concerns in the region, and London's future responses to American moves as well.

Nearly twenty-four months after the invasion, Grenada has receded

[1] Security Council Resolution, 3 Apr. 1982; *New York Times*, 4 Apr. 1982.

[2] B. Crosette, 'OAS, By 17–0, Calls for Truce in the Falklands', *ibid.*, 28 Apr. 1982.

[3] Remarks of President Ronald Reagan, 25 Oct. 1983, *Weekly Compilation of Presidential Documents*, 31 Oct. 1983; remarks of Deputy Secretary of State Kenneth Dam, 4 Nov. 1983, *State Department Bulletin*, 79 (1983).

[4] S. Taylor, 'International Lawyers Study the Muddied Waters', *New York Times*, 8 Apr. 1982.

[5] See H. Wiarda, *In Search of Policy: The United States and Latin America* (Washington, DC, 1984), pp. 14–15.

from public view. The Falkland Islands issue, however, though much older, continues to simmer, and to flavour Anglo-American concerns in the region. This is so because the efforts to find a negotiated solution have come to a stalemate. American policy-makers are persuaded that it would be to the advantage of the United States in its own dealings with Latin America if Britain could more actively pursue a *rapprochement* with Argentina. Some movement would strengthen the hand of President Alfonsin, who is now the centre of all hopes that the democracy of the nation can be preserved, the hyperinflation brought under control, and the economy restructured.

In short, while Grenada and the Falklands War may not go to the heart of the 'Special Relationship' between the United States and the United Kingdom, the lesson to be drawn is that the relationship cannot be counted upon to guarantee mutual support for a common policy in Latin America.

ASYMMETRIES ON THE MAINLAND: CENTRAL AMERICA

The longer-lasting conflict in Central America is another area where there has been little joint action or evidence of a common attitude, though the opportunity for both has certainly presented itself at least once.

Central America captured Washington's attention at the beginning of the decade, and still holds it. At first the primary focus was on establishing a successful democracy in El Salvador. More recently, following the consolidation of the position of President Duarte, attention has been riveted on Nicaragua. The focus has become clear. El Salvador has conducted two elections, culminating in the defeat of the right wing and the weakening of its hold on the legislature, and President Napoleon Duarte has been able to consolidate his power to the point of taking the first tentative steps towards talks with the rebels. The military situation is in stalemate, but at least the danger that the rebels might succeed in overthrowing the central government in San Salvador has receded. Nicaragua has now become the centre of the conflict. The anti-Sandinista forces—the 'Contras'—have grown to upwards of 20,000 men. Whether and how the United States should support them has become a permanent struggle in Congress and a principal element in the evolving heated debate over whether the United States should adopt a world-wide forward strategy to carry the fight to Soviet allies by funding anti-Communist rebels in Angola, Afghanistan, and Camboc'a as well. Apprehensions in Nicaragua and Washington that the Administration might even be contemplating direct intervention were ignited by the American invasion of Grenada and by the substantial buildup of the American force infrastructure in Honduras in alleged support of American training exercises there. All these have elevated the Nicaraguan element of the Central American crisis to an issue of commanding proportions for the United States. There is no sign that the conflict will be resolved in the near future.

It is an issue, however, on which there is ample difference of opinion, even within the Administration itself. The centre of the debate is whether the rise of the Sandinistas and the conflicts in Central America pose a security threat to vital United States interests. Europeans, perhaps because they have lived for the past four decades in such close proximity to the Soviet Union and its pliant satellites, are often unwilling to accept American assertions that Marxist regimes and leftist guerrillas are a real danger to the United States.[6] Congressman Michael Barnes, Chairman of the Subcommittee on Western Hemisphere Affairs of the House Foreign Affairs Committee, claims that 'it is difficult to identify vital interests that the United States has in Central America', except, he admits, 'preventing the emplacement of outside military capabilities . . . that could directly affect the United States'.[7] The former Mexican President, Lopez Portillo, noted, 'The U.S. problem is not with Nicaragua or with Cuba . . . The U.S. problem is with the Soviet Union.'[8]

The National Bipartisan Commission on Central America, appointed by President Reagan in early 1983 and chaired by Henry Kissinger, though not originally designed to serve that end, produced a final report which might have opened the door to a more constructive and balanced European engagement in the Central American dilemma. And the Commission's effort certainly provided the most significant opportunity for Europe to bring itself gracefully into the picture. The Commission's report, submitted on 10 January 1984, was gloomy enough. It concluded that 'war and the threat of war [were] everywhere'.[9] The challenges throughout the hemisphere were both economic and political, and these challenges were most acute in Central America.

The Commission rejected the notion that there could be a one-dimensional military solution. It urged support for the Contadora process of multipartite diplomatic negotiations on Nicaragua. More generally, it emphasized the need for a balanced and co-ordinated effort on the economic, political, social, and military fronts. The Commission

[6] Ibid., p. 15.

[7] M. Barnes, 'U.S. Policy in Central America: The Challenge of Revolutionary Change', in *Third World Instability*, p. 79.

[8] Kristol, 'Should Europe be concerned about Central America?', pp. 59–60.

[9] H. Kissinger *et al.*, *Report of the National Bipartisan Commission on Central America* (Jan. 1984), p. 84.

proposed stepping up both long- and short-term economic aid, the objective being to raise the standard of living to the level of the late 1970s.

The most significant aspect of the Commission's recommendations, however, was not quantitative, important as its proposal of $8 billion of economic assistance was, but concerned the way that assistance, and United States policy in general, should be managed. The Commission suggested something sharply at variance with the bilateralism which had traditionally dominated American relations with the region, but which owed a good deal to the Alliance for Progress experience. A Central American Development Organization (CADO) would be constituted, consisting of representatives of the Central American states, the United States, and the Contadora countries of Mexico, Venezuela, Panama, and Colombia. And, importantly, the Organization was to be open to membership by extra-regional powers who had an interest and were prepared to back that interest with contributions of economic assistance and diplomatic effort, as in the case of the Inter-American Development Bank.

It would be a responsibility of CADO to monitor progress by the five Central American states on a number of fronts. Not only would the Central Americans be asked to produce economic development programmes to make explicit their own internal efforts towads expanding their economies. In addition, they would undertake to open their political systems and move toward democracy. Externally, they would eschew intervention in the affairs of their neighbours, reduce their military inventories, and agree to peaceful settlement of disputes. The proposal even contained firm commitments with respect to human rights. The notion was to spur democratization in Guatemala, international restraint and elections in Nicaragua, curtailment of the death squads in El Salvador, and more rapid economic progress in Honduras —all under the spur of a collegiate, multinational review process which would tie outside assistance to a country's actual performance across the full range of economic, social, political, and security criteria, and invoke the collective power of world opinion in the search for peace.

This was an opportunity for Europe. Though the Commission itself did precious little to inspire a quick and enthusiastic European response, it hoped that the other industrial democracies would make a bid for a chair at the table of Central American policy-making when the Report was published. There was no response from Europe, however. Those who hoped that the 'Special Relationship' would express itself in an effort to join constructively in the pacification and development of Central America were disappointed.

In large part because the international response to the effort to put

Central American diplomacy on a multilateral basis fell so flat, the Kissinger Commission proposals received rather limited treatment in the United States Congress. The support for large-scale aid has been accepted by the Congress. But the notion that the United States engagement in the region should be tempered by more explicit considerations of the interests of the other members has been lacking.

The one-dimensional nature of Congressional response to the Commission's work, which had been sent to Capitol Hill with the President's hearty endorsement, is reflected in the Foreign Aid Bill which was signed by President Reagan on 8 August 1985. The Senate specifically implemented the Kissinger aid proposals, including a broad statement of policy, while also authorizing $1.2 billion in aid for the region for each of the fiscal years from 1987 to 1989 inclusive. The legislation produced by the House was similar in content, though the Foreign Affairs Committee declined to refer explicitly to the Kissinger recommendations. What emerged from the conference committee contained a House rewrite of the Commission's statement of policy, to the effect that the social, economic, political, and regional security issues are interrelated, and that none can be resolved in isolation. But the Congressional action, in 1985 as in previous years, could only air, not resolve, the basic American attitude toward political change and violent revolution in the region.

The Central American conflicts have become a proxy for the broader debate about how the United States can and should deal with the Soviet Union itself. In this sense European interests are directly engaged in the American anguish over hemispheric policy. Europe's real concern with the conflict in Central America is not so much what happens in Managua or San Salvador, but rather with the response in the United States to the regional eruption, and the conclusions America will draw about the nature of the larger East–West conflict and how it should respond.

For the heart of Washington's dilemma in Central America is whether its objective should be the pacification of the region and the containment of Nicaragua, or include the end of the Sandinista rule. The United States has not yet decided whether it will have secured its interests in a tolerably satisfactory fashion if Nicaragua commits itself to reduce the level of its military force and pledges not to interfere with its neighbours. Will the presence of an avowedly unfriendly regime in Managua, with its capabilities for surreptitious trouble-making in the region and its symbolic significance to leftist revolutionaries in Costa Rica, Honduras, Guatemala, and El Salvador, be consistent with peace in the region? Or must the United States accept the continued existence of the Sandinistas in Managua—or indeed their friends in Moscow—who by their very nature pose enduring and permanent threats, and from this derive the lesson that there can be no coexistence, that American security in the end will be assured only when these regimes pass from the face of the earth?

There is an intuitive understanding in Europe of the role Central America plays for the United States as a proxy. Western Europe is absorbed by what is happening there because it is a test of American leadership, and of the clarity of Washington's assessments of world affairs. The debate which has raged publicly throughout the United States and privately within the Administration as to how best to deal with the Central American conflicts reflects the larger debate about how best to deal with the Soviet Union. Europe has grasped this point at least.

But beyond this, there is little common policy. The interests of the United States and the United Kingdom scarcely coincide in Central America. Washington is increasingly inclined to interventionist military measures—funding anti-Sandinista forces, beefing up the military capability of the Hondurans; stiffening the antiguerrilla effort in Salvador with modern air weaponry, small-group tactical training and enhanced communications and intelligence, and a rapid rise in raw firepower; muscle-flexing naval displays in the waters around Central America—and less inclined to the diplomatic route. And in this again, Central America is proxy to the larger issue, for what is happening there is one manifestation of that bolder, more forward attitude in the Reagan Administration which argues that it is now time in the East–West struggle to carry a fight over to the other side wherever possible.

There is, in short, an asymmetry between Europe and the United States as to Central America, in terms of interests, objectives, and means—and no very early prospect that that asymmetry will be rectified. Their interests are of vastly different intensities, with the United States deeply concerned and Britain only slightly. The State Department and Whitehall diagnose the disease differently and prescribe different remedies.

SYMMETRY AT THE CENTRE: THE LATIN AMERICAN FINANCIAL CRISIS

Quite the opposite is the case with respect to the rest of the hemisphere. Central America and the smaller states in the Caribbean are special cases. Mexico and the continental land mass of South America hold much the larger share of the resources, the productive capacity, the diplomatic weight, and the population of the region. The issues there are profoundly different, and the significance for American and British interests much more equally balanced.

With the exception of Peru, there is only a slight threat of revolutionary change. The issue is not East–West as in Central America. The geostrategic significance of Latin America in the equation of world power-politics is less than that of Asia or Africa. History demonstrates that Latin America is less capable of inspiring or contributing to international military crises than any other region. The issue there is quite simply the viability of fragile democracies in a time of global economic distress—whether the democratic experiments in Brazil, Argentina, Uruguay, Peru, and Ecuador will survive or succumb to the mass frustration caused by adjustment programmes, and whether those nations, in collapsing, would tear a gaping hole in the international financial system.

The interests of the United Kingdom and America are virtually the same with respect to that issue. If the 'Special Relationship' is to find expression in a common foreign policy for any part of the Third World developing area, Latin America should be that area for the last half of the 1980s.

Certainly, the United States has not moved in an aggressive fashion to monopolize the solution to the problem on its own. Indeed, though the Latin American debt crisis exploded on the world like the Central American conflict at the beginning of the Reagan era, Washington's response to the two Latin American issues has been profoundly different. In Central America, the United States elbowed its way to a responsibility which left little room for European involvement. On the other hand, Washington's official reaction to Latin America's debt difficulties has been notably passive.

The opening gun of that crisis was fired by Mexico in August of 1982 when the new de la Madrid Administration was forced to recognize that it could no longer service its international payment obligations. The United States together with other nations and the International Monetary Fund cobbled together an emergency bridge financing effort. This permitted Mexico a breathing space to develop a slightly longer two-part plan. The first part consisted of an agreement with the International Monetary Fund; the second (for which the first was a distinct precondition) involved an agreement with the international commercial bank creditors of Mexico, in which, of course, American and British interests were salient. That agreement eventually produced a restructuring of Mexico's debt servicing obligations, stretching them out over a number of years and rearranging those obligations in a way which was less burdensome to the Mexican economy.

That pattern of *ad hoc* adjustment-cum-restructuring has been followed in the case of each of the other Latin American debtors—Brazil, Argentina, Peru, Colombia, Venezuela, and Chile. What has emerged is a series of arrangements with a tripartite pattern involving the International Monetary Fund, the debtor countries, and the American, British, European, and Japanese commercial banks. Governments of the creditor nations have been conspicuous only by their absence from the bargaining table.

This is not to say they have played no role. In Washington, the usual mechanisms of foreign economic policy, the Department of State and the Treasury, have been uninterested and ineffectual. But the Federal Reserve Board, acting quietly and behind the scenes through the impressive person of Paul Volcker, has been a commanding voice in the American efforts for the first three years to stave off disaster. (There may be some ironic justice to this. Latin America accumulated its mountain of debt in the 1970s when world-wide inflation made real interest on the debt negative over extended periods of time. Under those circumstances, it was almost unpatriotic not to borrow. Thus it was that when Volcker put the brakes on the American economy the accumulation of debt was suddenly transformed from an opportunity into a hideous burden, as a result of the extraordinary rise in interest rates in the early 1980s in consequence of the Fed's anti-inflation policy and the simultaneous downturn in the American business activity.) Nevertheless, it is fair to say that the tripartite answer to the payments difficulties of the Latin American debtors has been almost all economics and virtually no politics. Certainly, though Volcker's voice has been heard loudly in the design of the adjustment programmes and in the definition of Fund policy in general, he has stoutly resisted any move towards a broader overarching political solution in which governments would play an active role in expanding resource transfers to Latin America. And there has been little dissent in European circles from the view that the Fund and the markets can arrange things.

It has been a remarkable coincidence that the debt crisis, and the consequent necessity to move towards harsh adjustment programmes, has occurred at the same time as the rebirth of democracy throughout much of the hemisphere. The relationship is clearly more than historic accident. But the precise nature of the interaction between the two phenomena is subject to considerable debate. Certainly the economic crisis has had a severe effect on the political processes. The per capita income levels of Latin America have retrogressed sharply from the levels reached in the early 1980s to something like those of the mid-1970s. And there is precious little prospect that they will recover the lost ground much before the 1990s. The people of all of Latin America are, in short, eating less, driving fewer cars, and enjoying far fewer European and Florida vacations than was the case a mere half decade ago. And there is a hideous concomitant to the decline. Health standards have gone down; the numbers of refuse pickers have increased; disease is on the rise; education, already dismal enough in the hemisphere, has suffered a blow. Unemployment has grown. The numbers of the jobless in Mexico, already at nightmare proportions before the debt crisis, are beyond counting. All this has generated massive desperation.

And yet there has been no political explosion, no collapse, and no violent leftist revolution. The difficulties have been high inflation and low economic growth. The purchasing power of workers has been reduced by about one-third since 1982. In Venezuela, the price of milk has doubled. Meat is rare on the tables of the less privileged. Chileans' wages went down 13 per cent, after adjustment for inflation, in 1982, and 4.5 per cent in 1984. In Bolivia, workers staged an average of one and a half strikes per day in 1984. Yet for the most part, Latins have accepted their hardships. Indeed, in the face of all this, the two largest countries in South America, Argentina and Brazil, both moved from authoritarian military rule to authentic multiparty democracies, pledged to respect human rights, and with flourishing press freedom.

What happened? Certainly there is a good case to be made for the proposition that Margaret Thatcher is as responsible as anyone for clearing out the generals from the Casa Rosada in Buenos Aires, and putting President Alfonsin where he is today. Certainly the Falklands War, with its roller-coaster impact on Argentine self-perceptions—from glorious euphoria to the humiliation of defeat and the dawning realization that the nation had been ill-led and lied to by the military— ended whatever lingering hopes the Argentine Army had of continuing in power. The generals and the admirals were discredited. The return to multiparty civilian rule became a lively option in part because of the Falklands. But the military defeat only partially explains the democratic resurgence in Argentina, and not at all the Brazilian adventure. The more common experience of economic austerity suggests another important relationship as an explanation of the new democratic wave in the hemisphere in the early 1980s.

Economic constraint probably has increased the Latin incentive for democratization.[10] Certainly, as Pinochet is discovering in Chile, even the toughest general sits uncomfortably on his throne when the misery index goes up. Had the military stayed in Brazil, Argentina, and Uruguay, the probability of a revolutionary explosion in reaction to the economic crisis would have been considerably higher. With elective representatives in power, there has undoubtedly been a greater

---

[10] See generally R. Feinberg, 'Overview: The Adjustment Imperative and U.S. Policy', in *Adjustment Crisis in the Third World*, ed. Richard E. Feinberg and Valerina Kallab (New Brunswick, 1984), p. 12, for more on the proposition that the economic difficulties have actually increased pressures for democracy.

willingness to accept the sacrifices that the adjustment programmes have exacted. In short, those who suggested that democracy was less viable during economic crises, and that austerity would create a need for a tighter fist and more repression, have been proved wrong in Latin America.

These conclusions reflect importantly on the decision in Washington to avoid a political response to the economic crisis. If economics and politics are interrelated domestically in Latin America, the same may be true on the international plane. And it is in this that Britain and the United States should find common ground. In the years ahead, just as they have a shared interest in avoiding a breakdown of the international financial system, so too they share a common necessity to preserve and encourage the democracy that has sprung up so tenderly in the region. They both have much at stake. Mexico, Brazil, Argentina, Venezuela, and Peru, by working their way back to self-sustaining growth under democratic rule, can count for much in the world; if they fail, they will do grievous damage to the international financial system whose principal participants are Britain and America, and to the hopes for democracy everywhere.

22

America, Europe, and the Imperial Legacy

EDWARD MORTIMER

AT this point in the book Hedley Bull intended to insert a contribution of his own, commenting further on the Beloff thesis that decolonization was a catastrophe. Hedley would have argued for a less bleak view of decolonization and its consequences. He would have urged that the process should not be seen primarily as resulting either from failure of will on the part of the imperial powers or from pressure exerted by their allies or rivals, but from the world-wide 'revolt against Western dominance'—the theme of a book on which he was working in the last years of his life.

'The Beloff thesis', Hedley wrote in a letter to his co-editor, 'conveys perhaps dangerously to the United States today the message that with more will or more intellect applied to the problem it could find solutions by filling the vacuum, which tends to mean returning to a cruder form of imperialism. The forces in the Third World that primarily overthrew colonialism still exist, or are perhaps stronger; and it is in this context that the United States (and the rest of the West) have to work out their policies. This can only be done by taking the measure of these forces and arriving at some compromise with them; there can be no question of ignoring them, or proceeding as if they could be pushed aside if only we displayed a little nerve.' From there he went on to a favourite leitmotiv of his later writings: the 'need to build a new international order covering the extra-European or extra-western world in the wake of the age of empire'. Hedley, alas, did not live to write the essay.

Rather than attempting to try to reconstruct Hedley's argument, I shall offer some reflections of my own on the 'Beloff thesis' and, more generally, on the theme of this section of the book: the differences in perspective between America and Europe (including Britain) in their approaches to the rest of the world.

Lord Beloff's key argument is: 'The difference between the United States today and the old imperial powers—and indeed the Soviet Union with its own specific form of imperialism—is that while they had conscious or unconscious philosophies which to their ruling élites, and at times to wider strata of society, seemed to justify their status and activities, the United States is clearly still reluctant to accept its imperial role as anything but an expedient resorted to in self-defence.' Americans in general, he argues, are 'suffused with neo-Wilsonianism', meaning essentially the belief that the overriding benefits of self-government and self-determination are equally applicable to people in any part of the globe.

The United States, Lord Beloff said, had been 'sucked into the assumption of responsibilities in parts of the Third World through the diminution of the power of Britain and other European countries'. Its preoccupations had been governed by the fear that the alternative would be Soviet rule—a fear not taken so seriously in Britain or elsewhere in Europe. Secondly, the United States was 'without an adequate doctrine' or rather, saddled with 'a doctrine which is itself inhibiting'. Its failure to achieve military solutions, for instance in Vietnam, had something to do with this lack of a political doctrine. Americans had sought to overcome their doctrinal contradictions by resorting to what had been known in the older empires as 'indirect rule', which meant, broadly, to 'assume there is a group which can be trusted (in the country you are trying to influence or control) and give it what support you can'. This, Lord Beloff observed, produces a 'situation which gives one very little leverage'. Was Israel, for instance, a satellite of the United States, or was the United States a satellite of Israel? Either could be argued with almost equal force. And the same was broadly true elsewhere—the extreme case being Ethiopia, which apparently retained the right to pursue policies 'of friendship to America's enemies and of economic disaster for its own people' without forfeiting American economic aid. What, Lord Beloff asked, can the West do about it?

He is surely right to sense a contradiction between the Wilsonian ideology and the reality of contemporary United States policy, reflecting as it inevitably does the interests, appetites, and responsibilities that come with being a major world power. It is true that there has never been, and indeed it is hard to imagine that there ever could be, an American equivalent of British India. It is also true that present-day American involvement in Israel—let alone in Ethiopia—is quite unlike 'indirect rule' as practised by Lugard in Northern Nigeria, or even by Lyautey in Morocco. But classical imperialism was not restricted to these forms. As L. Carl Brown has pointed out, the interaction between local rulers and external great powers is very similar in the Middle East today to what it was in the heydey of imperialism.[1] The United States clearly took the place of Britain in Iran—as it had done earlier in South America—and that of France in Indo-China.

[1] L. Carl Brown, *International Politics and the Middle East: Old Rules, Dangerous Game* (Princeton, 1984; London, 1984).

The United States was drawn into imperialist behaviour in spite of its Wilsonian ideology. Paradoxically the expectations, and even the demands, of former colonial countries may invite American intervention. The simple fact of American power prompts the assumption, in many parts of the world, that the United States is capable of preventing or fostering any given political development if it sees a need to do so. It is a short further step to the belief that whatever does happen must be willed by the United States. Those who do not like what is happening blame the United States for it and assert that it is the fruit of illicit American intervention. In vain do American officials protest that a particular government is not of their choosing. Such protests are liable to be seen by that government as deliberate encouragement of its opponents, yet regarded by those same opponents as hypocritical, since the government can, *ex hypothesi*, only continue in office with United States support. American policy-makers must thus anticipate accusations of responsibility for political events in other parts of the world, whatever choices they make.

Such 'responsibility' could perhaps be shrugged off as existing only in Third World paranoid fantasy, were it not that similar reasoning has come to be applied to foreign policy within the United States. The visitor to the United States is inevitably struck by the fact that discussion of international affairs is hardly ever conducted there in a neutral or detached way. The question is not 'What is really happening in country X?' so much as 'Are we—the United States, meaning in practice the US government—getting it right in country X?' In Iran, for example, the apparent assumption was that the revolution must somehow be the product of misguided Western policies rather than of developments within Iranian society. This view was expressed in its crudest form by no less a person than President Reagan in his foreign affairs debate with Walter Mondale in October 1984. 'The Shah did our bidding for a number of years', he said, '. . . and then we went and turned it over to that maniacal fanatic'—a confession of imperialism on which the most paranoid Iranian, whether pro- or anti-Shah, could hardly have improved. American administrations have thus conveyed to domestic as well as foreign audiences the idea of American responsibility for the course of events in foreign countries.

In addition, Americans can seldom feel indifferent to the outcome of such events because they tend to see all world politics as a competition between themselves and the Soviet Union. This too is a familiar feature to students of classical imperialism: the *horror vacui*, or fear that any space on the global chessboard left unoccupied will be seized by a rival and then used to threaten one's existing positions. We should not forget that it was Gladstone—a Wilsonian *avant la lettre*, believer in 'Egypt for the

Egyptians'—who occupied Egypt, in the fear that if he did not France alone would establish herself athwart the route to India; and from there it was but a few steps to the occupation of Uganda, lest Germany get there first and control the head-waters of the Nile.[2] The fact that in today's 'Imperial game' there are only two serious players makes the competition all the more frantic, since there is less chance of containing an adversary by organizing a defensive coalition of all the players against him. (China can perhaps be seen as a third player, but with a role so far limited to eastern and southern Asia.)

One of the reasons for the *horror vacui* is that the imperialist generally sees himself as on the defensive, yet his power gives him interests far from home. A challenge to those interests makes him feel 'vulnerable' and this justifies him, in his own eyes, in projecting and using his power. Until the 1960s Britain felt 'vulnerable' east of Suez. Today it is the United States that faces that predicament. In Richard Ullman's words, 'phenomena one cannot affect seem less harmful than those one can'.[3] To put it another way, the unthinkable remains unthinkable only for so long as one has power to prevent it.

I tend to agree, therefore, with Lord Beloff in seeing the United States as a *de facto* imperial power. Where I cannot follow him—essentially for the same reasons that Hedley Bull could not—is in believing that an explicit, overt, unashamed American imperialism would be either possible, or preferable to today's hangdog variety. Whatever one's view of the way the great European empires were wound down, the conditions in which they were created have gone forever. From a distance it may look as if the 'Third World' had simply reverted to pre-colonial chaos. But that is not really what has happened, and the very use of the expression Third World is evidence of it. Conditions in many Third World countries may actually be more chaotic and violent than they were in the pre-colonial period, but that is not the point. The very names and frontiers of the countries are, in many cases, colonial or post-colonial creations. The societies have been in every case transformed by the colonial experience. That is true especially of the élites who are now in power, and of the techniques by which they maintain themselves in power. However anti-Western and anti-colonial their ideology, these élites have adopted Western technology and colonial structures of government. This is true even of countries which did not go through the experience of formal colonization, such as Thailand or Iran. There, similar transformations were carried out by indigenous rulers following Western models—and what they wrought, despite appearances, has by

---

[2] J. Gallagher and R. Robinson with Alice Denny, *Africa and the Victorians* (New York, 1965; London, 1965).

[3] See Richard Ullman's chapter in the present volume, p. 106.

no means all been undone. Even Iran's Islamic Republic is built, in many respects, on the work of the two Pahlavi shahs. It certainly has little in common with the debilitated Qajar polity which the Pahlavis inherited.

One crucial feature which these new states have in common—symbolized by the expression 'Third World'—is a sense of the world-wide arena in which they are performing. The pre-colonial élites were, by and large, easily manipulated to bring themselves and their peoples under Western domination. The present Third World élites, by contrast, are hypersensitive to imperialism and have considerable knowledge of Western—or northern—societies and ideologies. They know how to draft a UN resolution, how to address an American or European campus audience, how to play on the mutual fears and jealousies of the superpowers. They would certainly never accept without resistance a reassertion of direct Western control over their countries. Even in cases where their rule over their own peoples may objectively be more oppressive as well as less competent than was colonial government, ideology would enable them to mobilize mass resistance against any such attempt.

The withdrawal of the European powers from their respective empires was not caused primarily by a loss of will-power or nerve but by the rising cost of maintaining the colonial peoples in subjection—a cost not only financial but military, political, and moral. The new colonial élites challenged the metropolitan power with methods and concepts which they had learned from it, and against which it was ill-armed. Empires could only be held at the price of sacrificing values which were central to the European civilization in whose name the 'civilizing mission' had been undertaken. Similarly, the United States cannot now transform itself into a thoroughgoing old-style imperialist power, as Lord Beloff implies it should, without sacrificing the central values of American democracy.

I conclude that the contradiction between the Wilsonian theoretical commitment to equality among nations and the reality of unequal powers is unlikely to be resolved. With the United States today not only far and away the greatest Western power but, in most parts of the Third World, also far superior in influence to the Soviet Union, Americans will continue to wrestle with this contradiction among themselves. What attitude should the former imperial powers which are now America's allies take toward the American dilemma?

As former imperial powers watching a relatively new one at work, often in the same regions where we Europeans once held sway, we can hardly avoid speaking with the voice of the old hand, like a senior citizen no longer trusted at the wheel, but determined to influence the driver by offering advice from the back seat. Such advice is notoriously irritating to the person at the wheel. Yet only with difficulty will the occupant of the back seat be persuaded that he has no right to call out when he is convinced the car is on a collision course. After all, his survival is as much at stake as that of the driver.

It is similarly unrealistic for supporters of a given American policy in the region outside the NATO area to expect to impose silence on America's allies—if the latter are convinced that the policy in question is fundamentally misguided—by reminding them that their interests and survival are also at stake and are closely bound up with America's own. The more the allies are convinced of this, the more urgently will they seek to dissuade Washington from persisting with policies which they believe to be wrong. Therefore the American administration should be prepared to argue the merits of its policies, with its allies as with its domestic critics, rather than rely on tub-thumping appeals for loyalty.

A more pertinent response to criticism from allies may be to suggest that advice is not enough. European views would command more attention in Washington if Europe were making a bigger contribution to securing the interests of the alliance outside the NATO area, especially in a region where European interests are more directly at stake than those of the United States, such as the Middle East and the Persian Gulf. There is something to this argument, although Europeans also have some reason to feel the contributions they do make—including military and naval contributions, more or less discreet, in areas such as Africa, the Gulf, Lebanon, and Sinai, as well as important non-military roles such as that of Britain in South Asia—are insufficiently acknowledged on the American side. There are also doubts in Europe about the sincerity of American suggestions of a bigger European role. In the Middle East, especially, one has the strong impression that European attempts to 'get in on the act' are resented, and that American policy-makers would really prefer to be left alone.

Europeans tend to think that the United States is unduly obsessed with the Soviet Union, an obsession distorting American analysis. Attempts to exclude the Soviet Union from the Third World, however, create misgivings in Europe. Moscow may not be the only or even the primary source of regional trouble, but it clearly has a capacity, at the very least, to exploit trouble where it finds it; and it has a strong incentive to do so in any area where it is excluded from the diplomatic game. In European eyes, the Middle East in particular is an area where proximity to the Soviet Union, combined with the awkwardness arising from American identification with Israel, make it unwise and counter-productive to insist on 'keeping the Soviets out'. Europeans, not least the British, would like to see more thought given to ways of co-opting the

Soviet Union rather than confronting it in the handling of Third World problems.

In his address to the UN General Assembly in September 1984, President Reagan declared that 'spheres of influence are a thing of the past'. It is hard to see how this statement reflects the realities of Eastern Europe or Central America. The 'old hands' in Europe—and also their counterparts in Washington—worry about this rhetoric, fearing the consequences of upsetting a relatively stable European status quo and perhaps provoking Moscow itself to adopt more aggressive policies. On the other hand there are those in Europe, especially perhaps in the younger generation, who chafe at the bipolar world into which they have been born and would like to see the spheres of influence of both powers eroded. They would be less willing than some people in Washington to resign themselves to a 'long-term win' for Moscow in Afghanistan, but would also contest Washington's right to dictate the social and political course of Nicaragua. They would be ready to support 'liberation movements' in Third World countries cursed with dictatorial regimes, whether the latter were diplomatically aligned with East or West.

The bipolar world is the exception, not the norm, in a historical perspective, and for Europe—effectively partitioned between the two poles—it is not specially congenial. European nations which have experienced the decline of their own imperial power do not readily accept the assumption that a decline of American influence must be equated with a rise in Soviet influence. Europeans find it easier to see the post-war period as one in which there has been a gradual loss of control over the international environment by *both* the superpowers, in whose hands world power had been concentrated to a quite abnormal degree. The resulting world of the late twentieth century is an unpredictable and dangerous place in which to live, but for many peoples it may also offer a wider range of political choice.

COMMONWEALTH

23

The Transformation of the Commonwealth and the 'Special Relationship'

A. P. THORNTON

READERS of a book which tells how power has been used and what emotions it has stirred in the world since 1945 may wonder why it includes a chapter which concerns itself with the British Commonwealth of Nations. They may suspect they are being faced with another version of the old joke about the elephant[1]—in other words, with an insistence that everything fits into one particular context, and that perception thrives best in a tunnel. Since the Commonwealth deals less in power than in hope, and does not seem to be directed towards anything more concrete than its own continuation, these thoughts are not out of place. They warrant a reply.

In this century the Anglo-American relationship, whether 'special' or routine, has continued to turn exclusively on a London–Washington axis. Washington saw London as the controller of a world-wide system of authority and influence. Americans therefore believed that, since this British Empire existed, it would always operate an imperialist policy in its own interest. Many were the self-confessed imperialists in England who would have liked this to be true, who longed to be governed by skilful politicians capable of just such craft. In fact the Americans have sometimes been too suspicious, finding plots where there were not even plans. On the other hand the British have been too apt to deny any motivation whatever.

Some doings in the British world drew regular American attention. Successive United States governments, although reckoning all Anglo-Irish relations repulsive, usually muted this opinion. Americans expressed themselves more strongly about India, and in World War II greatly exasperated the British government, which had no policy towards India worthy of the name and so could not reasonably object to criticism of this omission. They have insisted on maintaining an

---

[1] French in origin. An Englishman, a German, and a Pole are asked to write about the elephant. The Englishman produces a manual on big-game hunting; the German a treatise on the natural history of pachyderms; and the Pole a thesis on 'The Elephant and the Polish Question'.

automatic friendship with Canada, without ever working much to keep it in good repair; and they became familiar with the geography if not with the politics of Australia, New Zealand, and (sometimes with the help of British Admiralty charts dating from the 1860s) a number of islands in the South Pacific. Some among the higher officials in Washington may early have learned to distinguish between the self-governing states of the Commonwealth and the dependent Crown Colonies—but there were never too many of these, and this story of gradual enlightenment may fittingly begin on 5 September 1939. On that date the United States Secretary of State, Cordell Hull, telephoned Canada's Prime Minister, Mackenzie King, to ask him whether Great Britain's declaration of war on Germany issued two days previously meant that Canada was at war too. American readers of this book will know that the answer to this was no it didn't and no it wasn't: but very many of Mr Hull's well-educated contemporaries would have shared his uncertainty, and some of the contemporaries of the American readers of this book may still do so.[2]

For the United States reckoned that British territories inhabited by the King's subjects were so much British territory, so many branches of the main store. Enquiries and complaints should therefore always be directed to the head office in London. If this was a misconception, what was its basis?

A dealer in ambiguity has a duty not to be ambiguous. So it is best to work from the known to the unknown, and to begin with a look at the Commonwealth of Nations as it exists at present before discovering how it reached that point in that particular shape, and why its aspirations have not been 'transformed' at all. At first sight incomprehensibility appears to be alive and well and propagating more of the same. At what exactly is one looking, when observing the Commonwealth? What are its credentials? Plainly it is not a formal institution, as the diplomatic fraternity understands the term, since the Commonwealth does not work out of a head office, and does not post accredited envoys to foreign capitals. What the observer is in fact looking at are the credentials presented by history itself—for the single qualification for membership in the Commonwealth is that the member-country should once have served its time as a component part of the British Empire.

The immediate result of winding the sheet of Empire, during the process of decolonization which was mounted in London from the late 1940s through the 1970s, was the extension of the bounds of the

---

[2] This subject is fully treated with range and insight in three fine books: Nicholas Mansergh, *The Commonwealth Experience*, 2 vols. (second edn., Toronto, 1983); W. David McIntyre, *The Commonwealth of Nations: Origins and Impact, 1869–1971* (Minneapolis, 1977); and J. D. B. Miller, *Survey of British Commonwealth Affairs: Problems of Expansion and Attrition, 1953–1969* (London, 1974).

Commonwealth. This activity was at once consistent, convenient, and commonsensical. 'Dominion status', which white men had invented in the 1920s for the benefit of other white men, in the style and practice of a gentleman's club, first opened up its doors and privileges in August 1947, in order to give political breathing-space to the newly arrived and innately hostile states of India and Pakistan. These were therefore able to begin their international independent careers on an equal footing. So were those who followed them. After 1957—the year Ghana and Malaya achieved independence—the new nations entered in orderly procession. They passed, under due ceremony of flag and (usually) a royal benediction, 'from an era of dominance to one of negotiation'.[3] One by one the ex-colonies arrived on the stage of the world by way of this companionable greenroom.

The arrival was done with dignity. This was the keynote: this was the point of arriving at all. This abstract concept was very much more to the nationalist point than any concrete case about economic viability. Asians and Africans bred to the British imperial experience had all sat in schoolrooms where liberal texts were indeed taught, but in a context of paternalism and trusteeship. Outside the school the Commonwealth already existed: these new graduates could make their way to it by applying the rules laid down for decolonized whites thirty years back. They had been Canadians looking for a place to stand, Irishmen and Afrikaners working out the blueprint for an escape-hatch, who had devised the guide-lines. 'Dominion Status', which had confused Mr Hull, had become something of a cliché when the Indians and the Pakistanis and Lord Louis Mountbatten exhumed it from the textbooks and put it to use again. The Irish principle of 'external association'— keeping the English devil, if not out of one's life, at least at arm's length—served to provide Jawaharlal Nehru and other ranks of ex-British subjects with a means of staying on the nominal roll while free of all duties. Once they had taken up residence in the Commonwealth, Asians and Africans were able to assert their own national identity and promote their own personal lifestyle—including a return to their own clothes, which perhaps were invented (as those of the Scots had once been) for the occasion. They could also define the meaning and function of their membership as they pleased. This too, from year to year since, they have done.

The troop of five members of the Commonwealth in 1939 (i.e. Australia, Canada, Newfoundland, New Zealand, the Union of South Africa; the Irish Free State (1922–49) was in its habitual condition: an anomalous position) has today become a squadron of 49—this figure

---

[3] Editorial, 'Crown and Commonwealth', *The Round Table*, no. 202, Oct. 1984, p. 355; cf. Sridath Ramphal, *One World to Share* (London, 1979), p. 64.

having climbed from 10 in 1957 to 21 in 1965 to 31 in 1970. Burma never came in, and only Pakistan and South Africa have gone out. 'Great empires when they crumble', Lord Rosebery told an Adelaide audience in 1884, in a speech wherein the word 'Commonwealth' was first aired, 'are apt to crumble exceedingly small.'[4] The evidence before us a century later proves him a prophet. The Queen of the United Kingdom is 'Head of the Commonwealth' in 18 states: this is a formula originally devised by the British to keep India, although openly tending towards a republic, as a member. (The Irish have confessed they would have welcomed the idea in 1949.) There are now 26 republics. Six states have their own monarchs. The population is less than one million in 27 states, and less than 200,000 in 15. Some of Lord Rosebery's crumbs have proved too minuscule even to sweep up. Such properties as Bermuda, Pitcairn Island, and St Helena have passed from the control of the Colonial Office (abolished 1966) to that of the Foreign Office, together with 12 others—including the Falkland Islands, that monument to the principle of self-determination.

The doctrine of the brotherhood of man has always lacked a family to promote it, but membership in a club at least promotes civility and a standard of acceptable behaviour: 'We all need to share a planet' was an opinion expressed even on such raucous battlegrounds as the rugby field, the cricket pitch, and the Olympic Games. Sharing is not necessarily the same as interference in misfortune. 'All I want', President Lyndon Johnson told Prime Minister Harold Wilson in 1968, 'is a battalion of the Black Watch'—but he did not get it, and Australasians alone broke the chain of Commonwealth non-involvement in America's adventure in Vietnam.

It was Kwame Nkrumah of Ghana who in 1964 suggested the setting up of a Commonwealth secretariat to act as a clearing-house for a host of common problems. Bad rows can occur even in good clubs: Malaysia expelled Singapore in 1965, which was the same year that the India–Pakistan war was resolved not by the mediation of the Commonwealth but by that of the Russians at Tashkent. Nehru's moral platform has stayed vacant since his death, but the organization has had what it considers its successes, such as the conversion in 1979 of white Rhodesia into black Zimbabwe. It has also coped resiliently with emergencies, such as the Turkish invasion of Cyprus in 1974 and the American invasion of Grenada in 1983. The 'Imperial Conferences' once summoned by and held in London have been replaced by Commonwealth Heads of Government Meetings (CHOGMs), eleven of which have been held anywhere convenient since 1965. These, via the secretariat,

---

[4] Quoted in W. K. Hancock, *Survey of British Commonwealth Affairs: Problems of Nationality, 1918–1936* (London, 1937), p. 54.

have arranged a network of mutual aid, technical co-operation, and educational development. It is a structure, and it stands.

Modern commentators, perhaps surprised that it does any such thing, often choose the role of apologist. This is in sharp contrast to the bounce and assurance of their forebears. But the commentary itself has a familiar ring. In the 1920s foreigners were neither expected nor wanted to grasp the mysteries devised by the British for their own use and entertainment. In the 1980s the London mandarins have fallen to baffling themselves. In October 1984 the editor of *The Round Table* (the in-house journal of imperial England since September 1910) intoned that 'the Commonwealth is not a simple but a complex and sophisticated thing, and it requires some sophistication properly to appreciate it'. The unsophisticated are soon joined in the street outside by persons more learned but equally wrong, for the editor of *The Times*, writing in the same issue, adds: 'One has to beware of subjecting symbols to the austere stare of the logician or the jurist'.[5] One, or quite possibly both, may be joking: but that the joke is also in-house, a piece of private idiom, is the telling point.

So, like the British constitution, the Holy Roman Empire, or the hundredth name of Allah, the Commonwealth is an artefact which attracts abstract speculation. It has done this since its first days, in the era after World War I—when, as Bruce Miller has noted, its affairs 'remained wrapped in a cocoon of theory, from which would emerge from time to time the formidable voice of Professor Berriedale Keith'.[6]

The presence of such a sage was never essential to the general understanding. The British Empire, Queen Victoria somehow still presiding, was a fact in everyone's life. Nobody needed to speculate about what was marked red all across the map. In the 1920s and 1930s French officers in the Levant tallied the daily quota of perfidy from Albion; George Orwell went forth to shoot his Burmese elephant for the honour of the Empire; and Swedish sea-captains paid its harbour-dues. Empire was a system of control. The British were the people who ran that system, who regulated both its markets and its habits. If as they did so they changed its name from Empire to Commonwealth, what did that signify? They continued to sit self-approving on their verandahs, fanning themselves with their liberal principles. Complacency interwoven with eccentricity had always been their style. Liberalism, like every other political theory, was a product of power, although no liberal would ever face this fact. The most revolutionary recipes issued by the

[5] *The Round Table, loc. cit.* pp. 353, 364.

[6] J. D. B. Miller, *Britain and the Old Dominions* (London, 1966), p. 105. Berriedale Keith was Professor of Sanskrit and Comparative Philology at the University of Edinburgh. Lacking pupils in this field, he turned to the Commonwealth, equally arcane.

Left Book Club, as Orwell delighted to infuriate his socialist companions by rubbing in, were ultimately protected by Scotland Yard at home and by the Royal Navy abroad.[7] To those who lived abroad, this had never been news.

Americans as a matter of instinct had always kept watch on the actions of the successors to the advisers of King George III. In September 1942 a visitor to wartime Washington from the British Foreign Office, Richard Law, reported home on how the ghosts of Lord North and the Hessian troops still haunted the American scene—

it may be these ghosts will never be laid, and that it will not be possible to instruct the American people in the real nature of the British Empire.[8]

It was not for want of trying. Three months later his colleague Sir George Sansom, fresh from some bruising experiences at an international conference in Quebec, as safe a venue as could then be found, noted that it was not difficult for the Americans and indeed the Canadians and the Australians to give an impression of high ideals and lofty purpose so long as they were not required to define in exact terms the meaning of freedom; democracy; racial equality; the common man; imperialism; colonialism; 'and other popular abstractions'. Obvious too, was

an American attitude which seemed to derive from a passion to extract assurances of good behaviour from the British Empire, and a determination not to believe them.[9]

Lord Hailey, out of India, out of Africa, the Colonial Office's top guru, was at Quebec and had done his incomparable best to convince his audience that the British, far from being motivated by imperialism, genuinely wished to see colonial peoples attain self-government and freedom. Sansom was ready to admit that Hailey's arguments

might have been more persuasive if they had been less finished in manner, less reasoned in content, but more evangelical in tone. It wanted, I am sure, but very little effort of imagination for some of his audience to see him addressing the mob from a tumbril in 1789.[10]

Patricians of Hailey's (and Sansom's) type naturally saw themselves as the true and only guardians of that 'real nature' of the British Empire. They were also its self-appointed evangelicals. They worked hard and

---

[7] Sonia Orwell and Ian Angus, eds., *The Collected Essays, Journalism and Letters of George Orwell* (London 1970), vol. ii, p. 169.

[8] Nicholas Mansergh, ed., *Constitutional Relations between Britain and India: The Transfer of Power 1942–7* (London, 1971), vol. iii, p. 253.

[9] Mansergh, *Transfer of Power*, pp. 521–2. Cf. W. R. Louis, *Imperialism at Bay: The United States and the Decolonization of the British Empire 1941–1945* (New York, 1978), pp. 11–12. At this Quebec conference, 'American anti-colonial sentiment reached its wartime peak.'

[10] Mansergh, *Transfer of Power*, vol. iii, p. 523.

long to make the name of Commonwealth a permanent fact in the consciousness of all those others in the world who had not had the benefit of the British imperial experience. A new name was certainly needed. During World War I a battering propaganda against Empire and imperialism had deeply impressed all political opinion in the United Kingdom. Widely publicized by South Africa's General Smuts, 'Commonwealth' had obvious appeal—and not only to Afrikaners who had fought, lost to, and finally got rid of the 'imperial factor' in their country's history: the century's first British act of decolonization dates from 1909, the formation of the Union of South Africa. It held overtones of welfare and democracy, as Oliver Cromwell himself had once remarked. It dodged Lenin's question—who is in charge of whom?—by calling it irrelevant. In these sunlit times who needed to be in charge of anybody? Imperial dominance did not suit a Commonwealth which was not mechanistic and did not rely on regulations for its spiritual health. Like-mindedness, common institutions, and a shared philosophy of life were their own best guarantees. They would all thrive together hereafter in an unguarded place. The old days had been bad days because controlled by power-brokers and war-mongers, imperialists to a man. But those days had gone, and would stay gone, if careful men took care.

Those who dedicated themselves to the Commonwealth and its cause, like those who strove to make the League of Nations succeed (and a lot of them were the same people) were always more at home with thoughts than with things—too much so, for their rhetoric may have repelled as many as it attracted. (Lionel Curtis's three-decker *Civitas Dei* is unreadable today.[11]) The enthusiasts for colonial emancipation were however luckier in their generation than those who sank their emotional capital in Geneva, for they did not have to cope with what finally brought the League down: 'its deep and grave weakness', its own historian has pronounced, was that the experts did not want it.[12] In contrast, the golden afternoon of the British Empire produced a great many experts who put their trust in progress, seeing in the concept of a commonwealth of nations a means to achieve this. Imperial power, hitherto concentrated in London, should devolve on those colonials who clearly deserved it, since they, all responsible men, would never misuse responsible government. A partnership of free societies would then exercise a powerful moral influence on world affairs. What was at stake here, everyone agreed, was the future of civilization itself. They did not think primarily in institutional terms, although those in London who agreed with the aim naturally continued to believe that all ideas needed to be systematized, and that a bureaucracy staffed by the sensible would

---

[11] Lionel Curtis, *Civitas Dei*, 3 vols. (London, 1934–7).
[12] F. P. Walters, *A History of the League of Nations* (London, 1952), vol. i, p. 16.

always be required to point out to the faithful the paths they should follow to reach the goal they sought.

In such terms did the concept of the Commonwealth collate and express the hopes of the group of former white colonies in the British Empire which, largely on their own initiative—whether in times of peace (the Dominion of Canada in 1867, the Commonwealth of Australia in 1901) or as the upshot of war (the Union of South Africa in 1909, the Irish Free State in 1922)—had become self-governing states. What their leaders hoped for was plain enough to the point of simplicity: to continue their steady enjoyment of a quiet life, in world conditions which when they changed, as doubtless they would, would do so only for the better—deepening the peace, increasing the prosperity, and broadcasting even further goodwill among men. As Adolf Hitler had already noted in *Mein Kampf* (1923), only to the satiated bourgeoisie in a pluto-democracy could such a notion occur. The colonial politicians did on professional occasions indulge in dinner-table platitude, but they were in the main a hard-headed and commonsensical body of men, and they knew they were asking a lot: still, they did not think it either wrong or absurd to try to set up a context wherein such hopes could gravitate from the Utopian to the practicable. Those in charge in Ottawa and Canberra and Pretoria and Wellington did not visit one another's capitals. They did not study the conditions of one another's countries. They most certainly did not want to be told about the problems of Dublin and Delhi, those insoluble fixtures on London's agenda, although they were ready enough to make allowance for one another's intensities, such as the drive in Irishmen towards a republic and the passion in Afrikaners to preserve their cultural identity. But they had always made it a habit to stay in touch with London's current attitudes, the more so since the government there had always made it familially easy for them to do so. In doing this, they knew, they kept in touch with the real world.

From their own shared experience they drew their strength, and announced it under the name of Dominion Status. They were justifiably proud of their effective belligerence in the Allied cause between 1914 and 1918. This paid them a notable dividend. By 1919 they had won themselves their international diploma, in the shape of a recognized presence: there was to be no further argument about their claims to national existence. They arrived among the peacemakers at Versailles as victors by right—even though France's Clemenceau never rid himself of the thought that all these bulky dominions had been invented by Lloyd George as a ploy to put at his own and Great Britain's disposal five unanimous brute votes at European conference tables. By 1931 the five white dominions, with the painstaking assistance of English jurists, had attained full domestic autonomy and a juridical status among the nations. And they did not fail to make use of the forum now open to them in Geneva itself.

In 1926 England's elder statesman Arthur Balfour had carefully instructed them how they were now to think of themselves. They were

autonomous communities within the British Empire, equal in status, in no way subordinate one to another in any respect of their domestic or external affairs, though united by a common allegiance to the Crown, and freely associated as members of the British Commonwealth of Nations.

Smuts later interpreted these runes as 'the grand equation of the commonwealth which equates Great Britain with the dominions . . . Freedom, equality are the essence of it.'[13] The essence is in fact less abstract, for the keywords in Balfour's declaration are only two: 'freely associated'—which signalled to the world-strewn subjects of King George V that they could in future associate with or dissociate from whomsoever as they pleased, even from King George V. This point was not emphasized, at least in public. 'Secession' never became a general topic of conversation within the Commonwealth, although every British government knew how firmly the Irish kept this notion at the front, and the Afrikaners at the back, of their respective minds.

One other thought may have existed without surfacing in those peaceable days when liberalism was king: an awareness that freedom of choice must presuppose the freedom to choose. Smuts's grand equation in fact does not stand close inspection, and did not indeed do so even when Smuts himself celebrated it in 1934. A status whose moral and physical security depended on the continued protection of someone else's liberal principles, and accordingly on the continued health of these same, had clearly only a shaky foundation. Stature, in contrast, is not arrived at by wishful thinking—for if its foundation is shaky it does not exist at all. It is another name for power perceived, in a calculated and unsentimental assessment from the outside. None of the dominions in the 1920s and 1930s owned that stature or had ambitions towards it. They remained privileged bystanders. (That such privileges might be revocable and the bystanding brought to an end was a thought that readily occurred to Australians in the spring of 1942 as they monitored the southward march of the Japanese.) Their role was still that of watchers by the threshold. The threshold belonged to a distant but long-familiar power-house—that headquarters in London from which for centuries past had issued the imperial decrees.

Thus, during the 1920s successive British governments had made good their commitments to carry into action their liberal opinions on the

---

[13] Miller, *Britain and the Old Dominions*, pp. 39–50.

value and utility of colonial self-government. But they devolved the power and movement of the Royal Navy on nobody. They never once considered ridding themselves of the responsibility for the defence of what everyone still called the imperial lifelines. They did not submit their foreign policy for approval beyond Parliament: London might consult, but it did not have to comply with, dominion views. The security of the white self-governing states of the Commonwealth, like that of the sixty-one coloured territories controlled by the Colonial Office within the British Empire 'proper', thus continued to depend on the existence and successful assertion of the power of the United Kingdom, the only 'Great Power' in the entire system, the only one with any stature at all. *Pax Britannica* therefore still lived. It was indeed not the awareness of this truth that caused agitation in the dominions, it was the fear that the old Victorian umbrella might be coming apart, might no longer be stout enough to shelter those dependent on it from a coming storm.

But, as the Victorian hymn had so ringingly served notice on all Christian soldiers,

> Crowns and thrones may perish,
> Kingdoms rise and wane

—although the Raj in India had never allowed this possibly encouraging but certainly subversive idea to ignite the imagination of any loyal subject, Christian or other, who found himself in a church.[14] Very little out of the 1920s has survived in the collective memory, and still less in the popular affections, of the European states. Everyone has suffered too harshly from the perishing and the waning. But the British and their kin are an exception. Although their kingdom has assuredly waned, they are unable to look back to that dim decade with the same feelings of distaste. For them these old days were not such bad days—not at all. They had been imperial days, when the 'Ten-Year Rule' had simplified the strategic thinking of the imperial general staff; when the world was safe for democracy; when the nationalist principle had been recognized in the drawing of a new map for Europe; when in magical fashion strong words at Geneva would solve the issues of collective security; and when for very different reasons both the United States of America and the Union of Soviet Socialist Republics were thankfully absent from regular diplomatic activity. And it was in those same sunny days that in a burst of optimism the Commonwealth had come into being.

British argument in the 1980s still insists—in however low-key and ironic a style—that this optimism of the 1920s has been justified.

[14] Cf. N. Gerald Barrier, *Banned: Controversial Literature and Political Control in British India 1907–47* (Columbia, Mo., 1974), for full and fascinating information on this theme.

Everything else perceived in that era may have been mistaken: but not its sole survivor, the Commonwealth of Nations. Here was one kingdom that had not waned, whose bounds had indeed been set, like Sir Edward Elgar's 'Land of Hope and Glory' (1902), 'wider still and wider'. It was the appeal of human dignity, vivid in both decades, vivid ever, that had done this. It was in answer to this appeal that the Americans had originally decolonized themselves, and had gone seeking a status that their history to date had denied them. By freeing themselves, they had set out to attain their own stature. From this American Revolution the British too had learned a lesson—that empire, like other forms of government, depends ultimately on the consent of the governed. When for whatever reasons the consent evaporates, when acceptance such as India had given the Raj is withdrawn, empire itself evaporates and withdraws. The American Revolution was therefore not replayed into the British record. British politicians wrestled with obstruction and disappointment as they followed the process of decolonization, but they were not confronted with the degree of disaster that broke the Belgian rule in the Congo, or drove the French fighting for their imperial cause in Indo-China and Algeria to a bitter end indeed.

In the other half of their hearts they may have agreed with Prime Minister Lord Salisbury, who a century back had denied any right of self-rule to Irishmen, Indians, and Africans because he distrusted what they would do with it; with his nephew Arthur Balfour, who in the 1920s had warned that 'constitutions are easily copied, temperaments are not';[15] with Labour's Herbert Morrison, who thought in 1943 that giving the African colonies independence was like giving a child of ten a latch-key, a bank account, and a shotgun; and with Iain Macleod, the Conservatives' colonial secretary who accelerated the pace of imperial hand-over and then stated publicly in 1961 that he had never believed the colonies were 'ready' for self-government. But the day of their graduation as nations could no longer be delayed by the timetable constructed by their imperial tutors. Whatever the terms of the 'trust', the wards made it plain it was time to wind it up. In the aftermath the trustee did not always reap the respect he felt he deserved. In 1965 Prime Minister Wilson saw no irony in the situation when African fellow-members of the Commonwealth combined to attack him for his hands-off policy on Rhodesia. Responding to the attacks after Rhodesia had

[15] Hancock, *Survey*, p. 429. Balfour continues: [If a people] 'have no capacity for grading their loyalties as well as for being moved by them: if they have no natural inclination to liberty and no natural respect for law: if they lack good humour and tolerate foul play: if they know not how to compromise or when . . . : if corruption does not repel them: and if their divisions tend to be either too numerous or too profound, the successful working of British institutions may be difficult or impossible.'

declared itself unilaterally independent Wilson exclaimed: 'Britain is being treated as if we are a bloody colony!'[16]

From the outset, Commonwealth propagandists had concentrated on one doctrine only, 'the government of men by themselves'.[17] People who believed in this, as Nicholas Mansergh pointed out in 1952, did so because

they regarded colonialism as a stage necessary for the bringing of backward peoples to political maturity, but of its very nature transient. In the end Indians must govern India, Africans must govern Africa.[18]

The Commonwealth, still based on that doctrine, remains today in the world, revolving around no axis, a presence if not a force, a project more than an achievement. The British will always see it as a monument to the vanished empire. They can make a case for doing so, and they take what advantage they can from it. As one example, in November 1983 the Foreign Secretary Sir Geoffrey Howe declared his satisfaction in the thought that its existence gave to the United Kingdom an immediate and a privileged entrée to the governments of thirty per cent of the United Nations.

At the University of Michigan in 1966, the Commonwealth's first secretary-general, Arnold Smith, spoke to its ideas. He told the students that

What matters most in shaping history are such intangibles as attitudes, values, intuitions, motivation, faith. It is in this field that the Commonwealth operates.[19]

This is a large claim. The boundaries of that field are not easily ascertainable, and maps of it are not usually the first to be consulted in either the Politburo or the Pentagon. Power continues to matter in the shaping of history. So does perception of it. When power is suddenly used, the bystander has to decide, and fast, whether the man armed with it is a cop or a robber. Since both are probably wearing uniforms this is a hard choice to make in the dark. Compare the British reaction in April 1982 to the invasion of the Falkland Islands by the Argentine Republic, to their assessment in October 1983 of the arrival in Grenada, another Commonwealth country, of the United States Marines. The British, perceiving the Argentinians to be burglars, mounted an old-style 'punitive expedition' against them, with signal success. In contrast, they were ready to identify the Americans in Grenada as agents of a rescue

[16] Arnold Smith, *Stitches in Time* (London, 1981), p. 65.
[17] Nicholas Mansergh, *Commonwealth Experience*, vol. ii, p. 243, quoting Lionel Curtis.
[18] Nicholas Mansergh, *Survey of British Commonwealth Affairs: Problems of External Policy 1931–1939* (London, 1952), p. 7.
[19] Smith, *Stitches in Time*, p. 39.

service—which was the same view the Americans themselves took: they were there for the Grenadians' own good. Ready, but not keen. Here was one more case where 'the cousins'—the in-house name for these particular 'special relations' in the files of the British intelligence network—had weighed up and acted on somebody else's situation faster than anybody else liked.[20]

The House of Commons therefore heard Sir Geoffrey Howe musing that on Grenada there was room for two views, and that the consultation between London and Washington on the matter had been 'regrettably less than we would have wished'. The Prime Minister, Margaret Thatcher, later declared that she was always personally delighted when people had the yoke of Communism lifted from their shoulders—but 'that does not mean that you are entitled to go into every country . . . which is under communist oppression'. That, as *The Round Table* pointed out, was as far as Mrs Thatcher was prepared to go by way of condemnation of the American invasion. It was enough to indicate her views, no doubt,

and no more than she could say without imperilling the special relationship with Washington that she so valued.

But *The Round Table*, although a conservative journal, thought poorly of this. Howe's formula is characterized as lame, and it is emphasized how no member of the Thatcher government could be induced to use the word 'condemn' to describe the American action.[21]

Relations may be special, but as every family knows, they can also be something of a trial. They still have to be tolerated. So too must the world itself—which regrettably is not in the condition any sensible inhabitant of it would wish. The role of the bystander, of the watcher by the threshold, lacks dignity. Small states, however polished their desks and their limousines, know this is so. They know what it is and how it feels to spend their time whistling in the dark. Lack of economic viability is endurable, but political invisibility is not. For forty years the Commonwealth of Nations has developed a 'special relationship' within itself, between a small group of secondary powers and a swathe of the totally powerless. In doing this it has kept at least thirty per cent of the world in countenance, and has thus done more for that percentage than will a constant taking of Washington's temperature, or a hopeful waiting for its word.

Yet the weather and the wait have not always been adverse. So long as

[20] Cf. John le Carré's novel, *The Honourable Schoolboy* (London, 1977), p. 199. He is describing a conference in Whitehall of high-level British officials: 'Before each pair of hands . . . lay a pink folder, like a dance programme. It was marked Top Secret Withhold. The withhold meant keep it away from the Cousins.'
[21] Anthony Payne, 'The Grenada Crisis in British Politics', *The Round Table*, pp. 407–8.

the Western bloc believes, at base, that the Commonwealth's claim to shape the future by way of a particular set of intangible values is a claim that is good and true, it will keep the moral edge over the opposing system of Communism—whose own intangible core of morality, indeed whose own ideology, has been worn away by its own record of brutalities. If the Commonwealth by habit still inclines too much to smugness in its public relations, and strews its language too much with truisms, none the less the fundamental characteristic of truisms is that they are true.

'Equal rights for all civilised men', was the political nostrum which Cecil Rhodes, the most heartily devoted of all the British imperialists, let loose in the 1890s into the unlikely context of South Africa.[22] Have men in our own time—whether in South Africa or anywhere else—come up with a better idea?

[22] Rhodes's definition of a civilized man is: 'A man whether white or black who has sufficient intelligence to write his name, has some property or work, in fact is not a loafer.' Quoted in Hancock, *Survey*, p. 188 n. 1.

24

The 'Special Relationship' in the Pacific

J. D. B. MILLER

ASIA and the Pacific are not Europe. The point is childishly simple, yet it needs to be kept constantly in mind if one is to understand the limitations of the 'Special Relationship'. One of the consequences of World War II was that large areas of Asia and the Pacific ceased to be the property of Europe and became independent; moreover, the influence of the Soviet Union moved beyond the borders of China to distant places in South-east Asia, while that of the United States became significant and often dominant in areas far beyond the traditional spheres of concern in Japan and the China ports.

It is in the context of this massive shift in international affairs since World War II that the 'Special Relationship' in the Pacific has to be seen. Briefly, while the United States has been prepared to see conditions in Europe as requiring constant co-operation with allies—among which Britain has been especially influential—it has not been prepared to see the Pacific in the same light. There, Britain has been not so much a permanency as a transitory colonial power; its one-time colonies of settlement, Australia and New Zealand, have been enthusiastic supporters of alliance with the United States, yet often disturbed by the problems of living with a giant, and apprehensive of what might ensue. In these circumstances their membership in the Commonwealth of Nations (like Britain's) has been a diplomatic resource to be used occasionally but never in order to outface the United States. The roots of the situation go back to the war itself.

I

The British role in the Pacific war was relatively slight, following the initial débâcle in Malaya and the loss of Hong Kong and Burma. It was confined to the defence of India, and, in due course, to the brilliant campaign by General Slim which regained Burma. That campaign received little public recognition in either Britain or the United States. So far as British public opinion was concerned, the Pacific war took second place to what was happening in Europe. Churchill was concerned that the United States should concentrate its efforts in Europe, and not succumb to Australian pleas that power should be concentrated against Japan. In this he was successful. As far as he could, he assumed with Roosevelt a leadership of the British Commonwealth throughout the world which he sustained for the time being but which became impossible to perpetuate when the war was over. In the United States the Pacific war was widely seen as a one-man campaign by General MacArthur, who had his headquarters in Australia; the other command, involving New Zealand and largely naval in character, got much less attention, certainly none in Britain. Between the British and American governments, however, there was considerable disagreement about what should happen to British colonies in Asia after the war.[1]

The debate was about colonialism generally, but had extra relevance to Asia and the Pacific because of President Roosevelt's special interest in China. This made Hong Kong a particularly important element in the discussion; moreover, the ignominious British failure in Malaya made Singapore another issue. The British presence in India occasioned special attention from Roosevelt and those around him; they reasoned that, unless the British made specific promises of independence to India, the Japanese might succeed with their propaganda about 'Asia for the Asiatics', and the task of defeating them would be made more difficult.

As other chapters in this volume indicate, Roosevelt was operating from a general anti-colonial position shared by the great majority of Americans. He added to this his own emphasis upon the need to placate and encourage China, and his scorn for British and French colonialism in South-east Asia. He was much taken with the idea of international trusteeship. In opposition to him was Churchill, an exponent of Empire in nineteenth- rather than twentieth-century terms, determined that Britain should give up nothing and should make its own arrangements with its dependencies. At the same time, Churchill was aware of the need for some movement in respect of India: the outburst in Bengal in 1942 and the creation of the so-called Indian National Army under Subhas Chandra Bose made it clear that action was necessary. Churchill was sure, however, that it should not be taken at American dictation.

Once the European war seemed likely to be won, the British government decided to be more active in the Pacific, so that Singapore and Hong Kong could be retaken by British rather than American forces. In December 1944 the first ships of the British Pacific Fleet under Sir Bruce Fraser arrived in Sydney harbour, and were received with

[1] In what follows I am very much indebted to Wm. Roger Louis, *Imperialism at Bay* (Oxford, 1977) and Christopher Thorne's two books, *Allies of a Kind* (London, 1978) and *The Issue of War* (London, 1985).

much acclaim; it was not at all plain, however, what part they would play in the final stages of the war against Japan. Admiral King, the United States Chief of Naval Operations, saw the Pacific as an American lake, and could find no reason why the British should take an active part there. In the event, the colonies were regained with no significant British losses because of the Japanese surrender after the use of the atomic bomb. Before long, the issue of colonialism had been largely abandoned by the American government, except for occasional philippics at the United Nations; the debates between Roosevelt and Churchill began to seem only a bad dream.

Nevertheless, the post-war situation of Japan showed that in East Asia the United States was accustomed to act on its own, without reference to allies, whether they were said to be in a special relationship or not. It had been broadly agreed that Britain, China, and the Soviet Union would be involved in policy towards a defeated Japan. Instead, the United States, acting through General MacArthur, took the whole responsibility to itself: both the Far Eastern Commission and the Allied Council for Japan proved to be of no account. So far as Britain was concerned, this did not greatly matter, but it was important to Australia and New Zealand. During the period of MacArthur's rule as Supreme Commander for the Allied Powers (SCAP), Britain had more to worry about than whether it had a say in the reconstruction of Japan. But the fact of MacArthur's supremacy indicated that the 'Special Relationship' was restricted to direct bilateral questions and to Europe: it had no currency in Asia and the Pacific, except when allies were needed to embellish a basically American initiative. This was true of the conduct of the Korean War. Britain participated, but in a strictly subordinate capacity.

Even though the Occupation ceased in 1951, Japan did not become a matter of concern to Britain, or to the United States in terms of its international connections, until the expansion of Japanese exports in the 1960s. By the time Japan had become a threat to domestic industries in Western Europe and North America, Britain was no longer a diplomatic force of significance. Complaints about Japan became a matter for the European Community at large, and distinctive British interests (which before World War II had been expressed in bilateral terms when Japanese textiles endangered British markets) were voiced through the European Commission.

We can thus see the 'Special Relationship' as operating in minimal terms towards Japan in both war and peace, even when it was at its height in other respects. Japan, as the principal Asian power, was the cause of controversy between Britain and the United States because of its success in seizing British colonies. That success helped to decide the

eventual form of the Commonwealth of Nations, and the attitude which
Britain would take towards decolonization; it also helped to determine
the roles which Australia and New Zealand would play in the Pacific,
and in relations with Britain and the United States. Their status as
members of the Commonwealth was very much involved in these
developments.

II

Any realistic discussion of the Commonwealth must acknowledge that it
has been different things at different times, though retaining its overall
nature as an association between Britain and its former colonies. The
state of current membership and the international environment have
been the two variables giving the Commonwealth its character at
particular times.

During World War II the Commonwealth was still composed of the
original Dominions, which, while widely recognized as autonomous, were
still relatively inexperienced in diplomacy in 1939. The international
stature and connections of the overseas members were greatly increased
(as was their tendency to act independently of Britain) by participation
in various theatres of war. This was especially true of Australia and New
Zealand. The British were no longer able to discourage them from
independent diplomacy, or to maintain that issues within the British
Commonwealth had some special status in international law. In various
fields British leadership was still accepted, but the course of the war had
shown conclusively that Britain could not hope to operate effectively
against a major power in the Pacific.

During the second half of the 1940s the membership changed
radically with the independence of India, Pakistan, and Ceylon, and
their acceptance into the Commonwealth (with the adjective 'British'
tacitly dropped). The Commonwealth was also affected by the
departure of Ireland. The previous assumptions about common action
between Commonwealth members were greatly weakened by differing
attitudes towards the United States. This involved not only the non-
alignment adopted by India (and, until 1954, by Pakistan) but also the
special needs of Australia and New Zealand for American protection.

These needs were expressed in the earnest search for a 'Pacific Pact' by
the foreign ministers of the two countries, Percy Spender and F. W.
Doidge, which culminated in the ANZUS Treaty in September 1951. In
the course of the negotiations the problems of applying the 'Special
Relationship' to Asia and the Pacific were clearly shown. John Foster
Dulles, on behalf of the United States, was reluctant to have Britain as a
member of the pact, in spite of mild yearnings by some members of the

Australian and New Zealand governments. If Britain were included, he would find it hard to exclude the Philippines. American opinion was unenthusiastic about the guarantees for British colonial territories which British membership would have entailed. Dulles was determined that, as far as possible, the pact should be confined to the United States, Australia, and New Zealand, and that discussions should be concluded quickly so that it could be signed at the same time as the peace treaty with Japan, about which the other two governments had earlier been somewhat obstructive.

From a British standpoint, there were both pluses and minuses in the ANZUS Treaty. On the one hand, there was much to be said for continuing the American responsibility for the security of Australia and New Zealand—a responsibility which the United States had discharged in World War II, and which Britain was patently unable to reassume. Also, it was congenial to British policy-makers that this should occur without giving the United States any special status in respect of Hong Kong and Malaya. On the other hand, there was the traditional concern that, if Australia and New Zealand grew closer to the United States, they would drift further away from Britain. In addition, there were technical considerations of co-ordinating military (especially naval) activity between Britain on the one hand and the ANZUS partners on the other.

The Attlee government was very quiet about the conclusion of the ANZUS agreement; Churchill's government, which took its place not long after the agreement was signed, was not. In 1952 and 1953 it sought to be associated with ANZUS, but to no avail.[2] It was noteworthy at the time that discussion in Britain concentrated on the effect which ANZUS might have on the Commonwealth connection with Australia and New Zealand, not on its effect on the 'Special Relationship'. It was as if that relationship had been tacitly accepted as applying only to bilateral issues and to those which arose in Europe, not to events in Asia and the Pacific.

It was also of some importance that, in the succeeding decade, ANZUS was not significantly tested, whereas the Commonwealth connection was. Australia and New Zealand were pleased that the United States initiated the treaty which led to the creation of SEATO (South-East Asia Treaty Organization) in 1954, which Britain signed. At the same time, while glad that American commitments in Asia were increasing, Australia and New Zealand were quite content that Britain should not commit its colonies in Malaya, Borneo, and Hong Kong to SEATO's care. These were recognized as, in a sense, Commonwealth

[2] See Nicholas Mansergh, ed., *Documents and Speeches on Commonwealth Affairs 1952–1962* (London, 1963), pp. 435–9.

responsibilities: Australia and New Zealand never sent troops to Hong Kong, but they were participants in the war against Communist guerrillas in Malaya, and later against Indonesian confrontation in Borneo. There was no American role in these campaigns: Britain was plainly in charge of the Commonwealth activities.

Yet, as the 1960s wore on, it became clear that the British, animated by a growing preoccupation with their economic future in Europe, and by a wish to disengage peacefully from their colonies in Africa, were paying less attention to Asia and to the considerations which the Australian and New Zealand governments regarded as paramount. At the same time, American concerns in Asia, centred upon the conviction that Communist China represented a maleficent force which could overrun South-east Asia and the Indian subcontinent, proved much more congenial to the Australian and New Zealand governments than to the British. The culmination was the participation of the two Pacific countries in the Vietnam War from 1965 onwards, while Britain and the rest of the Commonwealth stayed out.

Such a situation imposed strains upon the 'Special Relationship', and also upon relations between Britain and Australia; New Zealand, less deeply involved in the war and with a government somewhat more sceptical about it than the Australian, was less affected. The end of the Vietnam War and the effective departure of Britain from Asia, with its attendant close absorption in the affairs of Western Europe, were more or less coincidental in time but not coincidental in terms of secular change. Australia and New Zealand were now firmly linked with American policy, unless their domestic politics or their perception of trends in world affairs should force them to defy it.

At roughly the same time (i.e. the mid-1970s) a new development in Pacific affairs was giving both the Commonwealth on the one hand and Australia and New Zealand on the other an opportunity to extend their influence. This development was the acquisition of independence by a number of South Pacific island states, such as Papua New Guinea and Nauru (formerly administered by Australia), Western Samoa (formerly by New Zealand), and Fiji, Tonga, and the Solomon Islands (which had been British colonies). These and others came together with Australia and New Zealand in 1971 to create the South Pacific Forum, an international body which included neither Britain nor the United States. All were members of the Commonwealth, though the Forum was not envisaged as a specifically Commonwealth institution (and has not functioned as such). Their apparent unity, and the clear evidence of their independence of outlook in regard to French nuclear tests and matters arising from the UN conferences on the Law of the Sea, were a source of envy to the inhabitants of the United States' Trust Territory in

Micronesia, who saw themselves destined for local self-government modified by United States' supervision of foreign and defence policy till the end of time. What is most significant about the Forum in this context, however, is that it excludes Britain and the United States and functions as a truly regional body. Whether or not there is a 'Special Relationship' in the Pacific, it has no part in this organization.

The situation in the Pacific in the latter half of the 1980s is likely to be one in which Britain plays no role, the United States reverts to some forms of direct action after its ten years of self-imposed trauma over Vietnam, the small island states of the Commonwealth seek help from Japan, Australia, and New Zealand in order to preserve their precarious independence, Japan continues to be the major influence in the lives of most states, and Australia and New Zealand agonize intermittently over the possibly dire consequences of their association with the United States. New Zealand's refusal in 1985 to allow nuclear-armed ships into its ports has caused a minor rift within the ANZUS alliance; but there can be few people who doubt that, if war struck, the ports would be open to any American ship that wished to dock.

III

What can be said of the 'Special Relationship' in the Pacific, in the light of the changes since World War II? The main point must be that it was not of much importance at any time. The relationship has been effectively a European or Atlantic affair. As such, it has pleased both parties in different degrees at different times; but in Asia and the Pacific there has been no sign of concerted policies, and there have been numerous cases (mostly cited elsewhere in this book) of divergence. Starting with the now seemingly ridiculous row about colonialism, there have been the failure to act together in the Pacific War, the unilateral administration of Japan, the formulation of ANZUS, the British fears of what John Foster Dulles might do to China, the division over the Vietnam War, and the fading effect of British military power in Southeast Asia. Favoured though this power was by the United States, no attempt was made to bolster it, and none seems to have been asked for. To the extent that the United States and Britain have been active in Asia and the Pacific since 1945, each has acted in its own interest, and has disregarded the other. The absurdity of SEATO, so apparently similar to NATO in sound and propaganda, and yet so greatly different in practice, is an indication of how great the differences were.

Those differences caused major strains in the Commonwealth. In the long run, Australia and New Zealand, Malaysia and Singapore, and the island states of the Pacific, were there to stay; so was the United States, with a Pacific Fleet which nobody expected it to give up. Britain was not there to stay. It left. Now the Pacific is as if Britain had never been there, apart from the legacy of custom and language—and sometimes the investment—which it has left behind. The talk now is of a 'Pacific Community' which, however misty in its details, is assumed to include the United States and Japan as its twin pillars of economic strength, along with Canada, Australia, New Zealand, the ASEAN (Association of South-East Asian Nations) countries, and perhaps China and the Pacific islands. The European powers are not mentioned. Asia and the Pacific are not Europe; a Eurocentric world has disappeared; and the 'Special Relationship', fruitful and attractive as it has been, flourishes only in Atlantic water and European soil.

25

Afterword: The 'Special Relationship'

SIR MICHAEL HOWARD

IT would not be too much to say that the 'Special Relationship' was the creation of Winston Churchill, and that if it survives at all in the United States it does so mainly because of his memory. Churchill was indeed its embodiment. Genetically he was as much American as British, and throughout his long life he saw the two nations as artificially severed halves of a single community which he worked—not only as a statesman but as a historian and a publicist—to reunite. It was as much this emotional commitment as any calculation of power-politics that enabled Churchill to perceive, long before any of his British contemporaries, that the friendship and support of the United States was essential to the survival of Britain, both as a Continental and as an Imperial power. It was this that led him to cultivate his own 'special relationship' with Franklin D. Roosevelt as soon as he returned to office in September 1939 and to foresee, in the evening of his life, the catastrophic consequences of the policy pursued at Suez by his less clear-sighted successor. Churchill's 'Finest Hour' did not come during the Battle of Britain in 1940. It came three years later when he sat at the conference table with Roosevelt, to all appearances an equal ally, disposing with him of the destinies of the post-war world.

That was the 'Special Relationship', as David Reynolds has reminded us in his essay in this volume, which Churchill hoped to preserve after the war, and for whose revival he called in his speech at Fulton, Missouri, in March 1946: a relationship whereby the United States would accept and underwrite Britain's status as a coequal world power. Of course Churchill himself did not see it that way: taking Britain's status as a world power for granted, he regarded it as an alliance of equals in which any shortfall in Britain's economic power would be made up for by her political skills and historic wisdom. It was a view shared by many Englishmen at the time, but by curiously few Americans.

It is as well to remember how atypical, in the general perspective of Anglo-American relations, that moment of wartime euphoria was. Before the war the two peoples did not know one another very well or like one another very much. Only the rich could make the transatlantic voyage often, and though excellent relations were established between certain elements in the élites—relations which had after all produced Churchill himself—these did not extend deep into their respective societies. The Americans remembered clearly that the British had been the national enemy in two wars—episodes about which the British were prone to communal and genuine amnesia—and many saw Britain through the eyes of their Irish forebears. It was part of an old world from which they were glad to escape. Even those most friendly to the British held no brief for an Empire from which they had been the first to break away. The British in return tended to look on the Americans with the amused contempt portrayed by Trollope in *The American Senator*, and in Grossmith's *Diary of a Nobody* in the figure of Mr Hardfur Huttle—an attitude which, as David Watt points out, the exciting image of American society portrayed in the films of the 1930s did much to moderate. American neutrality during most of the First World War and its debt policy afterwards more than outweighed such brief wartime camaraderie as had been created in 1918. British statesmen between the wars regarded their American counterparts—with some reason, it must be said—as being long on unhelpful moralizing and short on serious action. As for the Second World War itself, the documents of the Chief of Staff reveal how persistent among the military leadership was the legacy of suspicious dislike on the American side and patronizing contempt on the British. The record makes clear the truly heroic role played by General Eisenhower and Field Marshal Sir John Dill in dissolving these antagonisms and creating a spirit of genuinely friendly co-operation which had by the end of the war become not the exception, but the rule.

So in spite of the inauspicious history of the relationship between the two peoples, by 1945 a unique and genuine 'Special Relationship' did exist, on three distinct levels. It existed first at the level of *Staatspolitik*, in that the United States and Britain appeared between them to control, however briefly, the destinies of the world. The Soviet Union was certainly a complicating factor in Europe from 1944 onward, but the great lines of world political and economic organization for the post-war world were being confidently drawn by American and British experts at San Francisco and Bretton Woods. At this level the relationship did indeed depend very largely on the intimacy which Churchill so sedulously cultivated with Roosevelt, and the disappearance of both statesmen in 1945 struck a blow from which it was never quite to recover. Attlee and Truman never really knew or wanted to know one another. Churchill's attempt to restore the relationship with Eisenhower when he returned to office was humiliatingly rebuffed, and Eden's attempt to take it for granted in 1956 was catastrophic. Under

Macmillan indeed the relationship enjoyed an Indian summer, whose sunset rays were to gild the Presidency of John F. Kennedy. But after that, Britain produced no Prime Minister (with the possible exception of Mrs Thatcher) whose personality and self-confidence carried serious weight in Washington, and the United States certainly did not produce a President sympathetic to British pretensions to equality. They might solicit British support, as Johnson did in Vietnam and Reagan has rather more successfully over Star Wars. They might listen respectfully to British advice. But there was never any question, in return, of supporting British claims to political parity or imperial power. Britain's role was now that of loyal and subordinate ally, or it was nothing. The leaders of that other loyal ally, the German Federal Republic, enjoyed at least equal esteem.

The 'Special Relationship' survived rather better at the second level, that of the officials. In spite of all frictions, a truly remarkable degree of friendly intimacy had developed during the war, especially among the military. Service in Washington with the Joint Staffs Mission, in north-west Europe with Allied Headquarters, and in North Africa and Italy, to say nothing of more intimate collaboration at Bletchley or with Special Operations Executive, had created a generation of officers and officials for whom transatlantic co-operation was second nature, its suspension at the end of the war a painful interruption, and its resumption with the establishment of NATO in 1949 a welcome restoration of normality. The links between the two intelligence communities obviously constitute the most enduring if the least publicized aspect of the 'Special Relationship', but Sir James Eberle's essay makes clear how far it extends within the armed services as well. The same habits persist to a large degree within the civilian bureaucracies, and any visitor to Washington must be impressed by the easy and intimate camaraderie that exists between British and American officials. It is of course made easier by the fact that the British are no longer trying to persuade their American colleagues to accept the unacceptable, whether a sterling area or a residual British Imperial presence in the Middle East. They have lost those battles (rather as their German colleagues lost other battles) and accepted defeat with a good grace. Neither does this ease of intercourse prevent frequent and sharp divergences of opinion, as was seen recently over technology transfers to the Soviet Union. Naturally any other foreign official sufficiently anglophone, well-informed, and impressive will be equally acceptable in the Washington corridors of power. But such figures are exceptional: the British have an inside track, and on the whole make good use of it.

The third level of relationship is the broad interface between the two societies, of which the interaction of the officials in Washington is only one aspect. The origins of this relationship can also be traced back to the war years, when a substantial number of American servicemen were stationed in Britain for anything up to two years. I know of no serious sociological survey of this interesting period, and certainly relations with the natives were not uniformly good. 'Overpaid, oversexed, and over here' was a sour and not untypical reaction. But many close friendships did result, innumerable false images were swept away, and the frequency with which the Americans concerned have returned to Britain with their families suggests that the experience was for them on the whole a pleasant and formative one. This traffic of course has been largely one way, and even mass air passenger transport has not overcome the financial difficulties in the way of large-scale British travel in the United States. But any British figure involved in business or in any of the professions is likely to be a fairly frequent visitor to the United States, and the ease with which students in both countries slip across the Atlantic and spend weeks in each other's countries with no visible means of support is a constant cause of amazement to their parents and teachers. Of course the same applies to nationals of other, especially European, countries; but unless their English is exceptionally good (as in the case of the Dutch and the Germans it often is) they will not be able to make themselves at home so easily as can the British in the United States, and the Americans in Britain.

At the level with which the contributors to this volume are most familiar, that of the universities and institutes, we almost have come to form a single community, engaging in a dialogue or series of dialogues in which our standpoint will not at all necessarily be determined by our nationality. Most of the great controversies in such areas as economics, foreign policy, and strategic studies have indeed been transnational, with the protagonists often seeking support from one another against the policies of their own government. Tensions at the level of *Staatspolitik* may indeed only strengthen these transnational links. British opponents of Reagan's policy on technology-transfers drew strength from their American counterparts, while the supporters of Reagan's Strategic Defence Initiative were able to recruit plenty of support in Britain in spite of the initially lukewarm response of Her Majesty's Government. It is a transatlantic community to which anyone can belong given a sufficient command of English: in my own field Helmut Schmidt, Karl Kaiser, Christoph Bertram, Johann Holst, Pierre Hassner, and the late Raymond Aron have been honoured members. But again, the British have, quite unfairly, an inside track.

But we must not make too much of this transnational community of professionals, least of all professional academics. Never was this sense of professional community stronger than in Europe before 1914. British visitors to the United States do not have to stray very far off the beaten tourist or conference track to find themselves in culturally alien country, and the same applies to Americans in Britain—especially to the tiny number that venture northward beyond the Trent. In spite of a cultural overlap broad enough for the short-sighted to take as total, there are areas of incompatible diversity between the two societies, and these areas are not shrinking. The religious fundamentalism which character-izes so much of the United States is to be found in Britain only among eccentric and politically inconsiderable groups; a difference which might be unimportant if its American manifestation were not so often linked with a militant ideological anti-Communism which finds little echo in Britain. The advent of a President who appeared so responsive to pressures from this sector of American opinion was therefore a source of understandable concern to British friends of the United States. Con-versely, the socialistic ideas which have been an intrinsic part of the pattern of British politics for the past hundred years have been equally marginal in the United States. Beyond the cultural overlap, British political culture extends as far to the left as American does to the right. Jesse Helms and Jerry Falwell no doubt have views about the 'Special Relationship' very different from those of Charles Mathias and Sam Nunn, while in Britain Arthur Scargill and Ken Livingstone look on the United States simply as the force which keeps the class enemy in power and drives on the Cold War. British apprehensions about the implica-tions of a Reagan Administration are echoed across the Atlantic when Americans contemplate the prospect of an ally ruled by Neil Kinnock and his associates. If things drift too far apart, for how long can the centre hold?

The relationship between Britain and the United States must therefore be seen, not as one between leaders or even élites, but between the societies which produce those leaders. Those societies are evolving rapidly, and it is by no means clear that evolution is taking them in the same direction. In America the old East Coast Atlanticists are losing their primacy to new elements rooted in the sunbelt of the South and West: people for whom Europe, and Britain with it, consists of far-away people of whom they know nothing, and who regard the world outside the United States primarily as an arena for a cosmic confrontation with the Soviet Union. Their interest in Britain is limited to her possible usefulness as an ally in that confrontation. Beyond that, they see her as a quaint amalgam of the Royal Family, pubs, Stratford-upon-Avon and the shade of Winston Churchill. Conversely in Britain the old ruling groups, who are interested in preserving Britain's status as a leading actor in international politics and see in the American connection the most effective way of doing so, are increasingly challenged by a 'counter-élite', one obsessed with domestic problems of welfare and consensus, anxious to escape from external entanglements, and resentful of the America who appears to create them, suspicious of their wealthy European neighbours, sympathetic to Third World socialism, indifferent to any dangers posed by Soviet expansionism, and hankering, consciously or unconsciously, after the neutral status of Sweden. As Britain grows increasingly impoverished, so the influence of these people increases. If the 'new Americans' regard Britain with indifference tempered by slightly contemptuous nostalgia, the 'new British' look on the United States with a dislike sometimes bordering on hatred. Neither group is as yet dominant in its own country, but each feeds on the image of the other. 'Special Relationship' or not, if they really represent the wave of the future it will be a disaster for our two nations, and for the world as a whole.

Index